The Italian Wars 1494–1559

The Italian Wars 1494–1559 outlines the major impact that these wars had, not just on the history of Italy, but on the history of Europe as a whole. It provides the first detailed account of the entire course of the wars, covering all the campaigns and placing the military conflicts in their political, diplomatic, social and economic contexts.

Throughout the book, new developments in military tactics, the composition of armies, the balance between infantry and cavalry, and the use of firearms are described and analysed. How Italians of all sectors of society reacted to the wars and the inevitable political and social changes that they brought about is also examined, offering a view of the wars from a variety of perspectives.

Fully updated and containing a range of maps as well as a brand-new chapter on propaganda and images of war, this second edition of *The Italian Wars 1494–1559* is essential reading for all students of Renaissance and military history.

Christine Shaw is Associate Member of the Faculty of History at the University of Oxford. She has published extensively on the political and military society of Renaissance Italy and her previous books include *Julius II: The Warrior Pope* (1993), *Italy and the European Powers: The Impact of War* (as editor, 2006) and *Barons and Castellans: The Military Nobility of Renaissance Italy* (2015).

MODERN WARS IN PERSPECTIVE

This ambitious series offers wide-ranging studies of specific wars, and distinct phases of warfare, from the close of the Middle Ages to the present day. It aims to advance the current integration of military history into the academic mainstream. To that end, the books are not merely traditional campaign narratives, but examine the causes, course and consequences of major conflicts, in their full international political, social and ideological contexts.

The Italian Wars 1494–1559

War, State and Society in Early Modern Europe

Second Edition

Christine Shaw

Michael Mallett

Routledge
Taylor & Francis Group

LONDON AND NEW YORK

Second edition published 2019
by Routledge
2 Park Square, Milton Park, Abingdon, Oxon, OX14 4RN

and by Routledge
711 Third Avenue, New York, NY 10017

Routledge is an imprint of the Taylor & Francis Group, an informa business

First edition published by Pearson 2012
Reprinted by Routledge 2014

British Library Cataloguing in Publication Data
A catalogue record for this book is available from the British Library

Library of Congress Cataloging in Publication Data
Names: Shaw, Christine (Italian Renaissance historian), author.
Title: The Italian wars, 1494–1559 : war, state and
society in early modern Europe / Christine Shaw.
Description: Second edition. | Abingdon,
Oxon; New York, NY : Routledge, 2019. |
Series: Modern wars in perspective | Includes index. |
Previous edition: The Italian Wars, 1494–1559: War,
State and Society in Early Modern Europe, by M. Mallett and Christine Shaw. |
Identifiers: LCCN 2018029758 (print) | LCCN 2018030604 (ebook) |
ISBN 9780429429354 (eBook) | ISBN 9781138739031 (hardback : alk. paper) |
ISBN 9781138739048 (pbk. : alk. paper)
Subjects: LCSH: Italy–History–1492–1559. | Italy–History,
Military–1268–1559. | Italy–Politics and government–1268–1559. |
Italy–Foreign relations–1492–1559. | War and society–Italy–History–To 1500. |
War and society–Italy–History–16th century. | France–History,
Military–1328–1589. | Europe–History, Military–1492–1648.
Classification: LCC DG541 (ebook) |
LCC DG541.M35 2019 (print) | DDC 945/.06–dc23
LC record available at https://lccn.loc.gov/2018029758

ISBN: 978-1-138-73903-1 (hbk)
ISBN: 978-1-138-73904-8 (pbk)
ISBN: 978-0-429-42935-4 (ebk)

Typeset in Sabon
by Out of House Publishing

Contents

Preface to the second edition

When I was originally writing this book, the only period of the Italian Wars that had been extensively studied was the first decade. In recent years, more and more work on later phases has begun to appear, which I have been able to make use of in preparing this second edition. There has been particular interest in propaganda and images of war, and I have added a chapter on that aspect.

The project to write a book on the Italian Wars began for me in the summer of 2008, when I was asked to help Michael Mallett complete the book on which he had been working for several years. He died before we could begin to work together, but he very much wanted the book to be completed. He had been prevented by illness from producing drafts of all the chapters he projected, and was far from satisfied with what he had written; most of his drafts had to be set aside. The chapters on the transformation and resources of war – his area of particular expertise – are still substantially as he left them; I have edited them again, to take into account changing perspectives on the organization of war in Europe during this period, and made further additions.

The coverage of secondary literature on the Italian Wars is still patchy, and consequently much of the narrative is based on printed primary sources, which fortunately are abundant. To avoid a heavy ballast of footnotes, detailed references in the narrative chapters are generally given only for matters such as troop numbers (where sources often differ greatly, so I wished to make clear those on which I have relied), or statements of plans and policies, so that the authenticity and reliability of the information can be checked. As well as references to works cited in the notes, the bibliographies include a guide to further reading with, so far as is possible, an emphasis on books and articles in English.

Naturally, I have taken the opportunity of this new edition to correct the errors (few and minor, but always regrettable) which have come to my attention.

MAP 1 *Italy in 1494*

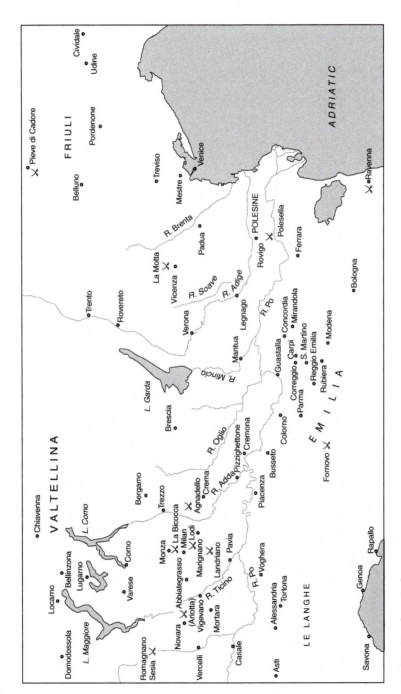

MAP 2 *Northern Italy*

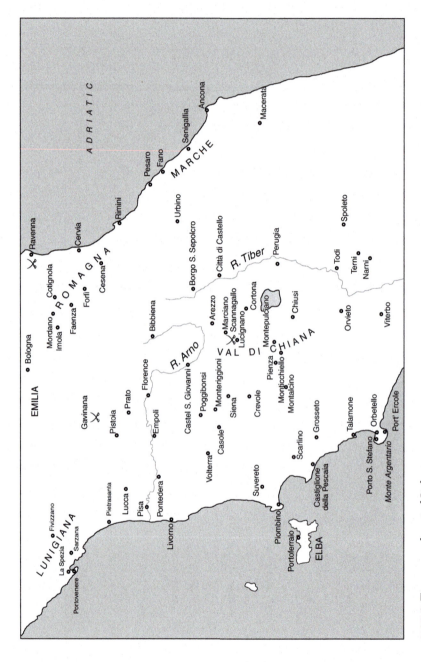

MAP 3 *Tuscany and central Italy*

MAP 4 *Southern Italy*

Introduction

The Italian Wars were a watershed in the history of Italy, of Europe, and of warfare. For over six decades, Italy was a focus of conflicts among the powers of western Europe. Eventually, victory went to the Spanish Habsburgs, who would be left with the two major states whose possession they had disputed with the Valois kings of France, the duchy of Milan and the kingdom of Naples. Spanish predominance in Italy was only one of the radical changes to Italian states and the system of relations among them that were brought about by the wars. Territories were won and lost, dynasties overthrown and new ones established, some states disappeared, others were created. In military history, the Italian wars were a proving-ground for developments in the constitution of armies, in tactics and in weaponry – for the strengths and limitations of massed pike infantry, the respective utility of heavy and light cavalry, the extensive use of handguns, for innovations in artillery and in fortifications. Soldiers from France, Spain, Germany, the Netherlands, the Balkans and all parts of Italy fought against and alongside each other, observed different weapons and tactics, and learned from each other while maintaining their own distinctive character.

Why did Italy become the focus of conflict between the two most powerful dynasties in western Europe? Essentially, because each had dynastic claims on Italian states. Both the French and Spanish kings had hereditary claims to the throne of Naples, the French as heirs to the Angevins, a cadet line of the Valois who had ruled Naples from 1265 to 1435, the Spanish as heirs to Alfonso V of Aragon, who had conquered the kingdom and separated it from his other realms, leaving it to his illegitimate son, Ferrante, in 1458. Another cadet line of the French royal house, the Orléans, claimed to be the rightful heirs of the Visconti Dukes of Milan, who had died out in 1447. In 1498, Louis d'Orléans, grandson of Valentina Visconti, became king of France, and his claim to Milan became part of the inheritance of the French crown. The duchy was an Imperial fief, which gave the emperor a claim to determine who should be ruler there. Indeed much of northern and central Italy was considered part of the territory of the Holy Roman Empire. This would become a matter of great significance when the emperor was Charles V, heir to the Spanish kingdoms as well as the lands of the Dukes of Burgundy.

The Italian state system was a complex one. Alongside the five largest, 'regional' states – Naples, Milan, the republics of Florence and Venice and the Papal States – were many lesser ones, including the republics of Siena, Lucca and Genoa and lordships ranging in size and importance from the territory of the Duke of Ferrara to tiny Imperial fiefs of a few square miles. Most of the smaller entities were linked to one or more of the larger by some form of alliance or agreement, bringing them under their 'protection'. Often such arrangements involved a military *condotta*, a form of contract to provide a specified number of troops in return for a set rate of payment, and usually an extra personal allowance for the lord. Such *condotte* were considered not only an honourable but, for many lords, an essential support.

The major Italian states and their lesser allies and satellites were usually grouped into leagues, generally presented as defensive but in reality vehicles for competing ambitions, for promoting as much as containing conflicts. They were far more conscious of the divisions, rivalries and enmities among themselves than of any common interests as constituent parts of 'Italy'. Yet they were also conscious of the distinction between Italian and non-Italian powers. The king of Aragon, for all that Sicily had been under the crown of Aragon for two centuries, was a foreigner; Ferrante of Naples and his sons, members of the same dynasty but ruling only an Italian state, were not. Italian states took little part in conflicts across the Alps. If Francesco Sforza, anxious for recognition after he had made himself Duke of Milan in 1450, valued his alliance with the king of France and sent troops to fight for him, his son Galeazzo Maria was less keen to respond to attempts by Louis XI and Charles the Bold of Burgundy to enlist his help in their wars.

On the other hand, Italian states were prepared to invite powers from outside Italy to take part in their disputes, especially the French king or the Angevins. Diplomatic intervention by the French or – as Ferdinand and Isabella consolidated their hold on their realms – the Spanish monarchs, was sometimes called in aid to negotiate peace settlements in Italy. But if an Italian state called on an ultramontane ally for military aid, they could be accused of betraying the interests of Italy. Such accusations could be more than a rhetorical flourish: a genuine sense of Italy as being a discrete political entity was sometimes evident. People from the next town could be regarded as *stranieri*, 'foreigners'; people from outside Italy could be generically dismissed as *barbari*, 'barbarians'.

In the high Middle Ages, the advent of armies from outside Italy and the claims of ultramontane rulers, notably the Holy Roman Emperor, to Italian states had brought prolonged wars and major changes in political structures and the patterns of relations between states. In the fourteenth and early fifteenth centuries, the Angevins had been one of the poles that gave a pattern to politics throughout Italy. For most of the fifteenth century, apart from the settlement of the Aragonese dynasty on the throne of Naples and Angevin attempts to dislodge them, foreign interventions had been pacific, like the French rule over Genoa from 1458 to 1461. Italians perhaps became lulled into a false sense of security. Some might warn of the dangers of inviting powerful foreign lords to intervene or come to Italy, but many, including those in positions of political power, believed there was no real peril, because such princes would not stay. There was a certain complacency among Italian politicians about their ability to make use of other powers to serve their own interests. Italians were slow to credit the persistence and the seriousness of intent of the kings of France and Spain and the emperor, the fact that they were coming or sending their armies to claim territories and states that they regarded as theirs and that, once gained, they intended to keep.

As they came to recognize the new reality of Italian politics, Italians tried to explain how it had come about, analysing and criticizing their own character, culture, and political and military systems and values. From these debates developed explanations that have long held sway: the political weakness of Italy, divided into many quarrelling states, confronted by the strength of the major European monarchies, of 'national' states; the military weakness of Italy, an over-reliance on mercenaries for whom war was a business, who put their own safety before the security of the states they served, and could not match the strength and determination of troops serving their king, or deal with the tactics and weapons of the Swiss and German infantry they brought or with their superior artillery, on the battlefield or in sieges.

It is difficult to argue against the significance of the imbalance between the resources the major European monarchs could muster and those of any Italian state, and difficult to deny that divisions between Italian states and their pursuit of self-interest, apparently blind to the wider consequences of their actions, obstructed the formation of lasting leagues which might offer determined, long-term defence of a common interest. It is also true that the armies who fought the major campaigns of the wars were usually greater in size than those that individual Italian states, with the possible exception of Venice, could field for any length of time, and that the bodies of troops that came over the Alps or across the sea to fight in the Italian Wars were raised and organized differently from those of Italian states.

The French could boast the finest heavy cavalry in Europe in the *compagnies d'ordonnance*, permanent units raised and paid by the crown, in which French nobles competed to serve. For infantry, the French had come to rely heavily on Swiss mercenaries. In the 1490s, the reputation of the Swiss stood very high. They were a different kind of 'national' army. A well-established system of training, organized by the governments of the cantons, resulted in a high proportion of able-bodied men having the strength and ability to handle pikes, halberds and two-handed swords, and the discipline to execute complex manoeuvres in formations of several thousand men. Other governments could hire companies of Swiss by arrangement with the cantons. In the early sixteenth century, the prowess of the Swiss pike squares was increasingly rivalled by that of the landsknechts. These were mercenaries, raised and organized by contractors or captains rather than governments, generally from southern Germany. The emperor considered he had first call on their services, but other powers also employed them. During the wars, the Spanish infantry also acquired a formidable reputation for their toughness and endurance, and for their proficiency in the use of handguns. The Spanish infantry companies that fought in the Italian Wars were essentially mercenaries, but generally fought for the Spanish monarchs, and could identify themselves with their interests and fortunes.

Of the major Italian states, Venice had the best-organized army, based on long-term, in some cases lifelong, contracts with *condottieri* and infantry constables. Under Francesco Sforza, Milan had had a strong army, but by the later fifteenth century the quality and loyalty of the permanent companies of cavalry had deteriorated, and Ludovico Sforza was increasingly reliant on Swiss and German infantry. In Naples, a permanent cavalry force, based on recruitment from the royal estates, had been created, in large part to reduce reliance on the forces raised and led by the barons. The Papal States produced many *condottieri* and, from the Romagna, some of the best-reputed infantry in Italy, but often the popes would not be their first choice as an employer. Popes were generally reluctant to maintain much of an army unless it was needed for a campaign. Florence, too, did not like to pay troops in peacetime, and depended largely on hiring *condottieri* to raise troops when required. So did all the other Italian states, to a greater or lesser degree. The *condottiere* with his own company recruited and maintained by him was the typical Italian military commander, their men generally the principal component of any Italian army.

Prominent among the *condottieri* were princes such as the marquis of Mantua and the Duke of Ferrara, together with the lords of smaller states and major barons. *Condotte* were often given for political reasons, to lords who might not take command in person. In itself, this system was perhaps no worse a hindrance to military efficiency than the customary appointments of major nobles to commands in the armies of the European monarchies. But it also meant that the lords of Italy were accustomed to switching political allegiance as opportunities for employment as a military commander appeared best. There were conventions about the circumstances and manner in which such switches could take place without the taint of unreliabilty or disloyalty. But such practices made Italian *condottieri* appear fickle and untrustworthy to princes and commanders from outside Italy. The kings of France and Spain and the emperor expected a greater degree of commitment from Italian lords, especially if *condotte* were part of a political agreement or alliance.

Nevertheless, there has been a fundamental revision to the long-prevailing view of the abilities of Italian soldiers and their part in the wars, of cynical, over-cautious professionals, unwilling to take risks, satisfied with securing minor advantages, concerned to avoid the shedding of blood (not least their own), no matter what the cost to their employer. Italian commanders took a prominent role in many of the campaigns and battles of the wars, and they had much to teach, as well as to learn from, the soldiers of other nations. If Italian infantrymen never became masters of the art of the pike square, they became respected as arquebusiers, and in the defence of fortresses and towns under siege; Italians also gained a reputation as light cavalrymen. Outdated military skills, and lack of martial spirit cannot furnish as large a part of the explanation for Italian defeats in the wars, and the ultimate predominance of the Spanish over much of Italy, as some contemporaries, and a long historical tradition, have given them.

CHAPTER 1

The genesis of the wars and the first French expedition

On 29 August 1494 Charles VIII of France set out from Grenoble with part of his army to make good his claim to the throne of Naples. After passing as an ally through the lands of the young Duke of Savoy, by 9 September he was in the Italian city of Asti, which could be considered French soil as it belonged to his cousin Louis, duc d'Orléans. Administrative officials, diplomatic envoys and advance troops in substantial numbers had already entered Italy during the previous months; Savoy, Piedmont, Genoa and the towns of western Lombardy were full of French soldiers in the late summer and autumn of 1494. But the origins of and preparations for this event, which was to set the Italian Wars in train, went back a long way.

Charles VIII and his inheritance

When Louis XI died on 30 August 1483, he left his son Charles a kingdom with a rapidly growing population, a flourishing economy and a monarchy that was increasingly secure. Far more of the kingdom was under the direct rule of the crown than there had been at Louis's accession. On the death of Charles the Bold, Duke of Burgundy in January 1477 without a male heir, the duchy of Burgundy itself, the heart of the state which his predecessors had been building up in the Netherlands and along the eastern frontier of France, reverted to the French crown. By an untimely use of force against Charles's daughter Mary, however, the king drove her to accept as her husband Maximilian, the son and heir of the Habsburg emperor, Frederick III. As a consequence of this match, the kings of France would henceforth have to be on their guard against the Habsburgs on their northern and eastern frontiers. Louis appeared to limit the immediate damage by arranging the betrothal in 1482 of his young son Charles to Margaret, the infant daughter of Mary and Maximilian, who was to be brought up at the French court. The year before, the extinction of the direct Angevin line of the royal house brought their lands, including Provence as well as Anjou, back to the crown.

Charles VIII was aged only 13 at the time of his accession. Although a formal regency was avoided, the king came under the tutelage of his elder sister Anne and her husband Pierre de Beaujeu, who resisted the efforts of Louis d'Orléans, his cousin, who was next in line to the throne, to overthrow them. The first part of his reign was dominated by a war against Brittany, where Louis had turned for support. This civil war had an international dimension, and far-reaching repercussions. Largely independent of France, the duchy of Brittany was subject only to the overlordship of the king. A military assault was launched on it in 1487. Duke Francis II was supported by an alliance of the Spanish monarchs, Ferdinand and Isabella, Henry VII of England, and Maximilian. But the military help sent by the allies, and diversionary attacks launched by Maximilian in Flanders, failed to prevent the rout of the Breton forces by the French army in July 1488; Louis d'Orléans was captured in the battle. Shortly after this, Francis died, leaving his eldest daughter, Anne, heiress to the duchy at the age of 11. Young as she was, she continued her father's independent policy, and her allies confirmed their support. In late 1490, Anne accepted a proxy marriage with Maximilian, who had been a widower for some years. A combination of French military and diplomatic pressure persuaded Anne to set aside her unconsummated marriage with Maximilian and marry Charles instead in December 1491.

For France, the resolution of the Breton wars promised closer integration of the duchy of Brittany into the kingdom, provided Charles and Anne produced an heir. Sustained and bitter campaigning had hardened the French army and given valuable experience to its leaders, and given Charles himself a taste for the excitement of going on campaign with his troops. But the wars left a legacy of international suspicion and hostility between France and the powers that had supported Breton independence. In particular, by marrying Anne Charles had not only deprived Maximilian of his bride, but had repudiated his longstanding commitment to marry Maximilian's daughter, Margaret. This humiliation rankled, adding a personal element to the burgeoning rivalry between the Habsburgs and the king of France.

The Angevin inheritance that came to the French crown in December 1481included the long-standing claims of the Angevins to the crowns of Naples and Jerusalem. The kingdom of Naples, a papal fief, had been first conferred on them by Clement IV in 1265, and the popes continued to assert rights not only to confirm by investiture the succession to the throne, but to nominate whom they chose. Papal approval was a consideration that Charles could not ignore, but it was not the decisive factor in determining who would rule in Naples. Influenced perhaps by one of his constant companions, Étienne de Vesc (who had acquired lands in Provence and adopted an Angevin outlook), by humanist tutors, and by Neapolitan exiles Vesc introduced to his court, Charles quickly showed an immediate interest in the claim to the Neapolitan throne. He asked for an enquiry into it in 1484, and in the next few years was constantly reminded of the issue by the exiles. Francesco di Paola, the saintly Calabrese hermit who had been summoned to the deathbed of Louis XI, remained close to Charles and filled his mind with ideas of freeing the Neapolitan people from the tyrannies of the Aragonese and the threats from the Turks.[1] His honour as king could not allow him to forget so significant an inheritance, quite apart from the reminders he received from others. But it was not until the early 1490s that the idea of activating the claim to the Neapolitan crown began to seem a practical proposition.

French interests in Italy

French political interests in Italy were rather unfocused. The kingdoms of Naples and of Sicily had been primarily the concern of the Normans and the Angevins, and their Mediterranean enterprises had been only peripherally linked to French royal policy. Intervention by the French kings there had been indirect, in support of the Angevins.[2] Control of Genoa had periodically attracted the interest of the French because of its proximity to France and its commercial importance. The republic had come under the dominion of Charles VI from 1396 to 1409 and of Charles VII from 1458 to 1461. Although neither king showed much direct concern for it, the submission of Genoa in 1396 gave grounds for an argument that it was legally subject to the French crown. An interest in Milan had been created by the marriage of Charles d'Orléans to Valentina Visconti, daughter of the Duke of Milan, in 1387, but it was Louis d'Orléans, Valentina Visconti's grandson, not Charles VIII, who claimed to be the rightful heir to the duchy. Of the other Italian states, the republic of Florence was the traditional ally of the Angevins in Italy, and Florentine merchants and bankers had important commercial links to France that made them susceptible to pressure from the king. And, of course, the French king needed to maintain some representation in Rome, once the papacy was re-established in Rome, after its 'exile' in Avignon and the disruption of the Great Schism, if only to deal with the business of appointments to benefices and ecclesiastical taxes.

With the accession of Louis XI in 1461, there was a significant increase in French royal interest in Italy. Louis had involved himself in Italian politics while he was still the dauphin, at odds with his father Charles VII. As king, he sent frequent envoys to Italy and welcomed Italian ambassadors to his court. He assumed a role as mediator and arbiter in Italian politics, as French diplomatic influence and support was sought by Italian states in their quarrels with each other. Charles was far too young and inexperienced to play the role his father had done in Italian politics, but the incentive to become directly involved in Italian affairs was even stronger for him. It was not just that the Angevin claim to the throne of Naples and the rivalry with the incumbent Aragonese dynasty had fallen to the French crown, nor that the Orleanist claim to the duchy of Milan was in the hands of the heir presumptive to the throne. With the integration of Provence and its long Mediterranean coastline, including the ports of Marseilles and Toulon, France now had the potential to be a Mediterranean power.

King Ferrante of Naples and the other Italian powers

Once Ferrante, on his succession to the throne in 1458 had fought off the challenge of René d'Anjou's son, Jean, and the rebellious Neapolitan barons who supported the Angevin cause, he had become a formidable, authoritarian ruler. He did not succeed in winning the love and loyalty of his subjects, many of whom harkened after the Angevins. Nor could he feel secure in the alliance of other Italian powers. They became increasingly wary of Ferrante's intentions, their suspicions heightened by the justified reputation he acquired for being devious and ruthless. Although the support, military as well as diplomatic, of Francesco Sforza, Duke of Milan had been crucial to Ferrante's victory over the Angevin challenge in the early years of his reign, and the two families were linked by marriages, in later years relations between the Neapolitan and Milanese rulers were poisoned by a family dispute. Ludovico Sforza, who became guardian of his nephew, the young Duke of Milan, Gian Galeazzo in 1480, and who aspired to supplant him permanently, found himself opposed by Ferrante, whose granddaughter Isabella was married to Gian Galeazzo. The popes resented Ferrante's growing interference in the internal affairs of the Papal States. Apart from joining in the competition among Milan, Venice and Florence for influence over the lords and communities of the northern Papal States, he deliberately set out to give *condotte* to Roman barons so that he could, when he wanted, bring direct military pressure to bear on the city of Rome and the pope within it.

The Venetians were concerned about the growth of Neapolitan interests in the eastern Mediterranean – Ferrante had competed with them for possession of the kingdom of Cyprus, acquired by Venice in 1473 – and did not want a stronger kingdom of Naples disputing Venetian aspirations to dominate the Adriatic; indeed, Venice hankered after control over some Neapolitan ports on the Adriatic coast. While the Florentines had been allies of the Angevin monarchs of Naples, they were more ambivalent towards the Aragonese dynasty there. The ambitions of Alfonso and Ferrante in southern Tuscany to control the lordship of Piombino with its strategically important port and, if opportunity offered, to establish dominance over the republic of Siena, aroused widespread resentment in Florence. On the other hand, the Florentines had important business interests in the kingdom of Naples, and there was a gradual shift among the leaders of the Medicean regime in the 1480s towards an alignment with Ferrante.

Invoking the threat of the Angevins, or the heirs of the Angevins, was a tactic that the other Italian states were quite willing to employ against Ferrante. During the War of Ferrara from 1482 to 1484, in which Ferrante was a member of the league opposed to Venice, the Venetians hired René, Duke of Lorraine (whose mother Yolande was the daughter of René d'Anjou) as a military commander. In the Neapolitan Barons' War of 1485–6 it was Innocent VIII who invited the Duke of Lorraine to go to Naples to claim the crown. At a moment of high tension between the pope and Ferrante in 1489, Innocent declared Ferrante deposed and formally offered the investiture of the kingdom to Charles VIII.[3]

By then, Ludovico Sforza was also seeking a closer understanding with France, to protect himself against the hostility of Ferrante. In October 1490 he sent a secretary to France to ask for investiture with Genoa (which had been subject to the Sforza from 1464 to 1478, and again from 1488), and the renewal of a league between Milan and Louis XI. Charles accepted Ludovico's homage for Genoa, and sent an embassy to Milan in January 1491 to discuss the investiture and the league; among the terms he wanted were the use of Genoa as a base for his fleet, and military support from Ludovico in any war.[4] While discussions about the alliance between France and Milan trudged on, in Rome Innocent VIII was finally ready to consider a reconciliation with Ferrante. A treaty was signed in late January 1492, and Ferrante got what he wanted most from this peace: papal recognition of his dynasty's claim to the throne. Ludovico's reaction to the unexpected entente between the pope and Ferrante was to speed up negotiations with France.

The death of Lorenzo de' Medici in April 1492, represented by the Florentine historian Francesco Guicciardini as a turning-point in the lead-up to the Italian Wars, was probably not that significant. Guicciardini, whose *Storia d'Italia*, written in the 1530s, has been the single most important source for accounts of the wars, portrayed Lorenzo as a beneficial and controlling influence in Italian politics in the later years of his life, and therefore emphasized that his death left a dangerous vacuum.[5] But Lorenzo's increasing preoccupation with establishing his own influence in Rome, and his leaning more towards Naples than Milan, had contributed to the growing tensions in Italy and to Ludovico Sforza's sense of isolation.

Piero de' Medici's continuation of his father's policy of friendship with Ferrante contributed to the diplomatic tensions in Italy following the death in August 1492 of Innocent VIII and the election of Rodrigo Borgia who took the title of Alexander VI. Borgia's main ally in the election was Cardinal Ascanio Sforza, Ludovico's brother, and it was therefore seen initially as a blow to Ferrante and a Milanese victory. Ludovico saw an opportunity to settle his differences with the king from a position of strength in alliance with the pope, but relations between Ferrante and Alexander were soured by the affair of the Cibo castles. Estates north of Rome, granted by Innocent to his son, Franceschetto Cibo, were bought by Virginio Orsini, the most powerful Roman baron in Ferrante's service. Despite the fact that Franceschetto had married Lorenzo's daughter, Maddalena, Lorenzo had planned this transfer of the lands to Virginio before his death, and Piero helped to arrange it. Alexander objected to the transaction, but put the blame principally on the king, who he accused of wanting to increase his own power in the Papal States by arranging this accession to the already formidable strength of Virginio Orsini.[6] He sent a secret envoy to Charles, urging him to invade the kingdom of Naples; the French diplomat, Philippe de Commynes would claim that the pope's exhortations had at one stage been the principal reason for Charles's determination to come to Italy.[7]

Preparations for the Italian enterprise

For all the intrigues in Italy that prepared the way for the French invasion of 1494, it has to be seen as primarily a French initiative conditioned by events and attitudes in France. The single most important factor in bringing it to fruition was the attitude of the king himself. He had a strong sense of his honour and a determination to pursue his rights. He was also a deeply religious man, and took seriously the threat to Christendom posed by the Turks.[8] Whether the idea of Charles leading a crusade is seen as being a realistic possibility by historians depends to some extent on their estimate of the continued power of the idea of crusade to evoke effective support in the late Middle Ages. It also depends on an assessment of whether the kingdom of Naples was indeed the best base from which to launch a powerful army against the Turks. As Ludovico Sforza pointed out, the obvious route for an army was to go through Hungary, but to engage on that crusading front would mean co-operating with Maximilian.[9] French propagandists were ready to celebrate the divine mission of their king, to hail him as a new Charlemagne. Many Italians would also present this image of himself to the king on his way through Italy, urging him to act as a liberator, a reformer of the Church. To say that most of such hopes placed in Charles were doomed to disappointment is not to deny that these ideas and images might appeal to him.[10] But what drew him to Italy was his claim to the throne of Naples, not visions of going on crusade or emulating Charlemagne.

Charles was also eager for an opportunity to lead his army and his nobility on an active campaign. He had developed a considerable interest in military affairs, in the organization of war and the practice of war. Undoubtedly he underestimated the problems posed by an Italian expedition, and found it difficult to steer a course through the cross-currents of advice that he was offered. Most of the advisers who encouraged his interest in Italy were seeking to further their own interests in one way or another, but the majority of his councillors were opposed to any expedition to conquer Naples, particularly one to be led by the king in person. In the last resort it was Charles's own resolve that got the expedition going, after a long period of preparation and debate.

The initial area of preparation was diplomatic. The settlement of the problem of Brittany had left a legacy of hostile encirclement of France, largely orchestrated by Ferdinand of Aragon. To counter this, separate treaties were made with the three main powers involved, treaties that have often been seen as strongly detrimental to France's interests, sacrificed to a desire to set aside all other problems and concentrate on Italy.[11] Yet the threat to France from the coalition created by Ferdinand was very real in 1492.

The most immediate threat was from England. Dismayed as he was by the loss of English influence in Brittany, Henry VII was more upset about the non-payment since the death of Louis XI of an annual pension promised to the king of England in 1478. In October, an English army was landed at Calais and began a siege of Boulogne. At this point Maximilian was not yet ready to join the offensive against France, and Charles's diplomats were soon able to agree terms with the English. The Treaty of Étaples of 3 November 1492 stipulated the return of the towns taken by the English during the expedition and the settlement of all debts to the English king. On the day that this treaty was signed Charles announced his intention of returning to the kingdom of Aragon the counties of Cerdagne and Roussillon on the Pyrenees frontier, occupied by Louis XI in 1463. He undertook to return them in a treaty signed at Barcelona on 19 January 1493, although he reserved his rights to reclaim them (this was by no means the final settlement of this dispute). Meanwhile, Maximilian had gone on the offensive to recover the dowry lands of Margaret, which Charles had still not restored. By early 1493 he had regained most of them, and a truce in March was followed by a peace treaty, agreed at Senlis on 8 May. Maximilian implicitly accepted the marriage of Charles to Anne of Brittany, and Margaret was returned to her father after spending ten years in France. Artois and Franche-Comté were handed over to Maximilian's son, Philip.[12]

These treaties cannot be seen solely in the context of preparing for the Italian enterprise. Yet the moment the treaty of Senlis was signed, the idea of the conquest of Naples moved to the stage of practical planning. On 15 May Charles announced the establishment of a commission to consider the affairs of Italy, whose members would plan and launch the expedition. A special envoy, Peron de Baschi, a veteran Angevin diplomat well-known in Italy, was sent to the main Italian courts, to sound out reactions and seek allies.[13]

Charles's advisers were still divided: the Angevins and Provencals were in favour of the proposed Italian expedition, while those from the northern provinces thought more about the threat from Maximilian. Doubtless, the reports of French disunity reaching Italy tended to foster the tendency of Italian governments to adopt their preferred policy of playing for time in the hope that the threat would go away. It was not until September 1493 that Ferrante himself began to address the French threat seriously and to prepare his defences. He sent urgent messages to Ludovico, exhorting him to think about what he was doing, and a series of envoys to the other Italian states to sound out opinions; an envoy sent to France was refused audience by the king.[14]

Then, on 25 January 1494, Ferrante died unexpectedly. By the time the news reached France, causing renewed enthusiasm for the expedition, Alfonso, Ferrante's heir, had already acted decisively. Writing to Alexander with news of his father's death, he offered to meet onerous financial conditions attached to his investiture with the throne and to provide substantial advantages in grants of estates and offices for the pope's beloved children. Alexander would exact a high price for his agreement, but Alfonso was willing to pay this to obtain confirmation of the papal sanction of his position. When Charles's envoys arrived to state the claims of their king and to threaten an appeal to a council of the Church over the pope's head if necessary, their protests were politely turned aside, but alarmed the pope nonetheless. He wrote to Charles to express astonishment that the king could be contemplating attacking a Christian power while the Turks were threatening; if he believed he had a right to the throne of Naples, he should submit his argument to the pope.[15]

Remaining hopeful that the pope could be persuaded or bullied into changing his mind, Charles pressed on with his plans. In February he had begun to move towards Lyon and Provence where the army and fleet were assembling. The Milanese ambassador, Carlo da Barbiano, who accompanied the king throughout the final period of preparation for the expedition, reported on the slow progress in raising the necessary money, and on Charles's reluctance to spend time on the discussion of details and to impose his authority to settle the quarrels among his advisers. Nevertheless, the king was determined to go in person to Naples 'as he realised that the greater part of his kingdom opposed the enterprise but he also knew that if he spoke of going himself no-one would contradict him'.[16] The king's decision to lead the expedition himself had in fact been one reason for delay, because the marshal Pierre d'Esquerdes, an enthusiastic supporter of the enterprise when he thought that he would be given its command, had been slowing down the muster of troops after he realized that he would not. He died on 22 April, a few days after he had been publicly rebuked by his furious young king. Charles then took personal charge of the arrangements.[17]

The final months

There was still uncertainty about how big the invading army needed to be, which route it should take to Naples, how much money would be needed and how much friendly Italian states could be persuaded to contribute. The plans that were being prepared in Lyon in March and April 1494 envisaged two separate armies, one moving down the peninsula by the land route and the other being transported by sea with the king direct to Naples. Initially the proposal was to assemble a total of 1,500 lances and 12,000 infantry, and divide them roughly equally between the two armies. As news of Neapolitan mobilization filtered through, and doubts were raised about how many Italian troops were going to be recruited by Ludovico Sforza in Milan and Cardinal Ascanio Sforza in Rome to support the invasion, leading French advisers argued for a much larger French force. It was agreed to plan for a total French force of 1,900 lances, 1,200 mounted archers and 19,000 infantry, to be supported by 1,500 Italian lances and 2,000–3,000 Italian infantry.[18] The problem was that while a fleet of about fifty ships and galleys was being prepared, it was only capable of carrying about a fifth of this army.

Alfonso was putting his defences in order. He set about building up his army by renewing the contracts of some *condottieri*, including the Roman baron Fabrizio Colonna and the Milanese exile Gian Giacomo Trivulzio, and giving new ones, to Niccolò Orsini da Pitigliano among others. Offers of help from the Turkish sultan, Bayezid II, who had heard of Charles's declarations of intent to follow the conquest of the kingdom of Naples with a crusade against him, allowed Alfonso to boast that he could have the assistance of 20,000 Turkish troops against the French.[19]

Alfonso's defensive strategy was based on forestalling the French expedition, to stop Charles and his army ever arriving in the kingdom. Provoking a revolt in Genoa against Ludovico Sforza, to prevent the French fleet using it as an embarkation point for the troops who were to be sent by sea, would, he hoped, prevent them from mounting their assault that year. This was to be co-ordinated with a direct attack on the duchy of Milan by land. An advance party of 240 men-at-arms under the command of Alfonso's son Ferrandino was sent ahead, reaching the Romagna in mid-July. Passage through the Papal States for the Neapolitan troops was permitted because of Alfonso's alliance with the pope, but the original plan for Alfonso to follow with the rest of the army was compromised by Alexander's insistence that many of his troops should be deployed to defend Rome. The king himself would remain with 30 squadrons of men-at-arms on the frontiers of the kingdom; his Great Constable, Virginio Orsini, was to stay south of Rome with 200 men-at-arms. Command of the expedition against Milan was left to the young and inexperienced Ferrandino.[20]

The reactions of the Italian powers

Reluctantly, Italian rulers had to face the likelihood that the long-heralded arrival of the French could finally become a reality that year. Adjusting to this prospect was not easy even for Ludovico Sforza, despite all the encouragement he had given to Charles for many months, and his having provided the French with access to the port of Genoa to equip vessels, gather the fleet and embark a large part of the army. He had been expecting the French forces to reach Naples largely by sea, and had not expected that Charles would lead his troops in person. Perhaps he had envisaged something more along the lines of an expedition by the Angevin claimants to the throne, not this deployment of the full might of the French crown. He had thought only moderate numbers of French troops would come and that much of the army would be recruited in Italy, that the expedition would be strong enough to inflict defeat on Alfonso but not to dethrone him.[21] Troubled, vacillating, he sought ways to protect himself and the duchy of Milan. One expedient was to suggest to Charles that he needed to co-ordinate his attack with Maximilian, even suggesting Maximilian could be given command of the land forces, although this would surely not have been a guarantee of greater strength, as Ludovico argued, but a guarantee of delay.[22] In late July, he was still hoping to delay the French; he was said to be seeking talks with Louis d'Orléans in Alessandria.[23]

Ludovico's father-in-law and the brother-in-law of Alfonso, Ercole d'Este, Duke of Ferrara, was blamed by Guicciardini for advising Ludovico to incite the French to come to Italy, hoping that the resultant turmoil would furnish an opportunity for him to recover lands taken from him by Venice during the War of Ferrara, and to take revenge on Ludovico for insisting on peace terms to end that war which sanctioned this loss.[24] This accusation cast a long shadow over Ercole's reputation, although it was fundamentally unjust. Devoted to his Neapolitan wife, Eleonora, he had tried to mediate between her father, Ferrante, and Ludovico. Like other Italian princes, Ercole was trying to protect his own position, and from his perspective, there was more to fear from the ambitions of Venice that from those of Charles. While the Este had a long tradition of Angevin sympathies, it was perhaps as a precaution, as insurance, that Ercole sent one of his sons – ironically, named Ferrante after his grandfather – to the French court; Ferrante d'Este would accompany Charles to Italy. Ercole's own days as an active *condottiere* prince were over, and although he went to Asti to greet Charles on his arrival on Italian soil, he took no part in the expedition. Nevertheless, he would be considered a partisan of France, and the Dukes of Ferrara would be among the most consistent supporters of the French in Italy during the Italian Wars.

Many Florentines were more inclined to maintain their historic, and commercially important, ties of friendship to the French, rather than stand by Alfonso. Piero de' Medici, however, insisted they were bound to support Alfonso as his allies. When French envoys reached Florence in May and reiterated the requests that Charles had been making for months for support of his enterprise, or at least for transit and supplies in Florentine territory when his army came to Tuscany, the official response followed the line dictated by Piero, to the displeasure of the Florentine people. Losing patience, Charles dismissed the Florentine ambassadors in France and expelled the agents of the Medici bank. Other Florentine merchants and bankers were left in peace, because, Charles said, he knew that the people of Florence were sympathetic to him.[25]

The Venetians, in response to solicitations for support from Alfonso and from Charles, maintained a polite neutrality. Charles tried to woo them by offering them some ports in Apulia as well as in the Balkans, if they would join in his expedition to Naples and go on to attack the Turks. But the Venetians used their need to be on guard against the Turkish threat to their colonies in the eastern Mediterranean as a justification for neutrality in Naples. They did not want to believe that the French were really on their way. There was also concern that if he did come, Charles might be acting in concert with Maximilian, who would attack Venice while the French advanced on Naples.[26]

Neutrality might well have been the preferred option of the pope as well, but the pressures on him to choose sides were greater than on any other Italian power. Not only were the Papal States the immediate neighbour of the kingdom of Naples, the pope was the suzerain of the kingdom. Alexander had recognized Alfonso as the king, and reaped the rewards for this in benefits for three of his sons, so he had a personal stake in Alfonso's continuing to reign. On the other hand, Alfonso had maintained his father's policy of taking Roman barons into his service, giving him considerable influence over the security of Rome. Other powers followed this strategy too. As part of the preparations for his expedition, Charles, via the agency of Ludovico and Ascanio Sforza, was also giving *condotte* to Roman barons. Arguing that Alexander could feel more secure if he had the Colonna in his service, in March 1494 Ascanio arranged a joint papal and Milanese *condotta* for Prospero Colonna, whom he considered to be the head of the powerful baronial family and its faction. Neither Prospero nor Alexander knew that the French were expected to pay the Milanese share of his *condotta*, for Ludovico told Charles that Prospero had been hired to serve France.

The situation became still more complicated when Alexander's most determined and feared opponent within the College of Cardinals, Giuliano della Rovere, fled to France, believing his liberty, if not his life, was under threat from the pope. Welcomed and honoured by the king, from his arrival in Lyon in June, the cardinal joined the group of advisers around Charles, his energy and resolution bringing a fresh impetus to the military preparations. He also encouraged Charles in his scheme to call a general council to reform the Church if the pope would not help him. Giuliano della Rovere left his fortress at Ostia, at the mouth of the Tiber, and his fortified abbey of Grottaferrata south of Rome, in the custody of Fabrizio Colonna, who was still in Alfonso's service, although Ascanio was trying to hire him for Milan and France.

When Prospero and Fabrizio Colonna negotiated the surrender of Ostia to the pope in late May, Ludovico judged it to be a setback for the expedition. The Colonna were unwilling to declare open support for Charles, putting themselves and their estates at risk, until his army neared Rome. Indeed it was still unclear whether the *condotte* Ascanio had arranged were with Milan or with France. Alexander tried to get security from the Colonna and their allies, the Savelli, that they would not attack him, but in fact he wanted Alfonso to attack them. In these circumstances Alfonso had to appease Alexander's anxiety by deploying troops around Rome.[27]

Alfonso could have done without this distraction, as the French forces were beginning to make their way into northern Italy, and were gathering in Piedmont and Genoa. French officials had been in Genoa since the end of May, raising money and organizing the equipment of the fleet. Three ships were despatched to Aigues Mortes to load the heavy artillery and bring it there. In late June Louis d'Orléans, accompanied by Antonello da Sanseverino and other Neapolitan exiles, left Lyon for Genoa to take command. He arrived there just as the Neapolitan fleet carrying the Genoese exiles Obietto Fieschi and Cardinal Paolo Campofregoso appeared in Genoese waters. With the city full of Milanese and French troops, including 3,400 Swiss under Antoine de Baissey, the *bailli* of Dijon, there was no prospect of provoking a rebellion in the city, and the Neapolitans turned to the eastern Riviera, hoping to rouse the Fieschi and Campofregoso partisans. Their attempt to take Portovenere was beaten off, and the Neapolitans retreated before the French and Genoese ships arrived to challenge them.[28] This was the first engagement of the Italian Wars.

The march to Naples

News that the king had crossed the Alps and arrived in Italy in late August brought another attempt by the Neapolitan fleet, which had been given refuge in the Florentine port of Livorno, to disrupt French preparations. On 3 September 4,000 men under the command of Giulio Orsini and of the Genoese exiles Obietto Fieschi and Fregosino Campofregoso disembarked at Rapallo, twenty miles south of Genoa.[29] Weather conditions in the bay forced the fleet to withdraw, leaving the troops unprotected when Louis d'Orléans arrived by sea with 1,000 Swiss infantry and a further 2,000 Swiss with contingents of Milanese and Genoese infantry reached Rapallo from Genoa by land.[30] Battle was joined when some Swiss provoked a skirmish, but the terrain, a restricted area of level ground between a steep hill and a stream, did not allow the deployment of the Swiss pike squares, and much of the fighting was between the Italian infantry on either side while the artillery from the French ships fired on Rapallo. It ended in the rout of the Neapolitan troops, with Fregosino Campofregoso and Giulio Orsini among the captives. Although on a comparatively small scale, this was seen as a significant engagement. It put an end to Neapolitan plans to disrupt the invasion by precipitating a rebellion in Genoa, and it provided a foretaste to the shocked Italian troops of the cruelty of the Swiss mercenaries, who, as was their custom, massacred the wounded and sacked the little town.

Charles was at Asti when the news reached him. There, as he was preparing to go on his way to Genoa, he fell gravely ill. His return to France was seriously considered, and many of the French would not have been sorry to go back with him, but the king was resolved to press on. By the time he was sufficiently recovered to leave Asti, it had been decided that he should make his way to Naples by land, not by sea.

In the Romagna, Ferrandino, with the experienced captains, Gian Giacomo Trivulzio and Niccolò Orsini, conte di Pitigliano, commanded a mixed force of Neapolitan, papal and Florentine troops. They were confronted by Gian Francesco da Sanseverino, conte di Caiazzo, and his Milanese troops, and the growing number of French led by Bèraut Stuart d'Aubigny. Both sides were uncertain, because Giovanni Bentivoglio in Bologna and Caterina Sforza in Imola and Forlì, whose territories were on the major route south, refused to declare their allegiances; they were allies of Milan, but subjects of the pope. Finally, the Franco-Milanese forces made a move, investing the stronghold of Mordano in the territory of Imola on 19 October. Some of the defenders were Neapolitan troops, but Ferrandino would not come to assist them. After they refused to surrender on terms, despite a warning from the Milanese commander that the French fought like 'mad dogs',[31] Mordano was bombarded, and taken. It was full of refugees from the surrounding area, many of whom were slaughtered with the defenders. The sack of Mordano became part of the Italian narrative of Charles's expedition, as the first of a series of violent assaults on small towns and strongholds that dared to defy the French. After it, there was no further resistance to them in the Romagna. Caterina Sforza came to terms, and the papal and Florentine troops began to leave. Ferrandino withdrew his men to Cesena at the end of the month.

Ludovico Sforza was becoming increasingly concerned at the size of the French army and the intentions of its leaders. Louis d'Orléans was making no secret of the fact that he intended to use the campaign to press his claims to the duchy of Milan (and was prepared to broker an agreement that Alfonso should keep Naples, paying tribute to Charles).[32] Much of the burden of provisioning and supplying the French army was falling on the Milanese state. Adding to Ludovico's ambivalence was a secret deal his envoys had struck in early September with Maximilian for the ducal title to be conferred on himself and his heirs in the event of the premature death of his nephew Gian Galeazzo. The ailing young duke died suddenly – and to many minds, suspiciously – in Pavia on 21 October, only a few days after he had been visited at his bedside by Charles and promised French protection. Ludovico, who had accompanied the king through the duchy, abruptly left him and hastened to Milan. There he was invited by the Milanese notables to assume the title of duke, despite the claims of Gian Galeazzo's young son Francesco, and the pretensions of Louis d'Orléans. Charles had not treated Ludovico with great respect on his passage through the duchy, insisting on the surrender of the keys of the cities he passed through, and on setting his own guard in them while he was there, but he accepted the decision taken in Milan, and sent restrained congratulations to Ludovico.

When he joined his main force at Piacenza on 18 October, Charles consulted his commanders as to which route through Italy he should take, along the western or the Adriatic coast. He decided for the western route, and on 20 October ordered Gilbert de Montpensier to lead the advance guard of the army over the mountains towards Tuscany; he followed himself three days later. Negotiations with the Florentines to allow free passage and provision of supplies for a march through Tuscany had so far proved unsuccessful, and Florentine territory was treated as hostile. Fivizzano, the first of their fortresses, was taken by stealth, with the help of

Gabriele Malaspina, marchese di Fosdinovo, who had an hereditary claim to it. His men joined in its brutal sack, in which all the Florentine defenders and many of the inhabitants were killed; others were sent as prisoners to Lyon, to be held for ransom. Although local rivalries contributed to the ferocity of the assault on Fivizzano, it reinforced Italian apprehensions about what they might expect from the soldiers of the French king. Other Florentine strongholds in the Lunigiana hastened to surrender; those that refused suffered the same fate as Fivizzano.[33]

Within days the French were at the gates of the more formidable Sarzana. Ludovico had encouraged Charles to besiege it, believing that its modern fortifications could delay the French advance for a significant period. He had reckoned that the Florentine defences would be able to hold back the French for several weeks, perhaps long enough to halt the whole expedition.[34] They would not be put to the test. On his own initiative Piero de' Medici left Florence to go to the French camp: the Florentines favoured coming to terms with the king, and Piero hoped to shore up his crumbling personal authority by conducting the negotiations himself. When he met Charles on 30 October, he agreed to the surrender of the fortresses of Sarzana, Pietrasanta, Pisa and Livorno for the duration of the Neapolitan expedition. Although he had no authority from the republican councils to do this, he gave orders to the castellans to admit the French, which they obeyed.[35]

Going to Lucca on the invitation of the government, Charles took the opportunity of asking for a substantial loan from the government, and for custody of one of the republic's fortresses, Montignano (which the French soon decided was not worth guarding). While there he was visited by Cardinal Francesco Piccolomini (who Charles refused to receive as a papal legate, because his uncle, Pope Pius II, had invested Ferrante with the kingdom of Naples in 1459); by ambassadors from Siena, who promised to give the king's men unobstructed transit through Sienese territory; and by ambassadors from Florence, who followed the king as he made his way to Pisa on 8 November.

As he entered Pisa, which had been occupied by French troops under Montpensier a week before, Charles was received rapturously by the people. Entreated by the Pisans to free them from their detested subjection to the Florentines, the king signified his consent. He may well not have understood the full implications of what he agreed to; perhaps confusing the 'liberty' for which the Pisans pleaded with the 'liberties', the privileges, enjoyed by the civic authorities of towns in France. Hailing Charles as their liberator, the Pisans interpreted his words as a promise to protect their independence and hastened to assert it, expelling the Florentine officials who the king had expected to stay on.[36]

The Florentine ambassadors had already left, having assured Charles that he would be welcome in Florence. Far from supporting Piero de' Medici's position, the agreement he had made with Charles had fatally undermined it, and he was forced to flee the city on 9 November. Further attempts were made to negotiate with Charles before he entered the city in triumph on 17 November. He had about 10,000 troops with him. The king came as a conqueror: at his request the Florentines not only removed the gates where he was to enter, but made a symbolic breach in the city walls nearby.[37] His army paraded in triumph, many bearing their weapons as though advancing into action. The king himself was clad in bejewelled armour under his robes of velvet and cloth of gold, and carried a lance, although he wore a crowned hat rather than a helmet. The Florentines were at pains to make a show of greeting the king with joy, not fear, but throughout his stay in Florence they were wary, alert to any sign his soldiers might turn to pillaging. Still, Florence was more valuable to Charles as an ally than as a looted and hostile city. He had to think of keeping open routes through Italy for his army in the south, of the military and financial support that Florence could provide.

A deal was struck: the Florentines accepted the temporary loss of their fortresses but secured Charles's promise that they would be restored, including Pisa, at the end of the Neapolitan expedition. They also agreed to provide a subsidy of 120,000 florins to Charles, to accept two representatives of the king in the city who would attend all deliberations concerning France and the kingdom of Naples, and not to appoint a captain-general for their own troops until the expedition was over. Charles's attempts to reinstate the Medici in the city, even as private citizens, were resisted, but the Florentines did agree to refrain from retribution against the family. Finally, Florence was formally taken under his protection and her merchants were given back their privileges in France which had been withdrawn earlier in the year. This agreement was signed on 25 November and three days later Charles left the city to continue his journey southwards.[38]

Welcomed by the Sienese, Charles made only limited demands on them. They had already refused a request from two French ambassadors sent before the king to give him custody of their ports, and a loan of 30,000 ducats, and he did not ask for the surrender of any fortresses, and accepted their excuses for not lending him any money. The prospect of his arrival and his brief stay in the city did force the increasingly unpopular oligarchy that dominated Siena to make some concessions, but the king had nothing directly to do with this. Much of the army had already passed Siena before the king arrived there, and d'Aubigny brought his troops from the Romagna through Sienese territory in early December.

On leaving Sienese territory, the French entered the Papal States. The pope was beset by uncertainty. By December Ferrandino had completed his withdrawal from the Romagna and joined up with other elements of the Neapolitan army which had been left near Rome, so there were plenty of men to defend the city. Rome's supply route up the Tiber had been blocked in September, however, when Prospero Colonna with the assistance of French agents had taken over the fortress of Ostia by guile. He held it for Giuliano della Rovere, but that meant that it was at the disposal of the French. Charles was talking of calling a Council of the Church to discuss reform, and possibly depose the pope. The papal legates sent to try to persuade the king not to come to Rome had had no success; indeed one of them, Cardinal Raymond Péraud, had gone over to his side, and stayed with him. Charles sent envoys to the pope to ask for passage and supplies for his army and for investiture with the kingdom of Naples. Alexander turned to Ascanio Sforza, who agreed to go to Viterbo to negotiate with the king on behalf of the pope, but demanded a high price for the Milanese tutelage – rather than protection – of the pope that he offered. On 9 December, Alexander had both Ascanio and Prospero Colonna arrested. Despite the arrest of Prospero, the Colonna refused to surrender Ostia and continued to hinder the provisioning of Rome; Prospero was released, having agreed to accept a papal *condotta*, a promise he probably never intended to observe. Ascanio's arrest infuriated Ludovico Sforza and drove him temporarily back into the arms of the French, just when he was trying to distance himself from Charles; the king was quick to demand Ascanio's release.

As the French advanced, the towns of northern Lazio opened their gates to them. Columns were detached from the main army to link up with the Colonna in Ostia to the west of Rome, and to secure the routes into the Abruzzi region of Naples to the east. Before leaving to serve Alfonso in the kingdom, Virginio Orsini, with the agreement of the pope and Ferrandino, gave orders that the French should be allowed transit through his lands north of Rome; other Orsini followed suit. Alexander thought of flight but this could have been tantamount to resigning the papacy. Ferrandino wanted to withdraw his troops before his lines of retreat to Naples were blocked. A truce was accepted to allow the Neapolitan army to withdraw, Alexander released Ascanio Sforza and Rome prepared to welcome the French.

Montpensier with the advance guard began to enter the city on 29 December. Two days later, towards evening, Charles arrived with the main army. Through muddy, torch-lit streets, the king entered Rome, as he had done at Florence, as a conqueror, wearing armour and carrying a lance. On either side of the king rode the two cardinals that Alexander feared the most, Ascanio Sforza and Giuliano della Rovere.[39] The king took up residence at the imposing Palazzo San Marco, near the palaces of the Colonna and Cardinal della Rovere; around it was ranged his artillery, pointing outwards on the city. His soldiers behaved like an occupying force. Charles issued stern orders to repress the forced entries, looting and violence perpetrated by his men. Alexander at first refused to meet the king, and on 7 January he shut himself up in the main fortress of Rome, the Castel Sant'Angelo.

It was soon apparent that Charles had already rejected the option of taking any decisive action against the pope as head of the Church. Nevertheless, in the agreement which was finally ratified, nearly all his demands were met. The pope conceded free passage and provisions for the French army, and the temporary tenure by the king of key fortresses, including those of Ostia, the port of Civitavecchia and Terracina, a papal enclave in the kingdom of Naples. Alexander agreed to hand over the captive Turkish prince Djem – a crusade was still the ultimate justification for Charles's expedition, and Djem could be a useful weapon against Bayezid – but the pope retained the subsidy paid by the sultan to keep his brother, and rival for the throne, secure. The pope had to allow the king to take another hostage, his son Cardinal Cesare Borgia (who would leave with the French but soon slip back to Rome). But Cesare was not given powers to crown Charles king in Naples, as Charles had asked, and the question of investiture with the kingdom of Naples was deferred.[40]

Charles left Rome on 28 January. The bulk of the army was already on its way southwards, taking Montefortino and other fortresses and fortified villages of barons considered hostile, some sacked and burned 'with great cruelty', by 'these strange types, French, Swiss, Gascons, Picards, Scots and Germans', as the Venetian Marino Sanuto noted.[41] It was at this stage of the expedition when the French army would expect to face serious opposition and much harder fighting. Alfonso had a reputation for military skill and leadership, his army was intact, its leaders among the best in Italy; the routes from the border of the Papal States towards Naples were well-guarded. Yet before Charles had even left Rome, Alfonso formally resigned his crown to Ferrandino and prepared to leave for Sicily.

Alfonso had been contemplating abdication for some time,[42] but the final decision was apparently precipitated by a succession of reports reaching Naples of setbacks and reverses. News of the entry of Charles to Rome and the retreat of the Duke of Calabria with his troops to the kingdom was followed by reports of a revolt in the Abruzzi, fomented by French agents, and the news that the pope had made terms with the French king. Alfonso set sail for Sicily, taking with him the treasure he had gathered together, leaving his son with empty coffers, and a kingdom ready to surrender to the French.[43]

The failure of Alfonso and his allies to put up serious resistance to the French seems less surprising in retrospect than it did to some contemporaries. Charles did not set out to conquer the entire peninsula, but he did have to pass through several other states in order to reach Naples. The minor states – Savoy, Lucca, Siena – were prepared to let the French pass through their territory unhindered. Ludovico Sforza was Charles's ally, and the duchy of Milan was open to his army. The attempt by the Neapolitans to invade Milan from the south and through Genoa failed. Ludovico had expected the Florentine fortresses to hold the French up for weeks, but the Florentines were not of a mind to bear the brunt of the attack on behalf of Alfonso, and the nerve of Alfonso's mainstay in Florence, Piero de' Medici, failed. The pope was willing to stand by his ally only as long as that seemed to be the best safeguard for his own position. The Roman barons, who held much of the territory and many of the fortresses in the western and southern Papal States, were either in the service of Charles or not prepared to see their lands ruined and their strongholds destroyed in Alfonso's cause. The French army's progress through Italy had not been a destructive raid intended to weaken the resources and sap the morale of the enemy, but what resistance they had encountered had been met by sack and massacre when Charles's troops had shown the price to be paid for defying their might.

The kingdom of Naples had a taste of this too, when the commander of the fortress of Monte San Giovanni, which belonged to Alfonso d'Avalos, marchese di Pescara (whose family had been conspicuously loyal to the Aragonese dynasty since they came to Naples with Alfonso's grandfather, Alfonso V of Aragon) refused a summons to surrender, and mutilated the envoys who brought it. This breach of military protocol and insult to the French brought a terrible retribution when the place was taken after a few hours of artillery bombardment on 9 February. Of the several hundred inhabitants, only a few survived. News of this slaughter would do nothing to encourage other places to risk a similar fate.[44]

Alfonso's departure did not rouse the Neapolitans to make any great sacrifices for their new young king. The only chance for Ferrandino was to stand and fight Charles at the frontier, but the French army advanced rapidly along several routes converging on Naples, and he was out-manoeuvred. As the army pulled back, the towns opened their gates to the French. Ferrandino based himself at Capua, but he was forced to go to Naples to quell rising disorder there. While he was away, the commander he had left in Capua, Gian Giacomo Trivulzio, went over to the French, while Virginio and Niccolò Orsini withdrew with their men and attempted to do the same. All claimed they had Ferrandino's permission to do this, but while Trivulzio was given a *condotta* by Charles, the Orsini would be treated as prisoners of war. When Ferrandino approached Capua on 17 February, he was warned that the citizens intended to surrender to the French, and that he should return to Naples. Charles entered Capua the following day.[45]

Back in Naples, Ferrandino was unable to rally the population to his support – they were more intent on looting – and he had to seek safety in the fortresses of Castelnuovo and the Castel dell'Ovo. The ships in the harbour were burned on his orders, to prevent them falling into the hands of the French, as was the arsenal. French troops were already in Naples when Ferrandino finally took ship. But he did not go far, only to the islands off Naples, Procida and the stronghold of Ischia. The main fortresses of the city were still held for him, and exchanging fire with the French. Because of this, Charles's first entry into the city of Naples on 22 February was low-key, not the triumphant procession of his entries into other Italian cities to which he had no claim. Accompanied by a comparatively small escort, he was dressed in hunting clothes, not armour, he carried not a lance but a hawk, and rode a mule rather than a warhorse. He himself said he had decided not to have a formal entry that day, although his officials in France circulated accounts of a grand ceremony.[46] It took three weeks to overcome the resistance of the fortresses, partly because the French fleet had not arrived to take control of the bay, having been shattered by storms.

The speed and ease of the French conquest of Naples aroused astonished alarm in the other states of Italy. Not one person had been loyal to the Aragonese, commented Marino Sanuto, with only a degree of exaggeration; everything surrendered to the king of France without a fight.[47] Such swift ruin seems almost impossible to Ludovico Sforza and everyone else, Isabella d'Este wrote to her husband, Francesco Gonzaga: 'This should be an admonition to all rulers to esteem the hearts of their subjects more than fortresses, treasure and men-at-arms, because the discontent of subjects wages worse war than the enemy in the field.'[48] Even Charles seemed surprised at his welcome: 'You would not believe the great affection and goodwill that the nobles and the people show towards me', he wrote home to the duc de Bourbon.[49]

A request from Ferrandino to retain his title and the city of Naples, leaving all the rest of the kingdom to the French, was peremptorily dismissed by Charles, and a counter-proposal for Ferrandino to retire to France, without his royal title but with a generous allowance, was refused in turn. At last Ferrandino left his refuge at Ischia for Sicily.[50] Charles, with Naples now secure and only isolated pockets of resistance elsewhere, began to establish his government throughout the kingdom. Any plans for launching a crusade had received a serious blow a few days after he had arrived in Naples with the death of Djem. But this prospect was even more remote than ever. Charles planned to be back in France before the heat of the summer.[51] Within weeks of arriving at Naples, the French began to talk of his returning to France, perhaps deposing Ludovico Sforza on the way.[52] They were already aware that they might not be able to leave Italy without a fight.

The French in Naples

Throughout the winter of 1494–5 Charles had been aware of diplomatic moves underway to create a coalition against him. The prime mover was Ferdinand of Aragon, who had already begun to show disquiet about events in Italy in the late summer of 1494, sounding out the possibility of an anti-French alliance with Venice, and moving additional troops and ships to Sicily. It was not until the French invasion began directly to threaten the pope that he felt able to move more decisively from his position of neutrality, demanding in January 1495 that Charles should return Ostia to the pope. Already in negotiation with Maximilian for marriages between their families, he played on the growing resentment of the Emperor-elect (Frederick III had died in 1493) of Charles's successes in Italy, so that Maximilian was soon prepared to set aside his traditional hostility towards Venice. Since November, Venice had been encouraging Ludovico in his growing detachment from France and in his fear of Louis d'Orléans, who had remained at Asti throughout the French expedition southward.

In early March 1495 Milanese ambassadors with powers to negotiate an alliance joined Imperial and Spanish envoys in Venice for the final stages of the creation of the League. All the powers involved were anxious to avoid giving too overt an anti-French slant to the coalition they were creating; hence, the League of Venice or the Holy League, as it was sometimes known, which was agreed on 31 March 1495 was described as a defensive league against unprovoked aggression by any power holding a state in Italy – which would now include Charles – against any of the signatory Italian states.[53]

With the threat of the League hanging over him, the question of the king's return to France became more urgent. Nevertheless, he remained in Naples for a further six weeks, giving audiences and attending meetings with his counsellors in the mornings, but devoting his afternoons to the pleasures of the Neapolitan spring. All that would be needed to make a paradise on earth is Adam and Eve, he wrote.[54] His men were enjoying themselves too, in hunting, tournaments and feasting.

The administration which the French established in Naples during this first brief occupation of the kingdom was an uneasy compromise between arbitrary impositions and preservation of the status quo. No plans had been made for institutional changes; generally, Charles was simply distributing rewards and grants and responding to petitions. The seven great offices of state were divided between five Frenchmen and two Neapolitans, and members of the Council of State were French. Most of the major prizes, in terms of confiscated lands, lucrative monopolies and rich heiresses, went to French captains. All the governors of cities and fortresses were French.

Charles himself did not lack goodwill towards his new subjects, the people as well as the nobles. One lasting legacy of his time in Naples was the inclusion of a representative of the *popolo* of Naples among the nobles on the body that governed the city, the Tribunale di San Lorenzo. But if the nobility largely continued to enjoy their estates and local offices, their pride was hurt by French arrogance and condescension. Many of the French nobles were primarily interested in converting the lands and privileges granted to them into cash; they had no intention of settling in the kingdom or of establishing lasting connections with it.[55] Disenchantment with their new masters quickly developed among the Neapolitans.

Charles formally showed himself as sovereign to his people on 12 May, making a ceremonial entry to the city. This time he was dressed in royal robes, wearing a crown he had had specially made, and carried an orb and sceptre; he rode a fine horse, under a canopy borne by Neapolitan nobles, surrounded by his commanders, courtiers and officials. The procession ended at the cathedral, where Charles took an oath before the high altar to govern his subjects well.[56] This was not a coronation – Charles could not be crowned, for he had not received papal investiture.

The French retreat and the Battle of Fornovo

Charles VIII left Naples on 20 May. Some contingents of his troops had already begun their journey; around 1,000 lances and some 6,000 infantry marched northwards with the king and his household. Gilbert de Bourbon, comte de Montpensier, the viceroy, was left with around 800 French lances, 500 Italian lances, and 2,700 infantry.[57] There had been talk of Charles himself and at least a part of the army returning by sea; but too few ships were available, and anyway the king felt that it would ill-become him to show any sign of fear of the League. He was also hoping to have the opportunity to put further pressure on the pope to concede the investiture. But Alexander had no intention of meeting him. Accompanied by most of the cardinals, his own guards and contingents of troops sent by Venice and Milan, he left Rome for Orvieto on 27 May. Declaring himself disappointed not to find the pope in Rome, Charles entered the city peacefully on 1 June, and stayed only two days. He withdrew his garrisons from the papal cities of Terracina and Civitavecchia, but did not relinquish Ostia. As Charles continued his journey northwards, taking much the same route as when he had come, Alexander withdrew to Perugia.

By 13 June, the king had reached Siena. There, he was called upon to intervene in Sienese internal politics, and was asked by both the governing Balia and by the opponents of the regime to leave behind a French captain. Charles nominated Louis de Luxembourg, comte de Ligny, who left some troops but would not stay himself. This was not so much an attempt to occupy Siena as an opportunity for Ligny to claim payments from the Sienese. Unable to play any effective role in keeping peace between the Sienese factions, and probably without clear orders as to what he should be doing, Ligny's captain would withdraw from Siena on 1 August.[58]

In response to news of the mobilization of the League's forces in Lombardy and the Veneto, the king agreed to a proposal by Genoese exiles who were with him, Obietto Fieschi, and the cardinals Paolo Campofregoso and Giuliano della Rovere, to try to overthrow the Milanese regime in Genoa. A large detachment of troops was sent off through the Lunigiana with the two bellicose cardinals and Fieschi, to be joined by other soldiers who had recently come from France by sea.

At Siena, and as the king made his way to Pisa, Florentine envoys came to plead with him to honour his promises to restore Pisa and the other fortresses. Feelings against him were running high in Florence; nevertheless, the Florentines offered large loans, and to send troops with the French army up to Asti. Charles was torn between a wish to honour his word to the Florentines and advice from Ligny and others that it would be advantageous to the French to have Pisa and Livorno at their disposal to guarantee communications with Naples, especially if the enterprise to provoke rebellion in Genoa should be successful. The dramatic pleas of the Pisans impressed Charles's soldiers, let alone the king. Leaving Pisa on 22 June, he renewed the garrisons there and in the other fortresses held for him in the Lunigiana. He told the Florentines that they would have to wait for a final answer from him until he reached Asti safely.[59]

Immediately the League had been signed, Ludovico Sforza had sent Galeazzo da Sanseverino with a small army to summon Asti to surrender. Louis d'Orléans not only refused but seized the opportunity to sally out and occupy Novara on 10 June. Charles was not pleased: Louis was supposed to stay at Asti, guarding the passage out of Italy; instead, besieged by the Milanese forces sent against him, he was trapped in Novara. For their part, the Venetians had sent a fleet to harass the French in Apulia, and begun active mobilization of their army. Francesco Gonzaga was given the command as governor-general. At the end of June a substantial army was waiting near Parma for the French to come through the mountains.

The stage was set for the first major battle of the Italian Wars, the Battle of Fornovo. The French army of 10,000–11,000 men came down the valley of the Taro towards Parma. Gonzaga had about 20,000 troops, a quarter Milanese and the rest Venetian, and some Venetian militia. His instructions from Venice were to avoid battle if possible, and harry the French out of Italy. When Charles asked for a truce and free passage to the frontier, Gonzaga refused.

On 6 July the French set off down the left bank of the Taro, keeping the river between themselves and the army of the League. They imagined that the main battle would be fought by the vanguard in order to clear the road north, so half their forces, including all the Swiss infantry and the artillery, were placed there with Pierre de Gié and Gian Giacomo Trivulzio in command. Gonzaga's battle plan was elaborate, with four separate forces crossing the river. The Milanese contingent, led by Gianfrancesco da Sanseverino, was to engage the advance guard, two columns of heavy cavalry, led by Gonzaga and Bernardino Fortebraccio, to assault the right flank of the French centre and rear where the king and his bodyguards were, and the Venetian light horse, the stradiots, to circle behind the French to attack their left flank. Given the confined space available in the valley and a traditional Italian preoccupation with retaining large reserves, only about half the forces available were to be committed in these opening charges, and

the rest were to wait on the right bank of the river, to be called forward by
Gonzaga's uncle, Rodolfo, when needed.

Needless to say, the plan did not work. While Sanseverino managed
to cross the river and at least engaged the French vanguard, although
with questionable commitment, the state of the river, swollen by heavy
overnight rains, forced Gonzaga and Fortebraccio both to use the same
crossing point and gave the French time to form up to confront them.
Meanwhile, the stradiots, having temporarily distracted the vanguard,
turned back and found and sacked the baggage train. This ill-discipline
quickly spread to some of the infantry companies, and drew them away
from the centre of the fighting. Francesco Gonzaga and Fortebraccio found
themselves outnumbered in the centre and the death of Rodolfo Gonzaga
left no one responsible for bringing in the reserves. After an hour's fierce
fighting during which the king had been in considerable danger, the Italians
fell back across the river, allowing the French to reform and continue their
march.[60]

Both sides claimed the victory. The French had lost their baggage
containing more than 300,000 ducats' worth of booty, and abandoned
the field of battle; the Italians had suffered more severe casualties and had
failed to stop the French. The battle was really fought out by heavy cavalry, with the Italians failing to take advantage of their numerical superiority. Francesco Gonzaga had, however, challenged the French and come
reasonably close to defeating them; his reputation was greatly enhanced
by the whole episode, aided by his vigorous self-glorification.[61] If officially
Italians celebrated the Battle of Fornovo as a victory – to the surprise of
the French – privately, many were not so sure. Guicciardini's verdict was
that 'general consent awarded the palm to the French'.[62] Judgement of its
outcome and significance has been confused by the rapidity with which
it became mythologized, as the archetype of a new kind of battle, a new
kind of warfare, unpredictable, bloody, of a different scale of magnitude
to those with which Italians were familiar. There were marked differences
between the accounts of eyewitnesses and of contemporaries who were
not there, who described the battle as they would have expected it to be
fought, with a prominent role for the French artillery and rapid assaults by
the French and the Swiss.[63]

The French moved on in good order, followed at a distance by the army
of the League; neither side wanted a second battle. While Gonzaga's army
joined the Milanese besiegers of Novara, Charles reached Asti on 15 July.
There he was joined by the troops who had been sent to Genoa: there had
been no rebellion, and the French ships supporting the land forces had

been defeated and captured by the Genoese. A stalemate ensued for three months while Charles awaited funds and reinforcements, and the League hesitated to launch an assault on Novara. Louis d'Orléans hoped that the main French army would come to his aid, defeat the army of the League and overthrow Ludovico. But it was not until mid-September that Swiss reinforcements began to arrive in significant numbers, and by that time continued wet weather and signs of an early onset of winter led both sides to seek a settlement.

Charles had already signed on 26 August a treaty with Florentine envoys in Turin which gained him a loan of 70,000 ducats and a promise of 250 Florentine-paid lances to bolster his army in Naples, in return for another promise to restore the lost fortresses. Louis left Novara quietly on 22 September; three days later the much-depleted garrison straggled out. Only half of the 10,000 or so men had survived the three months of siege; only 500 or 600 were in a condition to bear arms.[64] Despite Louis's obvious desire to press his claim to the duchy of Milan, he was unable to do so without the agreement and support of his king. Charles showed little interest either in the claims of his cousin, or in taking over Milan himself. He agreed the Peace of Vercelli, signed on 9 October, which was more a unilateral settlement with Milan than a peace with the League. The objections of Spanish and Venetian envoys were ignored as Ludovico Sforza agreed to allow France free use of Genoa for its supply routes to Naples. For Charles, honour had been saved and valuable assistance gained for the defence of Naples, and he could return to France with an easy conscience.

The French loss of Naples

The French regime in Naples was not saved by these agreements, as Spain and Venice came to the aid of Ferrandino in the recovery of his kingdom. Gonzalo Fernández de Córdoba, whose qualities as a commander earned him the epithet 'El Gran Capitán', 'the Great Captain', disembarked in Calabria on 24 May 1495, just days after Charles had left Naples, with the small army which had been prepared in Sicily over the winter. With their support, Ferrandino was able to return to fight the French, but Ferdinand's help came at a price. Ferrandino had to agree to the annexation to the kingdom of Sicily of several important towns in Calabria, including Reggio.[65] Nor were the Spanish troops initially a match for the French. In a first confrontation with the seasoned heavy cavalry and Swiss infantry of d'Aubigny on 21 June at Seminara the combined Neapolitan and Spanish forces were badly beaten, although d'Aubigny reckoned they numbered 3,000–4,000 infantry and 800–1,000 horse against his 100 men-at-arms and 1,200 Swiss.[66] For several months, Gonzalo de Córdoba avoided further major confrontation while he built up his heavy cavalry and began to equip some of his infantry with pikes.

After the battle at Seminara, Ferrandino made his way to Messina; from there, with ships paid for by his father Alfonso, and some lent from Spain, he sailed for Naples. A popular uprising in Naples on the night of 6–7 July prepared the way for his return to the city that day, to an exultant welcome. After vain attempts to drive him out again, the French forces in the city retreated to the fortresses, which also provided cover for their ships at anchor in the bay. Among those who rallied to the young king were Prospero and Fabrizio Colonna; Prospero helped him direct operations in Naples. A relief force under François de Tourzel, baron de Précy, accompanied by pro-French Neapolitan barons defeated the larger force Ferrandino sent out of the city to confront them at Eboli. But Montpensier in the Castelnuovo did not hear of this French victory and, short of food, accepted an offer of terms on 4 October, agreeing to surrender if no help came within fifty days. The French relief force withdrew and, taking advantage of the lull in the fighting, Montpensier escaped by sea with many of his men to join d'Aubigny. Ferrandino consider this a breach of the truce, and resumed assaults on the Castelnuovo. It was the innovative use of a gunpowder mine, sprung on 27 November 1495, that allowed the Aragonese to breach the defences; the main fortress was surrendered on 8 December. The defenders of the Castel dell'Ovo, who had not participated in the truce, capitulated on terms two weeks later, finally surrendering on 17 February 1496.[67]

Despite Ferrandino's success in the city of Naples, much of the kingdom was still in the hands of the French and their supporters among the Neapolitan barons. As usual when the throne of Naples was at stake, the conflict was a civil war as well as an attempt to repel an invading army. In Calabria, Gonzalo de Córdoba was beginning to take the initiative, and to make progress in conquering that province. In Apulia, the Venetians were fighting in support of Ferrandino, but they also had their own agenda, for they had long aspired to possess strategic ports on the coast of Naples to reinforce Venetian control of the Adriatic. In June 1495, the commander of the Venetian fleet off Apulia, Antonio Grimani, was ordered to attack the ports held by the French; Monopoli was taken after a fierce assault on 1 July, before the ships were diverted to assist Ferrandino at Naples. In return for a loan of 200,000 ducats to Ferrandino, the Venetians were granted possession of the ports of Trani, Brindisi and Otranto, which they were to retain until the loan had been repaid. In the spring, the arrival of Venetian reinforcements of 700 lances and 3,000 infantry under the command of Francesco Gonzaga began to tip the balance against the French in the eastern provinces of the kingdom; Gonzalo brought his men to join the camp of the League in late June. Montpensier and his troops gradually lost heart as reinforcements and pay from France dwindled, and a Spanish fleet patrolled the coast, and on 27 July 1496 he surrendered his last main base at Atella. As Ferrandino still regarded Montpensier as having broken the terms of the truce agreed in Naples the previous October, the French commander and his men were interned, in malarial marshland near Pozzuoli. Many died of disease, including Montpensier, before the remnants of the army were allowed to embark for France. The French garrison of Gaeta held out until November; the last city to submit to the Aragonese king was Taranto, in February 1498 (after trying to surrender to the Venetians, who refused to accept it).

By then, Ferrandino had died of a fever in early October 1496; his father had died in December 1495. It was Federigo, Alfonso's younger brother, who took the throne, but he would struggle to assert full control over the kingdom. Furthermore, not only was the king of France not prepared to renounce his claim to Naples, but Ferdinand of Aragon thought his own claim to the Neapolitan throne was better than that of Federigo.

For most of Italy, the final departure of the French from Naples would have signified a return to normality. The most powerful king in Europe had come, passed through the peninsula with astounding, alarming ease, and conquered the largest Italian state – but he had soon left, and the elements of his army that remained in the kingdom of Naples had been unable to hold it for him. There was some concern that Charles would want to return, but no immediate prospect of that. In Milan there was a new duke and in Naples a new king, but they were still a Sforza duke and a d'Aragona king, as before. Alexander VI had survived what had appeared to be a serious challenge to his authority as pope. Only in Florence was the situation very different from that before Charles had come: the Medici were in exile, the prophetic friar Girolamo Savonarola had a powerful influence over the government and society of Florence, and the people of Pisa still defied their former Florentine masters.

Even for those Italians whose affairs and concerns in late 1496 were little different from those of early 1494, there was still much to reflect on. Not only might the French king come back, but the Spanish monarchs too had intervened decisively in the outcome of the war in Naples, and they and Maximilian were members of the League of Venice. This level of inter-national interest in the affairs of Italy had worrying implications if it were to continue – as it would do. There was further food for thought in some of the weapons and tactics that had been employed in the campaigns, an intimation that familiar Italian military customs and practices might not provide an effective response to those of the French or the Spanish. These considerations would only become of pressing concern if there would be further, large-scale, foreign military incursions into Italy. Which, of course, there would be – but even the most pessimistic of Italians in 1496 might not have foreseen the decades of warfare to come.

Notes

1 Labande-Mailfert, 174–92; Chevalier, 186–9.

2 Abulafia, *The Western Mediterranean Kingdoms*; Kekewich.

3 Pellegrini, 264–5.

4 Delaborde, 220–2.

5 Guicciardini, Book I, Chap. 2.

6 Shaw, *The Political Role*, 53–4, 159–60, 177–80.

7 Desjardins and Canestrini, I, 526.

8 Labande-Mailfert, 180–4.

9 Catalano, 184–6.

10 Denis.

11 Labande-Mailfert, 117–34; Knecht, 31–3; Potter, 252–60.

12 Labande-Mailfert, 119–22; Delaborde, 264–7.

13 Mallett, 157–8.

14 *Ibid.*,159; de Frede, *L'impresa*, 90–5.

15 Delaborde, 306–9.

16 Mallett, 160–1.

17 Delaborde, 331–2.

18 *Ibid.*, 324–5.

19 De Frede, 'Alfonso II', 195–204.

20 *Ibid.*, 205–19; Clough, 198–9.

21 Pellegrini, 501–4.

22 Catalano, 190–3.

23 ASF, Medici avanti il Principato, b. 50, 315: P. Alamanni and A. Niccolini, 29 July 1494, Milan.

24 Guicciardini, Book 1, Chap. 4.

25 Desjardins and Canestrini, I, 313–14.

26 Delaborde, 360; de Frede, *L'impresa*, 130; Catalano, 190.

27 Shaw, 'The Roman barons' 252–7; Shaw, *Julius*, 92–7.

28 Delaborde, 357, 375–7, 384; de Frede, *L'impresa,* 149–52; Pieri, 325–6.

29 De Frede, *L'impresa*, 177.

30 Pieri, 327–8.

31 Clough, 211.

32 Delaborde, 406–11; Desjardins and Canestrini, I, 574–5.

33 Delaborde, 433–4.

34 Pellegrini, II, 543; Segre, 'Ludovico Sforza', 18 (1902), 292–3.

35 Delaborde, 434–6; Desjardins and Canestrini, I, 587–93.

36 Delaborde, 448–51.

37 Sanuto, p. 131.

38 Capponi, 363–75.

39 Sanuto, 163–4; de La Vigne, 112–3.

40 De La Pilorgerie, 123–65.

41 Sanuto, 208.

42 Segre, 'Lodovico Sforza', 20 (1903), 74–5.

43 De Frede, *L'impresa*, 259–68; Galasso, *Il Regno*, 58–60.

44 De Frede, *L'impresa*, 272–3; Sanuto, 209.

45 De Frede, *L'impresa*, 280–7; Galasso, *Il Regno*, 62–75; Sanuto, 226–7; de La Pilorgerie, 176–85, 448–53.

46 De La Pilorgerie, 198–205.

47 Sanuto, 236, 262.

48 De Frede, *L'impresa*, 297.

49 Pélicier, IV, 516–7.

50 De Frede, *L'impresa*, 323–5; Galasso, *Il Regno*, 116–7; Sanuto, 260.

51 De La Pilorgerie, 214.

52 Sanuto, 248, 249.

53 Segre, 'Lodovico Sforza', 20 (1903), 368–405.

54 De La Pilorgerie, 216.

55 Cutolo.

56 Delaborde, 602–3; Galasso, *Il Regno*, 105–7.

57 De La Pilorgerie, 274–9.

58 Shaw, 'The French invasions', 171–2.

59 De Frede, *L'impresa*, 380.

60 Benedetti; Guicciardini, Book 2, Chaps 8–9; de La Pilorgerie, 353–8, 470–2; Pieri, 341–54; Santossuoso; de La Vigne, 158–67.

61 Chambers.

62 Guicciardini, Book II, Chap. 9.

63 'Introduction', to Boillet and Piejus, 8; Matucci.

64 Quilliet, 155–6.

65 Suárez, 288.

66 Pieri, 358–60; de La Pilorgerie, 392–3: d'Aubigny, 21 June 1495.

67 Pepper, 283–5; Delaborde, 675–6; de Frede, *L'impresa*, 418–24.

Bibliography

Abulafia, David (ed.), *The French Descent into Renaissance Italy 1494–5: Antecedents and Effects* (Aldershot: Ashgate, 1995).

Abulafia, David, *The Western Mediterranean Kingdoms 1200–1500. The Struggle for Dominion* (Longman, 1997).

Benedetti, Alessandro, *Diaria de Bello Carolino (Diary of the Caroline War)*, ed. and trans. Dorothy M. Schullian (New York: Frederick Ungar, 1967).

Biancardi, Silvio, *La chimera di Carlo VIII (1492–1495)* (Novara: Interlinea, 2009).

Blanchard, Joel, 'Political and cultural implications of secret diplomacy', in Abulafia (ed.), *The French Descent into Renaissance Italy*, 231–47.

Boillet, D. and M.F. Piejus (eds), *Les Guerres d'Italie: Histoires, pratiques, représentations* (Paris: Université Paris III Sorbonne Nouvelle, 2002).

Capponi, Gino (ed.), 'Capitoli fatti dalla città di Firenze col re Carlo VIII a dì 25 di novembre 1494', *Archivio storico italiano*, 1 (1842), 363–75.

Catalano, Franco, *Ludovico il Moro* (Milan: Dall'Oglio, 1985).

Chambers, David, 'Francesco II Gonzaga, Marquis of Mantua, "Liberator of Italy"', in Abulafia (ed.), *The French Descent into Renaissance Italy*, 217–31.

Chevalier, Bernard, *Guillaume Briçonnet (v.1445–1514). Un cardinal-ministre au début de la Renaissance. Marchand, financier, homme d'État et prince de l'Église* (Rouen: Presses Universitaires de Rennes, 2005).

Clough, Cecil H., 'The Romagna campaign of 1494: a significant military encounter', in Abulafia (ed.), *The French Descent into Renaissance Italy*, 191–215.

Coniglio, G., 'Francesco Gonzaga e la guerra contro i Francesi nel regno di Napoli', *Samnium*, 24 (1961), 192–209.

Cutolo, Alessandro, 'Nuovi documenti francesi sulla impresa di Carlo VIII', *Archivio storico per le province napoletane*, 63 (1938), 183–257.

de Commynes, Philippe, *Mémoires*, ed. Joseph Calmette, 3 vols (Paris: Librairie Ancienne Honoré Champion, 1924–5).

de Frede, Carlo, 'Alfonso II d'Aragona e la difesa del Regno di Napoli nel 1494', *Archivio storico per le Province napoletane*, 99 (1981), 193–219.

de Frede, Carlo, *L'impresa di Napoli di Carlo VIII: Commento ai primi due libri della Storia d'Italia del Guicciardini* (Naples: De Simone, 1982).

de La Pilorgerie, J.L., *Campagne et Bulletins de la Grande Armée d'Italie commandée par Charles VIII 1494–1495* (Nantes: V. Forest and É. Grimaud, 1866).

de La Vigne, André, 'L'Histoire du voyage de Naples du Roy Charles VIII', in Denis Godefroy (ed.), *Histoire de Charles VIII Roy de France* (Paris, 1684), 114–89.

Delaborde, H.F., *L'expédition de Charles VIII en Italie. Histoire diplomatique et militaire* (Paris: Firmin-Didot,1888).

Denis, Anne, *Charles VIII et les Italiens. Histoire et mythe* (Geneva: Librairie Droz, 1979).

Desjardins, A. and G. Canestrini, *Négociations diplomatiques de la France avec la Toscane*, 6 vols (Paris: Imprimerie Impériale, 1859–86).

Fletcher, Stella and Christine Shaw, *The World of Savonarola: Italian Elites and Perceptions of Crisis* (Aldershot: Ashgate, 2000).

Galasso, Giuseppe, *Alla periferia dell'impero: Il Regno di Napoli nel periodo spagnolo (secoli XVI-XVII)* (Turin: Einaudi, 1994).

Galasso, Giuseppe, *Il Regno di Napoli: Il Mezzogiorno spagnolo (1494–1622) (idem* (ed.), *Storia d'Italia*, XV, 2) (Turin: UTET, 2005).

Guicciardini, Francesco, *Storia d'Italia* (various editions).

Kekewich, Margaret L., *The Good King. René of Anjou and Fifteenth Century Europe* (Palgrave Macmillan, 1907).

Kidwell, Carol, 'Venice, the French invasion and the Apulian ports', in Abulafia (ed.), *The French Descent into Renaissance Italy*, 295–308.

Knecht, Robert, *The Rise and Fall of Renaissance France* (2nd edition, Oxford: Blackwell, 2001).

Labande-Mailfert, Yvonne, *Charles VIII et son milieu. La jeunesse au pouvoir* (Paris: Librairie C. Klincksiek, 1975).

Mallett, Michael, 'Personalities and pressures: Italian involvement in the French invasion of 1494', in Abulafia (ed.), *The French Descent into Renaissance Italy*, 151–63.

Matucci, Andrea, '"E vi farai alcun fiume": il mito della battaglia di Fornovo fra Leonardo e Machiavelli', in Boillet and Piejus (eds), *Les Guerres d'Italie: Histoires, pratiques, représentations*, 103–16.

Negri, Paolo, 'Studi sulla crisi italiana alla fine del secolo XV', *Archivio storico lombardo*, 50 (1923), 1–135, 51 (1924), 75–144.

Pélicier, P. (ed.), *Lettres de Charles VIII*, 5 vols (Paris: Renouard, 1898–1905).

Pellegrini, Marco, *Ascanio Maria Sforza. La parabola politica di un cardinale-principe del Rinascimento*, 2 vols (Rome: Istituto storico italiano per il Medio Evo, 2002).

Pieri, Piero, *Il Rinascimento e la crisi militare italiana* (Turin: Einaudi, 1952).

Pepper, Simon, 'Castles and cannon in the Naples campaign of 1494–95', in Abulafia (ed.), *The French Descent into Renaissance Italy*, 263–91.

Potter, David, *A History of France, 1460–1560:The Emergence of a Nation State* (London: Macmillan, 1995).

Quilliet, Bernard, *Louis XII* (Paris: Fayard, 1986).

Sakellariou, Elena, 'Institutional and social continuities in the kingdom of Naples between 1443 and 1528', in Abulafia (ed.), *The French Descent into Renaissance Italy*, 327–53.

Santossuoso, A., 'Anatomy of defeat in Renaissance Italy: the Battle of Fornovo in 1495', *International History Review*, 16 (1994), 221–50.

Sanuto, Marino, *La spedizione di Carlo VIII in Italia*, ed. R. Fulin (Venice: M. Visentini,1883).

Segre, Arturo, 'Lodovico Sforza, detto il Moro, e la Repubblica di Venezia dall'autunno 1494 alla primavera 1495', *Archivio storico lombardo*, 3rd ser., 18 (1902), 249–317, 20 (1903), 33–109, 368–443.

Segre, Arturo, 'I prodromi della ritirata di Carlo VIII, Re di Francia, da Napoli', *Archivio storico italiano*, 5th ser., 33 (1904), 332–69, 34 (1904), 2–27, 350–405.

Shaw, Christine, 'Alexander VI and the French invasion of 1494', *Jacobus*, 25–6 (2009), 197–222.

Shaw, Christine, 'The French invasions and the establishment of the Petrucci *signoria* in Siena', in Fletcher and Shaw (eds), *The World of Savonarola*, 168–81.

Shaw, Christine, *Julius II: The Warrior Pope* (Oxford: Blackwell, 1993).

Shaw, Christine, *The Political Role of the Orsini Family from Sixtus IV to Clement VII. Barons and Factions in the Papal States* (Rome: Istituto Storico Italiano per il Medio Evo, 2007).

Shaw, Christine, 'The Roman barons and the French descent into Italy', in Abulafia (ed.), *The French Descent into Renaissance Italy*, 249–61.

Suárez, Luis, *Fernando el Católico* (Barcelona: Ariel, 2004).

CHAPTER 2

Milan and Naples overwhelmed, 1496–1503

Charles VIII was never able to renew his attempt to conquer Naples, before his premature death in April 1498. While Montpensier's army still held out in Naples the king made efforts to supply and reinforce it, but there was little chance of a relief expedition. There were incursions into northern Italy. Charles gave his blessing to an unsuccessful attempt by Giuliano della Rovere and the Genoese exile Battistino Campofregoso to take Genoa and Savona in early 1497. He ordered Gian Giacomo Trivulzio, who commanded the French troops based at Asti, to detach some men to help them. Trivulzio obeyed reluctantly, because he wanted to concentrate his forces on an incursion into the duchy of Milan, which had rather more success. Several places on the border were seized, and Alessandria threatened. By mid-February, Trivulzio's troops were withdrawing back to Asti. Another, half-hearted, attempt on Savona came to nothing. Charles merely authorized these expeditions: the initiative came from the three exiles who led them.

The French king was not the only ultramontane ruler to be interested in Italy now. Ferdinand of Aragon claimed to be the rightful heir of his uncle Alfonso I of Naples (Alfonso V of Aragon), and some Neapolitan barons would have preferred him to Federigo. Although his representatives in Naples acknowledged Federigo as king, Ferdinand asserted his right through diplomatic channels, but at this time, rather than challenge Federigo directly, he used it as a bargaining counter in negotiations with France. Proposals for a partition of the kingdom of Naples between Ferdinand and Charles, or of an exchange of Navarre and Naples, were discussed but no conclusive agreement was reached.

This refusal by Ferdinand to recognize Federigo as the rightful king of Naples would eventually have momentous consequences for Italy. His decision a few years later to take the kingdom for himself would reunite Naples with the group of states under the crown of Aragon, and bring it into the inheritance that Ferdinand would pass on to his grandson Charles, the future Emperor Charles V.

Maximilian's expedition to Italy, 1496

Another presage of the future Imperial intervention that would reshape the entire Italian state system and the role of Italy in European politics also took place in 1496 – the first direct involvement of the emperor-elect, Maximilian, in the Italian Wars. It would have taken an observer of exceptional foresight to divine its full import, for at this stage Imperial authority was not backed by substantive power, and his intervention turned into a fiasco. Maximilian was encouraged to come to Italy by Ludovico Sforza, who thought he could use his support to strengthen his own position. The princes of the Empire did not approve of the expedition, and when Maximilian arrived in Italy in late August, it was with far fewer troops than he had promised. He expected Milan and Venice to subsidize him and help him raise some more men, but Venice refused, and Ludovico was unwilling. With the forces Maximilian had, Ludovico felt he might at least be able to help strengthen the western frontier of Milan, but Maximilian's attempt to use his authority to influence French partisans such as the Duke of Savoy and the Marquis of Monferrato was fruitless.

Before he came to Italy, Maximilian had said that he intended to go to Pisa to impose a solution in the conflict between Pisa and Florence. Maximilian told the Florentines he would use his Imperial authority to decide on their quarrel with the Pisans; their response was that they would not accept any judgement until they were back in possession of their rebellious subject city.[1] Sailing from Genoa to La Spezia with six Venetian galleys, Genoese ships carrying artillery and 1,000 German infantry, Maximilian then made his way to Pisa by land in late October. From there, he set about preparing to besiege Livorno, which the Florentines had retaken, with his own men, who included another 1,000 German infantry and 500 horse who had come overland, and with the Milanese and Venetian troops who were already defending Pisa. The Florentines were well-prepared to defend Livorno, and their morale was boosted by the fortuitous arrival of several French ships carrying grain supplies and 600 Swiss and Gascon infantry they had hired in France.

Having unloaded the troops and grain, the French ships left, escaping a storm that scattered the fleet that had brought Maximilian and sank some vessels. Even before this setback, Maximilian had decided to raise the siege, and he returned to Pisa, and then suddenly left for the duchy of Milan. From there he hurried back to his own lands, just as the French forces under Trivulzio were launching their assault on the Milanese. High-sounding claims to authority as emperor, backed by inadequate forces and compromised by lack of funds, were what Italians had come to expect of Imperial interventions in Italy, to which Maximilian added his characteristic touch of sudden and unexplained withdrawal.

The Pisan War, 1495–9

From one perspective, the war between Pisa and Florence that dragged on, with varying degrees of intensity, for fifteen years looks like a sideshow in the Italian Wars, but in the late 1490s this conflict became for a time the focal point of Italian politics. It was a type of war familiar in fifteenth-century Italy, one of raids and manoeuvres, of sometimes fierce conflicts over fortified villages and minor strongholds; a war that those who paid for it suspected the commanders were more interested in prolonging than in bringing to a decisive conclusion; a war shaped and complicated by military and political rivalries, suspicions, traditional alliances and enmities. Yet the determined resistance of the Pisans won the admiration of some contemporaries. Pisan commentators were not alone in seeing it as an exemplar of the valour and fighting spirit civilians could show in defence of their city and their liberty; even Florentines could be moved to praise their heroism.[2] Pisan defence was fuelled not only by republican and civic ideals, but by bitter memories of their treatment by the Florentines. Few if any Florentines were prepared to accept its loss, despite the cost of their efforts to recover it.

In the initial stage of the war, both sides looked to the French king. The Pisans hoped he would preserve them from renewed subjection to Florence, the Florentines, for the return of Pisa and of the fortresses in the Lunigiana still held by French garrisons. A sense of grievance at Charles's delay in restoring their fortresses was heightened by the assistance French troops gave to Pisan efforts to beat back Florentine attacks. Interpreting the true intentions of the king (assuming that he had come to a firm decision) was complicated by the ambivalent attitude of the French commander in Pisa, Robert de Balzac, baron d'Entragues, whose support the Pisans had courted.

Orders from the king to hand the fortresses over to the Florentines were obeyed by the castellan of Livorno. Balzac sold the main fortress of Pisa to the Pisans for 20,000 ducats, Sarzana and Sarzanello were sold to the Genoese for a comparable sum, and then in March Pietrasanta was sold by Balzac to Lucca for 15,000 ducats. Both Lucca and Genoa were keen to re-acquire places they had possessed in the past and considered rightfully theirs. Despite their disappointment, the Florentines persisted in their alliance with the French king, pressing him to help them recover Pisa.

The departure of the French did not leave the Pisans to face the Florentines alone. Already during 1495 they had received arms and money from Genoa, and horse and foot from Milan and Venice; even Maximilian, at the instigation of Ludovico Sforza, had sent a few German infantry. Any intentions Ludovico Sforza and the Venetians may have had of assisting the Pisans as a way of influencing Florence, soon gave way to the aspiration to bring Pisa under their own control. The Pisans were prepared to offer submission to either power, but not on the terms Ludovico wanted, while the cautious Venetians turned them down more than once, saying the time was not right and they did not want to anger Ludovico by accepting.[3] Rivalries between the Milanese and Venetians hindered the defence of Pisa. After Maximilian's abortive expedition to Pisa, Ludovico began to withdraw his men.

Fortunately for the Pisans, the Florentines were distracted from prosecuting the war with full vigour by their internal divisions. The major factions at this time were the supporters and opponents of Girolamo Savonarola, who preached in support of the new constitution, centred on the Great Council in which about 3,000 citizens were qualified to sit. There was in any case a lull in the fighting in 1497, as Pisa (nominated an adherent of Spain) and Florence were included in a six-month truce between France and Spain from late April. As the truce neared its end, the Venetians decided to send reinforcements for the 1,000 infantry, 1,000 horse and 100 stradiots they had in Pisa. But it was not until the following summer, after the political turmoil in Florence came to a crisis with the arrest and execution of Savonarola, that the war entered a new phase. His removal from the political scene prompted Ludovico Sforza (who had disliked his influence over the Florentine government) to lend more open support to Florence.[4]

Renewed Florentine resolution was manifested by the appointment of Paolo Vitelli, one of the most highly reputed Italian *condottieri*, as their captain-general. The Venetians began to employ a new strategy, diverting Florentine forces from Pisa by opening other fronts, and the focus of fighting shifted east to the hills of the Casentino. After the Venetians took Bibbiena in early October, with the help of Medici partisans in the town, and concentrated 700 men-at-arms and 6,000 infantry there, Paolo Vitelli and his brother Vitellozzo were sent to counter this serious threat. Vitelli succeeded in outmanoeuvring the enemy, and a Venetian attempt to send substantial reinforcements under Niccolò Orsini was blocked in the Appenines in February.[5]

With about 20,000 of their troops deployed, for the Venetians the war was becoming seriously expensive. By early 1499 other issues, closer to home, were taking precedence in Venetian councils: the looming threat to their overseas dominions from the Turks, and the plans of the new French king, Louis XII, to take the duchy of Milan. They were ready to accept the arbitration of Ercole d'Este, even though the terms he proposed were far more favourable to the Florentines than they had expected, and the indemnity that they were to receive from Florence, of 180,000 ducats paid over twelve years, much less than they wanted. After some debate, they decided that it was worth accepting these terms to be free of their involvement in the war.[6]

Despite the rapid withdrawal of the Venetian troops, the Pisans refused to accept their return to subjection to Florence, not trusting that the conditions elaborated by Ercole d'Este would effectively guard them from Florentine reprisals. With the Pisans now having to stand alone, the Florentines wanted Paolo Vitelli to press the advantage and make a direct assault on the city. Sections of Pisa's walls were smashed by Florentine artillery in August, but Vitelli held back from ordering the assault until further breaches had been made and he thought his men could attack without incurring heavy losses. On the day he planned to attack, however, too many of his men were sick – as was Vitelli himself – and the siege had to be lifted in early September. This was the latest of a series of episodes in which the Florentines believed their commander had shown insufficient zeal, and some believed him to be in contact with the Pisans. He was arrested, taken to Florence, tortured and executed. His execution did not encourage Florence's other *condottieri* to be loyal to the republic, or enhance the military reputation of the Florentines, which did not stand high.

Preparations for the French invasion of Milan

The accession of Louis d'Orléans as Louis XII, following the sudden death of Charles VIII on 7 April 1498, had significant implications for Italy.

From the beginning of his reign, he left no doubt that the rapid conquest of the duchy of Milan was a priority for him. But there were other issues to be dealt with, both urgent in their own right and needing to be settled in preparation for any Italian enterprise.

First of all, there was the question of his childless marriage to Charles's sister, Jeanne, and the position of Charles's widow, Anne. The solution to the problem of providing an heir to the throne, and maintaining the hold on Brittany which the marriage of Charles and Anne had achieved, lay in Louis obtaining a divorce from Jeanne and marrying Anne himself. Both the divorce and the remarriage required papal authorization. Alexander was open to persuasion. Ready to satisfy the wishes of his son Cesare to abandon his career as a cardinal, Alexander was looking for a way to set him up as a secular lord. Within a few months of Louis's accession to the throne, exchanges between the French and papal courts began concerning the estates and other benefits the king would bestow on Cesare, with the explicit understanding that in return the pope would smooth the path to the annulment of Louis's marriage to Jeanne.

One of the additional favours Cesare could expect from the king was help with gaining his chosen bride, Carlotta, daughter of King Federigo of Naples and his first wife Anne of Savoy, who had been brought up in France. Following his resignation from the College of Cardinals, Cesare travelled to France in October, bringing the papal dispensation necessary for Louis to marry Anne in January 1499. Louis had difficulty in keeping his side of the bargain, because Carlotta refused to marry Cesare. At last the king succeeded in finding an acceptable substitute, Charlotte d'Albret. In the marriage contract, signed in May, there was a clause in which the king expressed his expectation that Cesare and his family would aid him in the conquest of Naples and Milan.[7] All the obligations and interests that bound Alexander to Louis arose out of this marriage and the king's patronage of Cesare Borgia; there was no formal alliance between the papacy and France.

Like Charles as he had planned his expedition to Naples, Louis wanted to secure the borders of his kingdom before he crossed into Italy. There had been an incursion over the eastern border within a few months of his accession, as Maximilian launched an attempt to recover the duchy of Burgundy. Local forces repelled with ease the few troops Maximilian had brought, and Louis outflanked him diplomatically by negotiating with his son, Archduke Philip. Now of age to govern the lands he had inherited from his mother, Philip was ready to act independently of his father's tutelage, and was much less hostile to France. In a treaty concluded in August 1498,

Philip agreed not to claim either Burgundy or Picardy from the French crown, and to do homage for the county of Flanders, in return for three cities in Artois. Unreconciled, Maximilian could not make any effectual response. Further security was provided by the reaffirmation of the Treaty of Etaples, as Henry VII readily accepted Louis's offer to renew it in July 1498. Negotiations with Ferdinand and Isabella were more difficult, but by early August the Treaty of Marcoussis had been agreed. None of the outstanding territorial disputes between France and Spain were settled, but it was agreed that the two powers were to have all enemies in common, except the pope; there was no mention of any other Italian power.

Louis was also engaged in discussing an alliance intended to provide active support for an invasion of Milan, one with Venice. Both Louis and Venice were eager to establish good relations, and by July 1498 the decision had already been taken in Venetian councils – in principle – to join Louis in war on Ludovico Sforza. It was a sign of how bad relations between Venice and Ludovico Sforza had become that many Venetians were ready for the sake of getting rid of him to run the risk of assisting such a powerful prince as the king of France to become their neighbour and their competitor for domination over Lombardy. Others, including the doge, did not think the risk worthwhile, but they were repeatedly outvoted in the long debates that took place in the Venetian councils on this matter.

Differences over several significant issues prolonged the negotiations. Pisa was one: Louis wanted the city restored to Florence, or placed in his custody or in that of the pope; the Venetians wanted it to be independent. How much Milanese territory the Venetians would gain was another. Some optimistic Venetians even hoped that Louis might agree to their having the whole duchy, in return for an annual tribute; the more realistic hoped that he would agree to their having the territory on both sides of the river Adda. Louis considered this excessive, maintaining that they should be content with holding the left bank. Another point of contention was the French demand that the Venetians should provide them with 100,000 ducats towards their costs. The Venetians tried to argue that it was not honourable for the king to insist on such a payment, but Louis backed his ministers' demands, saying that he wanted to be able to tell the French people that Italians would pay the costs of the expedition.[8] The question of Pisa was removed from the agenda by the Venetian acceptance of Ercole d'Este's arbitration, and the Venetians resigned themselves to their prospective gains being restricted to the city of Cremona and all the territory to the east of the Adda not yet under their control, and to agreeing to pay the subsidy. They were to support the French conquest of Milan by attacking from the east, with 1,500 men-at-arms and 4,000 infantry, and not impede in any way Louis's conquest of Genoa; the French would provide naval support against Ottoman attack on the Venetians. The terms were concluded at Blois on 9 February 1499, but kept secret for some weeks.[9] Even after the publication of the alliance, there was still some scepticism among Italians about whether Venice really would support a French invasion of Milan, and a belief that without the support of the Venetians, the invasion would not go ahead.[10]

Louis also secured the alliance of the states on the western frontier of Milan. Persistent, patient French diplomatic approaches succeeded in winning over the young Duke of Savoy, Filiberto, helped by Ludovico Sforza's refusal to offer comparably attractive terms. According to the treaty finalized in June 1499, the duke was to have command of 200 French lances, and a pension; he was to provide a contingent of 600 light horse and 2,000 infantry, and allow French troops to pass through his territory. Louis also confirmed in his service Ludovico, marquis of Saluzzo (who had been with him in Novara throughout the siege in 1495), increasing his company from 60 to 100 lances; and he gave the command of 50 lances and 200 mounted crossbowmen to Costantino Arniti, who governed Monferrato for his minor nephew, Marquis Guglielmo. Attempts by Ludovico Sforza to counter these engagements were tardy and ineffectual.[11] The route to Italy was now open to the French forces.

Louis's declared intention was that the invasion should be paid for out of Milanese finances after the conquest[12], but money was needed for advance payments to the troops. The treasury was in deficit when he came to the throne, but Louis was much more astute financially (some said avaricious) than Charles had been. By April 1499 he claimed to have amassed sufficient to pay for two years of war.[13] He also had to reform the army, which was in disarray, building up and reorganizing the companies of heavy cavalry. In the summer of 1499, the recruitment of thousands of infantry, Normans, Picards, Gascons, English and Swiss, was ordered. It took some time and careful diplomacy to secure the services of the Swiss. The treaty of Lucerne in March 1499 renewed the alliance with the Swiss that gave the king of France, in return for payment of a pension of 20,000 livres to the cantons, the official sanction to raise as many men as he required and they could provide. To command the army, Louis chose Ligny, d'Aubigny and Trivulzio. It was Trivulzio, still based at Asti, where the army began to muster in May, who would lead the attack on the duchy of Milan.[14]

Ludovico Sforza's preparations to defend his state were not going so well. He had been comprehensively outmanoeuvred by the king's determined and consistent diplomacy. His own diplomatic efforts, if at times intense, were vitiated by bouts of indecisiveness or over-confidence. Within Italy, only Federigo would be ready to offer substantial support. Federigo had his own obvious reasons for opposing a French incursion into Italy, but he was not ready to compromise the defences of his kingdom in order to help Ludovico. The duke's main hopes for support rested on Maximilian. From 1493 to 1498, Ludovico had paid him about a million ducats, as the price of imperial investiture with the duchy and for the dowry of his niece, Bianca, who had married Maximilian in 1493. In return, he wished the duchy of Milan to be treated as an integral part of the Empire, one that Maximilian would defend if it were attacked. But the only support he received from Maximilian was a few diplomatic interventions. In response to the threat of the Venetians joining the French in attacking Milan, Ludovico sent envoys to Bayezid, offering money to subsidize a Turkish war on Venice. Such was his reliance on the power of money, he even tried in the autumn of 1498 to buy off Louis's claims, or to pay him an annual tribute.[15]

His money would have been better spent in putting his army into order. Milanese military capacity had been undermined by years of neglect, poor pay, and inadequate attention to retaining the services of good captains. Ludovico made some effort to secure the services of Francesco Gonzaga, but then lost him to the Venetians. Prominent among the commanders of the Milanese forces in 1499 were the Sanseverino brothers, who were not the equal of their father, Roberto. The duke's favourite and son-in-law, Galeazzo, shone on the parade-ground and in tournaments, but was not a competent field commander. In March 1499, Ludovico reckoned he had 1,500 men-at-arms, 1,100 light horse and at most 5,000 infantry – rather fewer cavalry, and only about half the infantry he believed Louis to have ready at the time.[16]

To counter the threat from Venice, he looked to Maximilian to invade Venetian territory with German troops paid by himself and Federigo. He also hoped that the Florentines would provide 300 men-at-arms and 2,000 infantry if needed, but they refused to promise this. Ercole d'Este sent only a few men-at-arms, and a conveniently timed attack of syphilis excused his son Alfonso, whose company of 200 men-at-arms was paid for by Ludovico, from going to support his brother-in-law. Federigo did send, under the command of Prospero Colonna, some of the 400 men-at-arms and 1,500 infantry he had pledged to provide Ludovico if he were attacked by the French, but far too late to be of any use. The only effective help that the Duke of Milan would receive from other Italian states was 500 infantry sent by his niece Caterina Sforza, who governed Imola and Forlì in the Romagna for her minor sons.[17]

It was not until July that he began to make serious efforts to hire foreign mercenaries. While thousands of Swiss came to take his pay, Ludovico could not hire the organized companies with which the Swiss authorities were providing Louis; the duke had to rely on an assembly of individuals and small groups, that would not be able to show the same discipline and tactical skills in the field. His efforts to recruit German infantry and Burgundian cavalry and artillerymen were just as tardy.[18] An artillery train was scraped together by denuding the duchy's fortresses of their guns. Nor were those fortifications in good condition. Efforts to make some repairs had been begun in April, only to be suspended. 'Wait to the last moment to resume them', he ordered Galeazzo da Sanseverino, 'calculating exactly how long they will take'.[19] Work only began again just as Trivulzio crossed the frontier on 15 July. The French invasion had begun, while Ludovico was still frantically trying to put his defences in order, and to raise and hire more troops.

He looked to his subjects to help defend the duchy, ordering a mass levy of infantry.[20] But Ludovico was not a popular prince. Under him, aspects of Sforza government which had aroused much discontent – the elevation of favourites perceived as lowly born over established aristocratic families with deep roots in local society, partial justice, high taxes, the interference of ducal officials in settled provincial power structures – had become more marked. Disaffection was heightened by a sense that the duke was governing and exploiting the resources of the state in his personal, private interests.

The French conquest of Milan, 1499–1500

Trivulzio's incursion in July, apart from an attempt to take Alessandria with the help of some conspirators inside the city, was limited to capturing some minor fortresses in the border province. In Milan and Venice it was believed that the underlying intention was to stimulate the Venetians into completing their own preparations for an attack on the duchy.[21] The Venetian army that crossed the river Adige into Milanese territory in late August, under the command of Niccolò Orsini da Pitigliano, numbered about 12,000 men, including around 1,600 men-at-arms and 600 light horse.[22] They encountered little resistance as they set about occupying the territory allotted to Venice under the Treaty of Blois; the main prize, the city of Cremona, surrendered to them on 8 September, its fortress a week later.

In the west, the campaign proper was not launched until mid-August. Louis himself was not sure how many men he had ready; he said 30,000. Best estimates were that the French had about 10,000 cavalry – 1,500 lances and 800 light horse – and 17,000 infantry, about 6,000 of them Swiss, the rest largely French, with 2,000 from Savoy, and 2,500 artillerymen.[23] Estimating the size of the Milanese army is more difficult, because Ludovico was still recruiting; Venetian sources gave a total of about 23,000.[24] A rapidly executed campaign was what Louis wanted: he said that he would rather put all to the hazard of battle than have his army engage in a series of lengthy sieges, and his intention was that the first place taken should be treated with great cruelty, to encourage the surrender of others.[25] Rocca d'Arazzo, about five miles from Asti, was the first Milanese stronghold to suffer this fate. After five hours of bombardment, the garrison of 400 men surrendered, but many of them and of the population were massacred. Several hundred people, including all the garrison, were put to the sword at Annona when that fortress fell on 19 August after four days of resistance. With these examples before them, cities such as Voghera and Tortona quickly offered to surrender rather than face a French assault, and soon French forces were encircling the city of Alessandria.

Ludovico planned to avoid battle, to force the French to waste their strength in sieges. Alessandria and Pavia were to be nodal points of this defence, giving him time to raise more troops.[26] This strategy relied on having money and time, which were both in short supply, and loyalty, which few of his subjects felt towards him. After only a few days' siege, his incompetent commander Galeazzo da Sanseverino abandoned Alessandria; there were 5,000 troops in the garrison, but the people made it evident that they were not prepared to sacrifice themselves for Ludovico Sforza. The next morning, 29 August, the French entered the city; most of the Milanese troops were more intent on making their escape than on putting up a fight, but about 3,000 were captured and disarmed. Pillaging there was, but no massacre. Galeazzo rode to Pavia, but the inhabitants refused to admit him and his men and he had to go on to Milan.

There a disheartened and irresolute Ludovico found himself almost imprisoned in the castle by an increasingly hostile population. With the French advancing, now virtually unopposed, from the west, and the Venetians moving in rapidly from the east, Ludovico fled north to seek the protection of Maximilian; his sons had already been sent ahead in the care of their uncle Ascanio. On 2 September, a few hours after the departure of the duke, Trivulzio and 5,000 mainly Italian troops began to enter Milan; Trivulzio took care to stop French soldiers coming in to treat it as a hostile city. After a few days, the French were dispersed to secure the rest of the duchy, apart from the area of the Ghiaradadda and Cremona occupied by the Venetians. The Milanese were not happy at the Venetians taking over this territory, and Trivulzio himself sympathized with their wish that the duchy should not be dismembered.[27] To the citizens of Milan, the lands of the duchy belonged to their city, as much as to the duke.

As news arrived of the easy progress of his army, Louis, who had remained in France, decided to go in person. On his journey, he heard of the surrender of the fortress of Milan on 17 September. The king's passage through his newly acquired duchy was a leisurely progress with pauses for rest and hunting, rather than the march of a conqueror come to enforce the submission of his subjects.

For his ceremonial entry to the city of Milan on 6 October, the king wore ducal robes, a white mantle trimmed with grey vair (squirrel-fur). An impressive cortege of French and Italian dignitaries rode with him through the streets. Among the Italians, alongside many nobles from the duchy, were the Duke of Savoy, the Marquises of Monferrato and of Saluzzo, and Cesare Borgia, who all held military commands from the king, but also the Marquis of Mantua and the Duke of Ferrara, who did not. Ambassadors from Florence, Genoa, Siena, Pisa and Lucca also took part, as did the papal legate, Cardinal Giovanni Borgia. Two other cardinals accompanied the king, Giuliano della Rovere and Georges d'Amboise. The streets had been sumptuously decorated, and the Milanese came dressed in their finery to watch – but few to cheer, at least with any enthusiasm, according to a Venetian report.[28]

It took a while for many Milanese to realize that they would be coming under direct French rule. Some, particularly from the leading civic families, hoped that Milan would be an autonomous republic, with authority over all the territories that had been governed by the Sforza (except Genoa), paying an annual census to the king. Other cities in the duchy, such as Pavia, wanted to be autonomous too, and not subject to the city of Milan. Louis and his entourage had little understanding or sympathy for such aspirations, but he undermined the administrative integrity of the duchy by generous grants of estates to many French nobles and commanders.[29]

During Louis's stay in Milan, the new administrative structure for the duchy was planned. The most lasting innovation was the institution of a Senate, in some respects like the judicial parlements of France, which was to supervise the civil administration of the whole duchy. The majority of the seventeen members appointed were Italians; the presiding chancellor was French. At the head of the financial administration would be a general of the finances, as in a French province. Military matters were the responsibility of the lieutenant, who would also be the most important political authority in the duchy, with powers analogous to those of French provincial governors; Trivulzio was to keep that position.

Even before the king left Milan on 8 November to return to France, there were signs of discontent. The day before the ceremony on 29 October in which representatives of the people of Milan formally swore fidelity to Louis, there had been a riot during which some tax offices were burned. Addressing the people to calm them, Louis said he had spent 400,000 ducats on the conquest of Lombardy, and he urged them to pay their taxes willingly, saying that the proceeds would benefit them, not the treasury.[30] Urban billeting of French troops was another cause of grievance, not only because of the swaggering arrogance of French soldiers rejoicing in their easy victory, but also because, under the Sforza, troops had generally been billeted in rural areas. Disciplinary edicts and exemplary executions had some effect, but resentment festered.

Trivulzio's position as lieutenant was another cause of grievance. Far from welcoming the appointment of a Milanese gentleman, many nobles resented being subject to the government of a man they could barely regard as their equal. Even more problematic was that he was a leading member of the Guelf faction. Part of the fabric of political society in the duchy of Milan at every level, Guelf and Ghibelline allegiances had to be taken into account, but what influence they might have in any given situation could be difficult to determine. Not all Guelfs supported Trivulzio or the French, despite the traditional links of Guelfs and Angevins; not all Ghibellines were opposed to them. It was through the Guelfs that Trivulzio sought to reinforce his personal authority throughout the duchy. It was to hostility to Trivulzio, not to the king, that Ghibelline nobles attributed their support for the return of Ludovico Sforza.[31]

The return and final defeat of Ludovico Sforza

Ludovico had always intended to return with troops raised in the Empire, using treasure brought from Milan. Rumours put the army he and Ascanio brought together, including mainly German infantry with some Swiss, Albanian light cavalry and Burgundian men-at-arms, at 30,000 men or even more; it was probably more like 8,000.[32] Trivulzio sent reinforcements to the northern frontier under Ligny. On 20 January the Sforza troops began to move south through the Alpine foothills, occupying Chiavenna, Bellinzona and Domodossola. French artillery fire repelled an attack on Como, led by Ascanio. Ligny wanted to resist, but was recalled south by Trivulzio, who was unable to contain the unrest which had broken out in Milan at the end of January. On 2 February, Trivulzio and Ligny were forced to withdraw from Milan leaving a strong garrison in the castle, and to fall back to the west on Novara. Ascanio occupied Como, and on 3 February was welcomed into Milan with a contingent of 6,000 German infantry. His jubilant brother made a formal entry into the city two days later.

Showing some awareness of past errors, Ludovico presented himself in addresses to the Milanese as a soldier prince, ready to defend his people from the French and from the Venetians; a wise prince, ready to consult and to take advice.[33] While he led his troops to confront the French, Ascanio was left in Milan to take charge of administering the duchy, struggling to keep order as the Ghibellines took revenge on the Guelfs, and to raise money for the army by voluntary subscriptions.

The Sforza found themselves with more men than they could pay for. At a review of his troops in mid-February, Ludovico had 6,000 German and 4,000 Italian infantry, and 500 men-at-arms; a further 15,000 Swiss, 1,500 Burgundian cavalry and 300 German men-at-arms ('*elmetti*') were supposed to be on their way, and Ludovico ordered the levy of several thousand more Italian infantry.[34] With the Venetians concentrating on securing the east of the duchy, Ludovico could focus his efforts against the French.

By 9 February, Pavia surrendered after prolonged artillery bombardment; Vigevano was surrendered a few days later, as his troops were preparing an assault. The armies were now within a day's ride of one another. The French had been augmented by a substantial contingent led by Yves d'Alègre that had been in the Romagna. D'Alègre was sent in late February with 100 men-at-arms and over 1,000 infantry to strengthen the defences of Novara, while the bulk of the French army, some 11,000 men, stayed at Mortara.[35] With further substantial French reinforcements having been despatched by Louis, Ludovico decided it was time to launch an attack on Novara. The siege began on 5 March; an assault penetrated the town but was repulsed. Soon after a concentrated bombardment began on 20 March, the terrified townspeople offered to surrender. Preferring to keep in good condition to fight another day rather than endure a prolonged siege, the French agreed terms with Ludovico, withdrawing two days later.

Ludovico's troops were undisciplined and short of food and money. By late March, 2,000 Swiss had already left his army, at a moment when thousands of additional Swiss had just been recruited by the French and were beginning to arrive at Mortara. Another arrival there was the experienced general Louis de La Trémoille, sent by Louis with 500 lances;[36] many French gentlemen were also hurrying to the army to take part in the fighting. La Trémoille assumed overall control and brought the troops to better order.

Under his command, the army marched on Novara, arriving there on 8 April. Ludovico deployed his troops in battle formation outside the city, with the infantry between the men-at-arms on the right and the light horse on the left. The French advanced on them, and after some cavalry skirmishes and exchanges of fire, the bodies of infantry confronted one another. But when the front ranks of Ludovico's Italian infantry began to waver, the Swiss and then the landsknechts refused to back them up, and soon Ludovico's forces were retiring in confusion back into Novara. During the night the Swiss on either side began to fraternize, as did the Burgundians with the French. The Swiss and Burgundians negotiated safe conducts for themselves, agreeing that if Ludovico was found among them they would not protect him; his other troops were forced to take their chance, pursued by the French as they abandoned the city. The Swiss were made to pass through the ranks of their compatriots in the French army so they could be recognized individually; eventually the disconsolate, corpulent, pallid duke, disguised as an unlikely Swiss infantryman, was identified and detained.[37]

On hearing the news of his brother's defeat and capture, Ascanio despatched Ludovico's two young sons to the care of Maximilian and himself tried to escape south, but he and his escort fell into the hands of Venetian troops. No resistance was offered to the French, as they moved swiftly to reoccupy all the places that had been taken by the Sforza or had declared for them. Fearing retribution, those who had been most conspicuous in supporting the return of the duke tried to find a way out of the duchy. Many were captured; some who thought they had found safety in Venetian-held territory were handed back to the French, as was Ascanio. He and Ludovico would be sent as prisoners to France: Ludovico would end his days there in close captivity; Ascanio would eventually be released.

French attitudes to the duchy and its people had been changed by the brief Sforza restoration, accompanied as it was by what they saw as rebellion by subjects who had pledged their allegiance to the king only a few months before. Violence and looting by French troops was worse than it had been after the conquest, and cities that had declared for the Sforza were obliged to expiate their crime by paying large indemnities. The first, dismaying demand to the city of Milan was for 800,000 ducats, the entire cost of the war; the citizens managed to negotiate that down to 300,000 ducats, still a crippling amount for even so rich a city as Milan to find. Parma, asked for 75,000 ducats, bargained down to 30,000; Pavia was to pay 50,000, Lodi 20,000.[38] In overall charge of settling the punishments, and reordering the administration, was Cardinal d'Amboise, who had been sent to Italy by Louis at the same time as La Trémoille. Having waited out the campaign in Vercelli, he entered the city of Milan with 2,000 troops on 14 April.[39]

The reorganized government of the duchy was much more military in nature than before; at the highest level there were only Frenchmen, not Italians. Louis appointed two lieutenants-general, d'Aubigny and Charles de Chaumont d'Amboise, a young nephew of the cardinal. La Trémoille returned to France in June, together with Cardinal d'Amboise and many Lombards, including Trivulzio, who had been summoned by the king. Large numbers of troops were left in the duchy, 1,200 lances and 10,000 Swiss, according to one estimate; a list perhaps compiled for La Trémoille totalled 845 lances.[40] Effective oversight of the government of the duchy for the next few years at least seems to have remained with Cardinal d'Amboise, reinforced during a long visit to Milan from June to September 1501.

The involvement of Louis's chief minister in settling the details of the administration of the duchy was one indication of the significance of Milan for the king; it has been described as the consuming passion of his life.[41] But he would pay only brief, irregular visits to his prize. Nor were the French captains and nobles who were granted estates there keen to settle. When the property of rebels was assigned to them, it was supposed to be on condition that they stayed for at least two or three years, and if they then wanted to sell the property and return to France, they could only sell half, forfeiting the rest. But this stipulation does not seem to have been enforced widely, if at all. There was an active market in the property of rebels, much of which finished up in the hands of their relatives, with the French and Italian beneficiaries of the grants preferring to convert them into cash.[42]

France as an Italian power

Louis's rule over the duchy of Milan was more securely and completely established than that of Charles VIII over the kingdom of Naples had ever been. The political influence of the Dukes of Milan had reached well beyond their duchy, not just as a participant in alliances and wars, but as the patron and 'protector' of lesser lords and of republics such as Lucca and Siena. Louis did not simply take over the role of the dukes in Italian politics; his power was greater, his interests different and wider. The equilibrium of the Italian state system was disturbed, and other Italian states each had to establish how they stood in the new order.

One state, Genoa, Louis considered to be his by right. Not only had it been under the suzerainty of Ludovico Sforza, but it had in the past been under the suzerainty of the king of France. On 6 September 1499, the Genoese formally decided to submit to Louis. An embassy of twenty-four citizens sent to the king in Milan had to wrangle with determined French lawyers over what the terms of submission should be. The Genoese wanted effectively to govern themselves; the royal lawyers wanted a much greater degree of direct control by the king's officials, and that the Genoese should be obliged to provide ships and soldiers to the king when he was at war. Among the compromises agreed were concessions recognizing the Genoese dependence on trade with other European powers; in time of war, they were to provide the king with ships but would not be bound to take an active part in hostilities against the kings of England or Spain or the count of Flanders (who was the Duke of Burgundy).[43] When Ludovico Sforza returned, the Genoese ignored his overtures, and offered him no help.

The French claimed that several minor Italian powers had betrayed their alliance or friendship with the king, including the marquis of Mantua, the Duke of Ferrara, Giovanni Bentivoglio of Bologna and the republic of Lucca. Envoys were sent to Venice in May 1500 to suggest the Venetians should join the French in attacking these states and taking their lands, on the pretext of recovering the costs their breach of faith had caused the allies. Interested in this proposition, the Venetians suggested Ferrara and Mantua as their share of the spoils. This idea had been mooted by the French even though they envisaged the Venetians yielding some at least of the Milanese territory they held, or exchanging it for part of the kingdom of Naples.[44]

Haggling over how the territory of northern Italy was to be shared between Venice and France was ended by the Duke of Ferrara and the marquis of Mantua concluding their own bargains with the French. The duke was suspected of equivocation during Ludovico's return to Milan: prompt payment of a large sum of money restored Louis's goodwill towards him. Paying reparations the French claimed the right to impose brought escape from the threat of military retribution for others too. From Francesco Gonzaga – compromised by promises of aid to Ludovico, and guilty of failing to serve with the company of 50 lances he had been given in October 1499, while his brother Giovanni had commanded the Milanese forces against the Venetians in March 1500 – Louis claimed 50,000 ducats. From the lords of Carpi, Correggio and Mirandola, who had sent some help to Ludovico, he demanded 25,000 ducats each, an impossible burden on such small territories. Costantino Arniti, the governor of the marquisate of Monferrato, who had not sent the troops he was obliged to provide, was declared deposed from his position. After the Marquis of Saluzzo, who was appointed governor in his place, behaved as though he had been made lord of Monferrato, Louis removed him and the young Marquis Guglielmo, who had the support of his people, took up the government under French protection.[45]

The civic government of the papal city of Bologna had to offer 40,000 ducats to the king to expiate the distrust shown towards French troops passing through Bolognese territory, as well as the congratulations and money sent to Ludovico on his return to Milan by Giovanni Bentivoglio. The Sienese were guilty of sending an envoy bearing 4,000 ducats to Ludovico in February 1500. Attempts to make a formal alliance with Louis the previous autumn had foundered, partly because the king had referred them to Ligny, who wanted reparation for the forced departure of the guard he had left behind after being appointed captain of Siena by Charles VIII in 1495; months of negotiations for a new contract for him as captain came to nothing. When they again asked for French protection after Ludovico's return, the Sienese were told that they would have to pay. Why the Lucchese were deemed to be at fault is not clear, but they were forced to hand over to the French Pietrasanta and Motrone – strongholds for which they had paid French captains hard cash only a few years before – and then to buy them back at the cost of 25,000 ducats.[46]

The readiness of Louis and of Cardinal d'Amboise to compound for cash payments the punishment of supposed treachery by so many minor powers calls into question whether there was ever a serious intention to conquer so much of northern Italy. Discussions with Venice over dividing up Mantua and Ferrara could have been a ploy to initiate negotiations for the restoration of Milanese territory held by Venice. Louis had declared his intention that Italians should pay for his conquest of the duchy of Milan before his army had crossed the Alps. After the capture of Ludovico Sforza, the French captains had discussed which Italian power each would champion at court; naturally, they anticipated their patronage would be worth a good price.[47] Like the French generals, Louis and Cardinal d'Amboise had no scruples about demanding money in return for protection. This was a fundamental change to the pattern of relations between the major and the lesser Italian powers. In fifteenth-century Italy, 'protection' usually involved subsidies, often in the form of military contracts; lesser lords, smaller states, expected to receive cash and benefits in kind from their patron, not to have to pay them. To the French, 'protection' was something that should be paid for, and they saw no dishonour in demanding money with menaces.[48]

The Florentines were to some degree accorded different treatment. They were able to negotiate an alliance with Louis in October 1499, by which he promised to help them recover Pisa. In return, they had to promise 400 men-at arms and 3,000 infantry to help defend Louis's Italian territories, and, should he undertake the conquest of Naples, 500 men-at-arms for the duration of the war. Debts owed to Ludovico Sforza were to be paid to the king. Once Milan was secured, Louis agreed to send a substantial detachment of troops who, it was assumed, would be able rapidly to subdue Pisa.[49]

While the king proposed to appoint the experienced Yves d'Alègre to command them, the Florentines unwisely preferred the incompetent Beaumont, because he had restored Livorno to them in 1496. Expecting to pay for 4,000 Swiss and 2,000 Gascon infantry, they had to bear the additional cost of the extra 1,500 men who turned up for the muster at Parma in May. After lingering for a month, at Florentine expense, to extort money from Bologna, Mirandola, Carpi and Correggio, the troops, already reduced in number by desertion, finally arrived at Pisa at the end of June. On the way, they had taken control of Pietrasanta, disappointing the Florentines by not handing it over to them.

A day's bombardment by the artillery brought by the French did create a substantial breach in the city walls, and the French troops launched a disorderly assault, which was blocked by an internal earthen rampart fiercely defended by the Pisans. No second attempt was made. Within ten days first the Gascons, then the Swiss began to head back to Lombardy *en masse*, and the humiliated Beaumont could not stop them. An offer to quarter a detachment of French men-at-arms over the winter in Florentine territory to keep up pressure on Pisa was declined by the Florentines, who had lost confidence in the efficacy of French troops to resolve their problem. While the episode irritated the French and the Florentines with each other, the Pisans tried hard to propitiate Louis. Even as they fought off the assault, they cried 'France' as well as 'Pisa', and after the departure of the infantry, the women came to find the sick and wounded who had been left behind and took them into the city to nurse them back to health.[50]

French military aid lent to another ally, the pope, was rather more successful. Once the initial conquest of the duchy of Milan was concluded, 300 lances and 4,000 mainly Swiss and Gascon infantry were dispatched to the province of the Romagna in the Papal States under the command of d'Alègre and of Cesare Borgia, who had been named the king's lieutenant for this expedition. Alexander had asked the king for aid in recovering for the papacy lands and cities that were governed by lords who nominally held them as papal vicars but who tended to act as, to all intents and purposes, independent rulers. Their lands were destined to form part of the duchy of Romagna with which the pope planned to invest his son. Louis had an interest in the expedition – apart from repaying his obligations to the pope for facilitating his divorce and remarriage – because the first targets of the pope's plans were the cities of Imola and Forlì, ruled as regent by Caterina Sforza, Ludovico's niece. The few hundred infantry she had supplied to Ludovico were enough to provide the king with a motive for wishing to punish her. His willingness to send the men the pope asked for was no doubt enhanced by the fact that Alexander would be paying for them.[51]

The city of Imola offered no resistance to the detachment of troops sent there in late November; the fortress did, until the garrison surrendered on 11 December. Caterina Sforza's presence in Forlì did not prevent the population of the city from yielding without a fight. She took personal command of the defence of the Ravaldino fortress, reputed to be impregnable. Her defiance and her spirited direction of the defence won the respect of the French, but the prolonged bombardment from the French artillery gradually created a breach in the walls, filling the deep moat with masonry and providing the foundation for an improvised causeway over which an assault could be launched on 12 January 1500. Caterina fell captive, while 400 men of the garrison were killed.

Cesare was heading for another Sforza lordship – Pesaro, governed by Giovanni Sforza, the discarded husband of his sister Lucrezia – when d'Alègre and his men were summoned back to Lombardy to confront the Sforza there. Cesare could not continue the campaign without them. His father soon provided a remedy, appointing him captain of the papal army in March 1500. Soon Cesare built up his own forces, so for his second campaign in the Romagna which began in October 1500 he was much less reliant on the aid of French troops. Giovanni Sforza fled Pesaro before Cesare's troops arrived; nor did Pandolfo Malatesta of Rimini wait for them before surrendering his territory to a papal official. The people of Cesare's next target, Faenza, were determined to protect their young lord, Astorre Manfredi, and a siege began in November which would last throughout the winter. A hundred French lances were sent from the Milanese in November; at Alexander's insistence, more cavalry and 4,000 Gascon infantry were sent in February and March.[52] It was not these reinforcements but exhaustion that finally brought the Faentini to negotiate an honourable surrender in late April 1501.

Louis had again sent men because he wanted the pope's support in Naples, but Cesare was warned that a move against Bologna or Florence would be a step too far.[53] This did not stop Cesare using threats before the French forces left him to make Bologna cede Castel Bolognese to him. He moved on to Tuscany, putting pressure on the Florentines to give him a *condotta* for 300 men-at-arms, but was again warned off by Louis, who ordered him to leave Tuscany. Before he did, he set about taking Piombino, whose lord, Jacopo d'Appiano, had not bought Louis's protection.[54] Cesare returned to Rome by sea in June 1501, just before d'Aubigny arrived there with an army bound for the kingdom of Naples. Louis now wanted Cesare and his father to pay back the loans of French troops by Cesare joining this expedition.

The conquest of Naples

One aspect of Louis's preparations to conquer Naples struck contemporaries as surprising, if not foolish: his agreement with Ferdinand of Aragon to divide the kingdom with him. By a treaty signed at Chambord on 10 October 1500 and in Granada on 11 November, Louis was assigned the title of king, with the city of Naples and the neighbouring province of the Terra di Lavoro, and the Abruzzi in the north-east of the kingdom; Ferdinand was to have the southern provinces of Calabria and Apulia, with the title of duke.[55] News of this secret arrangement leaked well before Alexander officially, at the king's request, confirmed the division as the French troops heading for Naples were already in Rome. The pope granted the title of king to Louis and of Duke of Calabria and Apulia to Ferdinand, who was to hold these provinces of the papacy.[56]

From the first, the motives of the two kings have been found puzzling. Officially, their reason was so that they could unite against the Turks. Ferdinand justified what could be seen as treachery to his cousin, by Federigo's dealings with the Turks in his search for support. He also claimed that he had agreed to divide the kingdom in order to preserve the peace with Louis, and argued that if Federigo was to lose his kingdom, better that Ferdinand should have half of it than lose the whole of what was his by right.[57] Why should Louis have been willing to share his prospective conquest? According to Ferdinand and Isabella, Louis had wanted to avoid any rupture of his peace with them on account of Naples, and as the kingdom belonged by right either to the French or the Spanish monarchs, said that he would like to share it with Ferdinand.[58] Forestalling opposition from Ferdinand is a possible explanation, although half the kingdom would be a high price to pay.

Whatever their motives, it seems likely that neither party envisaged this arrangement being a permanent one. Had they done so, they might well have drafted the terms more carefully. As it stood, not only did they provide for a process to ensure that both sides received equal shares of the Neapolitan crown's revenues – which was bound to cause problems – but no mention was made of two entire provinces, the Capitanata and Basilicata.

In order to be able to recruit some Swiss for the campaign, Louis had to make another sacrifice, and swallow the loss to them of Bellinzona, a town strategically placed at the head of a valley leading to important Alpine passes, which had submitted in April 1500 to Swiss troops returning dissatisfied from the campaign in Milan, and which the French had tried in vain to recover. The French army that was to be sent to conquer Naples left the duchy of Milan in early June 1501. War treasurers' accounts indicate that d'Aubigny had about 1,000 lances with him, and perhaps 7,000 infantry, the majority of them French, and 36 artillery pieces, a dozen of them large cannon.[59] Further troops were about this time being embarked at Toulon on a fleet commanded by Philippe de Ravenstein, heading for Naples to support the forces going by land.[60] Cesare Borgia had been appointed as one of Louis's lieutenants for the expedition. The company of 100 lances nominally under his command had been brought south by d'Alègre, and remained with the army when it left Rome on 28 June. Cesare himself followed slowly several days later with his personal guard, uncertain of his standing with the French.

By that time, the army had already advanced into the kingdom virtually unopposed and had reached Capua, from where Federigo withdrew to Naples. Apparently, he had been unaware of the carving-up of his realm between Louis and Ferdinand until it became public knowledge in Rome.[61] His forces had been concentrated in the north of the kingdom, and he did not try to oppose the landing of Gonzalo de Córdoba in Calabria in early July to take the provinces allotted to Spain. An attempt to muster troops by summoning barons to perform the military service they owed as fiefholders failed: such a method of gathering an army had not been used since the fourteenth century. Few Neapolitan barons were prepared to stand by him. At most, he might have had 700 men-at-arms, 500 light horse and 6,000 infantry.[62]

Among those who rallied to Federigo were Prospero and Fabrizio Colonna. Fabrizio was given charge of the defence of Capua, with a large part of Federigo's available forces, including some Fabrizio had brought from the Papal States. Bombardment by the French artillery of the bastions of Capua's outer defences was countered by the Neapolitan artillery. After four days the bastions were overcome, and the defenders slaughtered. Bombardment of the city walls began, and a breach was made. The people of the city and those who had taken refuge there were losing heart, and urged the negotiation of surrender. On 24 July, while these negotiations were proceeding, French troops entered by the breach and began to sack the city. Several hundred, by some reports thousands, died; Fabrizio Colonna was among the many prisoners taken, and had to pay a substantial ransom. The sack of Capua earned its reputation as one of the more horrific episodes of the Italian Wars.[63] One report spoke of Federigo's envoy arriving to discuss ransoms, and d'Aubigny ordering that he should be taken round the city to see for himself the effects of the sack, and telling him to let the Neapolitans know they could expect worse.[64]

When the French appeared before the city of Naples on 25 July, Federigo did not attempt to defend his capital, but made terms, withdrawing to the island of Ischia. Naples warded off the danger of sack by paying 60,000 ducats. On 2 August the garrison of the fortress of Castelnuovo surrendered to the French, and two days later, d'Aubigny entered the city. With the city of Naples and the Terra di Lavoro in French hands, a detachment of troops under Jacques de Chabannes, seigneur de La Palisse, was sent to take possession of the Abruzzi. Federigo had agreed to retire to Ischia while he settled with Louis the terms on which he would surrender the rights to the kingdom. Should no accord be reached within six months, he would be free to vindicate that right as he chose. On Philippe de Ravenstein's arrival at Naples with the fleet, claiming equal status with d'Aubigny as a lieutenant of the king, he denounced this agreement as disadvantageous to Louis. Little pressure was required to persuade Federigo to consent to travel to France; he was escorted from Ischia by French vessels in early September. Treated honourably on his arrival in France, he was given revenues of 50,000 francs a year; he would die there in 1504.[65]

Spanish forces did not make quite such rapid progress in taking possession of their share of the kingdom. Gonzalo de Córdoba landed in

Calabria from Sicily on 5 July with a much smaller army than the French had: 190 men-at-arms, 300 light horse and 4,000 infantry, by his own calculation.[66] Although French troops were soon encroaching on territory Ferdinand considered part of his share, Gonzalo had orders not to do anything that might lead to his fighting them.[67] For several months he was occupied in blockading Taranto. The city was well-supplied, and the determined defence, commanded by Antonio de Guevara, conte di Potenza, was made still more resolute by the presence in Taranto of Federigo's eldest son, Ferdinand. When Taranto finally capitulated on 1 March 1502, Gonzalo gave his word that the young prince would be allowed to go free, but instead he kept hold of him and after some months sent him to Spain, where he would live in gilded captivity for the rest of his life.[68]

The viceroy that Louis sent to Naples was keener to extend the French share of the kingdom than to ensure that the Spanish obtained all of theirs. Louis d'Armagnac, duc de Nemours, who arrived in Naples on 12 October to take charge of the government and of the army, was a young man with little to recommend him for such responsibility except his birth (he was related to the king through his mother, Louise d'Anjou). D'Aubigny for one was not impressed by this appointment to a role he felt he was better qualified to hold, and asked Louis for permission to leave, which was refused.[69] Officials were also sent from France to take charge of the administration, including Jean Nicolay, who was to be chancellor, and Étienne de Vesc, who died barely a month after he arrived. Cesare Borgia was thanked for his services and asked to leave Naples by the king; his company remained with the French army. Ravenstein, too, had gone, sailing to join up with the Venetian fleet to fight the Turks.

As with Charles VIII in 1495, Louis XII's principal initiatives in providing for the government of his new kingdom were the granting of estates, offices and benefices. As after the conquest of Milan, some of the beneficiaries were quick to sell their lands. Pierre de Gié, for example, given again the estates he had briefly held in 1495, promptly sold them to their original owner. Claims from Neapolitan barons and others who had lost their property under Federigo because of their support for the French also had to be considered.[70] 'Bon ordre, justice et police' ('Good order, justice, and upholding the law') was the motto Louis ordered for French government in Italy,[71] but despite the efforts of conscientious officials such as Nicolay, French government in the kingdom of Naples was redolent rather of greed and peculation, with captains and financial officials, not for the first time or the last, putting their own enrichment before the needs of the army, let alone the local people.

The Spanish expulsion of the French from Naples

Neither the French nor the Spanish troops were regularly paid, and the people of the kingdom suffered the inevitable consequences in robbery by the soldiers and episodes of retaliation by their exasperated victims. Still more serious problems of disaffection arose among the barons. Many held estates in both the French and the Spanish zones. Angevin factional allegiances were reinforced by the return of the French and of important exiles, such as Roberto da Sanseverino, principe di Salerno. The Sanseverino family, the most prominent Angevins, were major landholders in Calabria. Those barons who had supported the Aragonese dynasty were transferring their allegiance to Ferdinand. They included the d'Avalos, to whom the island of Ischia had been entrusted by Federigo when he left, and who refused to surrender it to the French. They also included Fabrizio and Prospero Colonna, who made their way to join Gonzalo at Taranto, and would become his valued captains and advisers.

And there was still the unresolved question of the provinces of the Capitanata and Basilicata, which both parties claimed belonged to their share. What was at stake was control over the lands on which the vast migratory flocks of livestock pastured; the tax levied on them, the *dogana*, was a principal source of revenue to the Neapolitan crown. From the start, it had been agreed that the revenues of the kingdom should be evenly divided, but neither side wanted to leave the other in charge of gathering this rich income. On the ground, the French and Spanish were both taking what they could. Discussion between Nemours and Gonzalo de Córdoba in April and June 1502 to decide the practicalities of who should hold and administer these areas until their masters had come to an agreement, failed to produce any workable arrangements.[72]

Gonzalo was still under orders to avoid fighting the French if possible. He would serve them better, Ferdinand and Isabella wrote, by preserving what they held in peace, than by giving them the whole kingdom by a war.[73] By the time these instructions were written, skirmishes between French and Spanish troops had already escalated into open warfare. Conscious his forces were inferior in number to those of the French, and of his lack of highly trained pike infantry who could match the Swiss that Nemours could deploy, Gonzalo withdrew to Barletta on the Apulian coast, leaving garrisons in a few outposts. This strategy conformed to the instructions he later received from Ferdinand, which accompanied the notification that the king and queen were now officially at war with Louis. As he would be outnumbered in the field, Gonzalo must ensure that he held on to key places and maintained good communications with the sea, where Ferdinand expected to have supremacy over the French; a relief fleet and reinforcements were on their way.[74]

It was a month after Gonzalo's withdrawal before the French advanced, laying siege to Canosa in mid-August. Canosa's garrison was commanded by Pedro Navarro, of repute as an infantry captain as well as a military engineer. Their resolute repulse of French assaults earned the defenders honourable terms of surrender, and they were able to withdraw to Barletta. After fruitless attempts to draw Gonzalo out of Barletta to give battle, Nemours dispersed his men across a wide span of territory to block supply routes. Nemours himself traversed Apulia, to bring the province under French control. He complained that the Venetians – who still held several cities along that coast – were helping the Spanish with supplies, but the Venetians denied it; they maintained they were neutral.[75] It was as neutral territory that one of their enclaves, Trani, was the site of some of the most famous of a series of personal challenges and combats between small groups or individuals among the French and Spanish troops, provoked by taunts and insults exchanged during skirmishes or in handling prisoners. Complaints about dishonourable treatment of prisoners and demands for excessive ransoms became so troublesome that Gonzalo and Nemours agreed set rates for different ranks.[76]

Nearly all the people of the kingdom of Naples, in the judgement of Venetian officials there, were on the side of the French in the autumn of 1502. Even if the rumoured reinforcements came, the Spanish would still be driven out, because by their arrogance they had forfeited the sympathies of those who had been their friends; the French would be the lesser of two evils.[77] According to a detailed list of troops in the kingdom, in late November the French had around 1,200 lances, 3,000 mounted archers and 6,000 infantry; the Spanish around 420 men-at-arms, 170 mounted crossbowmen, 250 light horse and 5,000 infantry.[78] The great disparity in the numbers of cavalry alone makes Gonzalo's avoidance of a set battle with the French understandable.

These figures did not include the Spanish reinforcements arriving in Calabria that autumn and early winter. By mid-November about 3,000 infantry, 300 light horse and 200 men-at-arms had come from Spain, Sicily and Rome (where 600 infantry had been recruited among Spanish troops in the service of the Borgia). Calabrian barons supporting the French asked Nemours for help, and at the end of the month he sent d'Aubigny with 100 lances and 1,500 Swiss infantry, giving the French with their allies among the barons about 400 men-at-arms, 600 light horse and over 5,000 infantry in the province. D'Aubigny caught up with the combined Spanish forces at Seminara. Heavily outnumbered by the French and baronial men-at-arms, the Spanish men-at-arms were soon overcome, and their infantry, already struggling against the assaults of the Swiss, Gascon bowmen and the light horse, could not withstand the French heavy cavalry when they joined the attack. Many of the Spanish infantry were captured, although much of their cavalry did manage to escape.[79]

As d'Aubigny stayed in Calabria after this second Battle of Seminara, the disparity between the French and Spanish forces in Apulia was not so marked. In the New Year, while Gonzalo still had fewer men, and difficulty feeding those he did have, there were signs his fortunes were starting to change. As the Spanish held on, and reinforcements were arriving, opinion in the kingdom began to shift, and victory for the French no longer looked certain.[80] Pushing into the Abruzzi, Gonzalo's men were able to collect part of the *dogana* on the migrant flocks; in mid-February, victory by the Spanish over a French fleet off Brindisi enabled grain ships from Sicily to reach Barletta. A few days later, Gonzalo finally led most of his men on a sortie out of Barletta, taking Ruvo, one of the French bases, and capturing the captain, La Palisse, with 150 men-at-arms and 800 infantry.[81]

Another celebrated challenge took place at this time, when thirteen Italian men-at-arms met thirteen French men-at-arms in the Venetian enclave of Trani on 13 February. The decisive victory of the Italians in this fight, which became known as the 'disfida di Barletta' ('the challenge of Barletta'), became a source of pride and consolation to Italians, part of the mythology of Italian patriotism for centuries to come.[82]

Further, substantial Spanish reinforcements had arrived in Calabria, enabling the commander there, Ferrando de Andrada, to inflict a heavy defeat on the French near Seminara (the third Battle of Seminara) on 21 April. Not only were the French men-at-arms shattered by the Spanish men-at-arms (who on this occasion outnumbered them) and the light horse, but 1,500 Swiss were overwhelmed by superior numbers of Spanish infantry, including recently arrived Galicians and Asturians armed with throwing lances, with the assistance of flank attacks by the cavalry.[83] The overall balance of forces was tipped still further in favour of the Spanish by the long-awaited arrival in Apulia of 2,000 landsknechts; Gonzalo now had pike infantry that could match the Swiss in the field. He left Barletta with his army on 27 April, and Nemours moved from his camp to confront him.

The armies met at Cerignola on 28 April. Gonzalo had reached it first, and ordered his tired men, on the advice of the Colonna, to deepen a boundary ditch, using the earth they dug out to raise an embankment on one side. He positioned his forces behind this, the landsknechts in the centre, covered by handgunners armed with arquebuses, 300 men-at-arms to the left, also covered by arquebusiers, a block of other arquebusiers with the artillery behind them, and 800 light horse to the right. At the rear, Gonzalo stationed 400 men-at-arms, and waited there himself. Arriving as evening began to fall, the French commanders disagreed about whether they should attack immediately. D'Alègre urged they should, and the commander of the Swiss, the seigneur de Chandieu, said his men were impatient to fight. At length Nemours gave in and ordered his army to advance.

Nemours launched a frontal assault at the head of 250 men-at-arms and 400 light horse, followed by a mass of 6,000–7,000 infantry, including 3,500 Swiss, with d'Alègre commanding the rearguard of 400 men-at-arms and 700 light horse. They had not reckoned with the ditch. The horses could not cross the barrier, which was defended by the German pikes, and repeated arquebus volleys, bringing down horses and men, increased the confusion in the killing ground before the Spanish position. Nemours himself was killed by arquebus fire as he tried to find a way around the obstacle. When the Swiss arrived, with their characteristic rapid march, they could not make headway across the ditch either; Chandieu was one of the many cut down by Spanish arquebusiers. Soon they were under attack on both flanks from the Spanish men-at-arms; Gonzalo brought his reserves into the action, and many Spanish infantry also left their positions and joined the assault. In less than an hour, the battle was over. French losses were estimated on the day at over 2,000 dead and many prisoners; all their artillery, tents and baggage were captured too. At least the French rearguard had been saved by d'Alègre, who had not committed them to join in the fighting. Gonzalo's own intervention with his reserves could be seen as a calculated risk that d'Alègre would not attack.[84] In later years Fabrizio Colonna ascribed the victory not to the actions of the soldiers or the valour of their commander, but to the ditch.[85] Nevertheless, Cerignola has been considered one of the pillars of the Great Captain's reputation, for the role of the arquebusiers as well as the use of the terrain, and as a school of tactics.[86]

In engaging in this battle, both commanders could be said to have disobeyed orders, because they should both have received notification of a peace treaty made at Lyon in early April by Louis and Philip of Burgundy.

Louis's 3-year-old daughter Claude was to be married to Philip's even younger son Charles, and they were to be endowed with the French and the Spanish shares of the kingdom of Naples; the disputed provinces were to be put under the charge of Philip and a representative of the French king. Pending ratification of these terms by Ferdinand and Isabella, Philip's parents-in-law, Louis sent to Nemours to order him to cease hostilities, and Philip wrote to Gonzalo. If Nemours received this message, he ignored it, while Gonzalo refused to accept Philip's authority to give him such an order. In fact, his monarchs refused to ratify terms so unsatisfactory for them, alleging that Philip had exceeded the powers they had given him. Louis himself signed and sealed a secret declaration on 30 April that any promise of marriage he made for his daughter to anyone but his heir, François d'Angoulème, should be considered null and void.[87]

This did not stop him complaining of the bad faith of Ferdinand and Isabella, as Gonzalo consolidated his victory. Prevented from pressing on the pursuit of the French forces who had survived the battle by his own soldiers' preoccupation with securing their booty, and then by a mutiny of Spanish infantry, Gonzalo could still enter the city of Naples on 16 May. The French withdrew before him, leaving garrisons in the city's fortresses, but abandoning Capua and Aversa without a fight, and concentrated in Gaeta. Most of the other places held for the French soon surrendered. Only Louis d'Ars, commander of the light horse at Cerignola, with a band of several hundred men gathered from survivors of the battle, took the fight to the Spanish from a base at Venosa in Apulia. The Spanish forces under Andrada consolidated control of Calabria as they made their way north, bringing d'Aubigny, who had been captured, with them, arriving in Naples in late June.

Castelnuovo had fallen to the Spanish on 12 June by assault. A gunpowder mine placed by Pedro Navarro and an Italian, Antonello da Trani, brought down a bulwark and the Spanish troops entered through the breach created. Gunpowder mines also contributed to the fall of the other major fortress of the city, the Castel dell'Ovo on 11 July. 'As new modes of attack are more frightening because the defences against them have not yet been thought out', wrote Guicciardini; such was Pedro Navarro's reputation after this operation that it was believed no fortress could hold out against his mines.[88]

Louis's reaction to the calamitous turn of events in Naples was determination to avenge the defeats, and to protect 'our honour and reputation' by sending a fresh army by land and sea.[89] In an angry letter to d'Alègre, he ordered him not to leave the kingdom, but to try to recover Capua, and wait there for La Trémoille, who would be coming soon with 6,000 Swiss, 4,000 crossbowmen, 900 or 1,000 men-at-arms, and a large artillery train.[90] Reinforcements for Naples had been on their way in April, but they were halted at Genoa after the treaty agreed with Philip of Burgundy. A fleet of galleys and grain ships under the command of Prégent de Bidoux, who had been harassing Spanish vessels off the coast of Naples in the winter, sailed with 1,200 crossbowmen. On board was Ludovico, Marquis of Saluzzo, who had been appointed to replace Nemours as viceroy months before.[91] (Louis had written to recall Nemours, whose competence he had every reason to doubt, in January.) Saluzzo and some the troops were disembarked at Gaeta on 11 June, where he set about ordering repairs to the walls and rallying the disheartened soldiers. A further 4,000 French infantry arrived at Gaeta by sea in early August.

At that time, the main body of reinforcements had barely left the Milanese. La Trémoille had arrived in the duchy with some troops from France in mid-June; other units came from those stationed in Milan. By no means all of them were content to be transferring to Naples, believing the kingdom to be as good as lost. Problems recruiting Swiss infantry caused delay. Another brief war with the Swiss on the northern frontier had only ended in April; the Swiss authorities did not want to send men for an offensive campaign, only to defend France or Milan; and many Swiss soldiers did not want to fight in Naples in any case. Antoine de Baissey, the French expert in recruiting Swiss infantry, was arrested and held prisoner for a month. Only inexperienced or second-rate men were prepared to defy their governments and agree to serve. Reluctant to leave until he had the numbers and quality of Swiss infantry he deemed necessary, La Trémoille lingered at Parma until news reached him of the fall of the Castel dell'Ovo; then, as he prepared to go, he fell gravely ill. It was early August before the army began to move south.[92] Contingents were provided by some Italian states, Ferrara, Bologna and Florence. When the army was at Rome, a Venetian counted 940 lances, 1,500 light horse and less than 4,000 infantry.[93]

It did not leave Rome until late September, having been ordered to stay there during the conclave that followed the death of Alexander VI on 18 August. Cardinal d'Amboise hurried to Rome, hopeful that he would be elected pope. After a lengthy conclave, the competing factions in the College of Cardinals agreed a compromise candidate, Francesco Piccolomini, Pius III. In need of protection, Cesare Borgia made terms with the French, promising to send his troops to join their army. In command of the army as replacement for the ailing La Trèmoille was Francesco

Gonzaga, Marquis of Mantua, who was, Louis assured Saluzzo, to work with him as an equal.[94]

Gonzalo had left Naples on 19 June. Not until Pedro Navarro joined him after the fall of the Castel dell'Ovo did the siege of Gaeta begin. Positioned on a hill outside the city, defended by earthwork ramparts, the French artillery caused significant casualties among the Spanish forces who entrenched themselves below. After the Spanish guns had bombarded the city for several days, a wide breach was created in the walls, but an attempted assault on 1 August was halted by the skilled French bombardiers. Gonzalo raised the siege, and concentrated on preparing to meet the French army slowly advancing south. Andrada and his men had joined him at Gaeta and the forces he had sent to the Abruzzi had now taken possession of the entire province.

As the French army under Francesco Gonzaga at last made its way into the kingdom, and was joined by many of the troops in Gaeta, Gonzalo withdrew behind the river Garigliano, which entered the sea a few miles south of the city. Determined defence of the fortresses on the inland route to Naples made the French decide to try the coastal route, but that was blocked by Gonzalo. Gonzaga's solution was to order Prégent de Bidoux to construct a pontoon. Having kept a careful watch on its progress, when the bridge was put in place and the French began to cross it on 6 November, the Spanish were in position to push them back. After some hard fighting the French were able to hold onto their bridgehead, but, hemmed in by the Spanish, could not bring the rest of their men across, or advance any further.[95]

Leaving his command on the pretext of sickness, Gonzaga set off to return to Mantua. He had failed to win the respect of the French captains, who blamed him for the army's lack of progress; his inability to speak French cannot have helped. The marquis of Saluzzo, if also an Italian, nevertheless was much more at home among the French and his authority when he took over the command was accepted.[96]

Incessant rains rendered living conditions for both armies miserable. The swollen river flooded their camps, sodden tents and makeshift huts could not keep out the rain, clothes became soaked, the men were perished with the cold and everywhere the ground turned to mud. In such conditions, sickness inevitably took hold. Supplies of food were short on both sides. The French comforted themselves with the thought that if conditions on their side were bad, the Spanish, they believed, were in an even worse plight.[97] Both they and Gonzalo's own men hoped that he would move his troops back, but although he had to move them to higher ground when a storm left their camp submerged, he would not withdraw and leave the French to cross. And if the French forces were being depleted faster than his – it was easier for the French to desert, and their cavalry was being weakened by losses among their mounts due to shortage of fodder – Gonzalo was receiving reinforcements.

These did not come from Spain, where Ferdinand had to confront French attacks along the borders; a five-month truce between France and Spain agreed on 11 November was for the border war only, not for Naples.[98] They came from Rome, where the Spanish ambassador and Gonzalo's agents not only took on Spanish soldiers who had served in the now disintegrating army of Cesare Borgia, but the *condottieri* of the Orsini family and faction. It had been presumed that they, as Guelfs and enemies of the Colonna, would serve the French, but the French ambassador in Rome, Louis de Villeneuve, perhaps took this too much for granted and failed to match the offers of the Spanish. The Orsini were given a contract for 500 men-at-arms to be shared among them.[99]

The most important captain this brought Gonzalo was the spirited Bartolomeo d'Alviano. It was he who incited Gonzalo to build his own pontoon, and who oversaw its construction a few miles upstream from the French bridge, and he who led the advance guard of 3,500 Spanish infantry and a few horse across the river on 28 December. They were followed by Gonzalo, with 2,000 German pike infantry, and 200 light horse under Prospero Colonna. The rearguard of 300 men-at-arms and another 5,000–6,000 infantry, under Diego de Mendoza, were to contain the French bridgehead. Taken by surprise, the French troops were pushed back in disorder, too scattered and demoralized to rally and mount a counter-attack, except for a stand made by some men-at-arms to protect the retreat of their infantry across a narrow bridge which was acting as a bottleneck. Much of the artillery, which was loaded on boats, was sunk by a storm. Within two days the Spanish had reached Gaeta. The French had had enough. On 31 December they came to terms, and the city was surrendered on 2 January.[100]

What remained of the French army was allowed to leave. Prisoners were released, including d'Aubigny and La Palisse, but Gonzalo insisted that the Neapolitan barons who had fought with the French were rebels. While the nobles and men-at-arms left by sea, much of the infantry had to make their way home on foot, penniless and disarmed. Many perished, either at the hands of vengeful civilians, or from cold and hunger. Those who had left Gaeta by ship and reached the duchy of Milan were also in miserable condition. Even d'Aubigny and other commanders 'look like death', the Ferrarese ambassador reported, most 'are ill and poor'; their men-at-arms were on foot.[101] Among those who died soon after reaching northern Italy was the marquis of Saluzzo.

Of the survivors who reached France, only d'Aubigny was welcomed by the king. Louis was furious with them, dismissed them from his service, refused even to acknowledge captains such as d'Alègre, holding them responsible for the debacle. The troops were blamed for indiscipline, their captains for being divided, too preoccupied with competing with one another for command. The tenacity of Louis d'Ars, who held out in Apulia until ordered by the king to leave in March because he could not send a relief force to him, only served to highlight the failure of the other captains.[102]

Gonzalo de Córdoba had been known as the 'Gran Capitán' before, yet this was the war on which his reputation as a significant figure in European military history has been principally based. Was Louis right to blame his own soldiers for being routed out of the kingdom of Naples, or was it Gonzalo's victory? Louis himself has to bear some of the responsibility, for he failed to provide his army with an undisputed, authoritative commander, first appointing several lieutenants, of apparently equal status, and then the incompetent Nemours. Despite Nemours's evident shortcomings as a general, however, Gonzalo long avoided confronting him, biding his time in Barletta. Most of the fighting took place in Calabria, and Gonzalo could not direct the Spanish forces there. And in his victory at the battle of Garigliano, it has to be asked how effectively he could have controlled his forces, as they were spread out in pursuit of the French over several miles.

Gonzalo's strategic patience – the winter in Barletta, the sodden months blocking the French advance at the Garigliano – tested the endurance of his men to the limit. Proverbially hardy as Spanish troops were, they could become mutinous if there was no pay or booty to be had. On more than one occasion, most notably after the victory at Cerignola, Gonzalo had to show patience in dealing with their demands, which were not always expressed with great respect for him. But once he had committed them to fight, he could be confident of their loyalty, and there was no doubting his personal courage or his tactical sense. I could not ask for anything else than to serve under such a captain, d'Alviano enthused. No wonder he wins victories, for it seems impossible to lose under his banner.[103]

There was no doubt of the valour with which French soldiers could fight, either, and for much of the war they had the numerical advantage, better heavy cavalry, and better pike infantry. Gonzalo's strategy and tactics did not give them the chance to exploit these advantages against him. He avoided battle until he had German pike infantry at his command. Simple field defence works, combined with his deployment of these pikemen with concentrations of arquebusiers, broke the impetus of the French attack at Cerignola; the surprise assault on the Garigliano gave the French no chance to draw up in battle order, even if the starved horses and dispirited men could have summoned the strength to make an effective charge over the muddy terrain. Gonzalo's qualities as a commander were undoubtedly one of the greatest assets the Spanish army in Naples had – but if the French had been better led, the war could still have had a very different outcome.

Notes

1 Foscari, 911–2: 5 Oct. 1496.

2 Luzzati, 15–18.

3 Lupo Gentile, 23–6, 36–7.

4 Sanuto, I, 697–8, 794, 801, 839, 861, 927.

5 Pieri, *Il Rinascimento*, 373.

6 Scaramella, 5–47.

7 Pélissier, 'Sopra alcuni documenti', 18 (1895), 133.

8 Pélissier, *Louis XII*, I, 276.

9 *Ibid.*, I, 238–310; the terms of the treaty are in Sanuto, II, 522–6.

10 ASF, X, Responsive 59, cc. 130–3: Cosimo Pazzi and Piero Soderini to X di Balia, 7 June 1499, Blois; d'Auton, I, 326–7: Ascanio Sforza to Lodovico Sforza, 5 May 1499.

11 Pélissier, *Louis XII*, I, 182–9; Gabotto, III, 123–37; Barbero, 251.

12 Baumgartner, 105.

13 Sanuto, II, 722.

14 Pélissier, *Louis XII*, I, 149–50.

15 *Ibid.*, 474–5; Pellegrini, 712.

16 Pellegrini, 728.

17 *Ibid.*, 728–9; Machiavelli, ed. Chiapelli, I, 191; Pélissier, *Louis XII*, I,194–5, 374–8, 436–8, II,19.

18 Pélissier, *Louis XII*, I, 438–41.

19 *Ibid.*, I, 423–4.

20 *Ibid.*, I, 425.

21 *Ibid.*, I, 505–6.

22 Sanuto, II, 1147–8.

23 *Ibid.*, 1059–60, 1097–9; Pélissier, *Louis XII*, I, 396–7; Pieri, *Il Rinascimento*, 379.

24 Sanuto, II, 998, 1084–5; Maximilian's ambassador in Milan gave the same figure, 11,000 horse and 12,000 foot, in late July (di Brazzano, 102).

25 Pélissier, *Louis XII*, I, 400; Sanuto, II, 721.

26 Pélissier, *Louis XII*, II, 2–18.

27 Sanuto, II, 1222.

28 *Ibid.*, III, 24–5, 32; Pélissier, *Louis XII*, II, 234–6; d'Auton, I, 92–111.

29 Meschini, I, 67–70, 81–2; Sanuto, II, 1302–4.

30 Sanuto, III, 44, 48.

31 Arcangeli, 'Gian Giacomo Trivulzio', 39–48; Pélissier, *Louis XII*, II, 239–52.

32 Sanuto, III, 89; Pélissier, *Louis XII*, II, 87–116; Pellegrini, 762–72.

33 Arcangeli, 'Ludovico tiranno?', 146–7.

34 Pélissier, *Louis XII*, II, 137–46, 150–3.

35 *Ibid.*, II, 168.

36 Contamine, 'À propos du "Voyage de Milan"', 82–8.

37 Pélissier, *Louis XII*, II, 180–6; d'Auton, I, 354–9: Louis de La Trémoille to Louis XII, 9 (10?) Apr. [1500]; Pieri, *Il Rinascimento*, 387; Meschini, I, 101–4.

38 Pélissier, *Louis XII*, II, 258–9, 262–5, 281–2; Meschini, I, 135–42.

39 Sanuto, III, 233.

40 Meschini, I, 195–6; Contamine, 'À propos du "Voyage de Milan"', 87; La Trémoille's list in d'Auton, I, 383.

41 Baumgartner, 105.

42 Meschini, I,173–5, 249, note 90.

43 Belgrano, 557–658; Shaw, 'Concepts of *libertà*', 185–6.

44 Pélissier, *Louis XII*, II, 471–7.

45 *Ibid.*, II,193, 361–76, 390–7.

46 *Ibid.*, 376–84, 397–404; Pélissier, 'Documents sur l'ambassade siennoise', 43–66; Shaw, *L'ascesa*, 125–9; Tommasi, 351–3.

47 Vissière, 'Une amitié hasardeuse', 163–4.

48 Shaw, 'The role of Milan', 32–5.

49 Pélissier, *Louis XII*, II, 384–8; Desjardins and Canestrini, II, 26–7.

50 Guicciardini, *Storia d'Italia*, Book V, Chap. 1; d'Auton, I, 275–7, 297–312; Machiavelli, *Legazioni*, ed. Bertelli, I, 61–6, 213–28; Desjardins and Canestrini, II, 36–7.

51 Bonvini Mazzanti, 93.

52 Woodward, 198, 203–4.

53 Pélissier, *Louis XII*, II, 418–9.

54 Woodward, 210–8; Mallett, 188–9.

55 Dumont, III, part 2, 444–7.

56 Fernández de Córdova Miralles, 427–8.

57 *CSPSpan*, I, 259–61; Fernández de Córdova Miralles, 419–20.

58 *CSPSpan*, I, 259–61.

59 D'Auton, II, 12; Sanuto, IV, 61.

60 D'Auton, II, 15–27, 78–84.

61 Hernando Sánchez, 52–3.

62 Volpicella, *Federico d'Aragona*, 34–45; Pieri, *Il Rinascimento*, 395.

63 D'Auton, II, 49–64; Sanuto, IV, 76–8; Pieri, *Il Rinascimento,* 396.

64 Sanuto, IV, 78,

65 D'Auton, II, 76–91, 148.

66 Rodriguez Villa, 29 (1896), 45: Gonzalo to de Rojas, 27 July 1501.

67 Serano y Pinceda, 21 (1909), 350–1: instructions to Gonzalo, 5 Sept. 1501.

68 De Torre and Rodríguez Pascual, 35 (1916), 422: Gonzalo to Ferdinand and Isabella, 10 Mar. 1502.

69 D'Auton, II, 92–8.

70 D'Auton, II, 248; Courteault, 139–48.

71 Courteault, 140.

72 D'Auton, II, 247–56; Suárez, 368.

73 Serano y Pineda, 21 (1909), 559: 13 July 1502.

74 *Ibid.*, 564–6: 13 Sept. 1502.

75 Sanuto, IV, 339, 421–2, 517.

76 Giovio, 83.

77 Sanuto, IV, 372.

78 *Ibid.*, 526–30.

79 Pieri, 'La guerra franco-spagnola', 28–30; Pieri, *Il Rinascimento*, 402–3.

80 Sanuto, IV, 638.

81 *Ibid.*, 839–42; Pieri, *Il Rinascimento*, 405.

82 Guicciardini, *Storia d'Italia*, Book V, Chap. 13; d'Auton, III, 127–33; Giovio, 90–8; Sanuto, IV, 777, 783; Pieri, *Il Rinascimento*, 404–5; Procacci.

83 Pieri, *Il Rinascimento*, 406–7.

84 *Ibid.*, 408–16; d'Auton, III, 168–77; Sanuto, V, 32–4 (including a letter from Gonzalo written on 28 April).

85 Giovio, 114–15.

86 Baquer, 371–2; Pieri, 'Consalvo di Cordova', 220–2.

87 Courteault, 182–3; d'Auton, III, 152–7; Sanuto, V, 34.

88 Guicciardini, *Storia d'Italia*, Book VI, Chap. 1; d'Auton, III, 181–5, 380–1; Giovio, 118–20; Giustinian, II, 40–1.

89 Courteault, 191: Louis to Neapolitan nobles, 12 May 1503.

90 *Ibid.*, 197–8: Louis to Yves d'Alègre, c. 20–25 May 1503.

91 Figliuolo, 405–6.

92 Meschini, I, 273–81.

93 Sanuto, V, 112.

94 Figliuolo, 408–9, 420.

95 d'Auton, III, 260–70; Giovio, 133–5.

96 Giovio, 135–6; Sanuto, V, 341; Vissière, 'Une amitié hasardeuse', 160; Figliuolo, 410.

97 Machiavelli, ed. Bertelli, II, 706: 2 Dec. 1503.

98 Sanuto, V, 542–4.

99 *Ibid.*, 177–8; Giustinian, II, 230–3, 237–9; Faraglia, 551–62.

100 Pieri, *Il Rinascimento*, 422–31; Giovio, 142–5; d'Auton, III, 297–305; Sanuto, V, 697–700 (letter from Bartolomeo d'Alviano), 711–3 (letter from Gonzalo), 754.

101 Meschini, I, 307.

102 *Ibid.*, I, 306–9; Antonovics, 23–9; d'Auton, III, 318–28, 337–48.

103 Sanuto, V, 699.

Bibliography

Abulafia, David, 'Ferdinand the Catholic and the kingdom of Naples', in Shaw (ed.), *Italy and the European Powers*, 129–58.

Abulafia, David (ed.), *The French Descent into Renaissance Italy 1494–5: Antecedents and Effects* (Aldershot: Ashgate, 1995).

Antonovics, Atis, '*Hommes de guerre et gens de finance.* The inquest on the French defeat in Naples 1503–4', in Shaw (ed.), *Italy and the European Powers*, 23–32.

Arcangeli, Letizia, *Gentiluomini di Lombardia: Ricerche sull'aristocrazia padana nel Rinascimento* (Milan: Edizioni Unicopli, 2003).

Arcangeli, Letizia, 'Gian Giacomo Trivulzio Marchese di Vigevano e il governo francese nello Stato di Milano (1499–1518)', in Arcangeli, *Gentiluomini*, 3–70.

Arcangeli, Letizia, 'Ludovico tiranno?', in Arcangeli, *Gentiluomini*, 123–48.

Arcangeli, Letizia (ed.), *Milano e Luigi XII. Ricerche sul primo dominio francese in Lombardia (1499–1512)* (Milan: FrancoAngeli, 2002).

Baquer, Miguel Alonso, 'La escuela hispano-italiana de estrategia', in Hernán and Maffi, *Guerra y Sociedad en La Monarquía Hispánica*, I, 367–77.

Barbero, Alessandro, 'La politica di Ludovico II di Saluzzo tra Francia, Savoia e Milano (1475–1504)', in Comba (ed.), *Ludovico II Marchese di Saluzzo*, I, 229–54.

Baumgartner, Frederic J., *Louis XII* (Stroud: Alan Sutton, 1994).

Belenguer, Ernest, *Fernando el Católico. Un monarca decisivo en las encrucijadas de su época* (3rd edition, Barcelona: Península, 2001).

Belgrano, Luigi Tommaso, 'Della dedizione dei Genovesi a Luigi XII re di Francia commentario', *Miscellanea di Storia italiana*, 1 (1862), 557–658.

Bonvini Mazzanti, Marinella, 'La valenza giuridica nell'impresa borgiana', in Bonvini Mazzanti and Miretti (eds), *Cesare Borgia*, 85–104.

Bonvini Mazzanti, Marinella and Monica Miretti (eds), *Cesare Borgia di Francia, Gonfaloniere di Santa Romana Chiesa 1498–1503. Conquiste effimere e progettualità statale* (Urbino: Tecnostampa Edizioni Ostra Vetere, 2005).

Breisach, Ernst, *Caterina Sforza. A Renaissance Virago* (University of Chicago, 1967).

Calderón, José Manuel, *Felipe el Hermoso* (Madrid: Espasa Calpe, 2001).

Calendar of State Papers, Spanish (HMSO, 1862–1964) [*CSPSpan*].

Cerretani, Bartolomeo, *Storia fiorentina*, ed. Giuliana Berti (Florence: Leo S. Olschki, 1994).

Chittolini, Giorgio, 'Milan in the face of the Italian Wars', in Abulafia (ed.), *The French Descent into Renaissance Italy*, 391–404.

Comba, Rinaldo (ed.), *Ludovico II Marchese di Saluzzo, condottiero, uomo di Stato e mecenate (1475–1504)*, 2 vols (Cuneo: Società per gli studi storici, archeologici e artistici della provincia di Cuneo, 2005–6).

Contamine, Philippe, 'À propos du "Voyage de Milan" (février-juillet 1500): Louis de La Trémoille, Louis II et Ludovic le More', in *Milano nell'età di Ludovico il Moro*, 2 vols (Milan: Comune di Milano, 1983), 79–82.

Contamine, Philippe and Jean Guillaume (eds), *Louis XII en Milanais* (Paris: Honoré Champion, 2003).

Courteault, Henri, 'Le dossier Naples des Archives Nicolay: Documents pour servir à l'histoire de l'occupation française du Royaume de Naples sous Louis XII', *Annuaire-Bulletin de la Société de l'Histoire de France*, 52 (1915), 117–245.

d'Auton, Jean, *Chroniques de Louis XII*, ed. R. de Maulde, 4 vols (Paris: Renouard, 1889–96).

Desjardins, A. and G. Canestrini, *Négociations diplomatiques de la France avec la Toscane*, 6 vols (Paris: Imprimerie Impériale, 1859–86).

de Torre, L. and R. Rodríguez Pascual, 'Cartas y documentos relativos al Gran Capitán', *Revista de Archivos, Bibliotecas y Museos*, 34–44 (1916–23).

di Brazzano, Stefano, *Pietro Bonomo (1458–1546). Diplomatico, umanista e vescovo di Trieste. La vita e l'opera letteraria* (Trieste: Parnaso, 2005).

Dumont, Jean, *Corps universel diplomatique du droit des gens*, 8 vols (Amsterdam, 1726–31).

Fanucci, Vittorio, 'Le relazioni tra Pisa e Carlo VIII', *Annali della R. Scuola Normale Superiore di Pisa*, 16 (1894), 3–83.

Faraglia, N.F., 'Gli Orsini al soldo di Spagna (1503)', *Archivio storico per le province napoletane*, 6 (1881), 551–62.

Fernández de Córdova Miralles, Álvaro, *Alejandro VI y los Reyes Católicos. Relaciones político-eclesiásticas (1492–1503)* (Rome: Edizioni Università della Santa Croce, 2005).

Fernando el Católico e Italia (V Congreso de Historia de la Corona de Aragon) (Zaragoza: Institución 'Fernando el Católico', 1954).

Figliuolo, Bruno, 'Viceré di Napoli (novembre 1502-gennaio 1504)' in Comba (ed.), *Ludovico II marchese di Saluzzo*, I, 405–21.

Foscari, Francesco, 'Dispacci al Senato veneto … nel 1496', *Archivio storico italiano*, 7 (1844), 721–948.

Gabotto, Ferdinando, *Lo stato sabaudo da Amedeo VIII ad Emanuele Filiberto*, 3 vols (Turin: L. Roux, 1892–5).

Galasso, Giuseppe, *Il Regno di Napoli: Il Mezzogiorno spagnolo (1494–1622) (idem* (ed.), *Storia d'Italia*, XV, 2) (Turin: UTET, 2005).

Giovio, Paolo, 'La vita di Consalvo Hernandez di Cordova, detto per sopranome il Gran Capitano', in Paolo Giovio, *Le vite del Gran Capitano e del Marchese di Pescara*, trans. Ludovico Domenichi, ed. Costantino Panigada (Bari: Laterza, 1931), 1–193.

Giustinian, Antonio, *Dispacci*, ed. Pasquale Villari, 3 vols (Florence, 1876).

Graziani, Natale and Gabriella Venturelli, *Caterina Sforza* (2nd edition; Milan: dall'Oglio, 1987).

Guicciardini, Francesco, *Storia d'Italia* (various editions).

Guicciardini, Francesco, *Storie fiorentine*, ed. Alessandro Montevecchi (Milan: BUR, 1998).

Hernán, Enrique García and Davide Maffi (eds), *Guerra y Sociedad en La Monarquía Hispánica. Politica, estrategia y cultura en la Europa moderna (1500–1700)*, 2 vols (Madrid: Ediciones del Laberinto, 2006).

Hernando Sánchez, Carlos José, *El reino de Nápoles en el Imperio de Carlos V. La consolidación de la conquista* (Madrid: Sociedad Estatal para la Conmemoración de los Centenarios de Felipe II y Carlos V, 2001).

Law, John E. and Bernadette Paton (eds), *Communes and Despots in Medieval and Renaissance Italy* (Aldershot: Ashgate, 2010).

Leverotti, Franca, 'La crisi finanziaria del ducato di Milano', in *Milano nell'età di Ludovico il Moro*, 585–632.

Lupo Gentile, Michele, 'Pisa, Firenze e Massimiliano d'Austria (1496)', *Annali della R. Scuola Normale Superiore di Pisa: Lettere, Storia e Filosofia*, ser.II, 8 (1939), 23–51, 131–67.

Luzzati, Michele, *Una Guerra di Popolo: Lettere private del tempo dell'assedio di Pisa (1494–1509)* (Pisa: Pacini, 1973).

Machiavelli, Niccolò, *Dell'arte della guerra* in *Arte della guerra e scritti politici minori*, ed. Sergio Bertelli (Milan: Feltrinelli, 1961).

Machiavelli, Niccolò, *Legazioni e commissarie*, ed. Sergio Bertelli, 3 vols (Milan: Feltrinelli, 1964).

Machiavelli, Niccolò, *Legazioni. Commissarie. Scritti di governo*, ed. Fredi Chiappelli, 4 vols (Rome: Laterza, 1971–85).

Malipiero, Domenico, 'Annali veneti', *Archivio storico italiano*, 7 (1843).

Mallett, Michael, *The Borgias* (Bodley Head, 1969).

Mantovani, Sergio, *Ad honore del signore vostro patre et satisfactione nostra: Ferrante d'Este condottiero di Venezia* (Modena: Deputazione Provinciale Ferrarese di Storia Patria, 2005).

Meschini, Stefano, *La Francia nel ducato di Milano. La politica di Luigi XII (1499–1512)*, 2 vols (Milan: FrancoAngeli, 2006).

Milano nell'età di Ludovico il Moro, 2 vols (Milan: Comune di Milano, 1983).

Negri, Paolo, 'Milano, Ferrara e Impero durante l'impresa di Carlo VIII in Italia', *Archivio storico lombardo*, 44 (1917), 423–571.

Pandiani, Emilio, 'Un anno di storia genovese (giugno 1506–1507), con diario e documenti inediti', *Atti della Società ligure di storia patria*, 37 (1905).

Pélicier, P. (ed.), *Lettres de Charles VIII*, 5 vols (Paris: Renouard, 1898–1905).

Pélissier, Léon-G., 'L'alliance milano-allemande à la fin du XVme siècle: L'ambassade d'Herasmo Brasca à la court de l'empereur Maximilien (avril-décembre 1498)', *Miscellanea di storia italiana*, ser. III, 4 (1898), 333–492.

Pélissier, Léon-G., 'Documents sur l'ambassade siennoise envoyée à Milan en octobre 1499', *Bullettino senese di storia patria*, 3 (1894), 43–66.

Pélissier, Léon-G., *Louis XII et Ludovic Sforza (8 avril 1498–23 juillet 1500)*, 2 vols (*Bibliothèque des Ecoles Françaises d'Athènes et de Rome*, vol. 75) (Paris: Albert Fontemoing, 1896).

Pélissier, Léon-G., 'Sopra alcuni documenti relativi all'alleanza tra Alessandro VI e Luigi XII (1498–99)', *Archivio della R. Società romana di storia patria*, 17 (1894), 303–73, 18 (1895), 99–215.

Pellegrini, Marco, *Ascanio Maria Sforza. La parabola politica di un cardinale-principe del Rinascimento*, 2 vols (Rome: Istituto storico italiano per il Medio Evo, 2002).

Pieri, Piero, 'La guerra franco-spagnola nel Mezzogiorno (1502–1503)', *Archivio storico per le province napoletane*, 72 (1952), 21–69.

Pieri, Piero, *Il Rinascimento e la crisi militare italiana* (Turin: Einaudi, 1952).

Pieri, Piero, 'Consalvo di Cordova e le origini del moderno esercito spagnolo', in *Fernando el Católico e Italia* (V Congreso de Historia de la Corona de Aragon) (Zaragoza: Institución 'Fernando el Católico', 1954), 209–25.

Portoveneri, Giovanni, 'Memoriale dall'anno 1494 sino al 1502', *Archivio storico italiano*, 6, part 2 (1845), 281–360.

Procacci, G., *La difesa di Barletta tra storia e romanzo* (Milan, 2001).

Quilliet, Bernard, *Louis XII* (Paris: Fayard, 1986).

Rodriguez Villa, A., 'D. Francisco de Rojas, Embajador de los Reyes Católicos', *Boletín de la Real Academia de la Historia*, 28 (1896), 180–202, 295–339, 364–400, 440–74, 29 (1896), 5–69.

Ruiz-Domènec, José Enrique, *El Gran Capitán. Retrato de una época* (Barcelona: Ediciones Península, 2002).

Sanuto, Marino, *I Diarii*, ed. R. Fulin et al., 58 vols (Venice: Reale Deputazione veneta di storia patria, 1879–1903).

Scaramella, G., 'Il lodo del Duca di Ferrara tra Firenze e Venezia', *Nuovo archivio veneto*, N.S. 5 (1903), 5–47.

Serano y Pineda, L.J. (ed.), 'Correspondencia de los Reyes Católicos con el Gran Capitán durante las campañas de Italia', *Revista de Archivos, Bibliotecas y Museos*, 20–29 (1909–13).

Shaw, Christine, 'Alexander VI, Cesare Borgia and the Orsini', *European Studies Review*, 11 (1981), 1–23.

Shaw, Christine, *L'ascesa al potere di Pandolfo Petrucci, il Magnifico* (Siena: Il Leccio, 2001).

Shaw, Christine, 'Concepts of *libertà* in Renaissance Genoa', in Law and Paton (eds), *Communes and Despots in Medieval and Renaissance Italy*, 177–90.

Shaw, Christine (ed.), *Italy and the European Powers: The Impact of War, 1500–1530* (Leiden: Brill, 2006).

Shaw, Christine, *Julius II: The Warrior Pope* (Oxford: Blackwell, 1993).

Shaw, Christine, 'The role of Milan in the Italian state system under Louis XII', in Arcangeli (ed.), *Milano e Luigi XII*, 25–37.

Suárez, Luis, *Fernando el Católico* (Barcelona: Ariel, 2004).

Tommasi, Girolamo, *Sommario della Storia di Lucca* (Lucca: Maria Pacini Fazzi, 1969; reprint of 1847 edition).

Vissière, Laurent, *'Sans poinct sortir hors de l'orniere'. Louis II de La Trémoille (1460–1525)* (Paris: Honoré Champion Éditeur, 2008).

Vissière, Laurent, 'Une amitiè hasardeuse: Louis II de la Trémoile et le marquis de Mantoue', in Contamine and Guillaume (eds), *Louis XII en Milanais*, 149–71.

Volpicella, Luigi, *Federico d'Aragona e la fine del regno di Napoli nel 1501* (Naples, 1908).

Volpicella, Luigi, 'La questione di Pietrasanta nell'anno 1496 dai documenti genovesi e lucchesi', *Atti della Società ligure di storia patria*, 54 (1926), fasc. 1.

CHAPTER 3

The conflict widens

Even after the defeat in Naples, France would still be seen as the strongest power in Italy. Rather than banding together against Louis, as they had done against Charles VIII, the Italian states tended to call on the king for his protection and intervention. His European rivals, Ferdinand and Maximilian, would be increasingly drawn into the Italian arena. A new pope, Julius II, who as Cardinal Giuliano della Rovere had already had an active role in the wars, would become the driving force of a coalition that would expel the French from Italy. But before that happened, Louis would spearhead a coalition against Venice, the League of Cambrai, one of the gravest threats the republic would ever face.

In July and August 1502, Louis XII paid a second visit to his duchy of Milan. As this was a visit of state, not a military expedition, he brought his courtiers with him, not an army. Representatives of all the major Italian states, and most of the lesser ones, came to Asti and Milan to pay him honour, to ask for his protection or his support. Several princes came in person, including the marquises of Mantua, Saluzzo and Monferrato, the Duke of Ferrara, the Duke of Urbino, Guidobaldo da Montefeltro, who had just been ousted by Cesare Borgia, and Cesare himself. On his journey back to France, the king went to Genoa, where he made a splendid ceremonial entry. With the war in Naples that had just begun going in favour of the French, this visit to Lombardy and Genoa marked the height of Louis's power and influence in Italy. But French dominance in northern Italy was not untroubled, even in the duchy of Milan. There were too many unresolved disputes and conflicting ambitions that could not be stilled by the word of the king alone, and there was no question of his being able to send troops to impose his will in every situation in which he was called upon to intervene, even if he had wanted to. Apart from the war in Naples, there was a continuing threat to the duchy of Milan to be faced.

This challenge came from the Swiss cantons, where there was much ill-feeling against him. He had promised them Bellinzona, but gone back on his word. Thousands who had served him and Charles VIII in Italy claimed they were still owed money. In August 1501 around 4,000 Swiss, together with 300 exiles from Lombardy, seized Lugano south of Bellinzona. The French took this incursion very seriously, deploying about 10,000 troops against them. After seventeen days, the Swiss withdrew, and in mid-September the French recognized the possession of Bellinzona by the forest cantons for two years, and arrangements were made for settlement of the arrears of pay.[1] This was only a provisional settlement, and after further negotiations failed, in mid-March 1503 15,000 Swiss descended on Locarno on the Lago Maggiore. Raids further into the Milanese provoked alarm and unrest. Wanting to concentrate on the war in Naples, Louis was ready to make concessions and cede Bellinzona. Although this was not enough to satisfy the forest cantons, the others were not prepared to continue the war for their benefit, and agreed the Peace of Arona with the French on 11 April. An attempt by the Grisons, immediately after this peace, to seize Chiavenna was quickly thwarted. But the French remained nervous about the northern frontier, and kept their most numerous garrisons in the duchy to guard it.[2]

The limitations on Louis's influence in Italy beyond his own dominions were most evident in the Papal States. Several of the envoys and princes who came to see Louis when he was in northern Italy wanted his protection against the ambitions of the Borgia. The king had no wish to see the Borgia grab yet more territory, but nor did he wish to make an enemy of the pope. While Cesare Borgia was no longer dependent on French troops to aid his conquests, he was still unwilling to break his connections with France, so Louis had some leverage with him. Alexander was less wedded to the French, however, and the king could not afford to push him towards a Spanish alliance, particularly when the fate of Naples was still undecided. The balancing of interests on both sides was illustrated by the question of Bologna. Not really in a position to tell the Borgia that the second city of the Papal States was not their concern, Louis took the line that his protection was of the Bentivoglio family, rather than of Bologna. Still, he left no doubt that he would not view favourably the incorporation of Bologna into Cesare's duchy of the Romagna, and Cesare held back. Louis's protection of the Orsini family posed a sharper dilemma. *Condottieri* from the Orsini family and the Guelf faction of which they were leaders, including the Baglioni of Perugia and the Vitelli of Città di Castello, had been mainstays of Cesare's army but this did not prevent the

Borgia from planning to dispossess them. Louis tried to restrain the papal assault on the Orsini family and their lands, but again his desire for the pope's support in Naples took precedence. The Orsini were saved by the death of Alexander in August 1503. An agreement negotiated then by the French in Rome with Cesare Borgia had a part in the Orsini choosing to accept the Spanish offers of *condotte* rather than those of the French, and going to join Gonzalo de Córdoba on the Garigliano.

Perhaps Louis was too preoccupied by events in the south of Italy to pay attention to what was happening in Cesare Borgia's dominions after the death of Alexander. Some of the dispossessed lords returned, including the Duke of Urbino, and the lord of Piombino, but the Venetians also seized the opportunity to extend their holdings in the Romagna. They took over Rimini and Faenza, much of the territory of Cesena and Imola, and valleys and fortresses that gave control of mountain passes and of recruiting grounds for the prized Romagnol infantry. Protests from the new pope, Giuliano della Rovere, who took the title Julius II,[3] were met with point-blank refusals by the Venetians to hand over any of the territory they had seized. Appeals from the pope to Louis, Ferdinand and Maximilian yielded no effectual help, and Julius could not take on the Venetians alone. But he would not lose sight of his goal of recovering not only the territory they had taken in 1503, but other papal cities – Ravenna and Cervia – that they had held for much longer.[4]

Florence and Pisa

Doggedly, the Florentines still looked to Louis for aid in recovering Pisa – 'nothing matters more to the city', they told their ambassador in France[5] – and for protection. In April 1502, menaced by Cesare Borgia, they accepted a new treaty with Louis, which gave the king's protection of Florence in return for a payment of 120,000 scudi over three years; Louis was to send 400 men-at-arms to defend Florence if need be.[6] That need soon arose, when two of Cesare's *condottieri*, Vitellozzo Vitelli and Gianpaolo Baglioni, invaded Florentine territory in June. From Milan, 400 French lances were sent to force them out, and the *condottieri* withdrew. Yet Cardinal d'Amboise took the Pisans, too, under the protection of the king. His suggestion that the Florentines should be allowed access to Pisa, paying tolls as outsiders while also paying for a French garrison there, did not, unsurprisingly, go down well in Florence.[7]

The Florentines continued to feel that some visible French military presence brought them additional security, and Louis was looking for ways to offload some of the cost of maintaining the French military presence in Italy. With Louis's agreement, the Florentines took on Jacques de Seuilly, bailli de Caen, with a *condotta* for 100 lances in 1503, but he and his men were sent as part of the French relief army to Naples (another 100 Italian lances in Florentine pay were also sent there), and he died at Gaeta after the battle on the Garigliano.[8] Occasionally, Louis suggested Italian commanders among his allies and clients that the Florentines might take on. For their part, the Florentines suggested Louis himself should take on more Italian commanders (taking example from the Spanish, they said); he was ready enough to do so, was the reply, but the Florentines should do it first.[9] In the end, neither party really got what they wanted. The Florentines would not spend as much on soldiers as Louis would have liked them to do; Louis would not give the Florentines the unequivocal support in recovering Pisa that they desired.

Unwilling to commit the resources needed to besiege Pisa, the Florentines relied on a basic strategy of trying to starve the Pisans, by hindering the sowing of their crops and ravaging what they did manage to produce. It was aid from Lucca, Genoa and Siena that helped the Pisans to continue their defiance of Florence, as the Florentines repeatedly reminded Louis. The Florentines found the interventions of Pandolfo Petrucci of Siena especially irritating. Louis had effected Pandolfo's repatriation in early 1503, after he had been exiled at the insistence of Cesare Borgia, and Pandolfo had promised to pay the king 20,000 ducats. As the money had not been paid, Louis regarded Pandolfo as an enemy and encouraged the Florentines to attack him with the help of French troops.[10] The Florentines found the idea of punishing their weaker neighbour, Lucca, more appealing, but the king's ministers warned them off; the Lucchese had paid for his protection, and they would have it.[11] Nor did Louis stop the Genoese giving the Pisans substantial help, until under pressure from the Florentines, he reined them in.[12]

More worrying still for the Florentines was that the Pisans had also turned to the Spanish for help. Terms proposed by the Pisans for accepting Spanish protection – including an obligation to recover Pisa's territory and ports held by Florence, and that Ferdinand should have a half-share of the revenues[13] – would have made Spanish interest in Pisa too patent. Ferdinand did encourage Gonzalo to keep up contacts and intrigues there (and elsewhere in Italy).[14] In March 1505, he told Gonzalo that he did not want to take Pisa under his protection at present, but Gonzalo was to foster the preservation of the city's liberty through the assistance of Lucca, Genoa and Siena.[15] A foothold in Tuscany was secured by extending

Spanish protection to the lord of Piombino, Jacopo d'Appiano; Gonzalo sent ships and infantry there.[16]

Florence became alarmed about signs of Spanish interest in Pisa, and fears were heightened when Bartolomeo d'Alviano appeared in Tuscany in August 1505, with a substantial company of men-at-arms. It was suspected that he had come with the connivance of Gonzalo, if not on his instructions. Part of the contract agreed by d'Alviano and the Orsini with the Spanish in October 1503 had been a pledge that once the kingdom of Naples was secured, aid would be given to restore the Medici to Florence.[17] For d'Alviano, as a zealous member of the Orsini faction, the restoration of the Medici – who were closely related by marriage to the Orsini – was a personal concern, so Gonzalo's refusal to provide the infantry he wanted to take to Tuscany was frustrating. He became disenchanted with Gonzalo, who had in fact been ordered by Ferdinand to tell the Orsini and d'Alviano that the *condotte* agreed in 1503 must be altered. They were to have only 200 men-at-arms between them, and were no longer to have *condotte*, only captaincies, paid at the usual rate.[18]

His expedition to Tuscany was made on his own initiative, against Gonzalo's orders, and Ferdinand wanted 'such public disobedience and rebellion' to be punished.[19] Florentine intelligence was that he had only 150–200 men-at-arms and 200 light horse.[20] In any case, he could not think of attacking Florence directly – the concern was he might take his men to Pisa. Fortunately for the Florentines, their commander, Ercole Bentivoglio, making effective use of his knowledge of the terrain, was able to draw d'Alviano's forces into an engagement at Campiglia near Pisa in which they were routed by the Florentine troops, bringing the incursion to a swift end.[21]

To follow up this success, Ercole Bentivoglio persuaded the Florentines to make another attempt to take Pisa by storm. A siege camp was rapidly assembled and took up position on 6 September. Artillery created a breach in the wall, but two half-hearted assaults by the Florentine infantry were beaten back with ease. News that Spanish reinforcements were coming to Pisa from Piombino strengthened the sense that the siege was hopeless, and it was lifted. The lamentable performance of the mercenary infantry during this episode persuaded the Florentines to agree to Niccolò Machiavelli's cherished project of raising and training a militia from among their own subjects, to free them from dependence on unreliable and expensive mercenaries.[22]

Ferdinand had probably not heard of this siege when he expressed his readiness to arbitrate between Florence and Pisa, either alone or with

Louis. In November 1505 the Pisan government declared that the city was under Spanish protection, making public, they said, an accord reached with Gonzalo earlier in the year.[23] Ferdinand never openly acknowledged that Pisa was under his protection, and he did not pay for the Spanish troops in the city. Yet their presence and the persistent ambiguity about Ferdinand's relations with the Pisans were enough to make the Florentines wary of launching further assaults. They did not want to risk offending Ferdinand by attacking Pisa; Ferdinand did not want to risk offending Louis by taking possession of Pisa.

The Pisans continued to receive help from Genoa and Lucca until 1509, which enabled them to hold out. But in January 1509, after a punitive raid by Florence, the Lucchese came to terms and agreed to give no further aid. The Genoese were ordered to desist by Louis after he and Ferdinand made a treaty with Florence in March 1509 by which, for a substantial price (100,000 ducats to Louis, 50,000 to Ferdinand), they promised no further support for Pisa should come from their dominions. Pisa was finally starved into surrender on 8 June 1509. So desperate were the Florentines to recover their prize, that they agreed to pardon the Pisans on quite generous terms.[24]

Ferdinand in Naples

There had been a fundamental change in Ferdinand's position, caused by the death of Isabella in November 1504. Isabella had been queen regnant in Castile; Ferdinand's power there had been as her consort. In her will, she appointed him governor of Castile for her heiress, their daughter Juana, who was in Flanders with her husband, Philip of Burgundy. It was generally recognized that Juana was too mentally unstable to be capable of governing, and Philip believed he should rule as king of Castile. When Philip and Juana arrived there in April 1506, the powerful Castilian nobility rallied to him. Recognizing his position was untenable, Ferdinand resigned his powers as governor in late June 1506, and left Castile. News of Philip's death from disease reached him as he was on his way to Naples with a new bride. During the contest with his son-in-law, Ferdinand had sought support in an alliance with Louis, signed at Blois in October 1505, which was sealed by his marriage to Louis's niece, Germaine de Foix. As her dowry, the French king surrendered to her his rights to the kingdoms of Naples, Sicily and Jerusalem; he was to receive an indemnity of a million ducats, to be paid over ten years.

In going to Naples, Ferdinand's intention was to remove Gonzalo de Córdoba from the kingdom. He had been dissatisfied with Gonzalo's government of Naples almost from the start. Confiscated estates, offices and castellanies had been assigned to Gonzalo's captains and associates without consulting Ferdinand. Reports of maltreatment of the people by ill-disciplined and unpaid soldiers brought reproaches from the king. He wanted the expenses of governing Naples to be met from the kingdom's own resources, and ordered the numbers of troops to be reduced. All Italian commanders, not just the Orsini, were to be given captaincies, not *condotte*, in future. The great majority of the men-at-arms should be Spaniards, as should all the light horse and infantry. These orders, given a year before, had still not been carried out by November 1505. Ferdinand does not seem to have appreciated the political patronage aspect of Italian *condotte*. To him, it appeared an unnecessarily costly system, one that did not give sufficient assurance of the quality of the soldiers that he would be paying for. In later years, the viceroy of Naples would become the commander of Spanish arms in Italy, and spend much time on campaigns in Tuscany and Lombardy. At this stage, although he had instructed Gonzalo to maintain contacts in other Italian states, Ferdinand had no plans for his forces to become actively involved outside the kingdom.

His focus was on the assimilation of Naples into the crown of Aragon. Gonzalo's primary allegiance as a Castilian nobleman had been to Isabella rather than Ferdinand, and there were rumours that he was inclined to support Philip. Gonzalo wrote to Ferdinand in July 1506, swearing that he would never recognize any king but him as long as he wanted him for his servant and vassal.[25] But he had not obeyed repeated summons from Ferdinand until he realized that the king was finally coming to Naples, when he sailed to meet him.

On arriving at Naples, Ferdinand made a formal entry, and Gonzalo had a place of honour at the head of the procession with Prospero Colonna; Fabrizio Colonna held the royal standard. Throughout the months of Ferdinand's residence in the city of Naples (he did not tour the kingdom), Gonzalo still formally kept his position as viceroy, and he was treated with honour and favour. But Ferdinand overturned many of the arrangements, the grants of estates and appointments to offices he had made. The king had brought with him a group of Angevin barons who had gone to France. In the treaty of Blois he had agreed that these barons should be repatriated, and their confiscated property restored to them. Other barons who supported the French and had been imprisoned by Gonzalo had only recently been released. Naturally, those who had been given estates taken from barons considered rebels were not pleased to be told to surrender them, Ferdinand's pledges of compensation

notwithstanding. Apart from his obligations under the treaty, the reconciliation of Angevin barons was an important part of Ferdinand's plans
for the settlement of Naples.

Under Gonzalo, Naples had to some extent been governed as a
conquered kingdom. Ferdinand, on the other hand, emphasized that it was
his realm as the legitimate successor. The kingdom would be governed by
viceroys, as other component states of the crown of Aragon were. In this
well-established system, the constituent states kept their own forms and
institutions of government, none subordinate to another, bound together
only by their common sovereign. Ferdinand received the homage of his
new subjects at a Parlamento – an assembly of barons, representatives of
the city of Naples and of towns in the royal demesne – that opened on 30
January 1507. Oaths of fidelity were pledged to Ferdinand and to Juana
and her successors; there was no mention of Germaine.[26] Yet he asked
the pope to grant investiture to him and Germaine and any children they
might have, as uniting the Aragonese and Angevin claims to the throne.[27]
His choice of his nephew, Juan de Aragon, conde de Ribagorza, to be the
new viceroy, could also be seen as a signal of the bringing together of the
Angevin and the Aragonese traditions, for he was the brother-in-law of
the leading Angevin baron, Roberto da Sanseverino, principe di Salerno.
This was one of a number of marriages Ferdinand had arranged between
Angevin and Aragonese noble families. When the king left Naples in early
June, Ribagorza stayed on as viceroy, while Gonzalo was to accompany
the king back to Castile.

Louis in Italy, 1507

Louis planned to go to Italy again for two main reasons: to meet the pope,
who wanted the king's help against the Venetians in the Romagna, and
to suppress a rebellion in Genoa. In the end, the pope evaded meeting the
king, partly because of his sympathies for the Genoese. Louis had already
helped him to oust the Bentivoglio from Bologna, when in the autumn of
1506 Julius led his own troops on an expedition to Perugia and Bologna,
and called on the king for aid. Gianpaolo Baglioni had the sense to submit
and was allowed to stay with his family in Perugia. Giovanni Bentivoglio
had the effrontery to dictate terms on which the pope might be allowed to
enter Bologna. In late October, the French troops – 800 men-at-arms and
4,000 infantry with 15 artillery pieces[28] – approached Bologna, and by 1
November the artillery was in position and began firing on the city. This,
coupled with warnings from Chaumont that if the Bolognese defied the

pope, Louis's protection would be lifted, convinced Giovanni Bentivoglio that the game was up. That night, he fled with his sons to Chaumont, who promised them they would be safe. The French would continue to provide a refuge for the Bentivoglio, who would in the future prove useful instruments against Julius.

A threat to use them came very soon, for Louis suspected, not without cause, that Julius was fostering the defiance of the Genoese; the king claimed that he could put the Bentivoglio back into Bologna by sending just one letter.[29] As it became apparent that Louis was coming to Italy, the pope became increasingly uneasy. Louis and his ministers felt that, after the protection he had received from the French while he was in exile as a cardinal, as pope he ought to show his gratitude by compliance to the wishes of the king. But Julius became suspicious that Cardinal d'Amboise wanted the king to make him pope in his place. Rather than wait for Louis to come to northern Italy, he hurriedly left Bologna in late February 1507 and returned to Rome.[30]

The rebellion at Genoa began in July 1506 as an uprising by the *popolari* against the nobility, not against the French, even though French favour to the nobles, especially in the Riviere, was a significant underlying cause of the bad feeling between the nobles and the *popolari*. The French governor Philippe de Rocqebertin approved changes to the constitution of the civic government reducing the nobles' share in office from a half to a third. Many nobles, unwilling to participate in the civic government on these terms, left the city; Savona, where d'Alègre (now restored to some measure of favour) was the governor, became their base.

The *popolari* declared their loyalty to the French king but Louis did not approve of the innovations. His disapproval intensified when the Genoese took control of the western Riviera – much of which had been placed by the French under the government of the powerful noble, Gian Luigi Fieschi – and of nobles' lands in the eastern Riviera, and then refused to hand them over to French officials. Louis, who had been thinking of imposing a financial penalty on the Genoese, by late November was beginning to plan a military expedition to bring them to heel. By late March, all the French officials had left Genoa and only a garrison remained in the Castelleto, the fortress that dominated the city. Hostilities between the garrison and the city had already begun, and the Genoese had also taken a small fortress outside the walls, the Castellacio, slaughtering its garrison. On 28 March a council declared that Genoa was at war with the king; a fortnight later, an artisan, Paolo da Novi, who had played a prominent part in the Genoese military enterprises, was elected doge.

At that moment, the Genoese were unaware that the king, with a powerful army, had already reached Piedmont. Perhaps mindful of the problems poor leadership had caused for his army in Naples, Louis had announced his intention of always leading any future expeditions in person.[31] Throughout his reign Louis had frequently been ill, but he asserted he was well again and as capable as ever of bearing arms.[32] He had 'a million in gold' available to prepare his army and to pay for the infantry, he boasted, and the men-at-arms, artillery and munitions were all in readiness: 'If I begin, you will see how I make war, without stint and always in person.' Not just the Genoese, but the Venetians and Maximilian were in his sights.[33] He brought with him to Italy around 800 lances and several thousand infantry. He asked the Swiss cantons for 4,000 men, and a further 2,000 volunteers came with them. There were many French volunteers, too, as well as contingents from the French forces based in the duchy of Milan. Around 20,000 men were involved in the expedition against Genoa.[34] D'Alègre and the Genoese nobles from Savona were gaining control of the eastern Riviera, and a fleet under the command of Prégent de Bidoux was in Genoese waters.

Chaumont brought the main body of troops near to Genoa on 22 April, but delayed the assault until the king, who wanted to be present, arrived. A detachment under La Palisse was sent to test the defences on the west of the city. After some fierce fighting, during which La Palisse was wounded, they drove back the Genoese and took an important redoubt on a height outside the walls. Two Genoese envoys were sent to the French camp to negotiate terms; the king referred them to Cardinal d'Amboise, who told them Louis would accept only unconditional surrender. Meanwhile, several thousand Genoese tried to retake the positions lost, with some initial success, but then had to retreat. Genoese resistance was at an end; the next morning, four envoys came to surrender the city to the king. They were at the king's mercy, but he did not want Genoa sacked.

On 29 April, the king entered Genoa in triumph as a conqueror. As he entered the Porta San Tommaso, the king struck it with the battle mace he carried, saying, 'Proud Genoa, I have won you by force of arms'.[35] The king was dressed in full armour, with his ostrich-plumed battle helmet, riding a black war-horse under a baldachin. With him rode five cardinals, Italian princes who had come to take part in the campaign – the marquises of Mantua and Monferrato and the Duke of Ferrara – and the French nobles and captains, and the men-at-arms. No infantry took part in the procession 'for greater security of the city',[36] although the king's guard of archers and their captains marched on foot.

While there was difficulty in restraining the soldiers, especially the Swiss and Germans who resented being kept out of the city, from violence and robbery, and some individuals, including Paolo da Novi, were executed, it was the pride and the purses of the Genoese that suffered most. They would have to pay 200,000 scudi for the expenses of the campaign, and 40,000 for a new fortress to be built. At a solemn ceremony, the Genoese swore fidelity to the king, the terms negotiated in 1499 were literally torn up and burnt, and the new privileges the king was granting were read out. These were not very different in substance, but as privileges, not agreed terms, they were revocable by the king at any time.[37]

The suppression of the Genoese revolt was hailed by the French as a glorious triumph for their king. Not for 200 years and more, one account circulated in France proclaimed, had any prince 'won so great a conquest with so little expense and so little bloodshed'.[38] It helped to expunge the abiding shame felt at their defeat in Naples. Louis was hailed as a victor as he passed through the duchy of Milan after leaving Genoa on 14 May. Triumphal arches greeted him as he entered the city of Milan, and celebrations continued throughout his stay, with jousts and tournaments and banquets.

The genesis of the League of Cambrai

Before he left Italy for France, Louis arranged to meet Ferdinand at Savona in late June 1507. The public ceremonial and lavish festivities Louis put on for his guest were designed to display trust and friendship between the two monarchs. Their private conversations were kept secret. From a memorandum that was prepared for Ferdinand, it appears that the talks centred on relations with Maximilian.[39] Louis's agenda at the meeting may have included an attempt to persuade Ferdinand to join him in a coalition against Venice. He had been harbouring resentment against the Venetians for several years – for not sending help when the Swiss had invaded the Milanese, and for (so he believed) favouring the Spanish during the war in Naples – and he wanted the territory now held by Venice that had been part of the duchy of Milan. War against Venice may have been the intended subject of future talks, to include the pope and Maximilian, that the kings agreed to arrange.[40]

The question of the desirability of cutting Venice down to size was moving to the top of the diplomatic agenda. Apart from the lands Louis wanted to reincorporate into the duchy of Milan, the Venetians still held several ports in the kingdom of Naples on the Apulian coast, and papal territory in the Romagna. As Duke of Austria, Maximilian had a number of disputes with them in the Austrian-Venetian borderlands, and as emperor-elect he had grounds to challenge their possession of cities such as Verona and Vicenza that were theoretically part of the Empire, because the Venetians had no Imperial investiture for them. Other neighbours of Venice, the Marquis of Mantua and the Duke of Ferrara, had lost valued lands to Venetian expansion in the fifteenth century. But before a coalition against Venice could come into being, in the League of Cambrai, other problems had to be resolved, in particular, Louis's relations with Maximilian.

For some months in 1507–8, it looked as though Maximilian would attack Louis in Italy. He had been speaking for years of coming to Italy to be crowned emperor, and to assert Imperial rights. In July 1507 an Imperial Diet promised him 12,000 men to accompany him; it was hoped that the costs could be recovered in Italy.[41] This was not enough to enable him to challenge the French in Milan, so he decided to attack Venice instead, on the grounds that the Venetians had refused to ally with him against France and persistently refused him permission to pass through their territory with an army, even if he was supposed merely to be heading to Rome for his coronation as emperor. In early February 1508, Maximilian declared war on Venice, which called on Louis, still an ally, for help. On the orders of the king, Chaumont sent several thousand troops, keeping the bulk of his forces on the alert in the duchy.

Initial incursions by Maximilian's troops into Venetian territory in early February soon faltered. Those he could muster were largely from his hereditary lands and what mercenaries his limited resources enabled him to hire. In late February, he sent a diversionary force under Sixt Trautson to occupy the Cadore region of the Dolomites. Bartolomeo d'Alviano (who had returned to the service of Venice in February 1506) was sent against them. Taking up a suggestion sent to him by men of the Cadore loyal to Venice, d'Alviano led 100 men-at-arms, 400 light horse and 1,500 infantry over mountain passes to take the German forces by surprise at Pieve di Cadore.[42] When the Venetian troops arrived on 2 March, the Germans prepared to retreat, but d'Alviano, urging on his tired men, confronted them on the level ground outside the town. Sending ahead his mounted crossbowmen and stradiots, d'Alviano positioned his pikemen behind a dry streambed. This obstacle disrupted the advance of the German pike infantry, who then found themselves under attack on both flanks from the Venetian horse. Two-thirds of them, including Trautson, were cut down; only a few hundred were able to escape to safety.[43] Within a few days of the crushing victory, d'Alviano's men, with the help of militiamen from Friuli, had recovered all the Cadore.

Maximilian's own advance south from Trent towards Verona was blocked by the main body of the Venetian army under their captain-general, Niccolò Orsini da Pitigliano, and the French troops sent by Chaumont, under Alessandro Trivulzio. Soon Maximilian was in retreat. The Venetians wanted to pursue their advantage and push into Austrian territory, but the French would not agree to this. To the east, however, d'Alviano, with 4,000 regular troops and thousands of local militia under the nobleman Gerolamo Savorgnan, rapidly took those areas of Friuli held by Maximilian, including Pordenone. They then pushed on into Imperial territory, taking the county of Gorizia and the port of Trieste, which surrendered on 6 May, and advancing into Istria. Maximilian's project to assert the power and authority of the Empire in Italy rapidly turned into humiliation.[44]

Unable to insist even on the return of his own lands, Maximilian proposed a truce. Both Venice and Louis were ready to agree, but the king wanted to cover all arenas of conflict between him and Maximilian. While the French delegates to the negotiations were waiting for further instructions, Venice and Maximilian concluded a three-year truce for Italy alone. Louis was named only as an ally of Venice who could accede to the truce within three months. Indignant, Louis took this as an insult, blaming the Venetians.[45]

Now the king was in the frame of mind to make a serious attempt to settle his differences with Maximilian, and for a coalition with him against Venice. There had been indirect negotiations between them (via Milan and Mantua) for a joint attack on Venice even while Maximilian had been threatening to invade Milan. Maximilian had proposed impossible terms, by which he would gain nearly all the territory they proposed to conquer, and Louis would have subsidized his campaign as well as providing an army of his own. For an alliance between them against Venice to become a reality, they had finally to settle the thorny question of the status of Louis's investiture with Milan, among other outstanding problems. This was accomplished in talks held at Cambrai in late November and early December 1508. In these, Maximilian was represented by his daughter Margaret – who was governing as regent in the Netherlands for the young Duke Charles, and was far more politically astute than her erratic father – and Louis by his chief minister, Cardinal d'Amboise.

Two treaties were agreed, both signed on 10 December. One was between Maximilian and his grandson Charles, and Louis and Charles of

Egmond, Duke of Guelders. This covered disputes over Navarre, Guelders, Flanders and Artois, and Milan. Louis was to receive a fresh investiture with Milan for himself and his heirs. The second treaty, which was not made public, was for a league in which the pope and Ferdinand were to join Louis and Maximilian in a co-ordinated attack on Venice, to be launched in the following April and to be continued until each had recovered all lands they claimed that were currently held by Venice. The Duke of Ferrara and the marquis of Mantua could join in the League too. In effect, the Venetians were to be stripped of all the lands they held in Italy, except the city of Venice itself.[46]

Ferdinand had been represented at Cambrai, but not the pope, because he had delayed too long in sending an envoy. It was Cardinal d'Amboise who took it upon himself to represent the pope in the negotiations and to promise to obtain his ratification. Eventually Julius decided that he could not pass up this opportunity, and ratified the treaty in late March. To the last the Venetians, who had soon got wind of the coalition against them, were hopeful that the pope's distrust of the French would keep him at least neutral, but in April 1509 they had to face the fact that they stood alone against an alliance of the pope, the emperor-elect and the two most powerful secular princes of Europe.

The beginning of the War of the League of Cambrai

Once they were convinced that it was necessary, the Venetians were able to mobilize their forces quickly. They mustered a field army of 1,650 men-at-arms and 22,000 infantry, of whom 9,000 were militia, as well as mounted 'crossbowmen' (who might carry an arquebus instead of a crossbow) and stradiots.[47] Their captain-general was the veteran Niccolò Orsini da Pitigliano; second-in-command, as governor-general, was Bartolomeo d'Alviano. As all the signs were that the first assault would come from the French, the Venetian army was sent to the Milanese border.

Energetic preparations for the campaign had been well underway in France in January. Louis would be going to Italy in greater strength than any French king had gone before, Cardinal d'Amboise affirmed; he would be strong enough to oppose Maximilian as well, if he did not stand by his promises. He could beat the Venetians, Maximilian and the pope combined, Louis himself asserted. The French reckoned they had 1,100 lances already in Italy, 500 more were to be sent from France, and 300 gentlemen and pensioners who owed personal service to the king were being summoned to accompany him.[48] Because the king was to be leading a major expedition in person, many gentlemen were keen to go as volunteers at their own expense. Orders also went out for infantry to be raised throughout France. This was an innovation. Louis wanted to raise six infantry companies of up to 1,000 men each, to be placed under the command of respected cavalry captains, who would keep their existing commands over companies of men-at-arms as well. It was hoped their association with the new infantry would raise its prestige and facilitate co-ordination with the cavalry.

Agents were also sent to raise some Swiss infantry, but there was a problem. The agreement Louis and the Swiss had made in 1499, allowing him to recruit whenever he needed their men, was due to expire, and the cantons would not renew it. Not really understanding the complex political processes of consultation among the cantons, the French trusted to bribes, gifts and pensions, freely distributed to influential individuals, to get them whatever they wanted. They were inclined to regard the Swiss as subordinates, who should accede to the wishes of the king, not as allies.

Resentment at this, coupled with failure to pay what soldiers who had served Charles VIII and Louis on previous campaigns claimed they were still owed, reinforced anti-French sentiments which had always been present. It also gave additional force to criticisms among the Swiss of those who took bribes and pensions from foreign powers. French proposals to renew the agreement with Louis were received coldly. Yet many poor Swiss still needed the money to be earned from service as mercenaries, and the backhanders accepted by some of the political elite who took the decisions about the provision of official contingents gave rise to some scepticism about orders that they should not take service with this or that would-be recruiter. Official bans were disregarded, and French agents were able to recruit several thousand volunteers, although these were considered inferior – less cohesive, less disciplined – to the bands provided by the cantons. In any case, Louis was not prepared to increase his offers to the cantons, and was ready to turn to the Grisons, and to landsknechts, to provide expert pike infantry while (it was hoped) French infantry could be drilled into effective substitutes.[49]

Although the king had given orders no attack should be made before he came, Chaumont, apparently hankering after a little personal glory, took a force across the River Adda on 15 April two days before Louis's herald arrived in Venice to declare war. Capturing a few Venetian settlements, including the stronghold of Treviglio, he withdrew after two days. All the ground he had taken was recovered by the Venetians by the second week of May. Louis arrived in Italy in late April, bringing more troops, and entered the city of Milan on 1 May. Now the French were ready to begin the war in earnest. By his own estimate, the king had 2,300 lances and 20,000 infantry, including 6,000 Swiss. More Swiss were arriving, and a week later he had 7,500 on his payroll, while thousands more were being turned back on his orders.[50] Louis was keen for his army to engage the Venetians in battle. The Venetian army had been ordered to avoid battle, and to defend the Veneto by manoeuvring and blocking the enemy's advance. Such a strategy accorded well with the views of Pitigliano; d'Alviano argued in vain for taking the fight to the enemy's lands.

The Battle of Agnadello and its consequences

On 9 May, all the French army crossed the Adda unopposed; the Venetians were considered to have missed a good opportunity to have caused real problems for the enemy. The two armies were now very close. As the Venetian troops were moving camp on 14 May, they were strung out for miles along the route. The French advance guard, commanded by Gian Giacomo Trivulzio, came into contact with the Venetian rearguard near Agnadello, and seized the chance to attack. D'Alviano, whose columns formed the rearguard, had gone on ahead to the new camp at Pandino: he hurried back when he heard of the engagement but initially it was the experienced infantry constables Piero del Monte and Saccoccio da Spoleto who placed their men in a defensive position behind a dry canal bed. The men-at-arms took up position to their right, keeping out of range of the French artillery which concentrated its fire on the infantry. Before the Venetian artillery was in a position to return fire, Saccoccio da Spoleto and the militia from Padua and Friuli crossed the canal bed and advanced on the French artillery positions, but were attacked on their flank by the French horse.

At this point, d'Alviano arrived and led the men-at-arms against the French cavalry, while the remainder of the infantry from the rearguard went to support the militia, as did a contingent from the next column of the Venetian army. For a while, it looked as though the Venetians would be victorious. The Swiss infantry of the French were hard pressed, and d'Alviano with his men-at-arms attacked the French centre where the king was. In response, Louis ordered 500 fresh men-at-arms to support the cavalry regrouping after being assaulted by the Venetians. The rest of the third Venetian column, which had no orders to attack – their commander was at Pandino – hesitated to join the battle, but found themselves under attack by Trivulzio's cavalry and the redeployed French artillery. Left to fight unsupported, d'Alviano and his column were overwhelmed.

Thousands of Venetian infantry were killed on the field of battle, among them Saccoccio and Piero del Monte. Thousands more were cut down by the pursuing French as they fled, their corpses strewn over the countryside for miles. Louis had ordered that no prisoners were to be taken, to avoid disorder among his own men. Such orders would not apply, of course, to Venetian commanders. D'Alviano himself was captured, wounded in the face, fighting on foot after his horse had been killed beneath him. The bulk of the Venetian artillery, around thirty pieces, had been with the rearguard, and that was captured too.[51]

D'Alviano would receive much of the blame for the Venetian defeat, because he had pressed the attack against the French rather than just extracted his men from the perilous position they were in. The dismayed Venetians blamed him for doing too much, and Pitigliano, who had not sent any help, for doing too little.[52] Nevertheless, they would have liked to get d'Alviano back, but Louis was determined to hold on to him and sent him to captivity in France.

Agnadello was one of the most significant battles of the Italian Wars, not because of the way it was fought, but because the Venetian defeat then led to the loss of nearly all the lands that Venice had acquired on the Italian mainland over a century, and heralded a climactic period in the history of the republic. Although the bulk of their army was still intact, having taken no part in the battle, it was demoralized. Anxious to preserve it, the Venetians ordered it to retreat eastwards. Refused admission within the walls of the major cities of the Terraferma by the citizens, the army finally encamped at Mestre on the lagoon, positioned to defend the city of Venice. By the time it reached Mestre, the army's ranks had been seriously depleted by desertion. Men from Brescia and Crema who had fought at Agnadello were home in time to be members of the deputations that surrendered their cities to Louis.[53] Within a fortnight, the French had taken all the territory Louis claimed. Then, to the relief of the Venetians, they halted.

Francesco Gonzaga had already begun to take the lands that he claimed in April. After Agnadello, Alfonso d'Este expelled from Ferrara the Venetian official, the *visdomino*, who took care of Venetian interests there, and rapidly recovered the Polesine and other lands the d'Este had lost to Venice. Characteristically, Maximilian was slower off the mark. Three detachments of Imperial troops – 10,000 infantry and 1,500 horse in all – crossed into Venetian territory on 1 June and began to penetrate the valleys of the Adige, the Valsugana and into the Cadore region.[54] Much of Friuli was overrun, and Gorizia and Trieste, which had fallen to the Venetians in 1508, were retaken. The two major Friulan towns, Cividale and Udine, were not conquered. In spite of the losses of Friulan militia at Agnadello, Antonio Savorgnan was able to muster thousands of men to complement the few Venetian troops in the province, and prevent Imperial troops from taking control.[55] West of Friuli, Treviso also held for Venice, although the citizens did consider surrendering to the Imperial army.

Treviso was the only city in the Veneto that did hold. Concerned that if they made determined efforts to defend the lands Maximilian claimed, it would provoke the French to advance, and calculating that it would be much easier to recover territory from Maximilian than from Louis, the Venetians permitted the citizens of Verona and Vicenza to acknowledge Imperial sovereignty if they chose, and withdrew officials and garrisons from them.[56] The rectors of Padua were also told to leave; these instructions were countermanded but too late, for the officials had already gone. Verona, Vicenza and Padua were prepared to acknowledge Maximilian, but there were no Imperial troops near to whom they could surrender. The Veronese sent envoys to him to offer their allegiance. Vicenza and then Padua were content to accept the assurances of a Vicentine exile, Leonardo Trissino – who only had a few dozen scruffy men at his command – that he had a mandate from Maximilian, and they submitted to him.

The Venetians were stunned at how quickly they had lost so much of the Terraferma. As well as blaming the commanders of their army, they blamed the leading men in their own government.[57] Some denounced the whole policy of expansion into mainland Italy. Through pursuing this goal, they argued, Venetians had raised up enemies against their state, and had themselves been distracted from their true, maritime, mercantile calling, enervated by luxury and the pleasures of owning landed estates and villas, and corrupted by the temptations of holding lucrative office on the mainland.[58]

Why were the cities of the Terraferma so ready to abandon their allegiance to Venice? One consideration was that the Venetians made their own priorities evident from the start: they preferred to keep their army intact for the defence of Venice rather than disperse their forces into garrisons to defend their subject cities. Like the citizen elites of the duchy of Milan a decade earlier, many citizens of Venetian subject cities in 1509 deluded themselves with pipe dreams of a foreign monarch being willing to exercise a distant overlordship over self-governing cities which would, crucially, enjoy full control over their own extensive subject territories. It was such dreams that made the civic elites, mindful of the effective independence of the great German Imperial cities, prefer to surrender to Maximilian rather than Louis. Paduan envoys told Maximilian that he had freed them from the tyranny of 3,000 Venetians (that is the nobles, members of the Great Council), who had taken all their buildings, their churches and benefices, their offices and honours, and their estates outside the city.[59] Venetians had indeed bought up much property there, and the Paduan civic elite felt they had been displaced and dispossessed. In other areas, resentment of the Venetians was not so intense.

The vexatious realities of living with the presence of French or Imperial troops would soon dissipate the political illusions of the civic nobilities and elites. There were some who would still prefer subjection to the Empire to subjection to a republic; others would remain loyal to Venice, serving in Venetian armies while their own cities were under French or Imperial rule.[60] For the majority, in all likelihood, and especially if their city changed hands repeatedly, longing for peace and for security for their families and their property were the feelings that were uppermost, not allegiances to one power rather than another.

Soldiers on both sides could rob and mistreat civilians, even when they were not campaigning. The Venetians did deliberately strive to restrain their troops in order to foster the goodwill of the population. Living with French or German forces was definitely a worse experience. They expected the people in town and country to provide them with billets, food, drink, fuel and other provisions, and often to supply money for their pay as well. Townsmen were not accustomed to having large numbers of soldiers living among them, and so resented it all the more.

Yet it was the rural communities who suffered most. They were also aware that the civic elites had seen the withdrawal of the Venetians as an opportunity to strengthen their own hold over the territories of their cities, and to enhance the privileges that citizens enjoyed there. These were the principal reasons for the marked preference of the rural population for Venetian government, rather than Imperial or French, and why they would made significant contributions to Venetian military efforts. They harassed French and Imperial troops behind the lines and aided the Venetian forces. Much of Venetian intelligence about enemy troops came from peasants. German troops did not dare to stay in districts where there was no fortress, according to a Vicentine chronicler.[61] In the Veronese, peasants formed organized bands, hundreds strong, to attack smaller groups of soldiers, dispersing before stronger enemy forces tracked them down.[62] Delighted Venetians were inclined to attribute the loyalty of the rural population to recognition of the superiority of mild, just Venetian government. There was some – but only some – element of truth in this. That the alternatives were so much worse was the most powerful motive, nevertheless.[63]

The Venetian rally

Before they could begin attempting the recovery of any of their lost territory, the Venetians had to look to the defences of their city. Unaccustomed
to having to plan for such a contingency, they had no organization for
a citizen militia, but started to assess what fighting-men could be found
among the inhabitants of Venice (a high proportion of whom were
immigrants). In order to reduce the threat they faced, they took some hard-
headed decisions to sacrifice yet more territory to try to thin the ranks of
their enemies.

The very day that news of the rout at Agnadello reached them, it was
decided that the Romagnol lands should be restored to the pope, and a
few days later, that the Neapolitan ports must be offered to Ferdinand.[64]
Papal troops were already in action in the Romagna, and having rejected
the offer of partial cession of the territories before the war, the pope was
happy to accept their full surrender now. He would send few troops to
support the armies of Louis and Maximilian. In the kingdom of Naples,
the Spanish campaign to take the Venetian-held ports had been delayed
by an illness of the viceroy. By the time the army, including 2,000 infantry
sent from Spain, arrived before the ports in early June, orders to surrender
may have reached the Venetians there. Within a few days, they had all
capitulated. Attempts to appease Maximilian by offering to return territory he claimed as Austrian and to recognize Imperial sovereignty over the
areas he claimed for the Empire, were not successful.

Now that their own claims had been satisfied, neither the pope nor
Ferdinand really wanted to see Venice annihilated and the whole of
Lombardy divided between Louis and Maximilian. Ferdinand had his own
reasons to remain in the League, for he still had to reckon with Maximilian's
claims to govern Castile for his grandson Charles, but he would not send
any troops north that year. Julius's active participation in the League was
effectively over, although he was apprehensive about provoking an attack
on the Papal States by Louis and Maximilian if he openly withdrew from
his alliance with them.

Cutting their losses had paid dividends for the Venetians, and they
were ready to begin their efforts to recover those lands they were not
prepared to lose for good. On 17 July Venetian troops, aided by civilians
from Venice, retook Padua, having seized a city gate by a trick. The garrison of German troops retreated to the fortress, but soon surrendered.
This success greatly heartened the Venetians, and another coup followed
in early August, the capture of Francesco Gonzaga. On Louis's orders, the

marquis was on his way with his company of French lances to assault the stronghold of Legnago for Maximilian, when he was taken unawares by Venetian soldiers as he was sleeping.

Imperial troops struggled to consolidate their grip on the lands that had fallen so easily into their hands. Their forces in Friuli were too weak to secure that region, and could not link up with the main army to besiege Treviso, as Maximilian had planned. Louis sent 500 lances under La Palisse to support his ally, but took the bulk of the army with him as he returned in triumph to Milan, which he entered on 1 July. There he fell ill, and in August, fearing for his health in the heat of an Italian summer, made his way back to France. Meanwhile Maximilian, who had finally arrived in Italy in mid-June, began to lay siege to Padua on 10 August.

This time the Venetians were in no mood to surrender it so tamely. Over 14,000 infantry, 500 men-at-arms, 600 mounted crossbowmen and 950 stradiots,[65] under the command of Pitigliano, were deployed to defend the city, supplemented by hundreds of Venetian nobles. While the nobles were put in charge of the gates, the principal reason for their presence was to show Venetian subjects, as well as the enemy, their commitment to keeping the city. As a precaution, suspect Paduans were sent to Venice. Defenders of Padua were told by the Venetian government that the eyes of all Italy, of the whole world, were on them.[66] Italian soldiers there were reported to be keen to vindicate the honour of Italy and the reputation of Italian arms, which they feared would suffer – harming their own career prospects – if they were beaten on this stage by French and German troops.[67]

Maximilian, too, felt that his reputation was at stake. He encouraged exaggerated reports of the size of the Imperial camp, said to be over 60,000 strong. The Venetians believed this, but it boosted their sense of their own fortitude rather than discouraging them. A total of 15,000–16,000 effective troops, including 4,000 French and small contingents of papal, Ferrarese and Mantuan soldiers, was nearer the mark.[68] Relations between the French and German soldiers were bad, making co-ordinated assaults difficult to organize. Ferrarese artillery caused the defenders some anxiety, without making sufficient impression on the walls of Padua, while the Venetian artillery forced the Imperial camp to change its position. There was a shortage of supplies in the camp, and of money to pay the soldiers. On 1 October, Maximilian had to raise the siege.

Leaving some forces near Padua, Maximilian went to Vicenza and Verona before heading for Trent at the end of October. The troops from his hereditary lands were coming to the end of the four-month term of service for which they had been granted, and he hoped to raise some more. Once he had left, the Venetians quickly recovered Vicenza, but they delayed too long in responding to appeals from Verona. By the time they were ready, the French had sent reinforcements there, as well as money to pay Maximilian's men.[69]

Another setback was inflicted on Venice by the Ferrarese. Alfonso d'Este had occupied the Polesine, the marshy area in the lower valley of the Po north of Ferrara that Venice had taken from his father. This the Venetians were not prepared to relinquish. In late November a fleet under the command of the captain-general of the sea, Angelo Trevisan, made its way up the Po, looting and burning the villages along the banks. As well as seventeen war galleys, there were a couple of dozen vessels of various sizes of the river fleet, and many others manned by volunteers eager for booty. Some horse and foot under Giovanni Paolo Gradenigo were sent by land in support, but there were not enough to protect the fleet. It penetrated to within a few miles of Ferrara, but was forced back by Ferrarese artillery, and Trevisan took it to Polesella, about ten miles from Ferrara. Defensive earthworks were constructed on the bank, but the troops were encamped some distance away, and there were difficulties in co-ordinating the land and river forces. Trevisan bound galleys together as a pontoon to bridge the river. High water raised the Venetian vessels, so that they were more exposed to fire from the bank. When artillery positioned covertly by Cardinal Ippolito d'Este, the duke's brother, opened fire before dawn on 22 December, the stationary galleys made an excellent target. Six were destroyed, nine were captured and only two escaped, while the smaller vessels had to run the gauntlet of artillery fire.[70]

On his return to Venice, Trevisan was tried and sentenced to three years' exile. Punishing commanders held responsible for a bad defeat was a typical Venetian response. To them, this defeat was as dispiriting as that at Agnadello. Not only had it been inflicted by the forces of the Duke of Ferrara, who they were used to regarding as a virtual Venetian client, but it was more of a blow than the defeat of their army, because they prided themselves on their naval prowess.[71] One good outcome was that it helped to clear the way for their reconciliation with the pope. There had been six Venetian ambassadors in Rome since July; negotiations had been difficult, and Ferrara one of the major sticking-points. Ferrara itself was a papal fief, but for two centuries the Venetians had enforced privileges there, and the pope was insisting that these be given up. After Polesella, the Venetians resigned themselves to relinquishing them, among many other concessions. In February 1510, Julius lifted the excommunication he had imposed on Venice.

The campaign against Venice in 1510

Throughout the winter, Maximilian and Louis had been discussing plans for the next campaign against Venice. Maximilian wanted Louis to provide the bulk of the troops, some to be at his expense, some to be paid for by the French holding territories they might recover for him – anything except Verona – until their costs had been recovered.[72] Unwilling to shoulder the burden of the fighting while Maximilian stayed in Germany, Louis's sights were set on Verona as his reward for assisting Maximilian. A substantial force of French troops was still there, and French loans were needed to pay the Imperial garrison; as security for these loans, in February 1510 they took possession of the two fortresses in the city.[73] Louis attributed his decision not to go to Italy in person but to direct the campaign from France to Maximilian's refusal to agree he should have Verona.[74]

Louis was even more distrustful of Ferdinand. To bind him more firmly into the League of Cambrai, he brokered a treaty between Ferdinand and Maximilian in December 1509. Maximilian agreed that Ferdinand should govern Castile for Juana and Charles until Charles was aged 20; Ferdinand reiterated his commitment to aid Maximilian against Venice until he had secured all the lands he claimed.[75] It was because of this treaty that Ferdinand sent a contingent of troops to join the campaign against Venice in 1510 – although they would arrive late, and play no great part in it.

The campaign began in May with a two-pronged assault. The French army under the command of Chaumont joined up with Alfonso d'Este and his men in the Ferrarese on 13 May and advanced on the area of the Polesine held by Venice. The Imperial forces under Rudolf von Anhalt advanced from Verona with the French troops who had been based there.[76] The Venetians had lost Pitigliano, who died in January, and Gianpaolo Baglioni was in command. Strategy was decided by the Venetians and remained the same: to avoid pitched battles, with the overriding priority being the defence of the city of Venice by holding on to Padua and Treviso. In conformity with this, the Venetian army withdrew to Padua.

By the time the two armies of the League had come together on 23 May, they had taken the Polesine and Vicenza with its territory. An infamous atrocity took place in the Vicentino, when over 1,000 men, women and children who had taken refuge in a cave system at Mossano were suffocated by smoke from fires lit at the entrance by soldiers who wanted to plunder them. Legnago fell to the French, and then the League forces took several towns such as Bassano and Belluno which controlled the routes to major Alpine passes. Harassed by Venetian stradiots and hindered by passive resistance from peasants, they were unable to open the way, as Maximilian had wished, for von Anhalt's men to link up with the 4,000 men under Erich von Braunschweig, Duke of Brunswick, who were in Friuli.[77] Maximilian wanted either Padua or Treviso to be besieged. Before he would commit his forces to such an enterprise, however, Louis wanted to see Maximilian come to Italy.

Although the League armies were reinforced by 400 Spanish men-at-arms under the duca di Termoli, who arrived from Naples at the end of June,[78] the campaign was already running out of steam when Chaumont was ordered to withdraw with the bulk of his army to deal with threats to Genoa and Milan. Leaving 400 lances with the Imperial troops he returned to Milan in early August. Through desertions for lack of pay, the Imperial forces were dwindling. Soon the Venetians, now under the command of Lucio Malvezzi, began to advance. As the troops of the League retreated before them, the Venetians rapidly recovered all the territory they had lost, except for Legnago which was held by a French garrison. At the end of August they retook Vicenza. The Imperial army with the French and Spanish contingents fell back on Verona; they successfully resisted a Venetian assault on the city in mid-September, but were in no position to launch a counter-attack. Von Anhalt died of disease in early September; the Duke of Brunswick was to replace him as commander, but his contract ended in October and was not renewed. The German infantry was mutinous, demanding their pay. At the end of October, Ferdinand ordered Termoli to withdraw his men from Verona and return to Naples. Of all the lands Maximilian claimed from Venice for the Empire, only Verona and Legnago were still held by the League – and the fortresses of Verona and Legnago were in the hands of the French.

Julius II and the French

The pope had already decided that Louis, not Venice, was his primary enemy. He was behind both the attempt to overthrow the French regime in Genoa, and the Swiss invasion that had caused Chaumont to be ordered back to Milan. He was also attacking the Duke of Ferrara, not least because he was under the protection of the French king. Julius's animus against Louis had not been appeased by the death of Cardinal d'Amboise in May 1510. It was God's will that he should drive the French from Italy, he said.[79]

He proposed to start by driving them out of Genoa, which he thought could lead on to a rebellion in Milan.[80] Enlisting the help of the Venetians, he sent the papal fleet to try in mid-July to put ashore Genoese exiles of the Fregoso faction, and a small force of horse and foot under Marcantonio Colonna to advance on the city by land. This attempt was unsuccessful, but Julius tried again in early September, and in late October. On each occasion, as the fleet neared Genoa it was evident that the French forces there (which had been rapidly reinforced) far outnumbered them, and there were no signs of a rising against them.

The pope also endeavoured to set the Swiss against the French. His ally in this was Matthias Schinner, prince-bishop of Sion in the Valais region between the Swiss cantons, Savoy and the duchy of Milan. Capable, energetic and persuasive, he was not only the temporal as well as the spiritual ruler in the Valais, but he was also influential in the deliberations of the Swiss. Opposed to French efforts to treat the Valaisans as satellites, he preferred to have a Sforza duke rather than the king of France in Milan. In March 1510 he negotiated an alliance between the pope and the Swiss. They undertook to provide 6,000 men at the pope's expense when the papacy or its territory was threatened, and not to let their mercenaries serve the enemies of the pope.

In late July Schinner asked the Swiss diet to raise 6,000 men for the pope. The cantons decided their soldiers could fight their way through the Milanese to join the papal army, but not make the French their primary target. More troops than the pope asked for, up to 10,000 in all, turned up on the border in early September.[81] French resources were stretched – as Julius had intended they should be – between the defence of Genoa, supporting the Imperial troops against Venice and assisting the Duke of Ferrara. Chaumont aimed to contain the Swiss, and to deprive them of victuals. French troops shadowed them as they marched east in close order along the foot of the mountains. Food was hard to find, they had no money and there was no word from the pope. After a couple of days, they decided to turn back. They began to make their way home, pillaging as they went. Their withdrawal infuriated the pope, and his anger was stoked by an offer from the cantons to mediate between him and Louis. This he regarded as impertinence, and he refused to pay what the troops claimed he still owed them.[82]

Julius's justification for calling on the Swiss was that the French were supporting Alfonso d'Este. There were other causes of contention between Julius and Alfonso, but his association with the French was the most important. The campaign against him began in early July, with Cardinal Francesco Alidosi as legate in command. Alfonso tried to appease the pope, offering to give up some territory, but Julius was not open to offers.

Not only did he want Ferrara itself, he saw the campaign as a strike against the French. By early August, French troops were directly engaged in the defence of Ferrara. When Alfonso left the French camp in the Veneto with 150 men-at-arms to go to defend his lands, Chaumont sent with him 250 lances under Jacques Coligny, seigneur de Châtillon, and 3,000 Italian and Gascon infantry.[83] Alidosi put the papal army's strength at 1,000 men-at-arms and 10,000 infantry; another report put it at 700 men-at-arms and 8,000 infantry.[84] Papal troops entered Alfonso's second city, Modena, but the duke was able to reach Ferrara with some men in late August.

Suddenly, Julius decided to take charge of operations himself. Arriving at Bologna on 22 September, he soon fell ill, but still assumed active control of his army. In early October, Chaumont came on Louis's orders to reinforce support for Alfonso. He based his men at Reggio and Rubiera, while the papal camp was at Modena. His arrival was not the only obstacle to the papal army concentrating its attack on Ferrara, as Julius wished to do. Mutual dislike and rivalry between his commander, his young nephew, Francesco Maria della Rovere, Duke of Urbino,[85] and Cardinal Alidosi had reached such a pitch that they could not work together. Appointing Francesco Gonzaga (now released from captivity in Venice) his commander did not solve the problem, for Gonzaga stayed in Mantua. Some relief for Julius's frustration was on the way, in the form of reinforcements of Venetian and Spanish troops. The Venetian camp in the Polesine in early October had around 320 men-at-arms, 770 crossbowmen, 330 stradiots and 2,600 infantry, under the command of the commissioner Paolo Capello, and orders were given for another 100 men-at-arms to be sent there.[86] Ferdinand was sending 300 men-at-arms under Fabrizio Colonna. This was a condition of his investiture with the kingdom of Naples, which he had finally been granted by Julius, but the papal bulls were only to be handed over to him when Colonna arrived and promised to serve the pope with the men-at-arms. Julius had grounds for caution, because Ferdinand did not want to be a declared enemy of France. After some hesitation about what his troops could do, it was agreed they could fight French troops who were supporting Ferrara.

Chaumont decided to try to get control over Bologna before the Spanish and Venetian troops reached it; he had some Bentivoglio with him. He assumed Julius would retire from Bologna as he approached, but the bedridden pope stayed put when the French arrived on 19 October. The Bolognese were organizing to defend their city, not rising to welcome the Bentivoglio. Chaumont had not intended to lay siege to the city, especially with the pope inside it, and he withdrew. While the Venetians confronted

Alfonso d'Este's forces in the Polesine, some of their men joined the papal and Spanish camp, now under the control of Fabrizio Colonna, confronting the French. To cut costs on Louis's orders, Chaumont had to dismiss his Italian infantry. Leaving 500 lances and 2,000 infantry under Robert Stuart d'Aubigny,[87] he went to take up winter quarters at Parma.

Before Julius could attack Ferrara, he was advised he should take Mirandola. This strongly fortified little town was the centre of a small state belonging to the Pico family. At this time it was held by Francesca, the daughter of Gian Giacomo Trivulzio and widow of Lodovico Pico. She had accepted a French garrison there, and put Mirandola and her children under Louis's protection. Another Pico stronghold, Concordia, fell on 18 December, but Fabrizio Colonna and the Duke of Urbino agreed Mirandola should not be besieged in the prevailing bitter weather. Determined the siege should go ahead despite the deep snow, Julius left Bologna in early January 1511 to see to it himself. Exposed to the wind and snow, he watched the siege operations within range of the guns in the fortress. When the town surrendered on 20 January, he went around the streets to stop the soldiers plundering it.

Still he could not go on to attack Ferrara itself, for the French camp had moved, blocking the way. He returned to Bologna, and then went to Ravenna. Without his presence to infuse some vigour into the campaign, it languished. Perhaps anticipating that his men would not hold Modena against a French attack, and that the French would not attack Modena if it was held for Maximilian, in late January he gave orders for custody of the city to be handed over to an Imperial envoy, although he sent Marcantonio Colonna to command the garrison there. For some months Maximilian had been trying to reconcile Julius and Louis. His proposal of a general peace conference to be held at Mantua was greeted with enthusiasm by Ferdinand, more coolly by Louis. Julius was not really interested in peace, did not send a representative to the conference when it met in mid-March, and refused to discuss his relations with Louis with Maximilian's representative, Matthaeus Lang, bishop of Gurk, when he went to Bologna to meet the pope in April.

Lang's departure from Bologna heralded the resumption of hostilities. Concordia fell in early May to the French army, which was now led by Gian Giacomo Trivulzio following the death of Chaumont in March. The papal and Venetian forces fell back to protect Bologna. This time the pope did not wait there for the French, but left for Ravenna. The Bolognese rebelled, and partisans of the Bentivoglio sent for them to come. On 21 May, Alidosi fled, and the papal camp followed, leaving their baggage and artillery behind; the Venetian troops had little choice but to do the same. The French pursued, killing 3,000 infantry, Trivulzio claimed, and disarming the rest, in what he described to the king as an enterprise scarcely less honourable than the conquest of Milan.[88] The Bentivoglio returned in triumph, and urged the people on to destroy the new fortress Julius had built when it surrendered a few days later. On Louis's orders, Trivulzio left 400 lances under d'Aubigny in Bologna and took the rest of the army back to Milan; on the way, he captured Mirandola and put a French garrison in the fortress. The French triumph enabled Alfonso d'Este to recover easily the places papal troops had taken from him the year before.

In Ravenna, Julius blamed the Duke of Urbino as well as Alidosi for the loss of Bologna; the duke took his revenge by murdering the cardinal in the street. At this crisis of the pope's affairs, another serious attack was launched against him, one long premeditated and prepared by Louis, with the announcement by a group of cardinals estranged from the pope of their intention to hold a General Council of the Church. It was to meet in Pisa, which Louis was insisting the Florentines should make available. For someone other than a pope to summon such a council was a grave challenge to the authority of the papacy.

Julius was paying the price for such active involvement in the wars. Italian powers were accustomed to a pope behaving like a secular prince and waging war (admittedly not usually conducting military operations in person). For other European powers, a pope as the incumbent of the Holy See still retained a greater aura of spiritual authority. They might challenge him over ecclesiastical jurisdiction or appointments to benefices, but had more scruples than Italian princes did about waging war on him. For their part, popes had no scruples about using spiritual weapons for temporal ends, as Julius had excommunicated the Venetians in April 1509 and excommunicated Alfonso d'Este in August 1510. In a way, by raising the threat of a General Council against Julius because Julius was opposing him in Italy, Louis was taking on the pope at his own game. Julius's response was swift: he decided to summon a council himself, to meet in Rome. He returned to Rome, and in mid-July the convocation of his council was announced, and the Pisan council declared illegal. The prospects of peace between Julius and Louis were more remote than ever.

The campaign in the Veneto in 1511

Still intent on getting hold of the lands he claimed under the treaty of Cambrai, once again Maximilian called on Louis and Ferdinand to help him. Ferdinand did not send troops to join this year's campaign against Venice, and Louis gave up plans to come to Italy himself, to the relief of the nobles who would have been obliged to accompany him but were tired of Italian expeditions. Receiving no help from the Empire this time, Maximilian could not get together a stable, substantial field army to match the forces provided by Louis. If he managed to double the number of soldiers at Verona, the base of his Italian operations, there were still chronic shortages of money and supplies, and the hungry men were alienating the people by their thieving and brutality. Finding a commander was a problem, too. He appointed Francesco Gonzaga his captain-general, but Gonzaga again avoided taking up a command that would have compromised his stance of refusal to commit fully to any side. La Palisse was in command of the French contingent of 700–800 lances and the best part of 6,000 infantry, of whom 1,800 were Grisons.[89] French troops formed the bulk of the 10,000 foot and 3,000 horse that left Verona in early August.[90]

No satisfactory replacement had yet been found by the Venetians for Pitigliano as captain-general; the ailing Lucio Malvezzi had not renewed his contract as governor-general, and Gianpaolo Baglioni replaced him. The Venetians were having to give command to second-rank Italian *condottieri*, who had problems asserting control in the camp, and could not challenge or much influence the strategy dictated by the government. And so, in accordance with that strategy, the Venetian army again withdrew before the enemy advance, the unfortunate inhabitants of the Veneto were left to face occupation and plunder by Imperial and French troops, and Alfonso d'Este was able swiftly to retake the Polesine, while the Venetian forces concentrated on the defence of Padua and Treviso.

They were given time to reinforce the defences of Padua, where Baglioni took command, and Treviso, under the command of Renzo degli Anguillara da Ceri, who was rising to prominence as an infantry commander. Breathing-space was given to them by Maximilian's indecision about the next step. Eventually he decided to secure Friuli first, and the Imperial army with a small French contingent went there. La Palisse with the bulk of the French troops stayed north of Treviso on the Piave, where they were joined by 400 more lances under d'Aubigny, with Venetian stradiots imperilling their supply lines and disease in their camp.

Epidemics had been but one of the troubles afflicting Friuli during what had been a dreadful year. The province had also suffered an outbreak of vicious faction-fighting, peasant revolts against their castellan lords and a destructive earthquake. Understandably the people of Friuli were not able to put up as much resistance as in previous years to the Imperial army. Antonio Savorgnan, trying to protect the province and his own pre-eminence there, made terms with Maximilian. Nearly all of Friuli fell to the Imperial forces.

In early October, with Friuli apparently secured, the Imperial army rejoined the French. Maximilian ordered them to besiege Treviso, but a week into the siege, orders arrived from Louis for the French to withdraw. Nothing loath, his troops left on 15 October and the siege was ended, because the Imperial forces could not continue it alone. Nor were they strong enough to prevent the Venetians, before November was out, recovering Friuli (except for the important fortress of Gradisca), and pushing the Imperial troops back to Verona and Alfonso d'Este out of the Polesine. It would have been small comfort that Tyrolean troops continued the fight in the mountains, making some gains, including Belluno. Maximilian was pulling troops out even from Verona; by early December, most of the garrison was French.

The Holy League

Louis had ordered his troops to withdraw from the Veneto because of the new league of Julius, Ferdinand and Venice, proclaimed in Rome in early October.[91] It was called the Holy League, because it was supposed to be for the benefit of the papacy. Ferdinand, who had suggested the League and was to provide most of its military strength, had emphasized that it should not be explicitly against any power, but he intended it as a restraint on Louis. According to him, Louis aimed to conquer all Italy.[92] Julius was happy to agree to it, and the Venetians were pleased to be leaving their diplomatic isolation. Venetian obligations under the League were comparatively light: to contribute what troops they could, and their galleys; the pope was to provide 600 men-at-arms, under a commander supplied by Ferdinand. The king was to send 1,200 men-at-arms, 1,000 light horse and 10,000 Spanish infantry; the pope and Venice were to pay 40,000 ducats a month towards the cost of the Spanish troops.[93] Ferdinand was keen to include Henry VIII of England in the confederation (which Henry ratified), and he also made a separate treaty with him in which they agreed to attack France in Aquitaine.

Louis had hoped to avoid becoming involved again in war against the pope, by the threat of a Church council, but the prospects for that were unpromising. Few clergy, even from France, were willing to be associated with it. Maximilian's support was vacillating, Ferdinand was vehemently opposed, and none of the Italian states were in favour either. Reluctant hosts, the Florentines under pressure from Louis had allowed the council to be held at Pisa, but would not accept the escort of French soldiers the dissident cardinals claimed they needed, nor compel their own clergy to attend it. Even before the council was formally opened on 5 November, its failure was apparent. The council quickly decided to transfer to Milan, but was no better attended there.

As well as the threat from the Holy League to the south, the French in Milan were also facing a renewed threat from the Swiss in the north. There were various motives behind this, including a desire for revenge for the maltreatment of some Swiss envoys, and a desire to wage a more lucrative and successful campaign than that of 1510. Some hoped that they might be able to bring Louis to consent to more attractive terms than had been offered during negotiations that autumn.[94]

The king's wish to keep a check on expenditure was frustrating the French captains in Italy. Pitching their request high in the hope that he would at least agree to something, they asked him for authority to raise 20,000 infantry.[95] They had a new commander, the king's nephew, Gaston de Foix. Aged only 22 when he was appointed Louis's lieutenant in Italy and governor of Milan in October 1511, de Foix had already taken part in several Italian campaigns. In what would turn out to be a brief career as commander of the army, de Foix would prove himself a remarkable military leader. On the king's orders, he concentrated the bulk of the troops in the duchy at Parma, preparing to confront the Holy League. The papal troops in the Romagna, however, were biding their time until the Spanish army arrived from Naples.

The first test for de Foix would be dealing with an incursion by the Swiss. They began to muster on the northern Milanese border at the end of November. As he had to leave troops in Parma, Bologna and on the eastern borders of the duchy, de Foix had with him only 500 lances, 200 gentlemen and 200 mounted archers of the king's household, and 2,000 infantry.[96] Louis sent orders to raise 6,000 more infantry, and instructed de Foix not to attack the Swiss until they were on the plain, and then to fight them and force them to retire.[97] By the time he sent these orders the Swiss were already on the move. De Foix and his captains had decided to adopt the strategy of the previous year: to stay close to them, avoiding battle, trying to hinder them from finding supplies.[98]

By early December around 10,000 Swiss had gathered, and more were arriving; they chose Jacob Stapfer as their commander. Advancing towards Milan, they kept strict discipline and paid for their supplies. By 14 December they were in sight of the city, and they sent an appeal to the people, saying they came as liberators, not conquerors, in hopes the Milanese would rise against the French.[99] But the Milanese had agreed to provide 6,000 militia to help defend the city, and reinforcements were arriving from other parts of the duchy. The Swiss were not strong enough to lay siege to a city the size of Milan, and there was no sign of League troops arriving to support them. Negotiations began: the French were prepared to offer money, but the Swiss also demanded the cession of Locarno and Lugano, and unimpeded transit through the duchy, whenever they wanted, for Swiss soldiers going to fight for the pope – terms wholly unacceptable to the French.[100] Then, unexpectedly, the camp broke up. Disorganized bands of Swiss made their way home, devastating the country in their path.

Fortunately for the French, they had not had to deal simultaneously with an attack by the League. The Spanish troops, under the command of the viceroy of Naples, Ramon de Cardona, did not arrive in the Romagna until December. There was a desultory campaign in the Romagna before in late January the pope finally got his wish for a siege of Bologna. But by a rapid forced march over about thirty miles in bitter weather, de Foix brought reinforcements into Bologna on 5 February, taking unawares the Spanish and papal troops encamped to the south of the city. When Cardona learned of their arrival, he lifted the siege and withdrew.

No sooner had de Foix accomplished the relief of Bologna, than he was informed that Brescia had fallen to the Venetians. There had been several conspiracies against French rule there, for they had not endeared themselves to the Brescians. The latest had come to light in mid-January: a prominent Brescian noble, Luigi Avogadro, planned to co-ordinate an uprising in the city with the arrival of Venetian troops and of forces he and his allies would raise in the Bresciano. Outside the city when the plot was discovered, he insisted the Venetians should make another attempt. He entered the city at the head of 10,000 men during the night of 2–3 February, followed by Venetian troops. Revolts against the French broke out in the Bresciano, and in the city of Bergamo and its territory; French garrisons in Brescia and Bergamo took refuge in the cities' fortresses. As it was feared that other areas would also rebel, Gian Giacomo Trivulzio toured Lodi, Crema and Cremona with 2,000 infantry to secure them.

De Foix's response to the news was swift. He left Bologna on 8 February, and on 17 February reached Brescia, a journey shortened by three or four days by Francesco Gonzaga granting de Foix and his troops transit through his lands. On the way, they were joined by some landsknechts who had been in Verona. The Venetians in Brescia were surprised to see them, having no idea that the French could have come from Bologna in that time. Most of the men from the Bresciano who had come with Avogadro had been sent home, and the Venetians had few soldiers there.

On the night of 18–19 February de Foix led about 500 dismounted men-at-arms and 6,000 infantry by a hidden path into the fortress of Brescia, leaving d'Alègre with 500 men-at-arms to guard the walls. An assault was launched on the city, spearheaded by the men-at-arms, who crouched down when the ranks of the arquebusiers behind them fired their volleys.[101] The desperate defence was aided by women throwing tiles, stones and boiling water from the rooftops. Some stradiots fled the fighting through one of the city gates, only to run into d'Alègre's men, who were able to enter the city and join in the slaughter. By evening, the defenders had been annihilated; several thousand corpses lay in the city's streets.

A summons to surrender had been rejected by the Venetian authorities in Brescia, which meant the city was, by the laws of war, legitimately open to sack. De Foix gave his soldiers their reward, and for three days the people of Brescia suffered one of the most terrible sacks of the Italian Wars. The estimated value of the spoils was three to four million ducats, including the heavy ransoms imposed on individuals; 4,000 cartloads of goods were said to have been taken away.[102] So enriched were many French soldiers by booty and ransoms from Brescia that they left for home. Some blamed the decline of French fortunes in Italy on this depletion of their army: 'the capture of Brescia was the ruin of the French in Italy'.[103] The city of Brescia was also punished by heavy fines, the loss of its privileges and the exile of many citizens, as were Bergamo and other places that had rebelled, but they were spared a sack.

De Foix returned to Milan and then to Emilia. When Maximilian wanted to exploit the success of the French for his own ends and urged him to send troops against Padua and Treviso, de Foix replied that he could not do anything without orders from the king, that the first concern was the Spanish army, and that the Swiss might return. Louis's response was much the same.[104] He instructed de Foix to gather his army together, seek out the Spanish army and bring it to a decisive engagement. There was some sense of urgency behind this project for a resolution on this front, for Louis was mindful of the preparations being made for an English invasion of France.

Ferdinand, on the other hand, wanted Cardona to bide his time until preparations for attacks on the French in Lombardy by the Venetians and the Swiss, and in the south-west of France by the Spanish and English, were complete. Such instructions suited Cardona, who was naturally cautious – too cautious, some of his captains felt. So as the French army approached, the Spanish and papal forces drew back. The French were having serious difficulty in finding victuals, and could not afford to wait. After some debate among the commanders, it was decided to try to force the issue by attacking Ravenna, too important a city to be abandoned to them. An assault on 9 April was unsuccessful, but it did bring Cardona to approach to defend the city.

The Battle of Ravenna

Battle was joined on 11 April, Easter Sunday – from that very day, it was seen as an epic encounter. The Spanish and papal army took up a position south of Ravenna on the right bank of the river Ronco; the high embankments of the river were broad enough for large numbers of horse or foot to pass along them easily. Starting at right angles to the river, they dug a long, curving trench, leaving a gap at the river end. Their artillery was positioned at that end of the trench. The other units were drawn up in file, not to defend the line of the trench; the men-at-arms were nearest the river, the infantry in the centre and the light horse on the right wing. Pedro Navarro, who commanded the infantry, had placed in front of them about 50 light carts with projecting blades, protected by arquebuses. The French crossed the river near the city by a bridge de Foix had had built; d'Alègre was left with the rearguard to protect this. They took up position along the trench, the men-at-arms nearest the river bank, with artillery placed before them, separate units of German, French and Italian infantry side by side, and to the left the light horse and archers.

The Spanish and papal troops were outnumbered and they knew it: they had about 20,000 men, while the French had 30,000 or more.[105] Cardona had put 1,500 men under Marcantonio Colonna into Ravenna, and much of the papal army was not there, because the Duke of Urbino refused to be under the orders of the viceroy. Alfonso d'Este with 100 men-at-arms and 200 light horse was with the French. More significantly, he had brought his renowned artillery, giving the French perhaps twice as many artillery pieces as the League. Besides the guns positioned opposite the Spanish artillery, a couple of pieces were placed on the other side of the river, and d'Este with his artillery at the far end of the French line.

The battle began with an artillery exchange, unprecedented in its length – over two hours – and its ferocity. The Spanish guns were aimed at the infantry, causing significant casualties; the League's infantry were instructed by Navarro to move to a place where they could lie flat and evade the French and Ferrarese artillery. But there was no escape for their cavalry, who were caught in the crossfire. Eventually, the Spanish heavy cavalry were driven to leave their defensive position and attack the French men-at-arms. As they were trying to silence the Ferrarese guns, the Spanish light horse under the marchese di Pescara were attacked by the French light horse.

In the engagement between the French and Spanish men-at-arms, the Spanish were less disciplined and co-ordinated. D'Alègre and his rearguard joined the fight and turned the scales against the Spanish. Their rearguard under Alonso Carvajal broke and fled the field; Cardona left with them. Meanwhile the French infantry crossed the trench to attack the League's infantry, taking heavy casualties from the arquebuses as they tried to break through the barrier of the carts. The Gascons were put to flight along the river bank. As the Spanish infantry units and the landsknechts of the French army were locked in fierce combat, the French cavalry, having overcome the Spanish, were able to come to the aid of their foot. Fabrizio Colonna rallied what men-at-arms he could to defend the League infantry, but could not prevent their defeat. Although 3,000 Spanish infantry were able to retire in good order along the river bank, the rest were killed, captured or dispersed.[106]

By mid-afternoon the hard-fought battle was over. Contemporaries, appalled at the scale of the slaughter, considered it to be the bloodiest fought on Italian soil for centuries. It was estimated that upwards of 10,000 men were killed; some put the total as high as 20,000. There were disagreements about which army had suffered the greater mortality. It was probably the League, whose losses may have been three times those of the French. In one significant respect, the French losses were greater – among the commanders. While the Spanish lost some experienced and valued captains, the more prominent were captured rather than killed, including Pedro Navarro, Fabrizio Colonna and Ferrante Francesco d'Avalos, marchese di Pescara; the papal legate, Cardinal Giovanni de' Medici, was also taken prisoner after the battle. French losses among their commanders and nobles were heavy. Among the fallen were Gaston de Foix, apparently killed by Spanish infantry, Yves d'Alègre and his son, Soffrey Alleman, seigneur de Mollart, the captain of the Gascon infantry, and Philip of Fribourg and Jacob Empser, captains of the landsknechts.

For the French, the death of de Foix cast the greatest shadow over their victory. If his bravery had bordered on the foolhardy, in his brief period as commander of the army he had shown himself an inspiring leader, always in the thick of the action. Cardona, by contrast, seems to have left leadership to his subordinate commanders; he was widely blamed for their defeat. 'In truth, he knows nothing of warfare', was the verdict of Vich, Ferdinand's ambassador in Rome, 'and everyone complains that he never asks for advice or comes to a decision'.[107] Others have judged the outcome of the battle the result of the devastating effect of Alfonso d'Este's deployment of his artillery: 'the true cause of the French victory', according to Pieri.[108] The French themselves were more critical of his role, for his guns had caused many casualties among them too, as he continued to fire once the troops were engaged.[109]

The killing continued the following day, as the city of Ravenna, after an offer to capitulate had been made, was sacked by unrestrained Gascons and landsknechts who entered by a breach made in the walls by the earlier bombardment.[110] Within a few days, nearly all the Romagna had surrendered to the French, only the fortresses holding out a little longer. This conquest was not due to any concerted effort by the French, for the weary troops were occupied in looking after their wounded and their booty from Ravenna. La Palisse, as the senior captain, had assumed command. He quarrelled with the Duke of Ferrara, who left the camp with his surviving men, some of the wounded and his prisoners, including Colonna and Pescara. News arrived that the English and Spanish had invaded France, that Maximilian had made a truce with Venice, and that the Swiss were again threatening Milan. Nevertheless, to save money, 4,600 infantry were dismissed.

La Palisse left for the Milanese on 20 April with more than half of the remaining troops. Cardinal Sanseverino, in his capacity of legate of Bologna for the schismatic council, and his brother Galeazzo, with 300 lances and 6,000 infantry, stayed to complete the conquest of the Romagna in the name of the council.[111] When Louis's orders – issued when he was unaware of the real state of affairs in Italy – arrived, they were for the army to press on to Rome. The army commanders decided the threat to Lombardy was more urgent.[112]

The expulsion of the French

Despite the heavy defeat their forces had suffered, both Ferdinand and, after some initial dismay, the pope were determined to continue the fight against the French. Dismissing fears that the kingdom of Naples was in danger, Ferdinand ordered reinforcements be sent to Cardona. The viceroy had in fact returned to Naples in early May, but after reorganizing the army he left for northern Italy again at the end of the month. Julius also soon set about reordering his troops. The Duke of Urbino was now back in the fold, after considering going over to Louis, and would be in command. La Palisse would have been aware that the papal and Spanish armies were being renewed, but his more immediate problem was the Swiss.

Swayed by the strength of popular anti-French sentiment, the authorities of the cantons had decided to side with the Holy League. Twelve delegates had been sent to Venice to negotiate with Cardinal Schinner, who had been appointed papal legate to the Swiss. The Venetians had hoped they had come to negotiate with them, so Schinner included them in the talks. It was decided that the Swiss would provide the 6,000 men the pope was asking for, under the terms of their treaty with him and not, nominally, to the League; nevertheless, Venice and Ferdinand were to contribute to their pay. This agreement, made in Venice in early April, was approved by the Swiss diet a fortnight later. Permission was given for volunteers to go as well as the officially raised contingents. It was also decided that the Swiss would fight the French on their own account. The Swiss were acting in something more than their traditional capacity of suppliers of mercenaries, but not quite taking on the role of a member of an international league. The army that assembled at Trent numbered about 24,000, all but 6,000 of them volunteers. As usual, the army elected its own commanders, Baron Ulrich von Hohensax and Jacob Stapfer.[113] The cantons were not proposing to pay any of these men themselves, and the League found that they were expected to provide for the volunteers as well. But such a strong force – if the resources could be found to pay and supply them – promised to bring decisive success against the weakened French.

The situation of the French in Milan was deteriorating. Louis had recalled his household troops and an additional 200 lances.[114] Many of the remaining French troops were longing to go home as well, and many people in the duchy heartily wished they would, having had more than enough of French troops and officials and their demands. La Palisse lacked support. Other commanders, such as d'Aubigny and Trivulzio, were not prepared to accept him as their superior; Louis had confirmed him as commander of the army, but had not appointed him lieutenant in Milan. If the Florentines had finally fulfilled their treaty obligations to Louis by sending 200 lances to Lombardy, no help was to be looked for from Maximilian, who was hedging his bets. He ratified his truce with Venice in May, and without declaring support for the League had allowed the Swiss troops to pass through the Tyrol and muster at Trent. When the Swiss moved on to Verona, where they arrived on 25–26 May, they were welcomed by the

Imperial officials there. The French garrison had left the day before, to join La Palisse.

The Swiss were behaving like a mercenary army. They refused to move on from Verona until they were assured of supplies, and they were demanding their pay. In a letter to Venice, their captains threatened (probably not seriously) that they would go over to the French if the money was not forthcoming.[115] The Venetians, the pope and the viceroy found enough to get the Swiss on the move, promising them money from places they conquered in the Milanese. Cardinal Schinner's arrival in Verona helped, as he combined his authority as papal legate with his personal influence over them.

Schinner and the other representatives of the League discussed what to do. Papal troops were recovering the Romagna. When the Bentivoglio left Bologna on 10 June, the last French troops in the province left too. It was decided not to wait for Cardona, but to press on into the duchy, as the Venetian army – 550 lances, 1,200 light horse and 5,500 infantry, with an artillery train – joined up with the Swiss on 1 June.[116] Intercepted letters from La Palisse revealed he had only 8,000 infantry and 700– 800 ill-equipped lances.[117] He lost the best infantry he had when 4,000 landsknechts obeyed a summons from Maximilian to leave the French, although several hundred remained. He abandoned Cremona to the advancing Swiss and Venetians. Schinner accepted its surrender in the name of the League, and an indemnity of 40,000 ducats helped keep up payments to the Swiss. La Palisse retreated to Pavia, but after a few days of siege decided he would have to withdraw. What could have turned into a disastrous rout was made easier for him by the Swiss at one stage refusing to fight, believing the Venetian troops were trying to take the honour of blocking the French retreat. While the Venetians wanted to pursue the French, the Swiss refused to go on without another instalment of pay that Pavia was to provide.

In fact, the French army was abandoning the duchy, and was back in France by early July. Throughout the duchy, French officials and partisans were leaving; some were killed as revolts broke out. Genoa was lost to them too, as the exile Giano Campofregoso came with partisans and some troops provided by the Venetians, and on behalf of the League summoned the city to surrender. The French governor took refuge in the new fortress on the harbour, and on 22 June Campofregoso entered the city; a week later he was elected doge. By July, scattered garrisons in fortresses in Genoa and Lombardy were all that was left of Louis's dominions in Italy.

Notes

1 Meschini, I, 213–16; d'Auton, II, 109–34; Ostinelli, 97–101; Kohler, 14–17.

2 Meschini, I, 245–68; Kohler, 18–19.

3 Elected on 31 October after the brief pontificate of Pius III.

4 Shaw, *Julius II*, 127–39.

5 Desjardins and Canestrini, II, 91.

6 Machiavelli, ed. Chiappelli, II, 572.

7 Luzzati, 49.

8 Machiavelli, ed. Bertelli, I, 554, II, 563; d'Auton, III, 305; Machiavelli, ed. Chiappelli, II, 589–90.

9 Machiavelli, ed. Bertelli, II, 770, 783, 821–2.

10 Desjardins and Canestrini, II, 161–2: Francesco Pandolfini, 9 Mar. 1506; Shaw, *L'ascesa*, 132–7.

11 Desjardins and Canestrini, II, 124–6: Francesco Pandolfini, 7 Sept. 1505. Louis's protection over Lucca, agreed in 1501, was confirmed in February 1510: ASLucca, Capitoli, 20, ff. 279–81.

12 ASLucca, Capitoli, Reg. 50, f. 17; Luzzati, 67.

13 Desjardins and Canestrini, II, 82.

14 Serano y Pineda, 26 (1912), 307; 27 (1912), 517.

15 *Ibid.*, 28 (1913), 114.

16 Machiavelli, ed. Bertelli, II, 847–9; Giustinian, III, 377; Dupré-Theseider, 33–7.

17 Faraglia, 561.

18 The implication of Ferdinand's instructions seems to be that they would not be paid for companies they raised themselves, but be given commands of men-at-arms who were directly in the king's service: Serano y Pineda, 27 (1912), 514–17: Ferdinand to Gonzalo, 3 Nov. 1504.

19 *Ibid.*, 29 (1913), 456–7: Ferdinand to Gonzalo, 21 Sept. 1505.

20 Machiavelli, ed. Chiappelli, IV, 220, 246.

21 *Ibid.*, 398–402; Guicciardini, Book VI, Chap. 14.

22 Guidi, 220–6; Machiavelli, ed. Chiappelli, IV, 257–87, 402–4.

23 Luzzati, 70–3.

24 Guicciardini, Book VII, Chap. 13, Book VIII, Chaps 2,8; Desjardins and Canestrini, II, 256–95.

25 Ruiz-Domènec, 398–9.

26 Hernando Sánchez, 125.

27 Terrateig, II, 26–7: instructions to Vich, 14 Apr. 1507.

28 D'Auton, IV, 70–1.

29 Desjardins and Canestrini, II, 220: F. Pandolfini, 16 Feb. 1507.

30 Shaw, *Julius II*, 211–16.

31 Desjardins and Canestrini, II, 128–9: F. Pandolfini, 10 Sept. 1505.

32 *Ibid.*, 190: F. Pandolfini, 25 Oct. 1506.

33 *Ibid.*, 196: F. Pandolfini, 14 Dec. 1506.

34 *Ibid.*, 231, 233; Kohler, 38–40; Pieri, 446; Meschini, I, 396–8.

35 Pandiani, 399–400.

36 Sabattini, 148: Alberto Pio, 1 May 1507, Genoa.

37 Pandiani, 272–7, 405–7, 533–50; d'Auton, IV, 252–80; Taviani, 216–22; Pacini, 59–78.

38 Baumgartner, 186.

39 Doussinague, 143–6.

40 De Maulde, 589–90.

41 Wiesflecker, III, 354–79.

42 Pieri, 450.

43 *Ibid.*, 450–1; Sanuto, VII, 347–52 (Bartolomeo d'Alviano's account, 10 Mar. 1508).

44 Pieri, 448–55; Wiesflecker, IV, 15–20.

45 Meschini, I, 476–9.

46 Le Glay, I, 225–43.

47 Sanuto, VIII, 150–2, 134.

48 Desjardins and Canestrini, II, 265–9.

49 Baumgartner, 194–5; Kohler, 119–44; Schmidt, 'Le défi européen', 118–23; Schmidt, 'Les Suisses en Milanais', 119–23.

50 Desjardins and Canestrini, II, 312, 322.

51 Pieri, 459–69; Sanuto, VIII, 248–51, 256–7, 268–70, 286–9, 325; Desjardins and Canestrini, II, 326–8, 331, 338.

52 Sanuto, VIII, 257, 265–6.

53 Meschini, II, 590, 593.

54 Wiesflecker, IV, 51–2.

55 Trebbi, 96.

56 Finlay, 39–40.

57 Sanuto, VIII, 265–6, 374.

58 The best-known jeremiads on this subject are those of the Venetian diarist, Girolamo Priuli: for example, Priuli, IV, 49–53.

59 Sanuto, VIII, 468–9.

60 Mallett and Hale, 341–2.

61 Guerin-Dalle Mese, 193.

62 Varanini, 'La Terraferma al tempo della crisi della Lega di Cambrai', 424–5.

63 Mallett and Hale, 344–6.

64 Sanuto, VIII, 252, 291.

65 *Ibid.*, IX, 57–60.

66 *Ibid.*, 114–5.

67 *Ibid.*, 189.

68 Wiesflecker, IV, 56.

69 Finlay, 44–5.

70 Mazzetti; Finlay. The Ferrarese claimed to have captured 13 galleys and some other vessels, 28 large artillery pieces and 140 smaller guns: Mazzetti, 273.

71 Finlay, 56–62.

72 Le Glay, I, 277–91: instructions of Maximilian to his envoys to Louis XII, 26 Nov. 1509.

73 Meschini, II, 684–5.

74 Desjardins and Canestrini, II, 490.

75 *CSPSpan*, II, 32–3.

76 According to Pieri, 478, 500 lances, 600 light horse and 4,000 infantry advanced from Verona, 1,700 lances, 3,500 light horse and 12,000 infantry into the Polesine, while the Venetians had 600 men-at-arms, 2,000–3,000 light horse and 8,000 infantry.

77 Wiesflecker, IV, 73.

78 Terrateig, I, 183.

79 Sanuto, X, 539.

80 ASVen, Archivio Proprio, Roma, Reg. 3, no. 61: Girolamo Donà, 15 May 1510.

81 Kohler, 181.

82 *Ibid.*, 189–91.

83 Meschini, 730.

84 Sanuto, XI, 83, 42.

85 He had become Duke of Urbino at the age of 18 in 1508, on the death of Guidobaldo da Montefeltro, his uncle and adoptive father.

86 Sanuto, XI, 499–500.

87 Meschini, 782.

88 Godefroy, II, 233–5: Gian Giacomo Trivulzio to Louis, 22 May 1511.

89 *Ibid.*, III, 1–2: list of companies to be sent; Meschini, 862.

90 Wiesflecker, IV, 87.

91 Desjardins and Canestrini, II, 539.

92 Terrateig, II, 167–74: Ferdinand to Vich, 16 July 1511.

93 Sanuto, XIII, 89–93.

94 Kohler, 229–30.

95 Desjardins and Canestrini, II, 540–1.

96 Meschini, 916.

97 Le Glay, I, 463.

98 Desjardins and Canestrini, II, 544.

99 *Ibid.*, 612–4: Swiss captains to citizens of Milan, 15 Dec. 1511.

100 Desjardins and Canestrini, II, 546.

101 Pieri, 488–9.

102 *Storia di Brescia*, II, 248–70.

103 Le Loyal Serviteur, 568.

104 Le Glay, *Négociations diplomatiques*, I, 482–3.

105 Pieri, 491, gives figures of 1,900 men-at-arms, 3,000 light horse and 18,000 infantry, with 50 artillery pieces, for the French, and 1,700 men-at-arms, 1,500 light horse and 13,000 infantry with 24 artillery pieces for the Spanish and papal army. A document in Sanuto, XIV, 170–4, lists for the French 1,690 lances (plus the rearguard), 2,000 light horse and 1,000

dismounted archers, and 21,400 infantry (9,500 Landsknechts, 8,000 French and 3,900 Italian); and for the League, 1,725 lances, 6,000–7,000 Spanish and 2,000 Italian infantry, and 1,500 light horse. A Spanish eyewitness account, the 'Relación de los sucesos de las armas de España en Italia', 276–7, gives the strength of their army at 2,200 men-at-arms, 6,000 Spanish and 1,500 Italian infantry, and 2,500 light horse.

106 Taylor, 119–22, 180–215; Pieri, 491–8; 'Relación', 276–92; Sanuto, XIV, 126–80 (176–80, account of the battle by Fabrizio Colonna); Canestrini, 310–12; Shaw, 'La battaglia e il sacco di Ravenna', 78–82.

107 Terrateig, II,184: Vich to Ferdinand, 15 Apr. 1512.

108 Pieri, 496.

109 Meschini, II, 1008.

110 Shaw, 'La battaglia e il sacco di Ravenna', 82–3.

111 Meschini, II, 1010.

112 *Ibid.*, 1011–12.

113 Kohler, 324–5, 338, 344–5.

114 Meschini, II, 1019.

115 Kohler, 344–5.

116 Sanuto, XIV, 276.

117 Kohler, 364.

Bibliography

Baumgartner, Frederic J., *Louis XII* (Stroud: Alan Sutton, 1994).

Belenguer, Ernest, *Fernando el Católico. Un monarca decisivo en las encrucijadas de su época* (3rd edition, Barcelona: Península, 2001).

Bowd, Stephen D., *Venice's Most Loyal City: Civic Identity in Renaissance Brescia* (Cambridge, MA: Harvard University Press, 2010).

Calendar of State Papers, Spanish (HMSO, 1862–1964) [*CSPSpan*].

Canestrini, Giuseppe, 'Documenti per servire alla storia della milizia italiana', *Archivio storico italiano*, 15 (1851).

Contamine, Philippe and Jean Guillaume (eds), *Louis XII en Milanais* (Paris: Honoré Champion, 2003).

d'Auton, Jean, *Chroniques de Louis XII*, ed. R. de Maulde, 4 vols (Paris: Renouard, 1889–96).

de Maulde, R., 'L'entrevue de Savone en 1507', *Revue d'histoire diplomatique*, 4 (1890), 583–90.

Desjardins, A. and G. Canestrini, *Négociations diplomatiques de la France avec la Toscane*, 6 vols (Paris: Imprimerie Impériale, 1859–86).

Doussinague, José, 'Fernando el Católico en las vistas de Savona de 1507', *Boletín de la Academia de la Historia*, 108 (1936), 99–146.

Dumont, Jean, *Corps universel diplomatique du droit des gens*, 8 vols (Amsterdam, 1726–31).

Dupré-Theseider, Eugenio, 'L'intervento di Ferdinando il Cattolico nella guerra di Pisa', in *Fernando el Católico e Italia* (V Congreso de Historia de la Corona de Aragon) (Zaragoza: Institución 'Fernando el Católico', 1954), 21–41.

Faraglia, N.F., 'Gli Orsini al soldo di Spagna (1503)', *Archivio storico per le province napoletane*, 6 (1881), 551–62.

Fernández de Córdova Miralles, Álvaro, *Alejandro VI y los Reyes Católicos: Relaciones político-eclesiásticas (1492–1503)* (Rome: Edizioni Università della Santa Croce, 2005).

Finlay, Robert, 'Venice, the Po expedition and the end of the League of Cambrai, 1509–1510', in Robert Finlay, *Venice Besieged. Politics and Diplomacy in the Italian Wars, 1494–1534* (Aldershot: Ashgate, 2008), Essay VI.

Frati, Vasco et al. (eds), *Il sacco di Brescia. Testimonianze, cronache, diari, atti del processo e memorie storiche della 'presa memoranda et crudele' della città nel 1512*, 3 vols (Brescia: Comune di Brescia, 1990).

Gagliardi, Ernst, *Der Anteil der Schweizer an den italienischen Kriegen 1494–1516* (Zurich, 1919).

Galasso, Giuseppe, *Il Regno di Napoli: Il Mezzogiorno spagnolo (1494–1622)* (idem (ed.), *Storia d'Italia*, XV, 2) (Turin: UTET, 2005).

Gilbert, Felix, 'Venice in the crisis of the League of Cambrai', in J.R. Hale (ed.), *Renaissance Venice* (Faber and Faber, 1973), 274–92.

Giustinian, Antonio, *Dispacci*, ed. Pasquale Villari, 3 vols (Florence, 1876).

Godefroy, J. (ed.), *Lettres du Roy Louis XII et du Cardinal d'Amboise*, 4 vols (Brussels: Françoise Foppens, 1712).

Guerin-Dalle Mese, Jeanine (ed.), *Una cronaca vicentina del Cinquecento* (Vicenza: Accademia Olimpica, 1983).

Guicciardini, Francesco, *Storia d'Italia* (various editions).

Guidi, Andrea, *Un segretario militante: Politica, diplomazia e armi nel Cancelliere Machiavelli* (Bologna, Il Mulino, 2009).

Hernando Sánchez, Carlos José, *El reino de Nápoles en el Imperio de Carlos V. La consolidación de la conquista* (Madrid: Sociedad Estatal para la Conmemoración de los Centenarios de Felipe II y Carlos V, 2001).

Kohler, Charles, *Les Suisses dans les Guerres d'Italie de 1506 à 1512* (*Mémoires et Documents publiés par la Société d'Histoire et d'Archéologie de Genève*, ser 2, vol 4) (Geneva, 1896).

Le Glay, M. (ed.), *Négociations diplomatiques entre la France et l'Autriche durant les trente premières années du XVIᵉ siècle*, 2 vols (Paris: Imprimerie Royale, 1845).

Le Loyal Serviteur, *La très joyeuse, plaisante et récreative histoire du bon chevalier sans paour et sans reproche, gentil seigneur de Bayard*, in Joseph Michaud and Jean Joseph François Poujoulat (eds), *Nouvelle collection des mémoires pour servir à l'histoire de France*, Ser. 1, 12 vols (Paris: Guyot, 1850), IV.

Luzio, Alessandro, 'Isabella d'Este di fronte al Giulio II negli ultimi tre anni del suo pontificato', *Archivio storico lombardo*, Ser. 4, 17 (1912), 245–334; 18 (1912), 55–144, 393–456.

Luzzati, Michele, *Una Guerra di Popolo: Lettere private del tempo dell'assedio di Pisa (1494–1509)* (Pisa: Pacini, 1973).

Machiavelli, Niccolò, *Legazioni e commissarie*, ed. Sergio Bertelli, 3 vols (Milan: Feltrinelli, 1964).

Machiavelli, Niccolò, *Legazioni. Commissarie. Scritti di governo*, ed. Fredi Chiappelli, 4 vols (Rome: Laterza, 1971–85).

Mallett, Michael and J.R. Hale, *The Military Organization of a Renaissance State: Venice c. 1400 to 1617* (Cambridge: Cambridge University Press, 1984).

Mazzetti, Adriano, 'Polesella 22 dicembre 1509: l'armata veneta marittima "ruynata" in Po', *Archivio veneto*, 175 (2010), 255–84.

Meschini, Stefano, *La Francia nel ducato di Milano. La politica di Luigi XII (1499–1512)*, 2 vols (Milan: FrancoAngeli, 2006).

Ostinelli, Paolo, 'Il Ticino tra Milano e la Svizzera. Le "Guerre milanesi" nella regione subalpina', in Viganò (ed.), *L'architettura militare nell'età di Leonardo*, 97–111.

Pacini, Arturo, *I presupposti politici del 'secolo dei genovesi'. La riforma del 1528* (*Atti della Società ligure di storia patria*, 104 (1990), fasc. 1) (Genoa, 1990).

Pandiani, Emilio, 'Un anno di storia genovese (giugno 1506–1507), con diario e documenti inediti', *Atti della Società ligure di storia patria*, 37 (1905).

Pecci, Giovanni Antonio, *Memorie storico-critiche della Città di Siena*, 2 vols (reprint, Siena: Edizioni Cantagalli, 1997).

Pieri, Piero, *Il Rinascimento e la crisi militare italiana* (Turin: Einaudi, 1952).

Priuli, Girolamo, *I Diarii*, ed. Arturo Segre and Roberto Cessi, *Rerum Italicarum Scriptores*, 24, part 3 (Bologna, 1912–38).

'Relación de los sucesos de las armas de España en Italia en los años de 1511 y 1512, con la jornada de Ravena', in *Colección de documentos inéditos para la Historia de España,*112 vols (Madrid: Academia de la Historia, 1842–95), LXXIX, 233–98.

Ruiz-Domènec, José Enrique, *El Gran Capitán. Retrato de una época* (Barcelona: Ediciones Península, 2002).

Sabattini, Alberto, *Alberto III Pio. Politica, diplomazia e guerra del conte di Carpi. Corrispondenza con la corte di Mantova, 1506–11* (Carpi: Danae, 1994).

Sanuto, Marino, *I Diarii*, ed. R. Fulin et al., 58 vols (Venice: Reale Deputazione veneta di storia patria, 1879–1903).

Schmidt, Hans-Joachim, 'Le défi européen des Suisses. Confrontations et coopérations vers l'an 1500', in Viganò (ed.), *L'architettura militare nell'età di Leonardo*, 113–32.

Schmidt, Hans-Joachim, 'Les Suisses en Milanais: coopération et concurrence avec Louis XII', in Contamine and Guillaume (eds), *Louis XII en Milanais*, 189–225.

Serano y Pineda, L.J. (ed.), 'Correspondencia de los Reyes Católicos con el Gran Capitán durante las campañas de Italia', *Revista de Archivos, Bibliotecas y Museos*, 20–29 (1909–13).

Shaw, Christine, *L'ascesa al potere di Pandolfo Petrucci, il Magnifico* (Siena: Il Leccio, 2001).

Shaw, Christine, 'La battaglia e il sacco di Ravenna', in Dante Bolognesi (ed.), *1512. La battaglia di Ravenna, l'Italia, l'Europa* (Ravenna: Longo Editore, 2014), 77–84.

Shaw, Christine, 'Julius II and Maximilian I', in Michael Matheus, Arnold Nesselrath and Martin Wallraff (eds), *Martin Luther in Rom. Die Ewige Stadt als kosmopolitisches Zentrum und ihre Wahrnehmung* (Berlin and Boston: de Gruyter, 2017), 155–68.

Shaw, Christine, *Julius II: The Warrior Pope* (Oxford: Blackwell, 1993).

Shaw, Christine, *The Political Role of the Orsini Family from Sixtus IV to Clement VII. Barons and Factions in the Papal States* (Rome: Istituto Storico Italiano per il Medio Evo, 2007).

Shaw, Christine, *Popular Government and Oligarchy in Renaissance Italy* (Leiden: Brill, 2006).

Storia di Brescia, vol. II, *La dominazione veneta (1426–1515)* (Brescia: Marcelliana, 1963).

Suárez, Luis, *Fernando el Católico* (Barcelona: Ariel, 2004).

Taviani, Carlo, *Superba discordia. Guerra, rivolta e pacificazione nella Genova di primo Cinquecento* (Rome: Viella, 2008).

Taylor, Frederick Lewis, *The Art of War in Italy 1494–1529* (Cambridge: Cambridge University Press, 1921; reprinted Westport: Greenwood Press, 1973).

Terrateig, Baron de, *Politica en Italia del Rey Católico 1507–1516*, 2 vols (Madrid: Consejo Superior de Investigaciones Científicas, 1963).

Trebbi, Giuseppe, *Il Friuli dal 1420 al 1797. La storia politica e sociale* (Udine, Casamassima, 1998).

Varanini, Gian Maria, 'La terraferma di fronte alla sconfitta di Agnadello' in Giuseppe Gullino (ed.), *L'Europa e la Serenissima. La svolta del 1509. Nel V centenario della battaglia di Agnadello* (Venice: Istituto veneto di scienze, lettere ed arti, 2011), 115–61.

Varanini, Gian Maria, 'La Terraferma al tempo della crisi della Lega di Cambrai. Proposte per una rilettura del "caso" veronese (1509–1517)', in Gian Maria Varanini, *Comuni, cittadini e Stato regionale: Ricerche sulla Terraferma veneta nel Quattrocento* (Verona: Libreria Editrice Universitaria,1992), 397–435.

CHAPTER 4

New orders struggling to be born, 1512–19

So swift was the collapse of French power in Italy that it took all their enemies by surprise. No plans as to what should happen to the territories that had been under French dominion had been agreed by the members of the Holy League with each other or with the Swiss. Each had different ideas on crucial matters, notably on what territories should be included in the duchy of Milan, and who should govern there. These disagreements, added to existing conflicts, would bring shifts in alliances and significant changes to the political geography of northern Italy.

One focus of future military and diplomatic conflict was created when Julius II claimed Parma and Piacenza for the papacy, on the most tenuous grounds. In Piacenza the dominant Guelf faction instigated an offer of submission to him in early July 1512. Parma stood out longer, until in early September the papal governor of Reggio, backed by the forces of faction leaders from the Reggiano, came and took possession of the city.

Reggio itself had submitted to the pope in early July as papal troops drew menacingly closer. Julius was still set on getting hold of the rest of Alfonso d'Este's territories. After his French protectors had been hustled out of Italy, Alfonso went to Rome, where he was formally absolved by the pope and treated quite well, but pressed to surrender Ferrara. Refusing to give it up, he left Rome against the pope's wishes on 19 July, escorted by Fabrizio Colonna (who had been treated courteously as a prisoner in Ferrara after the Battle of Ravenna), and was given refuge on the Colonna estates. Alfonso returned to northern Italy with Spanish troops led by Prospero Colonna going from Naples to Lombardy; he arrived back in Ferrara in mid-October. Julius tried in vain to persuade his allies to join him in another campaign against the duke.

The assistance Alfonso received from the Colonna provoked harsh exchanges between the pope and the Spanish ambassador, Jeronimo Vich. There was already discord between them, because Julius was refusing to pay any more for Spanish troops he said were no longer needed in northern Italy. Ferdinand was aggrieved that neither Julius nor Venice would subsidize his army, as he argued they were still obliged to do by the terms of the Holy League, and he also knew that Julius wished the Spanish to leave Italy too. Determined to have a say in the disposal of the duchy of Milan, Ferdinand wanted to keep his army in northern Italy to strengthen his hand, but was unable or unwilling to find enough money to maintain it.

When Cardona brought the army back from Naples in July, he seemed to be looking for something to do. Leaving his men at Modena, Cardona went to a conference convened in Mantua by Cardinal Lang, who was striving to assert his right as Imperial representative to have the leading role in the disposition of Lombardy. (Despite the affairs of Milan being high on the agenda, neither Schinner, the Swiss nor the Milanese were invited to send representatives.) Cardona would take his troops to work in concert with the Imperial forces in Lombardy. But first, it was agreed at Mantua, he would lead them to Tuscany to restore the exiled Medici to Florence, overturn the pro-French regime there and gain some money to help sustain his army, an enterprise Ferdinand would fully endorse.[1]

The restoration of the Medici to Florence

Cardona went to Florence in the name of the League, but had only his own troops – 5,000 infantry and 200 men-at-arms[2] – with him. Julius approved the plan, and Cardinal Giovanni de' Medici was with the army as papal legate, but no papal troops took part. On 28 August the army reached the Florentine subject town of Prato, which was defended by more than 3,000 militia. The Spanish soldiers were desperate with hunger, for no supplies were to be found. Having just a few light artillery pieces with them, the Spanish could make only a modest breach in the town's walls, but the infantry, living up to the Spanish reputation for courage in assault during sieges, tested it, and entered the town. Within an hour the defenders were overcome, no match for the battle-hardened professional soldiers. Prato suffered a brutal sack. What I saw and heard will make me feel sick for a week, wrote one Italian observer with the Spanish camp. 'Oh God, oh God, oh God, what cruelty!'[3]

Rumours reached Florence with refugees from the sack of 5,000 or more dead, terrifying the Florentines. Their resolution to defend the regime headed by Piero Soderini, and not to admit the Medici, crumbled. A group of young aristocrats ejected Soderini from the government palace, and he went into exile. Giuliano de' Medici, Cardinal Giovanni's brother, came to the city without pomp on 1 September, and two days later terms were agreed with Cardona. Acting on behalf of the Holy League and as the representative of Ferdinand, Cardona took Florence into his protection. Reciprocal promises were made to send troops if Florence or Naples came under threat of attack. All the Medici and their followers were to have a full pardon, and their property was to be restored to them. If the terms were ratified by Maximilian or an Imperial representative, the Florentines were to pay 40,000 ducats.[4] According to Florentine sources, they also promised to pay 80,000 ducats to Cardona for his soldiers, and 20,000 to him personally. As he headed for Lombardy with his army, the viceroy also extracted money from Lucca and Siena.[5]

Haggling over reform of the government had already begun in Florence before the conclusion of the treaty with Cardona. Aristocrats persuaded the amenable Giuliano to accept arrangements that gave no special role to the Medici. Dissatisfied Medici partisans called on Cardinal Giovanni to intervene. Using the leverage given him by the presence of the Spanish army near the city, he ensured that before it left foundations were laid for Medici dominance of Florence, although many constitutional adjustments were still to come.

The settlement in Milan

Finding a settlement for the duchy of Milan was a complex problem – one impossible to resolve satisfactorily for all the interested parties. The Venetians were set on recovering all the territories they had held before 1509, but their claims conflicted with those of Maximilian, who wanted Bergamo. The Swiss were establishing themselves in the lands at the mouths of the Alpine valleys; the Grisons had opportunistically seized Chiavenna and the Valtellina in June, and did not intend to give them up. None of the other powers approved of the pope's annexation of Parma and Piacenza. Nor did the Milanese, who thought the duchy should have the same borders as under Ludovico Sforza, with an independent duke.

Their choice for their duke was Ludovico's 19-year-old son Massimiliano, who had been brought to Innsbruck from Flanders where he had been under the tutelage of Margaret of Austria. He was the most generally acceptable candidate, although Ferdinand and Maximilian were floating the suggestion that one of their grandsons, Charles or Ferdinand, could be made duke. Massimiliano was held back from going to Milan while the grandfathers tested how this idea might be received (not well), and also because if he was to be duke, Lang was disputing with Schinner and the Swiss who should install him and control him. While Maximilian claimed the right as emperor, the Swiss asserted their right as the victors in the field. Intent on securing the territorial, financial and commercial fruits of victory, the Swiss made a treaty of perpetual alliance with the provisional Milanese government. Recognizing Massimiliano as duke, the cantons undertook to support him; he was to pay the troops sent to protect him. A pension of 40,000 ducats a year was to be paid to the cantons, and their possession of Lugano, Locarno and Domodossola was confirmed. Swiss merchants were to be exempt from tolls from their borders to the gates of Milan.[6]

When Massimiliano was finally permitted by Lang to enter his own capital on 29 December, the Swiss and Imperial representatives disputed who would hand him the keys of the city; the Swiss prevailed. Competition between the Imperial representatives and Schinner and the Swiss for mastery over Massimiliano continued. With no experience of rule and showing little sign of aptitude for it, the young duke was more interested in enjoying himself than in the business of government. His subjects, watching him grant away and dissipate much of what revenues his allies and protectors left to him, were soon disenchanted.

The Venetians stand apart

The Venetians had not joined in this competition for mastery over the young duke. Pulling back their army to the east, they concentrated on trying to reduce the remaining French garrisons in cities they claimed. More than 1,000 men-at-arms, 1,600 light horse and 10,000 infantry were engaged in besieging Brescia in August 1512.[7] Suspecting, rightly, that the Swiss and Milanese would object to their having all the territory in their sights, the Venetians did not want their allies' forces to join them. Their conflict with the emperor was still unresolved and they were coming under pressure from Julius and Ferdinand to make concessions to him – although Ferdinand was concerned they should not be provoked into an alliance with France.

The pope's priority was to secure Maximilian's adherence to the Lateran council. In November 1512 Lang came to Rome to give this and to repudiate the schismatic council of Pisa, as well as to conclude a defensive alliance with Julius. The Venetians were to be considered excluded from the Holy League and Julius promised to use military means and spiritual sanctions to force them to yield to Maximilian.[8] While he did threaten them with excommunication if they did not agree to Maximilian's demands, he made no preparations to go to war with them; he hoped to avoid driving them into the arms of the French.

This treaty, however, was one of the spurs to Venice allying with Louis. Another had been Cardona taking possession of Brescia, as captain-general of the League, on 25 October. On his way from Tuscany to Lombardy, the viceroy had met Lang in Modena in late September, and agreed with him that he should go to take Brescia from the French to prevent the Venetians getting it. D'Aubigny, the French commander there, preferred to surrender to Cardona; he and the garrison were allowed to leave for France. Rejecting all suggestions that they should compromise with Maximilian, the Venetians chose instead to make a new alliance with Louis in March 1513, even at the cost of accepting that he would not allow them to have Cremona and the Ghiaradadda. Brescia, Bergamo and Crema were to be theirs in return for their assisting Louis to recover the duchy of Milan. Venetian prisoners held in France were to be released.[9] These included Bartolomeo d'Alviano, who made his way back to Venice and was appointed captain-general in late May.

The French invasion of Milan, 1513

By the time this treaty with Venice was concluded, Louis was rid of one of his most determined opponents. Julius II died during the night of 20 February 1513. The new pope was Giovanni de' Medici, who took the title Leo X. Much younger than Julius, he was not so belligerent and was far more subtle and changeable in diplomacy. Those who dealt with him would find him hard to read, except they soon discovered his fixed purpose to elevate the Medici into a princely dynasty: domination over Florence was not enough. Inevitably, his elevation to the papal throne strengthened his family's position in Florence, and Leo would effectively dictate Florentine foreign policy.

As he prepared to try to recover Milan, Louis could not be sure what the new pope would do, nor count on the Florentines as allies. He might have hoped to have neutralized at least one opponent in Italy, making a truce with Ferdinand in April for a year. But the truce covered the border war between France and Spain, not Italy, so Ferdinand could still oppose the French there. Nevertheless, Cardona had already been ordered to return to Naples with the army, leaving the infantry behind in the pay of others, if possible.[10]

Cardona had not left before the French invaded Milan. Under the command of La Trémoille and Gian Giacomo Trivulzio, the French troops – 1,200–1,400 lances, 600 light horse, and 11,500 infantry – crossed the Alps and mustered in Piedmont in mid-May, with 2,500 Italian troops.[11] In late May Massimiliano was reported to have 1,200 Spanish and Neapolitan men-at-arms, 1,000 light horse, 800 Spanish infantry, 3,000 Lombard infantry and 7,000 Swiss.[12] But Cardona, having sent troops to help Massimiliano defend the north-west of the duchy, quickly withdrew them, thus facilitating the rapid French advance. He kept his men at Piacenza, which he had taken over with Parma for Massimiliano after the death of Julius. In order to secure the pope's support against the French, Massimiliano agreed to give them up to Leo, but no papal troops were sent to help him. The duke was left with the Swiss and what Lombards rallied to his defence. On the other side, d'Alviano was under orders from Venice to join up with the French only if the Spanish joined up with the Swiss. The Venetians were confident that, lacking men-at-arms, the Swiss alone should not pose much of a problem for the French, and the campaign would soon be over.[13]

By early June, the French had overrun much of the west of the duchy. In Genoa, with the aid of a French fleet, the Adorno and Fieschi deposed Doge Giano Campofregoso and Antoniotto Adorno became governor there for Louis. In the east, the Venetian army under Bartolomeo d'Alviano took Cremona; Lodi and the Ghiaradadda rose against Massimiliano. The city of Milan, where a French garrison still held the fortress, was in confusion, waiting to see the outcome of the campaign. Only the areas around Como and Novara, where the Swiss were concentrated, still held for Massimiliano, who was at Novara.

Throughout the winter, Louis had been trying to come to an accord with the Swiss. The seriousness of his intent was signalled by his sending La Trémoille and Trivulzio to Lucerne to conduct the negotiations, and his ordering the surrender of the fortresses of Locarno and Lugano to the Swiss. Happy to have the fortresses, but not to have the French back in Milan, in response to the invasion the Swiss rapidly organized and despatched several thousand reinforcements. These headed for Novara; news of their approach made La Trémoille decide on 5 June to raise the siege of the city that had just begun. A column of 7,000–8,000 Swiss skirted the French positions and entered Novara that day, to join the 4,000 already there with Massimiliano.

By nightfall, the French had travelled only a few miles, and the units made camp where they halted, dispersed as they were for the march.

Consequently, they were ill-prepared for the attack launched by the Swiss before dawn. The Swiss had little artillery and only a few light horse with them, and the terrain, divided by ditches bordered by bushes, could have favoured the defenders had they had time to take position behind them. But the Swiss kept their disciplined battle order under fire from the French artillery and overcame the infantry. The stiffest resistance they encountered was from about 6,000 landsknechts, who took the heaviest casualties when they were left to fight alone after the French and Italian infantry were routed. The French men-at-arms made little effort to defend them; the ground was not suited to the deployment of heavy cavalry. Nearly all the French horse escaped unscathed, abandoning their pavilions and the baggage train to the Swiss. Their artillery was captured too, and the elated Swiss dragged it back to Novara, with their own wounded men.[14]

The battle of Ariotta (Novara) marked the zenith of the military reputation of the Swiss during the Italian Wars. Around 10,000 men, the majority of whom had reached Novara only hours before after several days' march (and without waiting for 3,000 further reinforcements who were hard on their heels), with virtually no supporting cavalry and very little artillery, had routed a numerically superior French army, including a contingent of landsknechts almost as large as the main battle square of around 7,000 men the Swiss had formed, over terrain ill-adapted to manoeuvring such a large formation in good order. It was a tribute to the training and discipline, as well as the bravery and physical hardiness, of the Swiss infantry. The element of surprise had, of course, helped them, together with the fact the French army had been so widely spread out and had not prepared a defensive position, but this did not detract from the achievement of the Swiss or the humiliation of the French.

After the rout of the French army, the Spanish finally joined the Swiss to drive them out of Italy. Cardona sent 400 lances under Prospero Colonna to support Massimiliano. He also sent the marchese di Pescara with 3,000 infantry and 200 light horse to Genoa, to assist the Fregoso faction in deposing Antoniotto Adorno on 17 June and replacing him with Ottaviano Campofregoso as doge. This displeased the Swiss, who had already made advantageous terms with Adorno. The Swiss took Asti, advanced in Piedmont and pillaged much of Monferrato.

It was evident that Louis could not send another expedition to Italy that year. In France, he was facing an invasion in the north by Henry VIII of England and Maximilian; Henry took Thérouanne and Tournai, and in August inflicted another humiliating defeat on the French at Guinegatte. That month the Swiss invaded Burgundy, laying siege to Dijon. La

Trémoille made a treaty with them promising large payments and renouncing the king's claim to Milan. The Swiss withdrew, but Louis would not ratify the treaty.

More than ever, the Swiss dominated the duchy of Milan. Massimiliano acknowledged the debt he owed for the blood they had shed to secure his rule, and agreed extra payments and compensation to those who had fought for him, totalling 400,000 Rhenish florins. But he did not have the money to satisfy them, nor could he afford to pay them to attack the Venetians, as Cardinal Schinner suggested.[15]

War in the Veneto

It was left to the Spanish and Imperial forces to continue the war against Venice. Ferdinand was content it should be so, for he envisaged the lands finally to be wrested from the Venetians being given to his grandson Ferdinand.[16] The Venetians had been making progress, occupying the city of Brescia (but not its fortress) on 31 May, but they withdrew after hearing of the French defeat. Renzo da Ceri was left with a garrison to defend Crema. A lightning attempt to take Verona by storm, led by d'Alviano, was repelled on 18 June. As usual, the main Venetian army fell back on Padua, where d'Alviano based himself, and Treviso, where Gianpaolo Baglioni was in command. Cardona brought his army to join the Imperial troops in early July; he was captain-general of the combined forces, Lang the governor.[17] They were joined by 200 papal men-at-arms, as the Venetians continued to refuse Leo's mediation if that would entail their accepting the loss of Verona and Vicenza.

At Lang's insistence, an attempt was made to lay siege to Padua, but its futility was soon recognized and the siege was lifted after eighteen days on 17 August. Some weeks of inactivity followed before, spurred on by the need to find some means of sustaining the troops, the combined army swept through the area between Padua and Venice. Intended to humiliate the Venetians as well as damage their resources, the raid targeted the villas of Venetian nobles. Mestre was burned so the flames could be seen from Venice, and taunting artillery shots fired across the lagoon. With the Venetian army intact, and Padua and Treviso on its flanks, the allied army could not remain there for long, yet the Venetians were provoked into allowing d'Alviano to bring their army into the field to prevent further damage to their lands.

Attempts to block the retreat of the enemy ended in a heavy defeat for the Venetian army near Vicenza on 7 October. D'Alviano's disposition of his forces was quite elaborate. Two separate groups of light horse and part of the heavy cavalry under his command aimed to flank the allied army to the left, where there was also a large force of infantry and peasants stationed on a hill waiting to fall on the enemy. Gianpaolo Baglioni, with the rest of the heavy cavalry, was sent to outflank them on the right. The main body of infantry was drawn up in two battle squares. Cardona and Prospero Colonna placed most of their cavalry in the centre, with a square of landsknechts, one of whose captains was the charismatic Georg von Frundsberg, on one side and a Spanish pike square commanded by Pescara on the other. Faced by the disciplined Spanish and German squares, the Venetian militiamen lost their nerve and could not keep their position within the Venetian infantry squares. Their collapse and the subsequent rout swung the balance against the Venetian cavalry which had had the upper hand against the Spanish and papal men-at-arms. The landsknechts, bent on revenge for the massacre of their countrymen at Cadore in 1508, were relentless in killing the fleeing Venetian infantry. All the Venetian banners and their artillery were captured; Baglioni was among the prisoners.[18]

The gravity of the defeat was compounded by the refusal of Teodoro Trivulzio, who commanded the garrison in Vicenza, to admit the Venetian troops into the city for fear their pursuers might enter with them; many Venetian cavalrymen drowned trying to ford the rivers nearby to make their escape. Vicenza fell to the Spanish and Imperial troops nevertheless. Inevitably, there were recollections of d'Alviano's defeat at Agnadello. Playing down the significance of the defeat, the Venetians stood by their captain-general. In fact, the consequences were limited to the loss of Vicenza, for the allied army could not follow up their victory. The Imperial troops retired to Verona, while Cardona's army established winter quarters in the Polesine.

To Maximilian's annoyance, Cardona would not support the campaign launched in Friuli. As always, the viceroy was short of money for his men; and in Ferdinand's complex diplomatic schemes, enlisting Venice into the League was still one option. The Imperial campaign – commanded by Cristoforo Frangipane, who had formerly been in the service of Venice – overran nearly all of Friuli apart from the Savorgnan fortress of Osoppo. Reluctant to allow d'Alviano to launch a counter-attack there, the Venetians finally consented in mid-March, and he quickly recovered the whole province, except for Gradisca and Marano.

The war in the Veneto continued through the summer and autumn of 1514. Cardona's army had been divided to ease supply problems, and the war became one of raids and skirmishes between detached units of the opposing forces. In June, d'Alviano was given permission to leave Padua and move the army to a more forward position, although he was under pressing instructions not to put it at risk. To the west, Crema was the focus of confrontation between the Venetian troops based there under the command of Renzo da Ceri and Milanese troops under Prospero Colonna, now Massimiliano Sforza's captain-general, and Silvio Savelli, who were encamped nearby. In late August Renzo da Ceri drove off Savelli's men and destroyed his camp. Insufficient Milanese troops were left to prevent a Venetian detachment from leaving Crema and occupying the city of Bergamo, but not its citadel, in mid-October.

Cardona had moved north in October with part of his army towards Verona; d'Alviano took advantage of his departure from the Polesine to attack and disperse the remaining Spanish troops there, and then headed for Legnago. He remained at Legnago when Cardona and Prospero Colonna joined forces to invest Bergamo, now defended by Renzo da Ceri, who had gone there in late October. The siege lasted only a few days, for the viceroy offered honourable terms of surrender, which Renzo da Ceri accepted on 15 November. On hearing this, the Venetians urged d'Alviano to safeguard the army and return to Padua. He was not looking to give battle, in any case. Neither he nor the Venetians had much confidence in their infantry – 'without even seeing the enemy, many take flight; nor can they keep in order', the Venetian government complained[19] – and he had heard that reinforcements of landsknechts were joining the enemy. Swiftly he pulled his army back to Padua and Treviso, while the Spanish troops settled back in the Polesine and the Germans in Verona.

Diplomatic conflict over Lombardy

The campaigns of 1513 and 1514 had their counterpart in complex diplomacy concerning the ultimate disposal of the duchy of Milan and of the Venetian lands in Lombardy. Much of this complexity was due to the apparent contradiction in Ferdinand's policies, which obscured the real consistency of his aims. One aim was to keep the French out of Italy. His truce with Louis in April 1513 excluded Italy, leaving him free to fight the French there. Another aim was to obtain subsidies for his army in Italy from other Italian powers, but he failed to convince them that they had any obligation to pay. Underlying both was his ambition to procure Milan or lands in the Veneto, or both, for one of his grandsons, preferably his favourite, Ferdinand (who had been brought up in Spain), and to govern these lands himself on behalf of the boy. This was why he kept his army in Lombardy, supporting Maximilian's war against the Venetians.

To get hold of the duchy of Milan he was relying not on military conquest, but on negotiation of a marriage alliance between his grandson Ferdinand and Renée, the younger daughter of Louis, with Milan as her dowry. Queen Anne liked the idea more than Louis did; her death in January 1514 made it even less likely to be realized. Louis soon married again, to Henry VIII's sister Mary, a match agreed as part of an alliance he concluded with Henry in August 1514. This alliance relieved Louis's diplomatic isolation and the threat to his kingdom (at the cost of the cession of Thérouanne and Tournai to the English king), and gave impetus to his plans to invade Milan again in 1515.

Maximilian was unconvinced by the proposed marriage alliance, and the idea that the boy should be given Venetian lands did not appeal to him at all. He insisted that he must have Verona, at the least, himself, and a substantial annual payment from the Venetians for those places – Padua and Treviso – he might agree to their keeping. The Venetians were pressed by Ferdinand and by Leo to make concessions to Maximilian, to free him to be able to concentrate his efforts against France. Both sides accepted Leo as arbiter, but neither would accept a decision they did not like. The Venetians were reluctant to contemplate the permanent loss of any territory they regarded as rightfully theirs, and certainly not of Verona.

The pope tried repeatedly to arrange a settlement between Venice and Maximilian, because he did not want Ferdinand's plans for his grandson realized. Nor did he want Louis to recover Milan. Leo's attitude to France was complicated, for he had Florentine interests as well as those of the papacy and his own family to consider. Florentine financial and trading interests in France were of prime importance to the city; many Florentines would rather see the French king than the Swiss in Milan. As the French had supported the regime in Florence during the exile of the Medici, Leo personally had cause to be less cordial towards them, but if they were to return to Milan, he wanted to be on reasonable terms with them, and to hold on to Parma and Piacenza. There were important ecclesiastical interests at stake, too, first and foremost the resolution of the schism. Louis's subjects were anxious for it to be ended, and in October 1513 he repudiated the Pisan council and acknowledged the Lateran council. Once that issue was settled, Leo's policy towards Louis was hard to decipher, if he had a coherent one at all, for he tried to keep on good terms with all the powers, but as an interested party, not a neutral one. Soon he acquired a reputation for tergiversation and dissimulation, as a man who was not just difficult to read, but who could not be relied on.

The advent of Francis I and the conquest of Milan, 1515

In the early hours of 1 January 1515 Louis XII died, his demise hurried on by his efforts to play the gallant lover to his beautiful young wife. His heir was his 20-year-old cousin, Francis. Physically strong, courageous, cultivated and somewhat conceited, the new king had been educated for rule under the careful supervision of his doting widowed mother, Louise of Savoy. Under Louis he had been given military commands and a seat in the king's council. The new king was full of confidence and eager to spread his wings. Hopes that he might not have inherited Louis's ambitions in Italy with the crown were soon dashed.

Concerted diplomatic preparations were made in the spring. Insurance against an invasion of northern France was provided by a treaty with Charles in late March 1515, in which Charles agreed to marry Renée (whose dowry would not include the duchy of Milan), and a renewal a fortnight later of the treaty with Henry VIII. The alliance with the Venetians was also renewed about this time; they were to help Francis conquer Milan, and he was to help them recover the lands in the Veneto still held for Maximilian. A secret agreement was reached in late April with the doge of Genoa, Ottaviano Campofregoso, who had been threatened by the Swiss; he promised he would send troops to help when the king came to Italy and acknowledge French overlordship of Genoa.[20]

Eager for military glory, the young king was spending freely the money accumulated by his financially prudent predecessor, and his military preparations were impressive. More than 20,000 landsknechts were hired, including the Black Bands, considered the most formidable landsknecht unit, and distinguished by their black clothes, arms and banners. Ten thousand French infantry were raised and placed under the command of Pedro Navarro. (In order to get his services Francis settled his outstanding ransom; as Ferdinand had done nothing to secure his release since he was captured at Ravenna in 1512, Pedro Navarro was now ready to serve the French king.[21]) As the king was to lead the expedition in person, the cavalry companies of the gentlemen pensioners augmented the 3,000 men-at-arms of the *ordonnance* companies.[22] A substantial artillery train was brought together, including, according to the memoirs of Robert de la Marck, who claimed to have been involved in their production, a new type of gun firing grape shot, devised by Pedro Navarro.[23]

To oppose this formidable army, Massimiliano Sforza should have had the support of the pope, Ferdinand, Maximilian and the Swiss who subscribed a mutual defence league in July 1515. As in 1513, however, in the event he would have to rely principally upon the Swiss. After some hesitation, Leo decided to stick with the League and sent troops north, but his principal concern was to hold on to Parma and Piacenza, where he feared French partisans would raise a revolt.[24]

Planning to confront the French as soon as they crossed the Alps, the Swiss and Milanese moved into Piedmont (the lands of the Duke of Savoy were considered neutral territory, accessible to both armies, even though the duke was Francis's uncle). After news arrived of French cavalry units appearing in Saluzzo on 11 August, the Swiss and Milanese captains held a council of war at Pinerolo. Trying to anticipate which passes the French would use, they decided that 10,000 infantry should go to Susa, and 8,000 with the Milanese cavalry under Prospero Colonna to Saluzzo (which had been occupied in large part by the Swiss since 1513). But while Francis sent some infantry and heavy artillery by the usual route French armies took over the Alps, that would bring them out at Susa, the bulk of the army and the king himself travelled by more difficult routes further to the west and south. Another detachment sailed from Marseilles to Genoa, and then, with some Genoese forces, crossed the Appenines and took Alessandria and Tortona. Three companies of French men-at-arms, led by La Palisse and d'Aubigny, took Prospero Colonna by surprise at Villafranca; Prospero himself and most of his men and horses were captured. The Duke of Milan had lost his captain-general and his cavalry, and the Swiss would have to face the French without cavalry support, unless they were joined by the papal or Spanish horse.

Withdrawing to the duchy of Milan, the Swiss were followed by 800 lances under Odet de Foix, seigneur de Lautrec. Another French detachment, commanded by Gian Giacomo Trivulzio with 700 lances and 10,000 infantry under Pedro Navarro, was sent to besiege Novara. The city had already been abandoned by the Swiss, and the fortress surrendered after a day or so; Francis entered on 30 August. Through the mediation of his uncles, Duke Charles and René of Savoy, the king opened negotiations with the Swiss. Although thousands of reinforcements were on their way, many of the Swiss in the Milanese were ready to leave, and a substantial number did not want to fight the French king. Some of the captains agreed terms; they were to leave the duchy, and relinquish the territory they held there except for Bellinzona; Massimiliano Sforza was to be given lands, revenues, and a wife in France. Francis was to pay the Swiss a total of one million écus, 150,000 immediately.[25] Hastily, he raised 150,000 écus from the gentlemen in his camp, and sent it off to the Swiss, despite doubts whether the treaty would come into force. In fact, Cardinal Schinner persuaded the majority of the Swiss, who had mustered at Milan, that it would be shameful to accept it, and that they should fight on.

The French army advanced to the south of Milan, blocking the route from Piacenza, where the papal troops had been joined by Cardona and the Spanish army. To the east, the Venetian army had come to link up with the French. As usual, the Venetians had ordered d'Alviano not to put their army at risk, and Francis had also asked them to keep it safe until his army was in the Milanese.[26] D'Alviano insisted that the Venetian troops must demonstrate to Francis that they were joining him in a common enterprise, not just pursuing their own interests, and brought the army, at the king's request, to Lodi, within a day's march of the French camp at Marignano (Melegnano). He went to consult with Francis who was planning to attack the papal and Spanish forces at Piacenza.[27]

The Swiss had other ideas. On 13 September, when the day was already well-advanced, moving swiftly in three large battle squares, they marched towards the French.[28] The French who watched them coming, raising a cloud of dust, were struck by their air of confidence, and their look of poverty – many without shoes and, as usual, most without any armour. They made an arresting contrast to the French army in all its pomp and heraldry, led by the glamorous young king, and even to the landsknechts, who were becoming noted for their extravagant dress. They had only a few artillery pieces with them, and virtually no cavalry.

The king was alerted that the Swiss were on their way in time to dispose his army into three battle groups. As at Novara, the terrain was cut by ditches, and it was not easy to manoeuvre large bodies of horse, but this time the men-at-arms would give full support to their infantry throughout what proved to be a long battle, charging the Swiss again and again. The vanguard, with much of the French field artillery, 9,000 landsknechts and French arquebusiers and archers, was backed by several hundred men-at-arms under the constable of France, Charles de Bourbon. These were attacked by the first Swiss battle square. In the hard fighting the Swiss were gaining the upper hand, despite their inferior numbers, the casualties caused by the artillery and missile infantry, and the charges of the men-at-arms, who themselves suffered considerable losses. It was difficult to see, first for the dust and then because of the gathering night. Fighting continued until it became too dark to see at all. Both sides slept on the field, close to each other. The king rested, in his armour, on a gun carriage. During the night, a letter was sent to d'Alviano, urging him to bring up the Venetian army.

At daybreak, the French rallied to the sound of their trumpets, the Swiss to their great battle horns. Francis placed his troops, still in three battle groups, in line, Bourbon commanding the right, Charles, duc d'Alençon (the king's brother-in-law), the left, Francis himself the centre. The Swiss kept their artillery, now including some French pieces captured the day before, in the centre, with about 7,000 men confronting the king, and two bands were sent to the left and right. On this day all three groups on both sides were engaged in the fighting. Despite being outnumbered and without cavalry, again the Swiss took the battle to the French, who were beginning to flag and to lose heart when their spirits were revived by the arrival of d'Alviano. He had ridden ahead with a small escort, but immediately threw himself into the fray. Soon more Venetian cavalry arrived, tipping the balance against the Swiss on that wing, who were overwhelmed. The two other squares, however, were able to retire to Milan in reasonable order with their wounded.[29]

The burial parties who interred the bodies of the fallen in mass graves estimated there were 16,500 dead; the great majority, the French claimed, Swiss.[30] This might well underestimate the scale of French losses. The disciplined Swiss had proved more than a match for the infantry of the French army, and their defence against the cavalry charges had been so fierce that some men-at-arms had left the field when they saw the Swiss attack again on the second day, not willing to face them.[31] The battle had taken a toll of the nobles, including the only son of La Trémoille, and François de Bourbon, the Constable's brother. The king himself had been struck by pike-thrusts several times, saved from injury only by his armour. Gian Giacomo Trivulzio, according to Guicciardini, said that he was a veteran of eighteen battles, but that all the others had been children's games, compared to this 'battle of giants'.[32] Chagrined by the poverty of their foes the French may have been, for there was little booty or ransom money to be gained from this victory, yet they kept a healthy respect for the fighting qualities of the Swiss. Debating with his captains whether to pursue the retreating Swiss, the king decided against it; he still wanted to come to terms with them, and to be able to call on Swiss infantry himself in the future.

Having placed 2,000 of their wounded in Milanese hospitals, and 1,500 able-bodied men in the Castello with Massimiliano Sforza and the 500 infantry he had there, the rest of the Swiss left for home. Cardinal Schinner went to Innsbruck to see Maximilian. The king stayed at Pavia, sending Charles de Bourbon and Pedro Navarro to Milan to direct the siege of the Castello. This was brief, for the Swiss in the fortress soon insisted it be surrendered. The Milanese had sent a delegation immediately after the battle to offer the submission of the city, and Massimiliano Sforza had no option but to make terms with the king.[33] With the promise of a generous income, he departed for exile in France. There he would be treated well, but he would never return to Milan. Francis made his entry into the city of Milan on 11 October, escorted by his household troops and around 1,300 select landsknechts; the Duke of Savoy and the marquises of Monferrato and Saluzzo were there to greet him. The king rode under a canopy, dressed in armour, but carrying 'the golden royal baton, with a hand on top', rather than a weapon.[34] This was the triumphal entry of a victor, emphasizing the military power and splendour of the king, but not that of a conqueror. Nevertheless, a punitive fine was imposed on the city, and some prominent citizens exiled. The rest of the duchy had capitulated; there was no further resistance.

Disenchanted with acting as a political power in Italy, the Swiss sent word to the king that they wanted an agreement with him. Francis was willing enough, and a treaty was concluded at the end of November. They were to surrender all the lands they held in the duchy of Milan; Francis was to pay a total of one million scudi in return for these lands and in settlement of sums owed to them under earlier treaties. He was to be able to recruit Swiss infantry for the defence of France and of Milan; and he was to send troops to help the cantons if they were attacked.[35] Only eight of the cantons signed up to this, however; the five most interested in holding on to the places south of the Alps were not reconciled to their loss.

The Spanish and papal troops had made no effort to support Massimiliano Sforza after the battle of Marignano. Cardona was quick to obey Ferdinand's orders to pull the army back to defend the kingdom of Naples. The pope's immediate reaction to the news of the battle was to seek assurance from Francis that he would not take Parma and Piacenza, and to offer peace terms. If there had to be one dominant foreign power in Italy, Leo argued, he would rather it was France than Spain or the emperor.[36] Such thinking was in line with the wishes of the Florentines, who also sent an envoy to Francis. By mid-October, Leo and Francis had agreed a treaty: the king took the Papal States, Florence and the Medici family into his protection, while the pope promised to defend Francis's possession of the duchy of Milan and to hand over Parma and Piacenza to the king.

It was also agreed that the pope and king should meet at Bologna. On his way there in early December, the king was welcomed into Parma and Piacenza, where his men had taken over from papal officials a month before. During his stay in Bologna from 11 to 15 December, the main business he transacted with the pope was an agreement there should be a Concordat concerning the respective powers of the pope and the king over the French Church. From later diplomatic exchanges, it is clear that other matters discussed included the French claim to the kingdom of Naples, and the Duke of Ferrara, who had managed to secure the protection of the king, to Leo's disappointment.

Francis returned to Milan to complete the process of restoring French government of the duchy. Already the Senate of Milan and other offices had been reconstituted as they were under Louis. Before he left the city on 8 January 1516, the king remitted the remainder of the fine levied on the Milanese, and offered pardon to rebels prepared to obey, and the Milanese took an oath of fidelity to him. Envoys from Genoa had sworn fidelity to him in October, but the French regime was not reinstated there. Ottaviano Campofregoso became governor for the king, instead of doge; otherwise there were no institutional changes, and no French officials were sent to share in the government.

When the king returned to France he left Charles de Bourbon as his lieutenant-general in the duchy. Much of the army remained as well, both to secure the duchy and to aid the Venetians. A substantial contingent had been assisting in the siege of Brescia since October. There was no respite for the Milanese. The financial exactions of the French were no easier to bear than the levies they had had to pay for the Swiss, and the French troops did not make themselves welcome. Neighbouring princes, the Dukes of Ferrara and Savoy, the marquises of Mantua and Monferrato, were called on to show their goodwill by providing billets for companies of French troops in their states, or to make 'loans' to the king to help pay for them, or to do both.

The invasion of Milan by Maximilian and the Swiss, 1516

Within two months of the king's departure from Milan, Bourbon had to defend the duchy against an invasion by Imperial and Swiss troops led by Maximilian in person. Among the instigators of this invasion was Henry VIII. Disconcerted by Francis's success in Milan, he sent money to pay the Swiss to drive the French out of the duchy, and then to push on into France while he would launch an attack in the north. The five Swiss cantons that had not signed up to the Treaty of Geneva with Francis were ready to provide the men. Meanwhile, Cardinal Schinner was urging Maximilian to attack the French in Milan. Old and sick as he was, Maximilian resolved to lead a campaign himself, but originally planned to attack the Venetians, while the Swiss were to invade the duchy. He could not raise the resources for this – his attempts to divert to himself the funds being sent to the English envoy with the Swiss, Richard Pace, failed – and he had to agree to join the Swiss. This would be a joint campaign, although it was generally seen as Maximilian's campaign, with the Swiss in his service. French plans to counter the invasion rested on the premise that Maximilian could not afford to stay in the field for long; they would avoid battle, try to hold the line of a river against him and defend the cities.[37]

In early March around 15,000 Swiss mustered at Trent, electing as their captain-general a Milanese exile, Galeazzo Visconti; they were met there by Maximilian. His army consisted of perhaps 10,000 German and Spanish infantry, many drawn from the garrisons of Verona and Brescia as the army passed by, and 4,000–5,000 horse.[38] After a few days spent trying in vain to take the Venetian fortress of Asola, the invasion force pressed on to Milan. Maximilian was confident there would be an uprising against the French in Milan, and that the Swiss with the French would not fight against the Swiss who were with him. Bourbon had decided to hold the line of the Adda, but being told it would be difficult to stop the enemy crossing the river, and hearing of unrest in Milan, he pulled back to the city to prepare its defences. French and Venetian troops who had been besieging Brescia came there too, and around 8,000 Swiss from the eight cantons allied to France. By the time the invasion force approached Milan on 24 March, the internal opponents of the French had been repressed and the city was prepared to withstand a siege.

Almost as soon as he arrived, Maximilian became fretful and melancholy, insisting he could not lay siege to the city because he had no money.[39] After a couple of days he departed, leaving his army to follow him. Most stayed in Lombardy, returning to Verona or Brescia, or going over to the Venetians. The indignant Swiss stayed at Lodi for a month, demanding their pay from Pace, holding him hostage with Galeazzo Visconti and Cardinal Schinner until an instalment of money from England arrived. Once this had been paid over, they left for home; some went to Verona.

Final stages of the war against Venice, 1515–16

The aid sent by Francis to his Venetian allies to recover their remaining territories did not being a speedy end to the war. The Venetians had lost their commander, d'Alviano, who died a few weeks after the battle of Marignano. His replacement, Teodoro Trivulzio, did not have the same authority. At Brescia, the Venetian and French commanders in the siege camp were at odds. Landsknechts in French service refused to fight landsknechts in the service of the emperor. Surrender terms agreed in December were nullified by the arrival of a German relief force. Odet de Foix, vicomte de Lautrec was sent to galvanize operations in February 1516, but then the camp had to withdraw before the invasion of Maximilian and the Swiss. When it resumed, the siege finally succeeded in large part because of discord between Spanish and German troops in Brescia; most had left to join the French or the Venetians. On 26 May the Spanish commander Icardo and what remained of the garrison surrendered to the French and left. Honouring Francis's agreement with Venice, Lautrec handed over Brescia to the Venetian commissioner, Andrea Gritti.

This left Verona, where the garrison of several thousand German, Spanish and Swiss troops was under the command of Marcantonio Colonna, who was now in the service of Maximilian. Lautrec (who replaced Bourbon as lieutenant-general) followed the Venetian forces there, but was not keen to press an attack on the city, and lodged his men in Mantuan territory. In late August, Venetian insistence at last brought a tightening of the siege. Several stretches of the city walls were brought down by artillery fire, but Colonna was vigilant in organizing the internal defences against any assault. The siege was suspended in mid-October after the arrival of several thousand German reinforcements. A month before this, Maximilian had asked Francis not to humiliate him by taking Verona by storm, promising he would surrender it, more honourably, to the Venetians in three months' time.[40] The surrender of Verona was negotiated in Brussels, with Charles signing the treaty in early December on behalf of his grandfather.[41] On 14 December Verona was formally handed over to the custody of Charles, who handed it over to the French, who handed it over to the Venetians, who entered the city on 17 January 1517.

For Venice, the war that had begun in 1509 was at long last over. There can have been few places in the Veneto that had not been directly touched by the fighting at some stage of the war; much of the territory had suffered from the presence of one army or another, some places for year after year. From the Battle of Agnadello in 1509 to 1517, one Vicentine chronicler calculated, there were 36 changes of regime in Vicenza – this might seem funny, he commented, if the consequences for his city had not been so tragic.[42] Areas such as the Veronese and Bresciano had had to sustain large garrisons, and sometimes siege camps, for several years. While a number of their subjects who had served or collaborated most enthusiastically with the Imperial forces were exiled or made rebels, the Venetians were more interested in reconciliation, in a return to normality, than in revenge. For the Venetians themselves, the war had been a sobering experience. Under the pressure of war finance, they had resorted to expedients that were distasteful to men who took pride in the institutions of their republic – in effect, selling government offices and positions in the Senate to the highest bidder. Venetians had already had to learn to live with the growing threat to their maritime empire from the Turks. There it was a question of whether they could hold on to what they had, not where could they expand further. Now they were in the same position in mainland Italy. They might still seize opportunities to take territory, especially if they saw a chance to recover an area they had held before, but they were no longer confident of their power to make further major acquisitions.

The quest for a Medici principate

Leo was intent on the promotion of the interests of his family beyond Florence. At first these ambitions were centred on his brother Giuliano and then, after Giuliano's death in March 1516, on his nephew Lorenzo. Optimistically, he hoped that Francis might yield his rights to Naples to Giuliano, whose marriage to the king's aunt, Filiberta of Savoy, took place at the French court a fortnight after the king's accession. But Francis was angling for a promise of papal investiture with Naples for himself. When Ferdinand died on 23 January 1516, leaving his 15-year-old grandson Charles the challenge of establishing his authority in the government of Castile and its dominions as well as Ferdinand's own realms, Francis hoped Charles might cede Naples to him in return for help in securing his Spanish inheritance. He was not ready to cede his own claims to Giuliano, or even to agree to his keeping Parma and Piacenza.

Leo had plenty of other schemes in mind. In Tuscany, not content with domination of Florence, he wanted to encompass Siena and Lucca in a Medici state. This idea found very little favour with others, and certainly not with the Sienese and Lucchese. As the regime of Borghese Petrucci in Siena was supposed to be under Ferdinand's protection, Leo saw the king's death as an opportunity to advance his plans. He helped Sienese exiles replace Borghese by his cousin Raffaele Petrucci, bishop of Grosseto, in March 1516; Raffaele had been in Leo's service since before he became pope, and he remained submissive to his will. Trying to contrive a way of getting hold of Lucca without encountering the opposition of other powers,

Leo obtained a promise from Francis that he would not renew Louis's protection of the republic. Ferdinand had made clear his disapproval of Leo's Tuscan schemes, suggesting that the pope might give his brother the duchy of Ferrara instead.[43] Although Leo would have been happy to add Ferrara to his brother's domains, Alfonso d'Este was able to keep the protection of France. Leo could not persuade Francis to abandon the duke, nor get other powers to help him use force against Alfonso.

Another suggested state for Giuliano was the duchy of Urbino. Mindful of the hospitality he had been given as an exile at the court of Urbino, Giuliano himself did not approve. Lorenzo had no such scruples. Papal troops under Lorenzo rapidly conquered the duchy in June 1516, and Francesco Maria della Rovere left for exile in Mantua. Lorenzo was invested with the duchy by the pope in August, but della Rovere had not given up. In January 1517 he went to Verona, where he gathered a small army from the soldiers of both sides who had been turned off at the end of hostilities.

By the beginning of February he had reached the Papal States with 7,000 infantry (two-thirds of them Spanish and the rest landsknechts, Gascons and Italians) and 600 horse. Leo was also hiring landsknechts and Gascons, and could raise more than double the number della Rovere had.[44] But the people of the duchy supported their former duke, not their new one, and della Rovere reconquered much of it, including the city of Urbino. After Lorenzo was wounded in the head by an arquebus shot at the end of March, the papal army lacked coherent direction, and the pope was struggling to pay it; some of the landsknechts and Gascon infantry went over to della Rovere in May. Leo asked for French troops from Milan on at least two occasions, only to change his mind. He placed his reliance on winning over dissatisfied soldiers in della Rovere's army, and the war ended when Leo succeeded in buying over the Spanish and Gascons in della Rovere's service. The troops also negotiated terms for the duke, which he had perforce to accept, and he left for Mantua again in mid-September.

Having secured a state for Lorenzo, Leo next found him a bride, Madeleine de la Tour, a relative of Francis. She died in childbed in April 1519, having given birth to a daughter, Catherine, the future queen of France. Lorenzo himself died a few days later. The duchy of Urbino was taken under the direct government of the papacy.

The Imperial election

At the time of Lorenzo's death, Leo was preoccupied by the consequences of another death, that of Maximilian in January 1519. Maximilian had been preparing the ground for his grandson Charles to be elected to succeed him. There were other candidates – Francis I and Henry VIII. The English king stood little chance; the king of France was a more credible pretender, not least because he was prepared to offer huge bribes to buy the votes of the electors. As the electors met in late June, however, Francis knew his cause was lost. Charles was elected unanimously. He was 19, and still not free of the tutelage of his councillors. He faced grave problems in Spain, where the avidity of his Flemish entourage was fuelling discontent that would soon erupt in rebellion. Yet there could be no doubt that his election would have momentous consequences.

Charles combined the wealth and resources of his Burgundian and now Habsburg inheritances, those of the Spanish kingdoms and their overseas possessions in the New World and in Italy, with the authority of the emperor. As the travails of Maximilian had shown, that authority could count for little when it was not backed by the resources to make it effective. Charles would be the most powerful monarch in Europe. Imperial authority would now count for more in Italy than it had done since the days of Frederick II in the thirteenth century. He and his agents in Italy would claim the right to intervene in the affairs of states throughout the *Regnum Italiae*, those regions of northern and central Italy that were considered part of the Empire. These included the duchy of Milan and, like Frederick II, Charles had inherited the kingdoms of Naples and of Sicily. Francis I held the duchy of Milan, and claimed the throne of Naples. Italy would become a major arena in which the rivalry between Francis and Charles and their heirs, between Valois and Habsburg, would be played out for the next forty years.

Notes

1 Godefroy, III, 300–1.

2 Terrateig, I, 326.

3 Guasti, *Il Sacco di Prato*, II, 135–6.

4 Doussinague, 547–9.

5 Guicciardini, Book XI, Chap. 4; Tommasi, 369; Pecci, I, part 2, 5.

6 Kohler, 500–1.

7 *CSP Ven*, II, 74–5.

8 Sanuto, XV, 406–8.

9 Gattoni, 318–21.

10 Doussinague, 599–600: Ferdinand to Cardona, Mar. 1513.

11 Lot, 37.

12 Godefroy, IV, 130.

13 Leonij, 227–9: Signoria to Bartolomeo d'Alviano, 5 June 1513.

14 Troso; Luzio, 18 (1912), 447–50: Massimiliano Sforza to Isabella d'Este, 8 June 1513, Novara; Gattoni, 84–8: Giovanni Gonzaga to Francesco Gonzaga, 7 June 1513, Novara; Pieri, 501–2; Vissière, 219–23.

15 Büchi, I, 235–8: Schinner to Massimiliano, 21 June 1513; 264–7: Massimiliano to Schinner, late Sept. 1513.

16 CSPSpan, I, 160.

17 Wiesflecker, IV, 133, put their strength at 10,000 men; Pieri, 503, gave a much higher figure:1,600 men-at-arms, 650 light horse and 12,000 infantry.

18 Pieri, 505–11; Filippi; Sanuto, XVII, 158, 172–3, 183–8.

19 Leonij, 293: Signoria to Bartolomeo d'Alviano, 20 Nov. 1514.

20 Pacini, 79. In August 1514 the French garrison who had been holding out in the fortress on the harbour of Genoa had surrendered; the Genoese had immediately demolished the fortress.

21 Le Glay, II, 81.

22 Barrillon, I, 68; Gar, 314.

23 Goubaux and Lemoisne, I, 174.

24 Wirz, 80.

25 Barrillon, I, 102–8.

26 Leonij, 240–1: Signoria to Venetian ambassador in France, 22 June 1515.

27 Sanuto, XXI, 77.

28 D'Alviano reported that Francis put their numbers at 24,000 (ibid., 100); in a letter to his mother after the battle the king wrote that there were 28,000 (Michaud and Poujoulat, V, 595).

29 Sanuto, XXI, 79–85, 96–7, 99–113 (report by Bartolomeo d'Alviano to Doge,100–2); Barrillon, I, 116–25; Michaud and Poujoulat, V, 595 (letter from Francis); Goubaux and Lemoisne, I, 189–99.

30 Barrillon, I, 125.

31 Ibid., 122–3.

32 Guicciardini, Book XII, Chap. 15.

33 Printed in Gattoni, 323–4.

34 Sanuto, XXI, 233–4, 236–8. Floranges in his memoirs described the entry as that of a conqueror, saying the king was carrying a sword, and was accompanied by 1,200 men-at-arms and 6,000 landsknechts (Goubaux and Lemoisne, I, 207–8).

35 Printed in Gattoni, 293–6.

36 *Ibid.*, 129.

37 Desjardins and Canestrini, II, 777.

38 Wiesflecker, IV, 242; Barrillon, I, 198–9; Guasti, 'I Manoscritti Torrigiani', 20 (1874), 38.

39 *LP*, II, part 1, lxx–lxxii: Richard Pace to Cardinal Wolsey, 1 Apr. 1516.

40 Tamalio, 313.

41 Barrillon, I, 253–60.

42 *Storia di Vicenza*, III/1, 78.

43 Terrateig, II, 297–8: Ferdinand to Vich, 10 July 1514.

44 Guasti, 'I Manoscritti Torrigiani', 20 (1874), 370, 372: Cardinal de' Medici, 10, 11 Feb. 1517.

Bibliography

Arcangeli, Letizia, 'Marignano, una svolta? Governare Milano dopo la "Battaglia dei giganti" (1515–1521). Note a margine di studi recenti', *Archivio storico lombardo*, 141 (2015), 223–63.

Barrillon, Jean, *Journal*, ed. Pierre de Vaissière, 2 vols (Paris: Renouard, 1897–9).

Benassi, Umberto, *Storia della Città di Parma*, 3 vols (reprint: Bologna, Forni: 1971).

Büchi, Albert (ed.), *Korrespondenzen und Akten zur Geschichte des Kardinals Matth. Schiner*, 2 vols (Basel: R. Geering, 1920–5).

Calendar of State Papers, Spanish (HMSO, 1862–1964) [*CSPSpan*].

Calendar of State Papers, Venetian (Longmans, 1864–98) [*CSPVen*].

Clough, Cecil H., 'Clement VII and Francesco Maria della Rovere, Duke of Urbino', in Kenneth Gouwens and Sheryl E. Reiss (eds), *The Pontificate of Clement VII. History, Politics, Culture* (Aldershot: Ashgate, 2005), 75–108.

Dennistoun, James, *Memoirs of the Dukes of Urbino*, ed. Edward Hutton, 3 vols (John Lane, 1909).

Desjardins, A. and G. Canestrini, *Négociations diplomatiques de la France avec la Toscane*, 6 vols (Paris: Imprimerie Impériale, 1859–86).

Doussinague, José M., *Fernando el Católico y el cismo de Pisa* (Madrid: Espasa-Calpe, 1946).

Ferri, Massimiliano and Luca Fois, 'Le terre ticinesi tra Ducato di Milan, Francia e Svizzeri dalla caduta di Lugano e Locarno all'alleanza di Lucerna (1513–1521)', *Archivio storico lombardo*, 139 (2013), 149–82.

Filippi, Elena, *Una beffa imperiale. Storia e immagini della battaglia di Vicenza (1513)* (Vicenza: Neri Pozza, 1996).

Gar, Tommaso, 'Documenti risguardanti Giuliano de' Medici e il Pontefice Leone X', *Archivio storico italiano*, Appendice, 1 (1842–4), 291–324.

Gattoni, Maurizio, *Leone X e la geo-politica dello Stato pontificio (1513–1521)* (Città del Vaticano: Archivio Segreto Vaticano, 2000).

Godefroy, J. (ed.), *Lettres du Roy Louis XII et du Cardinal d'Amboise*, 4 vols (Brussels: Françoise Foppens, 1712).

Goubaux, Robert and P. André Lemoisne (eds), *Mémoires du Maréchal de Florange dit le Jeune Adventureux*, 2 vols (Paris: Librarie Renouard, 1913, 1924).

Guasti, Cesare (ed.), 'I Manoscritti Torrigiani donati al R. Archivio Centrale di Stato di Firenze', *Archivio storico italiano*, 19 (1874)–26 (1877).

Guasti, Cesare, *Il Sacco di Prato e il ritorno de' Medici in Firenze nel MDXII*, 2 vols (Bologna: Gaetano Romagnoli,1880).

Guicciardini, Francesco, *Storia d'Italia* (various editions).

Knecht, R.J., *Francis I* (Cambridge: Cambridge University Press, 1982).

Kohler, Charles, *Les Suisses dans les Guerres d'Italie de 1506 à 1512* (*Mémoires et Documents publiés par la Société d'Histoire et d'Archéologie de Genève*, Ser 2, vol 4) (Geneva, 1896).

Le Fur, Didier, *Marignan 13–14 septembre 1515* (Paris: Perrin, 2004).

Le Glay, M. (ed.), *Négociations diplomatiques entre la France et l'Autriche durant les trente premières années du XVIe siècle*, 2 vols (Paris: Imprimerie Royale, 1845).

Leonij, Lorenzo, *Vita de Bartolomeo di Alviano* (Todi: A. Natali, 1858).

Letters and Papers, Foreign and Domestic, of the Reign of Henry VIII, ed. J.S. Brewer et al., 21 vols and *Addenda* (London: HMSO, 1862–1932) [*LP*].

Lot, Ferdinand, *Recherches sur les effectifs des armées françaises des Guerres d'Italie aux Guerres de Religion 1494–1562* (Paris: SEVPEN, 1962).

Luzio, Alessandro, 'Isabella d'Este di fronte al Giulio II negli ultimi tre anni del suo pontificato', *Archivio storico lombardo*, Ser. 4, 17 (1912), 245–334; 18 (1912), 55–144, 393–456.

Meschini, Stefano, *La seconda dominazione francese nel Ducato di Milano: la politica e gli uomini di Francesco I (1515–1521)* (Varzi (Pavia): Guardamagna Editori, 2014).

Michaud, Joseph and Jean Joseph François Poujoulat (eds), *Nouvelle collection des mémoires pour servir à l'histoire de France*, Ser. 1, 12 vols (Paris: Guyot, 1850).

Pacini, Arturo, *I presupposti politici del 'secolo dei genovesi'. La riforma del 1528 (Atti della Società ligure di storia patria*, 104 (1990), fasc. 1) (Genoa, 1990).

Pecci, Giovanni Antonio, *Memorie storico-critiche della Città di Siena*, 2 vols (reprint, Siena: Edizioni Cantagalli, 1997).

Pieri, Piero, *Il Rinascimento e la crisi militare italiana* (Turin: Einaudi, 1952).

Sanuto, Marino, *I Diarii*, ed. R. Fulin et al., 58 vols (Venice: Reale Deputazione veneta di storia patria, 1879–1903).

Storia di Milano, vol VIII, *Tra Francia e la Spagna 1500–1535* (Milan: Fondazione Treccani, 1957).

Storia di Vicenza, ed. Franco Barbieri and Paolo Prato, vol. III/1 *L'età della Repubblica Veneta (1404–1797)* (Vicenza: Neri Pozza,1989).

Tamalio, Raffaele, *Federico Gonzaga alla Corte di Francesco I di Francia nel carteggio privato con Mantova (1515–1517)* (Paris: H. Champion,1994).

Terrateig, Baron de, *Politica en Italia del Rey Católico 1507–1516*, 2 vols (Madrid: Consejo Superior de Investigaciones Cientificas, 1963).

Tommasi, Girolamo, *Sommario della Storia di Lucca* (Lucca: Maria Pacini Fazzi, 1969; reprint of 1847 edition).

Troso, Mario, *L'ultima battaglia del Medioevo. La battaglia dell'Ariotta Novara 6 giugno 1513* (Mariano del Friuli: Edizioni della Laguna, 2002).

Vissière, Laurent, *'Sans poinct sortir hors de l'orniere'. Louis II de La Trémoille (1460–1525)* (Paris: Honoré Champion Éditeur, 2008).

Wiesflecker, Hermann, *Kaiser Maximilian I: Das Reich, Österreich und Europa an der Wende zur Neuzeit*, 5 vols (Munich: R. Oldenbourg, 1971–86).

Wirz, Caspar (ed.), *Akten über die diplomatischen Beziehungen der römischen Curie zu der Schweiz 1512–1552* (Basle: Adolf Geering, 1895).

CHAPTER 5

The contest for supremacy in Italy, 1520–9

Before his victory in the Imperial election, Charles V had entered into treaties with Francis I which could be considered humiliating, including agreeing to pay the king of France 100,000 ducats a year in recognition of his rights over the kingdom of Naples. After the election, he wanted recognition from Francis of his new status, and a change to the terms that were supposed to frame relations between them. He was now emerging from the shadow of his counsellors, showing signs of independence of mind, of shrewd judgement and keen interest in affairs of state. The king was reluctant to acknowledge his new position, and was concerned that Charles would travel to Italy to be crowned emperor by the pope and take over more territory while he was there. Francis saw a window of opportunity while Charles was still struggling to establish his rule over his Spanish kingdoms and was yet to test his powers as emperor in Germany. To divert him from Italy, Francis funded an invasion of Luxembourg by Robert de la Marck in February 1521, and assisted Henri d'Albret to take Spanish-held Navarre.

Eager to prove himself, Charles was ready to face the challenge from Francis and retaliate for the attacks that had been launched, yet he was handicapped by his continuing difficulties in Spain and in Germany, where Martin Luther and his supporters were becoming a force to be reckoned with. Growing fear of Luther's influence was one factor that made Leo decide to ally with Charles rather than Francis, as Charles promised measures to contain the spread of heresy. The king's unwillingness to lose Parma and Piacenza, or relinquish protection of Ferrara, and his attempts to get Leo to commit himself to a campaign in Naples also told against him with the pope. The terms of the treaty Leo and Charles agreed in May 1521 were principally concerned with Italy and the interests of the Medici family. The French were to be driven out of Italy; Francesco Sforza (the younger brother of Massimiliano) was to be made Duke of Milan, Antoniotto Adorno, doge of Genoa. Leo was to have Parma and Piacenza and Charles was to assist him against the Duke of Ferrara and any other rebellious papal subject, and take the Medici under his protection. The pope promised to help Charles defend the kingdom of Naples, and in any future war against Venice. Each was to contribute 100,000 ducats to hire 16,000 Swiss; once Francesco Sforza was installed as Duke of Milan he was to pay 150,000 ducats to be shared between them.[1]

Some blamed Leo for bringing about an escalation of the war between Charles and Francis, and for re-igniting the war in Italy, rather than acting as a peacemaker. On the other hand, Mercurino da Gattinara, the Imperial chancellor, has often been held responsible for encouraging Charles to view Italy as central to his concerns as emperor. He certainly stressed the importance to Charles of an alliance with the pope, and that the only way to gain that was to support the pope in Italy.[2] In 1521, however, the attention of Charles and of Francis was focused on the north-eastern frontiers of France with Flanders and the Empire; the war in Italy was something of a sideshow. Only in retrospect would it be seen as the beginning of a decade of warfare, when Italy would become the main arena in which the rivalry of the king of France and the emperor was played out.

The expulsion of the French, 1521–2

The campaign began with attempts to see if the French could be expelled from Italy the easy way, by using exiles. A venture by Antoniotto and Girolamo Adorno to oust Ottaviano Campofregoso from Genoa with the aid of papal and Imperial galleys and some Spanish infantry in June failed. So did efforts by exiles from the duchy of Milan. They were too open in their movements, and the most visible result of their efforts to provoke uprisings in various cities was a spate of executions of those known or suspected to be their collaborators.

Prospero Colonna was placed in overall command of the papal, Imperial and Florentine troops. The commander of the papal forces was Federico Gonzaga, who had succeeded his father as marquis of Mantua in 1519. Securing the use of his territory had been a major motive for his appointment, yet at this stage of his career he proved to be more reliable than his father, actually taking the field with his troops, and he generally accepted Colonna's authority. The commander of the Spanish infantry, the marchese di Pescara, was less willing to defer to him, but he vented his rivalry by trying to outshine Colonna, not undermine him. Antonio de Leyva, experienced and respected, commanded the Spanish cavalry. The incompetent viceroy, Cardona, intended to come from Naples too; Prospero Colonna warned that he would leave if Cardona came.[3] No one wanted Cardona to take command; in the end, illness prevented his leaving Naples (where he died in March 1522).

The campaign hung fire until late August, as Colonna waited for the other commanders to arrive with their troops near Parma. There was concern that 6,000 German troops who had been recruited would be blocked on their way south by the Venetians, but they were allowed to pass through. As they were bound to do by their alliance with France, the Venetians sent a few hundred men-at-arms and a few thousand infantry under Teodoro Trivulzio to help defend the duchy of Milan, but wishing to avoid bringing war on themselves again, they would not attack from their own territory. The Swiss, who had treaty obligations to supply both Francis and Leo with troops, sent men to both sides. Siege was finally laid to Parma on 29 August, but abandoned after a fortnight as Lautrec was drawing near with the French army. There were also reports that the Duke of Ferrara was gaining ground, and might make an attempt on Modena. Some papal troops were detached to deal with this threat, while the rest of the army waited to see what Lautrec would do. On 1 October, the army crossed the Po into the Cremonese, where they lingered until they were joined by the Swiss brought by Cardinal Schinner at the end of the month. Four thousand men from Zurich, ready to defend papal territory but not to attack the French, had to be allowed to go to Reggio. In the other camp, Lautrec was losing his Swiss and Valaisans because he could not pay them. He was forced to dismiss more men, and pull back behind the Adda. His brother Lescun tried in vain to block the Imperial and papal troops crossing the river too.

By mid-November, the French and Venetians together had 8,000 infantry and 1,200 lances, heavily outnumbered by their opponents' 20,000 infantry and 1,500 lances.[4] They concentrated their forces in Milan, where Lautrec's measures to prepare for the defence of the city, including burning the suburbs, heightened the people's seething disaffection from the French. The weakness of the hastily constructed earthworks outside the walls was immediately apparent to the enemy when they arrived on 20 November. Pescara and Colonna pressed a sudden assault with the Spanish and German infantry, and the Milanese rose up in support. The Venetian troops abandoned the city, leaving the wounded Trivulzio behind to be captured; Lautrec pulled his own men out that night. The city of Milan had been taken in two hours. Other cities of the duchy, including Pavia, Parma and Piacenza, quickly surrendered. The French were left in possession of Cremona and some fortresses, including those of Milan and Novara. Francesco Sforza was declared Duke of Milan, and his lieutenant Girolamo Morone assumed the government of the city in his name. Lautrec took his troops to Venetian territory, where he would spend the winter; the reluctant Venetians, fearful of reprisals, insisted no attack should be launched from their lands.[5]

The work of expelling the French was not completed before impetus was lost because of the sudden death of Leo X on 1 December 1521. As a consequence, the Florentine troops with the papal army left, while the papal and Florentine funds that had largely paid for the League's forces dried up, forcing Colonna and Pescara to dismiss many more men. The contingent from Zurich was summoned home, and the other Swiss, no longer regularly paid, became disaffected. Some of the remaining papal troops went to Modena, others remained in the Milanese under Federico Gonzaga.

In the conclave the most prominent (although not the only) division was between French and Imperial partisans. No one was as surprised as the cardinals themselves when they realized that out of the politicking they had elected, on 9 January 1522, Charles V's former tutor and current regent in Spain, Adrian of Utrecht, who took the title Adrian VI. It would be the end of August before he reached Rome; in the meantime, the temporal affairs of the Church were directed by the cardinals.

This hiatus gave an opportunity for Francesco Maria della Rovere to recover the duchy of Urbino, in alliance with others who had been ousted by Leo, Borghese and Fabio Petrucci and Malatesta and Orazio Baglioni, the sons of Gianpaolo.[6] Alfonso d'Este, who had taken the opportunity to recover much territory he had lost to the pope, provided some funds which helped to raise a small army of 3,000 foot and 500 horse.[7] By the end of December, della Rovere had recovered the duchy of Urbino, Pesaro and Senigallia. In early January, Malatesta and Orazio Baglioni returned to Perugia, and then the allies' forces went on to Siena. There, the run of military success ended, as Florence sent troops to support Raffaele Petrucci and operations were hampered by heavy snow. Interim recognition of della Rovere's possession of Urbino by the cardinals (confirmed by the pope in May) led to an agreement with Cardinal Giulio de' Medici. Part of the territory of the duchy that Leo had granted to Florence was restored to him, and he was appointed captain-general of Florence for one year. Consequently, he did not aid another unsuccessful attempt in April to overthrow the regime in Siena, led by Renzo da Ceri, who had just been taken into the service of France.

In Lombardy, the French launched an attempt to recover Milan. Lautrec was sent 16,000 Swiss reinforcements,[8] who asked him to come to them at Monza to the north of Milan, which he did at the beginning of March. The French army was joined by the Venetian forces – 360 lances, 700 light horse and 2,500 infantry[9] – and by Giovanni de' Medici, who brought over his company of infantry and light horse. Medici had made a reputation for himself as a bold and vigorous commander in the previous campaign, when he had served his distant relation, Leo X. The combined forces approached Milan, but Prospero Colonna had ordered the construction of effective defensive earthworks to contain the French garrison still in the Castello, and to repel any attempts by the French army to get through to them. To aid in the defence of the city, Morone organized a militia among the Milanese, which provided several thousand men, and Lautrec failed to prevent Francesco Sforza reaching Milan in early April with 6,000 landsknechts he had brought down from Trent.

As Lautrec attempted to take Pavia, Prospero Colonna brought his army out of Milan to the Certosa of Pavia, forcing the French to move. The Swiss with the French army were growing impatient, threatening to leave, but were persuaded to stay for a few more days by the promise their pay would arrive soon. The French were planning to withdraw to Novara, which had been taken by Lescun, to await the expected arrival of Francis, and the Venetians to retire to Venetian territory. Charles V was annoyed by the loss of Novara, accusing his captains of having done nothing since they took Milan but waste time and money, without attacking the enemy.[10] The captains were willing enough to give battle, the Spanish commissioner with the army explained, but the terrain had so many ditches that whichever side attacked the other in their encampment was liable to be defeated, even if they were the stronger.[11] This observation proved prophetic. Following Lautrec from Pavia, Colonna encamped his men – 10,000 landsknechts, 4,000 Spanish and 4,000 Italian infantry[12] and a few hundred men-at-arms – at La Bicocca, a country house three miles from Milan with a park bordered by ditches and irrigation canals, constructing ramparts and platforms for his artillery. Lautrec recognized the strength of this position, but the Swiss were keen to give battle. Fighting battles, the Swiss (and the landsknechts) believed, was their proper role in warfare.

Against his better judgement, Lautrec ordered an attack on the encampment on 29 April. At their own insistence, the Swiss were to make a frontal attack on the position of the landsknechts; Montmorency and other French nobles went with them on foot 'for their pleasure and to acquire honour'.[13] Lescun took 400 men-at-arms on the left flank to a stone bridge to the rear of the camp; Lautrec led the remainder of his men, infantry and men-at-arms, to the right flank to attempt entry into the camp on that side. The Venetian rearguard appears to have been the reserve. Lescun's corps succeeded in penetrating the camp, causing some confusion and capturing much of the baggage of the men-at-arms. The Swiss had pressed ahead with their assault, but their approach was covered by the artillery of the camp. Those who survived this were confronted by an impassable ditch and rampart, and in this killing ground many fell victim to relentless fire from handguns. (Pescara was said, as a tactical innovation, to have organized the arquebusiers in four ranks, firing in sequence and kneeling down to reload as the rank behind fired over their heads.[14]) Swiss captains and French gentlemen who had placed themselves at the front took particularly high casualties among the estimated 3,000 men who died in this battle. The Swiss drew back and refused to make another attempt. Never again would Swiss infantry be so confident that they could overcome any enemy by sheer resolution and the shock force of their battle squares. Lescun's men were unable to sustain the attack that was turned against them, and had to withdraw across the bridge.[15]

The Swiss retired with Lautrec to Monza, but there they left the army and went home. The Venetians withdrew their army from the duchy of Milan. Lautrec departed for France, where he met with a frosty reception from the king. Lescun, who had been left in Cremona, having agreed terms of surrender with Prospero Colonna if no relief force should arrive from France within a set period, followed with the remainder of the army not long after. Only the fortresses of Cremona, Novara and Milan were still in French hands.

Colonna had agreed these terms because it had been decided that, rather than pursue the retreating French, the Imperial army should go to take Genoa. Raising some money was as much the objective as installing Antoniotto and Girolamo Adorno – who were with them and had fought at Bicocca – at the head of the government there. Pedro Navarro had been sent by Francis I with two galleys to help Ottaviano Campofregoso defend the city, but the people of Genoa were not ready to fight for Campofregoso and the king. Pescara with the Spanish and Italian troops reached Genoa from the west on 20 May, and began bombarding the city; Colonna brought the rest of the army to the east a few days later. Negotiations began, but while they were proceeding, on 30 May Pescara's Spanish infantry entered through a breach made in the walls by artillery fire, and met no resistance. The wealthy city was systematically looted; although the citizens had their homes ransacked, and were forced to pay ransoms, the soldiers seem to have concentrated on plunder, not slaughter.[16] Ottaviano Campofregoso and Pedro Navarro were taken prisoner and sent to Naples, on the orders of Charles V. Antoniotto Adorno was installed as doge of an independent republic under imperial protection, a republic in which the imperial ambassador kept a close watch on the government and expected to be consulted on all important matters.

The claims of the Empire

Charles V, his advisers and agents in Italy were ready to claim authority over the states and fiefs of Italy that were considered part of the Empire. After the French were expelled from Milan, Imperial officials and commanders demanded that Italian states that were presumed to be subordinate to the Empire should pay for the maintenance of the Imperial army in Lombardy. Money was extorted from Siena, Lucca and Florence – as fines for 'disobedience', for having had contacts with the French – under threat that troops would be sent to punish them if they did not pay. This did not yield as much as was demanded or required, and the states represented the payments as gifts and would not accept the principle that they should make regular contributions.

It had been generally believed when Adrian VI was elected pope, that Charles would also be able to control the papacy. He should be Charles's ally against Francis, the pope was bluntly told by Imperial envoys, and he should do as he was directed by the emperor. Refusing to be dictated to, the pope wanted to make peace between Charles and Francis, so that they could unite against the threat to Christendom from the Turks in Hungary and on the island of Rhodes (which fell to them in December 1522). He was angry that, on the instructions of Charles's ambassador in Rome, Juan Manuel, Imperial troops were quartered at Parma, Piacenza and Reggio.[17] They were sent there because it was impossible to find other quarters for them, was the justification he was given, and anyway, he was told, he was wrong if he believed these places belonged to the Church.[18] Another cause of dispute with Charles was the question of the status of Modena and Reggio. Both pope and emperor were willing to sell the rights to these cities to Alfonso d'Este for a substantial sum; Charles claimed they were Imperial fiefs, while Adrian claimed they belonged to the Church.[19]

Only towards the end of his brief pontificate (following hostile declarations by Francis, who objected to his efforts to impose a truce) did Adrian agree to a defensive league with Charles. This league was also supposed to include Henry VIII, Ferdinand, Charles's brother (now Archduke of Austria), Francesco Sforza, Florence, Siena, Lucca and Genoa. The Italian states were supposed to make regular financial contributions, but the Imperial agents in Rome may have included them in the treaty without consulting them, as they would do on other occasions; Cardinal de' Medici, who was named as a party to the treaty, probably promised for Florence.[20]

The French return to Milan, 1523–4

As soon as Adrian had signed this treaty in early August 1523, Charles hoped to turn it into an offensive league against France,[21] which he was planning to invade. Francis was planning to invade Milan, but this time he would have to do without the aid of Venice. After lengthy negotiations, Charles reached an agreement with Venice in late July 1523, including a Venetian commitment to defend the duchy of Milan.[22] (One consequence of this was that the pro-French Teodoro Trivulzio was replaced as governor-general of the Venetian army by Francesco Maria della Rovere.) Charles intended that Prospero Colonna should attack France in Provence, in concert with invasions from Spain and from England, and with a rebellion by the disaffected Constable of France, Charles de Bourbon. On the other hand, the French invasion of Milan was supposed to be co-ordinated by an uprising of French partisans in the duchy. Both conspiracies misfired. The Milanese uprising was mistimed, and an assassination attempt on Francesco Sforza failed. Discovery of Bourbon's conspiracy delayed the French; the king was informed of it while he was on his way south, and Francis decided to stay in France to investigate its ramifications. He also had to face an English invasion of Picardy that thrust towards Paris. Bourbon, however, was unable to organize an attack from Imperial territory to the east of France, where he had fled in early September, and the planned invasion from Spain foundered.

When Francis pulled back from going to Italy, he gave command of the expedition to Guillaume Gouffier, seigneur de Bonnivet, Admiral of France, who had already crossed the Alps. He had a large army at his disposal; one report was of over 2,200 men-at-arms, not counting the gentlemen who came as volunteers, and 36,000 infantry.[23] Prospero Colonna had a smaller army, perhaps 800 lances, 800 light horse and 15,000 infantry.[24] He thought to hold the line of the Ticino, but the river was low, and the

French were able to cross it easily on 14 September. Pulling his men back to Milan, Colonna was given valuable breathing space for a few days to repair earthworks and bring supplies into the city, as Bonnivet did not press on the advance. The Milanese, incited by Morone to defend their city, responded enthusiastically. Some support was provided by allied forces. At Colonna's request, Federico Gonzaga brought his troops, 500 lances, 600 light horse and 5,000 infantry, to Pavia.[25] (As well as being captain-general of the Church, since August 1523 he had also been captain of the Florentine troops and since 1522 held a *condotta* of 100 lances from the emperor.) The Duke of Urbino, under the usual orders from Venice to make his priority the preservation of their army, was given an excuse not to cross the Adda by the arrival of 2,000 Swiss on their way to join the French, who posed a threat to Crema and Bergamo. Bonnivet lifted the siege in mid-November and withdrew to winter quarters at Abbiategrasso, where he awaited further Swiss reinforcements.

The Imperial army was strengthened by the arrival in late December of the new viceroy of Naples, Charles de Lannoy, and Pescara, bringing troops from Naples. Lannoy, who had been appointed captain-general of the League, took command; this caused no difficulty with Prospero Colonna, for he died on 30 December, after a long illness. Colonna was one of the last of the generation of Italian *condottieri* who had been active commanders before the Italian Wars. Guicciardini credited him with changing the strategy of the wars, with finding a way of frustrating the progress of armies and avoiding battle so that states could no longer be won and lost by a swiftly executed military campaign.[26] Whether or not he was influenced by this example, Lannoy pursued a strategy of containing the French army, blocking their supplies, but not seeking battle. The main difficulty for Lannoy was lack of money to pay the troops, whose numbers had been increased by the arrival at the end of January 1524 of 6,000 landsknechts sent from Germany. Charles was warned that his army could disintegrate, that his honour and the kingdom of Naples were both at stake, and Lannoy urged him to seek a peace or truce with Francis.[27]

In accordance with the advice of the Venetian commissioner, Leonardo Emo, when the Venetians came to join up with the Imperial army in early February, the joint forces pushed the French back across the Ticino. Bonnivet's army was wasting away from disease and shortages. A diversion by Renzo da Ceri, who brought 5,000 Grisons into the territory of Bergamo, was repelled by a detachment of Venetian troops and Giovanni de' Medici, who had been sent with his infantry to guard Milan. Ten thousand Swiss reinforcements were not much help to Bonnivet, refusing to march to join him, demanding he must go to them at Gattinara on the river Sesia in Piedmont. On Bonnivet's arrival on the other bank of the river, on 28 April, the Swiss informed him they had come only to take home their countrymen who were already with him, not to advance into the duchy of Milan. The next day, the whole French army began to cross the Sesia near Romagnano, with Bonnivet commanding the rearguard covering their withdrawal. As they crossed, they were attacked by the Imperial army, with Pescara's handgunners pursuing them and inflicting heavy casualties. Bonnivet himself was wounded by an arquebus shot. The Swiss and the rest of the French army went their separate ways, without being pursued further, and the few places that were still held for the French – Lodi, Alessandria and Novara – soon surrendered.

Calculating that only 350 men-at-arms and 4,000 infantry had evaded death or capture during this campaign and made it back to France, Charles saw this as an opportunity for vengeance that he could not let pass.[28] He ordered Bourbon, who had come to join the Imperial army, to invade France from Italy. Appointed Charles's lieutenant in Italy, Bourbon was to share the command. This would cause problems. While the other commanders bowed to the emperor's decision and recognized Bourbon's social status and his courage and energy, they did not respect him as a military leader. Charles hoped that much of the money needed for the campaign could be found in France as the army advanced. These hopes were not realized, and nor were Bourbon's hopes of an uprising against Francis, or the plans for simultaneous invasions of Picardy by Henry VIII and Charles himself from Spain into Languedoc. Francis brought a powerful army to Avignon, while the invasion force came to a halt in mid-August besieging Marseilles, whose defence was directed by Renzo da Ceri. Lifting the siege on 29 September, the Imperial army rapidly withdrew back to Italy, chased by French men-at-arms under Montmorency.

Francis I's second expedition to Italy, 1524–5

The king followed after with his army, unopposed. By late October, the French army was at the city of Milan. This time the Milanese had no heart to mount a defence; they had suffered great mortality in an epidemic. There were only 3,000 Spanish soldiers in the city – just enough to man two of the nine miles of ramparts. The Imperial commanders (Bourbon and Pescara had rejoined Lannoy) abandoned the city, having strengthened the garrison in the Castello.[29] Rather than pursue them, Francis decided to lay siege to Pavia, which was defended by 300 men-at-arms and 5,000 infantry under Antonio de Leyva. The king's army was reported to number 30,000 infantry, 2,200 lances and 1,400 light horse.[30] He was confident of a quick victory, but an assault on a breach in the city walls created by his artillery failed, as did an attempt to divert the river Ticino away from the city. He felt his honour was at stake and refused to lift the siege, keeping his army encamped outside the city through the discomforts of a winter siege, rather than go to confront the Imperial field army that was being kept together with difficulty at Soncino.

The Imperial army was not being supported by the Italian states. Venice agreed a mutual non-aggression pact with Francis in December 1524, and began negotiations to renew their alliance. The Duke of Ferrara once again sought the protection of the French king, paying part of the price in munitions sent to his army. No help was forthcoming from the new pope, the indecisive, timorous, over-subtle Giulio de' Medici, Clement VII. As he had been considered head of the Imperial faction in the College of Cardinals, Charles hoped for his support against Francis, but Clement did not want to go to war or subsidize either side.

Clement was forced to abandon strict neutrality when Francis despatched John Stuart, Duke of Albany (an exiled member of the Scottish royal house) with 5,000 infantry, 500 lances and light horse to march on the kingdom of Naples.[31] This force was to be increased by other infantry brought from France by Renzo da Ceri and troops recruited by the Orsini in the Papal States. Fearful of the consequences for the Papal States and Florence if he refused, as Albany was crossing the Appennines into Lucchese territory in early January, the pope agreed to allow the troops free passage through his state, while Francis promised not to disturb the regime in Florence and to leave Parma and Piacenza in the pope's hands.[32] Yet, as well as allowing the Orsini to raise men in the Papal States to attack the kingdom of Naples, Clement allowed the Colonna to raise men to defend it.

While reminding Lannoy that his first responsibility was the preservation of Naples rather than of Milan, the emperor left it to him to decide what to do.[33] Lannoy had already decided to leave the defence of Naples to the Colonna and forces to be organized in the kingdom, and sent Ugo de Moncada money and men for a fleet to prevent French vessels taking troops south. Moncada's ships were based at Genoa; the French fleet, under Andrea Doria, was on the western Riviera. The French ships had carried several thousand infantry under Renzo da Ceri, and the Genoese withdrew as the French advanced, abandoning Savona to them. Francis sent the marquis of Saluzzo to continue the conquest of the Riviera, while

Renzo took his men to join Albany. An attempt by Moncada to block the French expansion in late January 1525 ended in defeat and his capture.

Renzo's men met up with Albany's army near Lucca. Having extorted money and a couple of artillery pieces from Lucca, but leaving Florence alone, Albany arrived at Siena in late January. Clement exploited the presence of Albany's army in Tuscany to strengthen his Sienese allies in the imposition of a more oligarchic regime (the Petrucci had been expelled in September 1524). Albany lingered to please the pope and to get money and more artillery from the Sienese. At the end of January he moved on to the Papal States. Renzo da Ceri went ahead to raise infantry there, but the Colonna, too, were raising thousands of men. By allowing both sides to recruit in his lands, Clement risked bringing war to Rome, with the French and Orsini pitted against the Colonna. Then news arrived of the momentous battle at Pavia.

The Battle of Pavia

The French army had been enduring the winter in their camp and trenches outside Pavia. In late January the Imperial army came, seeking to draw the French into battle before its own forces dispersed for lack of money. The main French camp was to the east of the city between the river Ticino that ran south of Pavia and the wall of a great park that stretched for miles up to the Certosa to the north. Their siege lines extended from the Ticino and into the park to its far walls. The men-at-arms pastured their horses in the park, and the king had the wall breached to facilitate communication between the park and the camp. On the other side of the French camp was a stream, the Vernavola, that also ran through the middle of the park.

On arriving at Pavia, the Imperial army set up camp on the other side of this stream, outside the walls of the park. There were several fierce skirmishes, but the French refused to join battle. Thinking, as Pescara wrote to the emperor, that for an army to disband in the face of the enemy was as bad as to lose a battle, the Imperial commanders decided to force the issue before their army fell apart. Because the king seemed to rely on the strength of the park walls to protect his position, Pescara suggested the army should approach through the park; the other commanders agreed.[34] A message was sent to de Leyva in Pavia to be ready to sally out with the garrison.

Estimates of the size of the armies vary considerably. Both had lost men in the skirmishes since the Imperial camp arrived, and through disease and desertion. Thousands of Grisons had just been recalled from the French camp. Floranges, who fought in the battle and was captured, put the numbers in the French army on the day as 600 men-at-arms and 17,500 infantry. He claimed to have heard in a debate over dinner at Pescara's table afterwards that there were 24,000 infantry, 1,200 men-at-arms and 1,200 light horse in the Imperial field army, and 8,000 infantry and 220 men-at-arms in the Pavia garrison.[35] This probably underestimated the strength of the French and overestimated that of the Imperial army. Francis himself spoke after the battle of having had 26,000 infantry.[36]

On the night of 23 February, the Imperial army made its way northwards along the wall of the park. At some point (the location is uncertain) the walls were breached. This took longer than expected, and it was dawn by the time the first troops entered the park. Three thousand German and Spanish infantry under the marchese del Vasto were sent to take a house, Mirabello, situated towards the centre of the park. Mostly civilians and camp followers were found there, so they did this quite easily. A detachment of French men-at-arms who had been there or nearby hurried back to the camp to raise the alarm. Already informed that the Imperial army was on the move, Francis seems to have assumed it was retreating, so he and his cavalry were arming for a pursuit. He set off with his cavalry and some light artillery to confront the enemy, leaving the infantry to follow behind.

The battle did not develop as the Imperial commanders had planned – their intention seems to have been to take up positions around Mirabello – and the French army was not deployed in an organized battle formation. Contemporary accounts of the course of the battle were contradictory, and in many details irreconcilable, but there is broad agreement among historians about the main outlines. The body of the Imperial army advanced along the Vernavola stream, heading towards Mirabello, the cavalry under Lannoy, Bourbon and Alarcon to the right nearest the stream, and to their left the infantry under Pescara; the artillery had had to be left behind near the park wall. Francis with his heavy cavalry charged the Imperial cavalry, gaining the upper hand. Pescara deployed his arquebusiers in uneven ground and copses on the flank of the French cavalry; their firing caused heavy casualties. The Imperial cavalry rallied and counter-charged. French artillery fire against the Imperial infantry was ineffective, as Pescara ordered them to lie in the hollows of the undulating parkland. After Vasto brought his men up to rejoin the main body, there was a fierce infantry engagement. The Black Bands of landsknechts on the French side were annihilated; the bodies of their commanders, François de Lorraine and Richard de la Pole, the exiled Duke of Suffolk, were found among the slain. The Swiss came under attack from the infantry of the main Imperial army and from the landsknechts of the garrison of Pavia, led by de Leyva (who was carried on a chair by his men, as he suffered from gout), and were also over-ridden by the fleeing French cavalry; they broke and retreated in disorder. The king himself, by all accounts, fought hard, as the nobles around him were cut down. Eventually, as he was trying to escape the field, his horse was brought down by an arquebus shot, pinning the king beneath it. He was captured, surrendering to Lannoy.

By midday the battle was over. The French army had effectively been destroyed: only the rearguard of the cavalry under Alençon escaped, breaking the bridge across the Ticino behind them, and thus adding to the losses as fleeing soldiers were trapped or drowned trying to swim the river. Estimates of the numbers of dead varied considerably, while generally agreeing the French losses were much heavier. Among the many French noblemen who perished were some who had commanded armies in Italy – La Trémoille, La Palisse, Bonnivet; Lescun died of his wounds. He was one of a rich harvest of ransomable prisoners. Apart from the greatest prize, the king himself, they included Henry, King of Navarre, René of Savoy (who also died of his wounds), Anne de Montmorency and François de Bourbon, comte de Saint-Pol. Of the great nobles with the army the only one to escape death or capture was Alençon, who died (some said of shame) soon after his return to France. The Imperial army struggled to cope with the numbers of prisoners that fell into their hands; thousands were stripped of their weapons and armour and sent on their way. Reports agreed that Imperial losses were much lighter. The only Imperial commander to be killed was Ferrando Castriota, marchese di Sant'Angelo, who had led the light horse; Pescara, de Leyva and Alarcon were wounded.[37]

This has often been presented as a battle commanded by Pescara, and much of the credit for the victory has been given to his planning and his deployment of the arquebusiers. He claimed it was his idea to attack through the park.[38] The contemporary historian Giovio said that Pescara had been given overall command of the army[39] but Imperial sources made no mention of this, although Pescara was singled out for praise for his valour and energy. In the field, Bourbon and Lannoy had taken the most honourable positions in command of the cavalry. Pescara himself said the emperor was as much indebted to the least of his soldiers for the determination and spirit they had shown.[40] It was such appreciation for the infantry who served under him that earned Pescara the loyalty and devotion of his men. But the Battle of Pavia was not a tactical victory for him, or any other commander; no one controlled the course of events in the park of Mirabello.

The aftermath of the Battle of Pavia

What was left of the French army was soon out of the duchy of Milan, the Swiss heading back across the Alps, the French making their way to France. The marquis of Saluzzo left the Riviera for France, and Andrea Doria's fleet went south to pick up the Duke of Albany and his men from the Papal States.

After nearly three months in the fortress of Pizzighettone, the king was taken to Genoa. From there, he was sent to Spain. This was Lannoy's decision, but Charles approved when he learned his prisoner was in Spain. Charles ordered that no prisoner of rank or captain – anyone who might be a useful leader of French troops – should be ransomed until the king had been freed.[41] In the event, Montmorency was exchanged for Ugo de Moncada, while Saint-Pol and Henry of Navarre would manage to escape before the king's release.

The emperor's response to news of the victory was restrained. Unsure what to do, and in receipt of much conflicting advice, he aimed for a lasting peace settlement, and to make Francis pay for causing the war. Thoughts of demanding much of the territory of France for himself and his allies were set aside in favour of more moderate demands for the duchy of Burgundy (which Charles regarded as his own rightful inheritance), recognition of his sovereignty over Flanders and Artois and the renunciation of French claims to Milan and Naples. To the French, these demands seemed excessive and humiliating, but Charles stood by them. Francis had hoped to benefit from some chivalrous gesture, but once he realized there would not be one, he was equally determined – above all, not to yield Burgundy. Anxious as she was for the release of her son, Louise of Savoy, the regent of France, thought the price Charles was asking was far too high.

The emperor also considered what to do about Italian states that had sided with the French, or at least not helped the Imperial army. How to handle Florence, Lucca and Siena was left to the discretion of Lannoy. Charles decided that it would be inexpedient to try to punish Clement or the Venetians, and that it would be better to come to agreement with them.[42] An alliance with Clement to which other Italian states might be admitted was signed at the beginning of April; Charles refused to ratify an additional agreement that Clement wanted, which included a guarantee Reggio should be returned to the pope (Alfonso d'Este had recovered Reggio in 1523 after the death of Adrian VI).[43] Venice was ready to negotiate, but not to accept the terms suggested. For the Imperial agents in Italy, as for Charles, chastising the Italian powers for their failings was, first and foremost, a pretext to get money to pay for the army. This was desperately needed: 600,000 ducats were owing to the troops up to the Battle of Pavia. Calculations were made about fines that could be levied. The Venetians, for example, considered culpable for not having sent their army to join the Imperial troops, could be asked for 130,000 ducats.[44] It was also hoped to impose regular contributions for the maintenance of the army on the Italian states.

It was not just in demands for money that the emperor's men were taking a high-handed attitude to the Italian states. The Imperial envoy in Genoa, Lope de Soria, told the Genoese that they were Charles's subjects, nothing more; confederates was the term the Genoese thought more accurate.[45] Imperial agents considered it to be open to them to intervene in the internal affairs of states that could be claimed as part of the Empire, to create governments that would be favourable to Imperial interests. Siena attracted their attention, as a state positioned between Florence and the Papal States. The regime there had soon decided that they had better come to terms with the Imperial agents, and was ready to pay 15,000 ducats. When an envoy came to collect the cash, the leader of the regime, Alessandro Bichi, was assassinated just as he was handing it over. This was an internal, factional matter, not an anti-Imperial protest; the new regime, dominated by the Monte del Popolo, described themselves as the true Imperial partisans. Nevertheless, they were not ready to accept the dictation of the duca di Sessa, the Imperial ambassador in Rome, who Lannoy ordered to reform the government.

The arrogance of Imperial agents aroused great resentment – one reason why the crushing military victory at Pavia did not translate into political hegemony in Italy, as they were assuming it would. Their problems in sustaining the army were widely known, and their efforts to force Italian states into paying for it backfired. As governments realized that the army was in danger of disintegrating, and could not be deployed, they saw no necessity to hand over the money demanded of them. Gattinara's argument that the way to get the Spanish out of Italy was to pay them to go was unpersuasive.[46] By July, Venice, the pope and the Duke of Milan were discussing an Italian league to drive the Imperial forces from Italy, and proposing an alliance with France, if all French claims in Italy were dropped.

The Imperial takeover of the duchy of Milan

The regions that suffered most from the problems of the Imperial army were the duchy of Milan and those neighbouring states that were also forced to provide for it. Units were sent to the lands of the Duke of

Savoy, to the marquisate of Saluzzo (which was taken over by Imperial troops in July 1525), and to small Imperial fiefs; some were sent to Genoese territory but were not accepted in Genoa itself. To the outrage of the pope, some were sent to Piacenza. Well aware of the problems the soldiers caused by their demands, the commanders feared for the safety of their men – it was not uncommon for them to be attacked, even killed by the civilians they lived among – but were in a quandary. The duchy of Milan had been stripped of resources by the war and could not support the army.

The generals knew of the proposals for an Italian league, not least because Girolamo Morone tried to draw Pescara, who was known to be discontented with the rewards for his services to the emperor, into a conspiracy. With the approval of the pope, Morone offered him the crown of Naples. Playing along, Pescara kept his colleagues and the emperor informed, and Charles gave him discretion to act as he thought best.[47] In mid-October, Morone was arrested. His confession implicated Francesco Sforza (who had finally been granted investiture with the duchy in late July for a total price of 700,000 ducats), giving a pretext for accusing Sforza of felony towards the emperor, and for the occupation of the duchy. Some places were taken by the troops, others Sforza was forced to cede, but he insisted on keeping the key fortresses of Milan, where he lived, and Cremona. Imperial troops surrounded them, while proceedings against him for treachery to Charles began.

The death on 3 December of Pescara – who had never wholly recovered from the wounds he received at Pavia – increased the problems of the army. Bourbon was appointed captain-general and Charles's lieutenant in Italy, but was still in Spain and would not return to Italy for some months. Pescara had left the army under the interim command of his cousin, Alfonso d'Avalos, marchese del Vasto, and Antonio de Leyva. Without money, and with all sources of credit exhausted, they struggled to keep it in being. The ambiguity about whether Francesco Sforza was to be left as Duke of Milan persisted. Bourbon was promised investiture with the duchy in February 1526, but Charles had not decided he should have it, and Sforza had not yet been found guilty of the charges against him.

The League of Cognac

Pining in his Spanish prison, Francis agreed terms with Charles in January 1526 in the Treaty of Madrid. The main territorial concessions were to be the surrender of the duchy of Burgundy and the renunciation of his claims to Naples, Milan and Genoa. The king never intended to abide by these terms, and once they became known, few expected him to do so. When he was at last back in France in mid-March, although his two sons had taken his place as hostages in Spain for his fulfilment of his obligations under the treaty, he refused to ratify it; his council declared that he could not give Burgundy away. Frustrated, Charles could not afford to mount a military campaign to take it.

The emperor was also trying to negotiate with Clement and Venice, but his continued equivocation over the fate of the duchy of Milan made them prefer to press on with the Italian league. Deeming it essential that Francis should be a member, they had been negotiating with Louise of Savoy during the king's captivity. On his return to France, they sent envoys to urge him to join them. He was willing to do so, and the Holy League of Cognac was concluded on 22 May 1526. As well as the three principal powers, it included Florence, coerced into association with it by the pope, and Francesco Sforza. Henry VIII, who it had been hoped would join and subsidize the League, was named as its protector; his natural son, the Duke of Richmond (who Henry fancied might become Duke of Milan) was to be given estates in Naples, as was his chief minister, Cardinal Wolsey.[48] Theoretically, the League was open to Charles V, but on conditions he would be sure to refuse, including guaranteeing the independence of Italy. Its aim was to drive the Imperial army from northern Italy; if Charles refused to negotiate, the kingdom of Naples was to be conquered and Clement would dispose of it as he thought fit.

For Francis, who had no more intention of promptly fulfilling his obligations under this league than those under the Treaty of Madrid, its primary purpose was to make Charles V more amenable, and to provide cover for negotiations with Henry VIII.

Venice and Clement, however, had already been preparing for the campaign, which they launched in June. While they wanted to take advantage of the disorder and demoralization of the Imperial troops, they hesitated to attack before they were joined by the Swiss they hoped to hire, and they disagreed over strategy. Their armies were moving to join up, when on 24 June the Venetian troops under Urbino were able to take Lodi, as one of the gates was opened to them by a disaffected Italian infantry captain.

Lodi had been garrisoned by Italian infantry because the Spanish infantry there had decided to go to Milan after rumours reached them that it was being sacked by their comrades, as they wanted to share in the plunder. There had just been an uprising in Milan, co-ordinated with the defenders of the Castello, but provoked by exasperation with the behaviour of the soldiers. A month after the uprising, Sforza's resistance was finally worn down, and he surrendered the Castello on 25 July. By the terms of surrender he was to go to Como, where he would be given the jurisdiction and revenues, plus extra income, pending judgement on whether he was guilty of felony towards Charles. Nothing had been said about the Spanish garrison there leaving, and when they refused to go, Sforza went to Venetian territory, to Crema.

The Imperial troops – 6,000–8,000 Spanish and German infantry and some Italians, 700 lances and about 1,200 light horse[49] – were concentrated at Milan, Pavia, Alessandria and Cremona. Despite the success in finally dislodging Sforza from the Castello of Milan, they were on the defensive, with widespread desertion and those troops who stayed refusing to take the field because they were owed so much back pay. Cremona came under siege from the League's army at the beginning of August, falling in late September. The League's fleet had reached Genoese waters at the end of August, and would stay there some months, although Clement withdrew his galleys under Andrea Doria in September. Pedro Navarro commanded the French vessels, but could not make an attempt on Genoa without the support of land forces. It was thought that the French troops who arrived in Italy in August, under the command of Michele Antonio, marquis of Saluzzo, might go there but they went to Lombardy instead, joining the League's forces at the end of September. Many of the 4,500 foot, 250 lances and 300 light horse[50] in the French contingent were Milanese exiles.

Some relief came for the Imperial army in Lombardy just as the French arrived, for the pope ordered his troops to withdraw, as he ordered his galleys to leave the fleet. Clement had been brought under increasing pressure for some months. Moncada had been sent to Rome in June with instructions from the emperor that if Clement had allied with France (as indeed he just had), Moncada was to come to terms with the Duke of Ferrara and to use the Colonna and the Sienese against the pope.[51]

Charles had been told by his officials in Italy that Siena was markedly loyal to the Empire, and he saw Siena as a potentially useful restraint on Clement. He was under the illusion that the Sienese would be prepared to quarter and pay for thousands of Spanish troops.[52] Clement, on the other hand, was keen to re-establish Medici influence over the government of Siena. Papal and Florentine forces were sent against Siena with Sienese exiles in July. The siege camp was on the point of breaking up when it was attacked by Sienese troops on 25 July. The jubilant Sienese claimed a resounding victory, and were still less inclined than before to accept the dictation of the pope or of Imperial officials, or to let their exiles return.

Alfonso d'Este's support was considered desirable by both sides in Lombardy. Personally, he still inclined to France, but Charles could offer the grant of Imperial investiture with Reggio. Among Alfonso's demands was appointment as Imperial captain-general in Italy. His appointment was not confirmed at this stage, but Charles did grant Alfonso investiture with Reggio and Modena, and with Carpi. Alfonso felt sufficiently committed to the emperor to refuse the offer of becoming captain-general of the League.

Plans by the emperor's agents to use the Colonna against the pope were put in train soon after Moncada arrived in Rome, and then went to stay on their estates. By early August, the troops gathered by the Colonna were reported to outnumber those Clement had in Rome.[53] After a French envoy, Guillaume du Bellay, arrived in Rome bringing excuses from the king, but no money or promise of troops, Clement was ready to reach an agreement, pardoning the Colonna. They in turn undertook to put down their arms. Moncada ordered the troops that had come from Naples to withdraw to the frontier, and Clement dismissed all but a few hundred men to save money. This was just what Moncada and the Colonna had hoped to achieve by making the agreement, planning to take Clement unawares.

Their intention was to threaten Rome, to enter the city if possible, and if not, to raid the surrounding countryside. The Colonna had over 300 horse beween them and more had come from Naples, and there were 5,000 infantry, apart from the men raised from the Colonna estates; the pope had only 100 horse and 200 infantry left in Rome.[54] When Moncada, Cardinal Pompeo Colonna and Ascanio Colonna came to Rome with their troops on 20 September, they entered the city without much difficulty. The Romans stood by, partly because they did not believe that the Colonna would do the pope any harm. But the troops looted the Borgo, the area near the Vatican where many members of the papal court and curia lived, and the papal palace, while Clement took refuge in the Castel Sant'Angelo. On the next day, Clement agreed a four-month truce with Moncada. The Colonna were to withdraw to Naples, and Clement to pull his troops out of Lombardy.

But Clement broke the truce, using the papal troops brought from Lombardy to attack the Colonna estates. He wanted to ruin them, and he used Orsini *condottieri*, who enlisted their own vassals and partisans to help. News that Renzo da Ceri, despatched by Francis to help the pope when he heard of the incursion into Rome, was at last arriving, cheered Clement. Renzo brought no money when he came in early January, but drew on the resources of the Orsini faction to organize the defence of Rome against the troops from Naples sent to support the Colonna.

Encouraged by Renzo and by the arrival of some subsidies from France and from England, the pope sent an expeditionary force into the kingdom. Renzo was able to take Tagliacozzo, a county long disputed between the Orsini and the Colonna, and to use the Guelf faction to turn L'Aquila against the Spanish. Papal and French galleys under Andrea Doria, with an Angevin claimant to the kingdom, Louis de Lorraine, comte de Vaudemont on board, sailed towards Naples and seized several places on the coast. By mid-March, both sides were ready to agree an eight-month truce. Lannoy, who had returned from Spain, was concerned about the security of the kingdom, whose people would not fight the invaders. Clement was short of money and his forces were disintegrating for lack of support and because the partisans raised by Renzo could not be kept in the field for long.

Clement dismissed many of his remaining troops, despite a looming threat to the Papal States and Florence from Lombardy. There the League was on the defensive, uncertain whether they could look to the pope for support. The Venetians left Monza in late November 1526, Saluzzo withdrew the French troops behind the Adda, and papal troops abandoned Piacenza. The Imperial army was reinforced by up to 16,000 landsknechts under Georg Frundsberg, who arrived in Lombardy in November. Many of them were Lutherans, fired by anti-papal zeal, and dreaming of the prospect of attacking the rich cities of Florence and the Papal States, to compensate for the fact they had so far received little money from Archduke Ferdinand or from Bourbon. Giovanni de' Medici, considered the best captain in the League's armies,[55] had been killed trying to oppose their crossing the Po. They spent months near Piacenza, enduring the privations of a bitter winter, waiting for Bourbon to bring his troops to join them. Bourbon feared the Milanese would rebel if the Imperial troops left, and doubted his troops would move unless they were paid. Eventually he gathered some funds and could join Frundsberg in February 1527. In early March, the army was said to consist of 700 lances, 800 light horse and 18,000 infantry, 10,000 German, 5,000 Spanish and 3,000 Italian.[56] Some persuasion was needed before Antonio de Leyva agreed to stay guarding Milan, because of the difficulties he justifiably feared he would face finding the money to maintain the garrison.

Bourbon and Frundsberg had serious problems too. In mid-March, the German troops threatened their commanders. Bourbon had to leave his pavilion to be ransacked, while Frundsberg suffered an apoplectic fit under the strain of trying to quell the mutiny, and left for Ferrara to recuperate.

When news came to the camp of the truce with Clement and the soldiers were told to return to Lombardy, they refused. They were set on going to Florence, if not Rome, and their commanders could not win them round. Bourbon sent to Rome to say that unless 150,000 ducats or more were paid, he would have no choice but to go on with the army. Lannoy, who came from Rome, was unable to get a different answer. As Bourbon would be disobeying Imperial orders by continuing, Vasto left the camp and Lannoy went to Siena. The army proceeded to Tuscany, beginning to look and behave less like an Imperial army and more like a fourteenth-century mercenary company.

The forces of the League shadowed it, but did not try to attack. Part of the Venetian army was left behind to guard eastern Lombardy. The Venetians had given their usual orders to their captain-general, who was also the commander of the League. Urbino himself made this explicit – they would do all they could to protect the territory of Florence and the pope, but 'always with the preservation of the Venetian states in mind, which depends on keeping our army intact'.[57] The rhetoric of the defence of Italy that had accompanied the negotiation of the League of Cognac did not mean that the perspective of the Venetians had changed. At this time they were also unsure what the pope would do. Saluzzo did not have enough troops to take the initiative against the Imperial army on his own, even if he had been inclined to; he was working in close co-ordination with Urbino. Considering the League dissolved by Clement's defection, the Venetians made a separate accord with Francis in late April,[58] unaware that in Rome Clement had switched again, and negotiated new terms with the French and Venetian ambassadors there. Defending the pope and the Florentines was to be the main purpose of the renewed league; France and Venice were to pay substantial subsidies to the pope.[59] Francis and the Venetians rejected these terms as placing too much of a burden onto them.

The Florentines also felt that Clement's demands on them were excessive, and there was growing discontent with the Medici regime there. The city refused to pay any more to support Clement's wars, but would contribute something to appease Bourbon's troops. Appeals were sent to the armies of the League to come to defend Florence, and when the Imperial army crossed the Apennines into Tuscany, they came too. Neither Francis nor the Venetians wished to see Florence sacked; they wanted to bring Florence into the League, separately from Clement. On 26 April, Saluzzo and Urbino went to the city; their arrival put an end to an uprising that had broken out on that day. It was agreed that Florence would enter the League, and contribute 5,000 infantry, 200 men-at-arms and 500 light horse.[60] San Leo, a fortress given to Florence by Leo X, was restored to the Duke of Urbino.

As attacking Florence, guarded by the forces of the League, now looked a lengthy and difficult enterprise, the Imperial army marched rapidly south to the Papal States. The League's army followed, at a more leisurely pace. Their commanders, above all Urbino, have often been condemned for failing to stop, or even attempting to stop, the Imperial army as it made its inexorable way to Rome. It is from the perspective of hindsight that their failings loom so large; they could not anticipate that the great city of Rome would fall to the assault of a mutinous army, in a single day.

The Sack of Rome

The army arrived beneath the walls of Rome on 5 May. Bourbon's demand that they be admitted to the city was rejected by the pope. Only 3,000 infantry were available to Renzo da Ceri, who was in command of the defences of Rome; some were inexperienced men recruited from the cardinals' households. Early on the morning of 6 May, the Spanish and German infantry scaled the walls of the Borgo, aided by a mist which prevented the artillerymen in the Castel Sant'Angelo from seeing their targets. They met little resistance, but they did lose their commander, as Bourbon was killed by an arquebus shot as he led the assault. The troops quickly overran the Borgo, slaughtering those who tried to defend it; Clement barely had time to escape to the Castel Sant'Angelo. Demands from the captains for quarters in the city and the payment of their arrears were refused – and the Sack of Rome began.

At last the soldiers had the opportunity for plunder they had been longing for through the hardships of the winter and the march south. They spared no one who came into their hands, man, woman or child, lay or ecclesiastic, Italian, French, Spanish or German. Even the Imperial agents in Rome, such as the embassy secretary Juan Perez (who had been acting as an envoy since the death of Sessa in August 1526), were forced to pay ransoms. The Colonna came to Rome on 10 May with men from their estates; when they fell to looting, Cardinal Colonna called them off, but could do nothing to stop the atrocities happening throughout the city.

The Lutheranism of many of the landsknechts gave an additional dimension to the acts of sacrilege – the looting of precious church vessels, the rape of nuns – that were often a feature of the sack of cities. Reliquaries were smashed, tombs, including those of the popes, rifled. Parody masses were held, and there was a parody election of a 'pope' by the landsknechts. Graffiti praising Luther can still be seen etched into the frescoes in the Vatican. It was such sacrilege in the city of the Prince of the Apostles, the profanation of relics and shrines in churches which had been visited by pilgrims from all over Europe, that was considered particularly shocking.

Equally lamentable to some, was the dispersal of the community of artists and scholars who had gathered in Rome, making the city a major centre of Renaissance culture. The members of this community were scattered throughout Italy; some returned to Rome in later years, but many did not, to the gain of other places and therefore, perhaps, ultimately to the cultural benefit of Italy. Rome would recover and become once again a centre of art and learning, but the spirit of the artists and scholars and of their patrons would be different. There would be less emphasis on Renaissance Rome as the revival of classical Rome. To many of those who experienced the sack, or only heard reports of it, it was a deeply sobering event that gave impetus to the desire for religious and ecclesiastical reform.

At the Imperial court there was general regret, rather than rejoicing. Letters were sent to other powers, denying the sack had been on Charles's orders or by his wish, arguing the pope had brought it on himself.[61] Others could also see it in that light, blaming Clement's political mistakes or his spiritual shortcomings or the sins of papal Rome, while still regarding the sack as a dreadful tragedy. There were fears that Clement, besieged in the Castel Sant'Angelo, might be carried to Spain and that the emperor would take control of the papacy. Some Imperial agents in Italy were indeed suggesting that. The emperor was also urged to make provision for the government of Rome, to consider himself to be lord of Italy.[62]

In fact, it was the soldiers who controlled Rome, and no one could control them. Bourbon's death had left them without a commander. Philibert de Châlons, the Prince of Orange, was of suitable rank, and was popular with the landsknechts, but the other Imperial generals and officials considered him too young and inexperienced for the position. The troops were unwilling to accept Lannoy as commander, after his efforts to persuade them not to come south, and when Lannoy came to Rome he soon departed for Naples. He suggested Moncada, who had arrived with del Vasto, Alarcon and troops from the kingdom, might take command of the army but Moncada was not keen. Charles was urged to appoint a captain-general; he thought the Duke of Ferrara would be suitable.[63] Alfonso, however, made his excuses, pleading ill-health. In reality he, like the others, did not want to take on responsibility for the troops who, despite all their loot, were still demanding their pay.[64] The Prince of Orange also became disenchanted with the idea of commanding such troops when they began to turn on him, plundering his lodgings, and he left Rome for Siena.

The number of troops in Rome had been swollen, not only by those brought from Naples but by thousands who came on their own initiative to join in the continuing sack. But many were dying from the epidemics infesting the city, along with the unfortunate inhabitants of Rome who had not yet fled, and suffering from the shortages of basic necessities for there was little to buy with their ill-gotten gains. Some took what they had and left. The generals wanted to move the army on – to Florence, to extort money to pay them and to prevent the Florentines helping the League, or to Lombardy to support de Leyva – but the Spanish and German captains were determined to have money from Clement before they would leave Rome, or let him leave the Castel Sant'Angelo.

Desperate as Clement's situation appeared, he still hoped the army of the League under Saluzzo and Urbino would come to his rescue. They approached Rome and there were some skirmishes, but their army was starving and diminishing. While he had hopes of help, Clement temporized, before agreeing terms on 5 June. The garrison of the Castel Sant'Angelo, with their commanders Renzo da Ceri and Orazio Baglioni, could leave unmolested. Clement was to provide a total of 400,000 scudi to pay the army, and hand over Ostia, Civitavecchia, Modena, Parma and Piacenza; as well as several hostages. When the first tranche of 100,000 ducats had been paid, Ostia and Civitavecchia were in Imperial custody and arrangements in train to fulfil the rest of the conditions, Clement and the cardinals with him could leave for Naples.[65]

A garrison of German and Spanish troops under Alarcon entered the Castel Sant'Angelo, guarding the pope. Ostia was soon handed over; Civitavecchia not until the end of June, because separate arrangements had to be made with Andrea Doria, whose galleys were based there. Parma and Piacenza refused to submit, encouraged by secret instructions from the pope, and Alfonso d'Este recovered Modena for himself. Elsewhere in the Papal States, others took advantage of the opportunity to revive their claims. The Malatesta returned in June to Rimini, from which they had been expelled by Cesare Borgia, holding on to it for a year. Venice occupied Ravenna and Cervia, initially to protect them from some Spanish troops that Bourbon had left at Cotignola, but then the Venetians decided to reinstate their own government there. Worst of all for Clement, perhaps, was the overthrow of the Medici regime in Florence, within days of the news of the Sack of Rome reaching the city.

Florence remained a member of the League, taking on some of the troops who had been in the service of Clement, including Giovanni de' Medici's former company, known as the Black Bands because of the mourning they wore for him. Orazio Baglioni was appointed captain-general of the Florentine infantry, and he and the Black Bands were sent to the League's camp. By late June, this was based in Umbria, waiting to see what the Imperial army in Rome would do, ready to block its return to Lombardy or to defend Florence.

During the period from July to September, many of the infantry in Rome moved out of the city to the south of Umbria looking for food and respite from the heat and epidemics. Thanks to the favour of the Colonna, Ghibelline towns such as Rieti and Terni were spared, and the troops concentrated their attention on Spoleto, Todi and Narni, towns dominated by Guelfs. Most of the fighting that did take place around Rome had more of the character of faction-fighting between Guelfs and Ghibellines, Orsini and Colonna, than of confrontation between the forces of the League and the emperor. At Rome the Colonna saw to guarding the city gates, and Cardinal Colonna was considered to have some influence with the German troops, who used the Colonna palace as a place to keep their hostages and held some of their meetings there.[66]

Neither Cardinal Colonna nor the Imperial commanders could control the infantry. The captains of the companies, who negotiated for them, acted more like spokesmen for the men than officers taking decisions on their behalf, and came under threat if they did not act as the men wished. Landsknechts were accustomed to debating and making decisions collectively. The Spanish and Italian infantry were not so organized or democratic in the way they formulated their demands, and were somewhat more tractable. When money was available to pay the troops, the Germans would be given priority, then the Spanish, then the Italians. The cavalry, quartered outside Rome, were last in line. The problem was that by the time money had been scraped together in Naples, extracted from the pope or even sent from Spain, to meet one set of demands, months would have passed and new arrears built up, so there would be further demands to be met. Until the men were satisfied, they refused to march back to Lombardy.

It took months to get through to Charles that his army was not heading back to Lombardy, and was not being supported, as he wished to believe, by money from the pope and Florence.[67] Eventually he began to order substantial sums to be sent, but then it could take months to arrange the transfer of funds. And Charles still had the problem of finding a suitable commander prepared to assume the risky responsibility for the army. Lannoy died in September; Moncada was appointed viceroy of Naples in his place and stayed there. The Duke of Ferrara continued to refuse the appointment, and then went over to the League. Charles then appointed the Prince of Orange, who returned to Rome in December and after some hesitation agreed, and the other commanders accepted him as captain-general.

It also took months for the emperor's orders that the pope should be released from detention in the Castel Sant'Angelo to be carried out. The landsknechts wanted to keep him as security for the money he had pledged to pay. To be liberated, Clement had to make two new treaties, both signed on 26 November. One was with the captains of the army concerning the payment of about 370,000 scudi, specifying how and when it was to be paid.[68] The other was agreed with a representative of the emperor, Francisco Fernández de Quiñones, the general of the Franciscan order. Clement promised to call a council to reform the Church and extirpate the Lutheran heresy, and to yield as security custody of Ostia, Civitavecchia, Civita Castellana and Forlì, as well as several hostages, including Ippolito and Alessandro de' Medici.[69] Clement was allowed to leave on 6 December, slipping away in disguise before daybreak (for the landsknechts were still unwilling to see him released), and going to Orvieto.

Again his obligations under these treaties were only fulfilled in part. Ostia and Civitavecchia were already in Imperial custody, but Civita Castellana and Forlì were not handed over, and he did not keep up the payments he had pledged to make. Ambassadors of the League hurried to Orvieto where Clement had set up his impoverished court. Before Clement would consider joining it again, however, he demanded that the Venetians must return Ravenna and Cervia, which they were determined to keep. Nor did he approve terms that had been granted to the Duke of Ferrara to win him over to the League, including recognition of his possession of Modena and Reggio. Another difficulty was that Florence, governed by a regime hostile to the Medici, was also a member.

The war in Lombardy, 1527–8

While the Imperial army in Rome was refusing to return to Lombardy, de Leyva was left to hold on to what positions remained there, with inadequate forces and funds. He had little contact with Spain, or with the other army. Although he felt abandoned, he carried on resolutely, despite the fact he could not rely on the troops, especially the landsknechts, to fight if their pay was in arrears, as it generally was.

De Leyva calculated that he was confronted by 13,000–14,000 infantry, 500 men-at-arms and 700 light horse of the Venetians and Francesco Sforza.[70] He believed his men were outnumbered four to one, but decided to go to challenge the Venetians and Sforza when they came to Marignano. On reaching Marignano, he attacked with only his Spanish and Italian troops – the Germans, not keen on night marches, had lagged behind – and succeeded in expelling them. They withdrew to a nearby encampment surrounded by ditches, where he penned then up. In late July, hearing that Giangiacomo de' Medici had arrived near Monza with several thousand Swiss in French pay, he went to attack them there. The Swiss and Grisons 'fought like devils', and he had never been in such a fierce fight in his life, the veteran commander reported to the emperor, but at the third assault his men had prevailed.[71]

Other Swiss had come and Lautrec had arrived in Lombardy with a French army. Francis had decided to send an army as soon as reports arrived of the Sack of Rome.[72] He also took Andrea Doria into his service with eight galleys. Doria joined the French fleet under Pedro Navarro blockading Genoa, and a detachment of French infantry under Cesare Campofregoso (the son of the former doge Giano Campofregoso) was sent to attack from the landward side. Genoa surrendered on 18 August. The day after, Teodoro Trivulzio arrived to be governor of Genoa for Francis. This was a considerable blow to the Imperial forces, especially in Lombardy. Genoa was their main channel of communication with Spain, and a major source of finance, as Genoese bankers were used to cashing Imperial letters of credit.

The loss of Genoa was followed by the fall of Alessandria to Lautrec on 12 September. De Leyva concentrated his remaining forces at Milan (2,200 Spanish, 3,400 Germans and 1,000 Italians) and Pavia (2,000 Italians, 30 men-at-arms and 100 light horse, under Lodovico Belgioioso).[73] Lautrec approached Milan, but then joined up with Francesco Sforza and the Venetians under Giano Campofregoso, who were still based at Marignano. Together, they went to attack Pavia. Artillery fire soon breached the crumbling walls of the castle. The city was taken on 5 October, and subjected to a vicious sack, as revenge for the king's defeat there.

Imperial forces still held Milan, Como, and the strongholds of Trezzo, Pizzighettone and Monza. The Venetians – estimated to have 6,000 infantry, 500 men-at-arms and 600 light horse[74] – returned to quarters near Milan. Lautrec, whose forces were said to have diminished with the departure of nearly all the Swiss to 8,000 infantry and 300 men-at-arms,[75] turned south. At the insistence of the Venetians, Lautrec had rather unwillingly handed over Alessandria to Francesco Sforza, and he put a French garrison in Pavia. Nevertheless, Sforza and the Venetians wanted him to continue the conquest of the duchy. Lautrec decided instead to carry on with his primary task, to go to Rome to free the pope, and then on to Naples. He took his men to Bologna, awaiting the arrival of reinforcements of landsknechts led by Vaudemont.

While waiting, he persuaded the Duke of Ferrara to come over to the League in mid-November. He was to provide 100 men-at-arms and 6,000 ducats a month, in return for benefits including the protection of the League and recognition of his possession of Ferrara, Modena and Reggio, and the marriage of his son Ercole to Renée of France, daughter of Louis XII.[76] Lautrec also brought Federico Gonzaga into the League in early December. He was to provide 80 lances and 6,000 scudi a month, to be appointed captain-general in Lombardy, and to be given revenues in Milan, Naples and Venice.[77]

The invasion of Naples, 1528

After Vaudemont had arrived with 3,000 landsknechts, Lautrec set off for the kingdom of Naples, heading for the Abruzzi, a stronghold of Angevin sympathies. A thousand landsknechts in the pay of Venice also joined the army on the way. It crossed the river Tronto into the kingdom on 10 February. Conquest of the Abruzzi, including the important city of L'Aquila, proved easy, as Imperial garrisons withdrew and the army was welcomed by many barons and communities, and Lautrec pushed on into Apulia. The French had reached the kingdom before the Imperial commanders could move their army from Rome. After a final effort to get together enough money to satisfy the troops, they were at last able to leave on 17 February. Orange decided to head for the city of Naples, but a council of war at Benevento then agreed that, leaving some troops to defend Naples and the surrounding provinces, the bulk of the army should go to Troia to confront Lautrec.[78]

Del Vasto went in advance and prevented Troia falling to the French; Orange arrived there on 4 March. Lautrec brought his troops up, and for a week or so the two armies were encamped within a few miles of each other. There was much skirmishing, but the Imperial commanders, knowing they were outnumbered, avoided battle. Lautrec's forces were increased during March by the arrival of the lances of Alfonso d'Este and Federico Gonzaga, of Saluzzo with his 1,000 foot and 100 lances, of the Florentine Black Bands a fortnight later, and at the end of the month of the Venetian commissioner Alvise Pisani with around 2,000 infantry.[79] The Imperial army, their numerical inferiority compounded by difficulties with supplies, fell back on Naples. Unsure of the temper of the Neapolitans and of the soldiers, the commanders had planned to defend the city from entrenchments outside the walls; then, fearing the soldiers would force their way in anyway, they moved them inside.

The League army proceeded to take most of the remainder of Apulia before turning for Naples at the end of March. Heavy rains and shortages of provisions slowed their progress. Having captured various strongholds in the area around Naples, such as Capua and Aversa, they settled to besiege the city. They were believed to have around 20,000 men, the Imperial forces 12,000 when the siege began at the end of April.[80] Naples was one of the largest cities in Europe. Elaborate siegeworks designed by Pedro Navarro were constructed slowly, and never completed. The main camp was situated on the hill of Poggioreale, with its luxurious villas and beautiful gardens overlooking the city. The artillery was placed on the heights, but its fire proved more of a nuisance than a menace to the city's defences.

The harbour was blockaded by eight galleys of Andrea Doria under the command of his nephew Filippino, not enough to cut off seaborne supplies completely. A Venetian fleet was expected to join them, but at this time it was off the coast of Apulia, helping to capture the ports Venice had held there at the beginning of the century and given back in 1509. Moncada decided to try to rid the harbour of Doria's galleys. Filippino Doria had warning of the attack, and took on board some troops from the League's camp. Moncada had six galleys to Doria's eight, but he also had a number of smaller armed vessels with him when he joined battle on 28 April off the Capo d'Orso. What ensued was the major naval battle of the Italian Wars. It ended in defeat for Moncada, who was killed; four of the Imperial galleys were lost; among the prisoners were del Vasto and Ascanio Colonna. Yet Doria's fleet was badly damaged too, and in no condition to enforce the blockade.[81] Moncada's critics may have exaggerated the significance of the defeat; Orange, his rival for the control of Naples, and his supporters had not approved the venture.

The arrival of a Venetian fleet of 16 galleys on 12 June tightened the sea blockade again, but the port of Gaeta was still open, so that grain ships from Sicily could unload there and some of their cargo could get through to Naples. The Imperial light horse was able to gather in supplies from the countryside, as well as harassing the League's outposts and foraging parties. There were few light horse in the League camp, and the French did not really know how to use them or fully appreciate their value. This

lack of light horse also told in the skirmishes, in which the League generally had the worst of it. The French men-at-arms were quartered away
from the camp, and would not mount effective patrols.[82] The troops in the
League's camp suffered even more than those in the city from shortages.
They also suffered more from epidemics of fever, which were exacerbated
by disturbances caused by the siegeworks to water courses flooding the
ground near the camp.

Lautrec's problems were multiplied by the attitude of his king, who
had already reduced the funding allocated to the army before it went to
Naples. Now he ordered Lautrec not to let the Venetians take over any
more territory in the kingdom. They were supposed to have half of any
conquests, and already felt they were not getting their share; Lautrec did
not try to implement this instruction.[83] Francis also lost him the support of
Doria's fleet. Even before the king demanded that Doria should surrender
Ascanio Colonna and del Vasto to him, he had been dissatisfied with his
treatment by Francis. During negotiations for the ransom of the prisoners,
who Doria had refused to send to France, his discontent was evident. So
eager were de Leyva and Orange to have him on their side, considering
how useful he could be in keeping open their lines of communication with
Spain, that they accepted as part of the terms of his contract an undertaking that Genoa when freed from French rule would be an independent
republic under no obligation to pay anything for Imperial protection.[84]

On the expiration of Doria's contract with Francis at the end of June,
his galleys left Naples (they would return, with Doria, bringing supplies
to the city). Then the Venetian fleet left for Calabria to pick up supplies
in mid-July. A few days later, the French fleet came, bringing only 800
infantry, and insufficient money to make up the arrears owing to Lautrec's
men. The new arrivals, who included Renzo da Ceri, had to fight their way
to the League's camp and the troops sent to escort them suffered heavy casualties. Lautrec was sick, but determined to persevere with the siege. Renzo
da Ceri had sufficient personal authority to speak freely to the haughty
Lautrec, who was not given to taking advice, and stressed the need for
reinforcements. He was despatched to recruit infantry and light horse in
the Abruzzi. It was too late. There not enough soldiers in the League camp
fit for active service to protect their own positions. Lautrec died during the
night of 15–16 August; Vaudemont, his second-in-command, was already
dead, as was the Venetian commissioner Pisani. Command of what was left
of the League's army fell to Saluzzo, who soon raised the siege.

On 29 August fewer than 7,000 men had enough strength to join the
retreat, leaving the sick, most of the baggage and the artillery behind.

Unwisely, Saluzzo divided the remnants of the army into the three classic units, enabling a few hundred Imperial light horse under Ferrante Gonzaga to disperse first the rearguard, then the battle; among those captured was Pedro Navarro. Saluzzo and the vanguard of around 3,000 men managed to reach Aversa. With no food, no artillery and no will to fight on, they could not hold out when the Imperial army came. By the terms of surrender dated 30 August, all the places held by the French and Venice in the kingdom were to be handed over.[85] Saluzzo soon died in captivity in Naples. Pedro Navarro, on the orders of Charles V, was sentenced to death; he died in prison, perhaps with some assistance, before he could be executed. Some Italian and German troops of the League were able to enlist in the Imperial army; few of the French and Swiss, stripped of their arms and armour, survived the perilous journey home on foot. Some were killed, many weakened by disease and privation died on the road. Another French army had been destroyed in the kingdom of Naples. The Black Bands, the only unit of Italian infantry to achieve a reputation as crack shock troops, split up.

Triumphant as the Imperial commanders were, they still had to face the problems of satisfying and controlling their army. Charles was warned that it was a matter of urgency to send them out of the ruined kingdom[86] – but first they had to be paid. The captains were demanding rewards and recognition for their services. Orange awarded pensions to the officers, and estates and titles provisionally to the captains, pending confirmation by the emperor. So many barons came under suspicion of collaboration with the French that their prosecution appeared to be driven by the need for money and property to give to those claiming reward. Charles was warned that three-quarters of the barons would be forced into exile; that the kingdom would be destroyed; that the soldiers to whom estates had been granted had already begun to sell them.[87]

The war in the kingdom of Naples was not over yet. There was still fighting in the Abruzzi and Apulia, where Renzo da Ceri was fighting for the French, based at Barletta, and the Venetians still held Trani, Monopoli and Polignano. They had some 10,000 infantry and 1,000 horse between them.[88] There were still strong Angevin sympathies in the region, among the barons and communities. L'Aquila and Amatrice rebelled; Orange went in person to suppress their revolts in February 1529. To punish L'Aquila, its extensive territory was divided up into about forty fiefs, that were given largely to Spanish captains. This was a grievous blow to the city, which never recovered control of its territory. Renzo da Ceri and the Venetians held on, their resistance aided by the difficulties the Imperial commanders had in getting their men to agree to go to the Abruzzi and Apulia to fight. The places they held would not be recovered by conquest but by cession in the treaty of Cambrai in August 1529 and the treaty the Venetians made with Charles at Bologna in December 1529.

The last campaign in Lombardy, 1528–9

During the siege of Naples, the Imperial army had been expecting the arrival of a relief force sent by the Archduke Ferdinand under Henry, Duke of Brunswick. It was reported that he would bring 20,000 infantry and 1,700 horse, but he probably brought far fewer.[89] Under orders from Ferdinand and the emperor to march to Naples, Brunswick showed little inclination to go. Charles had sent some money for these troops, but Brunswick anticipated they would largely be paid in Lombardy. Young and inexperienced, he was dependent on the advice of a council of captains who were not much interested in looking for a fight. Entering Venetian territory in early May, and having taken Peschiera, the army moved slowly to meet up with de Leyva with some of the troops from Milan. De Leyva had been taking the war to the League forces in the Milanese, capturing Pavia and Abbiategrasso, and together with Brunswick set siege to Lodi on 20 June. Disease soon broke out in the camp. Some of Brunswick's men had already headed home; at one point he had to leave the camp for his own safety after his men threatened to kill him if he did not pay them,[90] and they refused to assault Lodi. By late July, the camp was breaking up. Brunswick blamed the Imperial officials in Lombardy for not providing the funds he asked for; the officials and commanders blamed Brunswick's lack of experience and the insatiable, undisciplined German troops. This episode deepened the disillusion of the emperor's agents in Italy with using German troops there.

To counter Brunswick's forces, Francis had planned to send 400 lances and 10,000 infantry under the comte de Saint-Pol.[91] In the event, Saint-Pol only arrived in Piedmont, with rather fewer men, in early August. He joined up with the Venetian army under the Duke of Urbino, and they decided to attack Pavia. Taken on 19 September, the miserable city was sacked again. No quarter was given to the German and Spanish soldiers there; the Italian troops were spared. The fortress fell soon after.

Saint-Pol did not send reinforcements for Genoa requested by Teodoro Trivulzio, who was concerned for the security of the city; Trivulzio withdrew to the Castelleto. The French fleet, which had evaded Doria's vessels off Naples, came to Genoa, but when Doria's galleys approached, it sailed for the safety of Savona. Doria had only 500 infantry on board when he entered the harbour of Genoa on 12 September, but encountered no resistance in a city desolated by an epidemic. In early October, Saint-Pol brought his army up to Genoa to try to recover the situation and called on the citizens to submit. But the Genoese had gathered forces to defend themselves, Saint-Pol's own troops were deserting him, and he turned back. By the end of October, the French forces in Savona and in the Castelleto had surrendered.

Under the aegis of Andrea Doria, the Genoese were able to recover their independence, and to implement long-contemplated institutional reforms to eliminate the influence of the factions which the Genoese believed had been the cause of their domination by foreign powers. Doria would be the powerful *eminence grise* of what the Genoese called their 'new republic'. Opponents accused him of being the virtual ruler of Genoa, but he did not attempt to undermine the new constitution. His galleys and his reputation as a naval commander were of such importance to Charles V, who believed they were vital to control of the seas between Italy and Spain, that Doria was able to shield Genoa from pressure to accept subjection to the emperor.

Both the League and Imperial armies in Lombardy retired to winter quarters, de Leyva to Milan, the Venetians on the Adda, Francesco Sforza in Pavia and Lodi, Saint-Pol at Alessandria. Saint-Pol was the most active, launching assaults on Genoese territory. He went to attack the stronghold of Gavi in early December, and when Genoese forces moved up to defend it, tried a surprise attack on Genoa with 2,000 infantry and 200 horse. Appearing on 19 December, he saw the Genoese were prepared for defence, and retired. By chance, on that day and the next, a detachment of infantry arrived by sea from Spain.[92] The Genoese offered to raise 2,000 men and join de Leyva in an attack on the French, but de Leyva was unable to do so. In poor health throughout the winter, he still had problems with feeding, paying and controlling his men. By January, there were only 2,000 landsknechts left in Milan, with 800 Spanish infantry, some Italian troops and a little cavalry.[93] De Leyva and Doria asked Orange to send reinforcements from Naples, but there were insufficient troops there to send an army north as well as continuing the campaign in Apulia.[94]

No great sense of urgency marked the beginning of yet another season of the war in Lombardy. Doria sent the Spanish infantry at Genoa to Milan, which helped de Leyva make a sortie towards Pavia in late April. He returned to Milan as the Venetians and Francesco Sforza joined forces, and Saint-Pol, advancing from Alessandria, took Mortara and the fortress of Vigevano. The commanders of the League discussed investing Milan, but could not decide how best to do it, and did not really have sufficient men anyway, so Saint-Pol decided to make another attempt on Genoa. On 21 June, his army was at Landriano, in some disorder. Hearing they were on the move and vulnerable, de Leyva, carried in his usual chair, led his men on a night march from Milan and took the French by surprise as they were preparing to move on. Some resistance was put up by Saint-Pol's French and Italian troops, but his Swiss and landsknechts were unwilling to fight. Within a few hours, his army had been dispersed. Saint-Pol, having fought on foot with a pike, tried to escape on horseback, but was captured when his tired horse could not jump a watercourse. Few men died at Landriano, but many were wounded and around 3,000 were taken prisoner.[95] It was the last battle of the war in Lombardy. When he heard of the loss of the French army, Francesco Sforza panicked and fled from Lodi to Crema; the Venetians went onto the defensive, digging in near Cassano.

The Treaties of Barcelona and Cambrai

Even before Saint-Pol's army was scattered at Landriano, diplomatic settlements marking a significant stage in the Italian Wars were under way. News of the French defeat had little influence on their outcome. It was already clear that Charles had the upper hand, but he wanted a halt to his war with Francis as much as the king did. He had other pressing matters to attend to, especially the religious strife in Germany. Before he went to deal with that, he wanted to go to Italy to be crowned emperor.

As he had to be crowned by the pope, Charles needed to come to an understanding with Clement. The pope was ready to make a treaty with him. The obstacles to his joining the League remained, and Charles was prepared to make the promises he desired: that Venice would be made to restore Ravenna and Cervia, and the Duke of Ferrara yield Modena and Reggio; that Imperial troops would help the Medici return to Florence, and Charles's natural daughter Margaret would marry Alessandro de' Medici; that Francesco Sforza would be restored to the duchy of Milan, if he was found innocent; if not, Charles would not dispose of the duchy without Clement's approval. In return, Clement would renew the investiture of the kingdom of Naples, make concessions over benefices and taxes on the clergy and ecclesiastical property, and grant absolution for all those involved in the Sack of Rome. This treaty was signed at Barcelona at the end of June 1529.

Charles's project to travel to Italy had long been known. Keen to prevent it or forestall it, Francis had been discussing plans with his Italian allies for a new campaign, for the king to come to Italy himself or send an army to the Spanish frontier.[96] His allies were aware there was little prospect of either. Both Francis and Charles were ready for peace. Negotiations were conducted at one remove, through Charles's aunt Margaret, regent of Flanders and Francis's mother, Louise of Savoy. Much diplomatic spadework was put in before the ladies met at Cambrai in July, yet the talks there were no formality. The two tough, intelligent women were each determined to get the best terms they could. The fact the negotiations were conducted by them, not directly for Charles and Francis, permitted the exclusion of other powers, including the pope and the king of England. Several Italian powers had envoys at Cambrai, but they were anxious spectators, not participants. Francis promised his allies their interests would be looked after, but they were not.

In large part, the Treaty of Cambrai concluded in early August 1529 was a repeat of the Treaty of Madrid of 1526, with the significant changes that Charles would now accept a cash ransom for the sons of Francis, still held hostage in Spain, and would no longer insist on the cession of the duchy of Burgundy. Francis renounced all his interests in Italy, and would give up all territories still held for him there. He abandoned his Italian allies, offering lame excuses to their envoys for his breach of faith.[97] The Italian powers would be left to make the best terms they could for themselves with the emperor.

Notes

1   Gattoni, 306–12.

2   Rodríguez-Salgado, 28–30.

3   Guicciardini, *Carteggi*, IV, 132.

4   Sanuto, XXXII, 133.

5   De Leva, II, 175.

6   Gianpaolo Baglioni, who had been distrusted by Leo, had been summoned to Rome in 1520, and on his arrival there under a safeconduct from the pope had been arrested and executed; his position in Perugia had been taken by his more compliant cousin Gentile.

7   Dennistoun, II, 412–13.

8   Knecht, 114.

9   Sanuto, XXXIII, 7.

10 Pacheco y de Leyva, 251–2: Charles V to Najera, 11 Apr. 1522.

11 *Ibid.*, 263: Najera to Charles, 24 Apr. 1522.

12 *Ibid.*, 264.

13 Bourrilly and Vindry, I, 227.

14 Giovio, 290.

15 Bourrilly and Vindry, I, 224–30; Pieri, 541–6; Sanuto, XXXIII, 197, 198, 200, 211, 213–4; Pacheco y de Leyva, 268–71: Najera to Charles, 27 Apr. 1522, Bicocca; Giovio, 288–94.

16 Sanuto, XXXIII, 282–5; Pacheco y de Leyva, 298–301; Pacini, 86–101.

17 Gachard, 133–6: Adrian VI to Charles, 21 Nov. 1522.

18 *CSPSpan*, II, 484.

19 Shaw, 'The papacy', 113–14.

20 Guicciardini, *Storia d'Italia*, Book XV, Chap. 3; *LP*, III, part 2, 1333–4.

21 *CSPSpan*, II, 587–8: Charles to duca di Sessa, 2 Oct. 1523.

22 *Ibid.*, 570–1.

23 Sanuto, XXXIV, 420–1. According to du Bellay (Bourrilly and Vindry, I, 282), there were 1,400–1,500 men-at-arms and 24,000–27,000 infantry; according to Guicciardini, *Storia d'Italia*, Book XV, Chap. 3, followed by Pieri, 547, 1,800 lances and 31,000 infantry.

24 Guicciardini, *Storia d'Italia*, Book XV, Chap. 5.

25 *Ibid.*

26 *Ibid.*, Chap. 6.

27 Halkin and Dansaert, 209–12: Lannoy to Charles V, 21 Feb., 18 Mar. 1524.

28 *CSPSpan*, II, 639–40.

29 Halkin and Dansaert, 242–4: Lannoy to Charles V, 28 Oct. 1524.

30 Desjardins and Canestrini, II, 787: Gianmatteo Giberti, 12 Nov. 1524, camp at Pavia.

31 Desjardins and Canestrini, II, 800–1.

32 *Ibid.*, II, 812–14.

33 Halkin and Dansaert, 258–60: Charles V to Lannoy, 5 Feb. 1525.

34 Sanuto, XXXVIII, 21.

35 Goubaux and Lemoisne, II, 241–2.

36 Lot, 54.

37 Sanuto, XXXVIII, 12–16, 20–3 (letter from Pescara), 39–43, 45–7, 52–3; Bourrilly and Vindry, I, 352–8; Goubaux and Lemoisne, II, 222–42; *LP*, IVi, 492–3; Canestrini, 319–20; *CSPSpan*, II, 708–9; Casali and Galandra; Mayer; Pieri, 558–66.

38 Sanuto, XXXVIII, 21; Najera attributed the plan to Lannoy (*CSPSpan*, II, 708).

39 Giovio, 414–5, 422.

40 Sanuto, XXXVIII, 23.

41 Halkin and Dansaert, 268: Charles V to Lannoy, 27 Mar. 1525.

42 *Ibid.*, 268–9.

43 De Leva, II, 248–9, 273.

44 *CSPSpan*, III, i, 105–8.

45 *Ibid.*, 332–3, 342.

46 *CSPVen*, III, 461.

47 De Leva, II, 293.

48 Dumont, IV, 1, 451–5.

49 *CSPSpan*, III, i, 767.

50 *CSPSpan*, III, i, 947–8.

51 Lanz, I, 213–6.

52 *Ibid.*, 215.

53 Sanuto, XLII, 355.

54 *Colección de documentos inéditos*, XXIV, 463–4: Ugo de Moncada, 16 Sept. 1526.

55 *CSPSpan*, III, i, 1037.

56 *CSPSpan*, III, ii, 91: Najera to Charles V, 3 Mar. 1527.

57 Sanuto, XLIV, 536.

58 Fraikin, 353–4.

59 Bourrilly, 42–3.

60 Roth, 39.

61 Lenzi, 136–40.

62 *CSPSpan*, III, ii, 219: Najera to Charles, 27 May 1527.

63 Halkin and Dansaert, 322–3: Charles V to Lannoy, 30 June 1527.

64 *CSPSpan*, III, ii, 316.

65 Sanuto, XLV, 245–9.

66 *CSPSpan*, III, ii, 476–7: Juan Perez to Charles, 30 Nov. 1527, Rome.

67 Lanz, I, 251–2: Pierre de Veyre to Charles, 30 Sept. 1527, Naples.

68 Dumont, IV, 1, 486–7.

69 De Leva, II, 455.

70 Lanz, I, 235: Antonio de Leyva to Charles, 14 July 1527.

71 *Ibid.*, 246: de Leyva to Charles, 4 Aug. 1527.

72 Desjardins and Canestrini, II, 955–7: Roberto Acciaiuoli, 4 June 1527, Paris.

73 *CSSpan*, III, ii, 399: de Leyva to Charles, 29 Sept. 1527.

74 *Ibid.*, 421: de Leyva to Charles, 18 Oct. 1527.

75 *Ibid.*

76 *Ibid.*, 462–3.

77 *Ibid.*, 693.

78 Dandolo, 248–53.

79 Arfaioli, 108–11.

80 Sanuto, XLVII, 383.

81 Arfaioli, 198–203.

82 *Ibid.*, 123–31.

83 Lanz, I, 273–4.

84 *CSPSpan*, III, ii, 765–7.

85 Molini, II, 84–6.

86 *CSPSpan*, III, ii, 856: Perez to Charles, 28 Nov. 1528, Naples.

87 *Ibid.*, 894: Cardinal Santacroce to Charles, 15 Feb. 1529, Rome.

88 *CSPVen*, IV, 175.

89 *CSPSpan*, III, ii, 686; Pieri, 583, gives a figure of 600 horse and 10,000 infantry.

90 *CSPSpan*, III, ii, 733.

91 *Ibid.*, 691.

92 *Ibid.*, 867.

93 *Ibid.*, 873.

94 *Ibid.*, 927.

95 Piacentini.

96 Molini, II, 177–89.

97 Desjardins and Canestrini, II, 1107–8.

Bibliography

Arfaioli, Maurizio, *The Black Bands of Giovanni* (Pisa: Plus, 2005).

Bennato, F., 'La partecipazione militare di Venezia alla Lega di Cognac', *Archivio veneto*, Ser. 5, 58–9 (1956), 70–87.

Bourrilly, V.-L., *Guillaume du Bellay, Seigneur de Langey, 1491–1543* (Paris: Société nouvelle de librairie et d'édition, 1905).

Bourrilly, V.-L. and F. Vindry (eds), *Mémoires de Martin et Guillaume du Bellay*, 4 vols (Paris: Renouard, 1908–19).

Brandi, Karl, *The Emperor Charles V. The Growth and Destiny of a Man and of a World-Empire*, trans. C.V. Wedgwood (London: Jonathan Cape, 1939).

Calendar of State Papers, Spanish (HMSO, 1862–1964) [*CSPSpan*].

Calendar of State Papers, Venetian (Longmans, 1864–98) [*CSPVen*].

Canestrini, Giuseppe, 'Documenti per servire all storia della milizia italiana', *Archivio storico italiano*, 15 (1851).

Casali, Luigi and Marco Galandra, *La battaglia di Pavia, 24 febbraio 1525* (Pavia: G. Iuculano, 1984, 1999).

Colección de documentos inéditos para la Historia de España, 112 vols (Madrid: Academia de la Historia, 1842–95), vols XXIV and XXXVIII.

Dandolo, Tullio, *Ricordi inediti di Gerolamo Morone* (2nd edition, Milan: Tipografia Arcivescovile, 1859).

de Leva, G., *Storia documentata di Carlo V in relazione all'Italia*, 5 vols (Venice: Naratovich, 1863-Bologna: Zanichelli, 1894).

Dennistoun, James, *Memoirs of the Dukes of Urbino*, ed. Edward Hutton, 3 vols (John Lane, 1909).

Desjardins, A. and G. Canestrini, *Négociations diplomatiques de la France avec la Toscane*, 6 vols (Paris: Imprimerie Impériale, 1859–86).

Duc, Séverin, 'Pavie en état de siège (octobre 1524-février 1525)', in Guido Alfani and Mario Rizzo (eds), *Nella morsa della guerra. Assedi, occupazioni militari e saccheggi in età preindustriale* (Milan: FrancoAngeli, 2013), 47–73.

Dumont, Jean, *Corps universel diplomatique du droit des gens*, 8 vols (Amsterdam, 1726–31).

Firpo, Massimo, *Il Sacco di Roma del 1527 tra profezia, propaganda politica e riforma religiosa* (Cagliari: CUEC, 1990).

Fraikin, J., *Nonciatures de Clément VII* (Paris: Alphonse Picard et Fils, 1906).

Gachard, Louis-Prosper (ed.), *Correspondance de Charles-Quint et d'Adrian VI* (Brussels: Hayez, 1859).

Gattoni, Maurizio, *Leone X e la geo-politica dello Stato pontificio (1513–1521)* (Città del Vaticano: Archivio Segreto Vaticano, 2000).

Giovio, Paolo, 'La vita del Marchese di Pescara', in Paolo Giovio, *Le vite del Gran Capitano e del Marchese di Pescara*, trans. Ludovico Domenichi, ed. Costantino Panigada (Bari: Laterza, 1931), 195–474.

Goubaux, Robert and P. André Lemoisne (eds), *Mémoires du Maréchal de Florange dit le Jeune Adventureux*, 2 vols (Paris: Librarie Renouard, 1913, 1924).

Guicciardini, Francesco, *Carteggi*, ed. Roberto Palmarocchi, 14 vols (Bologna: N. Zanichelli, 1938–72).

Guicciardini, Francesco, *Storia d'Italia* (various editions).

Halkin, Léon-E., and Georges Dansaert, *Charles de Lannoy, Vice-Roi de Naples* (Paris,1935).

Hook, Judith, 'Clement VII, the Colonna and Charles V: A study of the political instability of Italy in the second and third decades of the sixteenth century', *European Studies Review*, 2 (1972), 281–99.

Hook, Judith, *The Sack of Rome* (London: Macmillan, 1972).

Knecht, R.J. *Francis I* (Cambridge: Cambridge University Press, 1982).

Lanz, K., *Correspondenz des Kaisers Karl V*, 3 vols (Leipzig: Brockhaus, 1846).

Le Loyal Serviteur, *La très joyeuse, plaisante et récreative histoire du bon chevalier sans paour et sans reproche, gentil seigneur de Bayard*, in Joseph Michaud and Jean Joseph François Poujoulat (eds), *Nouvelle collection des mémoires pour servir à l'histoire de France*, Ser. 1, 12 vols (Paris: Guyot, 1850), IV.

Lenzi, Maria Ludovica, *Il Sacco di Roma del 1527* (Florence: La Nuova Italia, 1978).

Letters and Papers, Foreign and Domestic, of the Reign of Henry VIII, ed. J. S. Brewer et al., 21 vols, and *Addenda* (HMSO, 1862–1932) [*LP*].

Lot, Ferdinand Lot, *Recherches sur les effectifs des armées françaises des Guerres d'Italie aux Guerres de Religion 1494–1562* (Paris: SEVPEN, 1962).

Mayer, Jean-Paul, *Pavie. L'Italie joue son destin pour deux siècles* (Le Mans: Éditions Cénomane, 1998).

Molini, G. *Documenti di storia italiana*, 2 vols (Florence: Dante, 1836–7).

Pacheco y de Leyva, Enrique (ed.), *La politica española en Italia. Correspondencia di Don Fernando Marín, Abad de Nájera, con Carlos I* (Madrid: Revista de Archivos, Bibliotecas y Museos, 1919).

Pacini, Arturo, *I presupposti politici del 'secolo dei genovesi'. La riforma del 1528* (*Atti della Società ligure di storia patria*, 104 (1990), fasc. 1) (Genoa, 1990).

Piacentini, Massimo, *La giornata di Landriano del 21 giugno 1529. Storia della battaglia e del paese nel Rinascimento* (Landriano: Comune di Landriano, 1999).

Pieri, Piero, *Il Rinascimento e la crisi militare italiana* (Turin: Einaudi, 1952).

Rivero Rodriguez, Manuel, 'Italia, chiave della *Monarchia universalis*: il progetto politico del Gran Cancelliere Gattinara', *Archivio storico per le province napoletane*, 119 (2001), 275–88.

Rodríguez-Salgado, Mia J., 'Obeying the Ten Commandments: the first war between Charles V and Francis I, 1520–1529', Wim Blockmans and Nicolette Mout (eds), *The World of Emperor Charles V*

(Amsterdam: Royal Netherlands Academy of Arts and Sciences, 2004), 15–67.

Roth, Cecil, *The Last Florentine Republic* (London: Methuen, 1925).

Sanuto, Marino, *I Diarii*, ed. R. Fulin et al., 58 vols (Venice: Reale Deputazione veneta di storia patria, 1879–1903).

Shaw, Christine, 'The papacy and the European powers', in Christine Shaw (ed.), *Italy and the European Powers: The Impact of War, 1500–1530* (Leiden: Brill, 2006), 107–26.

Shaw, Christine, *The Political Role of the Orsini Family from Sixtus IV to Clement VII. Barons and Factions in the Papal States* (Rome: Istituto Storico Italiano per il Medio Evo, 2007).

CHAPTER 6

Testing the boundaries, 1529–47

As the Treaty of Cambrai was being concluded, Charles V was already on his way to Italy. Traditionally, this trip to Italy and the settlement of Italian affairs while Charles was there were seen as marking the end of Italian political liberty and independence, the beginning of a long period of Spanish oppression. But there was still much room for manoeuvre and evasion left to even the smaller Italian states and princes under the new dispensation, not least because French aspirations in Italy were by no means at an end. When this is borne in mind, the emperor's visit in 1529–30 looks somewhat less epoch-making, even if it did mark a transition to a new era of Italian politics, and of the Italian Wars.

Other than an intention to be crowned emperor by the pope, probably in Rome, Charles's plans were uncertain. He came prepared to make war, if need be. On the fleet with him were 9,000 Spanish infantry and 1,000 horse, and 8,000 landsknechts had been recruited in Germany and were on their way to Lombardy.[1] De Leyva was keen for the war in Lombardy to be continued. Under the terms of the treaty of Barcelona, Charles was bound to assist Clement against Florence, and the prince of Orange was coming north from Naples with his army to support the pope. Charles was thinking of going to the kingdom of Naples, where Renzo da Ceri and his troops and the Venetian forces had not been dislodged from Apulia, and the government in Naples was badly in need of reform.

Arriving at Genoa on 12 August 1529, Charles waited there for confirmation of the conclusion of the Treaty of Cambrai before moving on to Piacenza, where he stayed for several weeks. Although it was some months before Charles finally decided against going to Rome and Naples, in mid-September he asked the pope to come to meet him at Bologna. He was under pressure from his aunt Margaret and his brother Ferdinand to settle affairs in Italy as quickly as possible and then go to help Ferdinand, who was facing a challenge for the throne of Hungary and an invasion of his Austrian lands by the Turks, as well as the religious conflict in Germany. Adding to the uncertainty of his situation, was the attitude of the French. When Francis had ratified the Treaty of Cambrai, he had protested that he could not renounce Milan, Genoa and Asti. Feelers were put out to test whether Charles might consent to some arrangement whereby Francis might have Asti, or even Milan.[2] Charles would not do that, but he knew the pope and other Italian powers would not accept his keeping the duchy for himself. He had thought of dividing it up, granting some lands in fief, selling other portions to neighbouring states. Nevertheless, he was aware that the least controversial solution would be to leave Francesco Sforza as duke.

Awareness of all Charles's difficulties encouraged the Venetians not to capitulate to Charles and to continue to support Francesco Sforza, and hostilities in Lombardy did not cease. The troops sent from Germany stayed in Venetian territory, burning and plundering, and skirmishing with the Venetian army. Those from Milan, under the command of Lodovico Belgioioso (de Leyva had joined the emperor in Piacenza) took Pavia. Charles felt he lacked the resources to defeat Venice, however. As he later explained to his brother, he was running out of money to pay the soldiers he had with him, and to continue to fight the Venetians and Sforza would be to have 'war without end' in Italy. He decided that he needed to negotiate, not enforce, a settlement of Italian affairs, and to try in the process to raise some money there.[3]

Charles V and Clement VII in Bologna, 1529–30

Etiquette dictated that the emperor should travel to where the pope was, so Charles waited for Clement to reach Bologna, which he did on 24 October. Charles arrived there on 5 November, escorted by hundreds of sumptuously dressed courtiers, many Italians, including Andrea Doria and Alessandro de' Medici, and thousands of soldiers – more an army than a military escort. The emperor himself wore armour covered with brocade, except that on his head he wore a black velvet cap rather than a helmet, and he carried a golden baton.[4] Clement awaited him seated on a tribune on the steps of the great church of San Petronio; there Charles dismounted and paid reverence to the pope.

The emperor and the pope were lodged in adjoining apartments in the Palazzo Pubblico by San Petronio. They would be there for nearly five months, an unusual length of time for any monarchs, let alone the heads of the spiritual and secular hierarchies of Europe, to be in such proximity. It is not known what they said in their many private meetings over the winter; it can be safely guessed that Italian matters loomed large.

One topic was certainly Milan. If it could not go to Alessandro de' Medici, Clement's preference was for Francesco Sforza to keep it. Sforza and ambassadors from Venice came to Bologna, and treaties with both him and Venice were concluded on 23 December. He was to remain Duke of Milan, although at the cost of pledging to pay a total of 900,000 ducats – a sum the ravaged duchy could hardly afford – for his investiture. Como and the Castello of Milan were to be held by Imperial soldiers as security for the initial payments.[5] Once Charles agreed to Sforza keeping the duchy, the Venetians agreed to surrender the cities they held in Naples. Better to secure the possession of the whole of his kingdom than to remain locked in disputes with Venice by excluding Sforza from the duchy, Charles reasoned.[6] The Venetians undertook to pay an indemnity of 100,000 ducats for the costs of the war, with other payments dependent on settlement of their outstanding territorial disputes with Ferdinand. Ravenna and Cervia were to be restored to the pope. Both Venice and Charles would be obliged to defend Milan, and Venice to send 15 galleys when required for the defence of the kingdom of Naples.

This treaty was cast as a confederation of Ferdinand, the pope and Francesco Sforza, as well as Venice and the emperor, and the allies of the parties to it were to be included; Charles nominated Genoa, Siena, Lucca, the Duke of Savoy and the marquis of Mantua.[7] It never really came into effect. Rather than establishing a new state system in Italy, it would be used by the emperor and his men in their unceasing efforts to get other Italian powers to support the burden of the army in Italy. Charles himself in his long letter of 11 January 1530 to his brother, setting out what he had been doing and why and what he was trying to accomplish during his time in Italy, made no mention of an Italian league.[8]

Charles decided that he had to move on to Germany without going to Naples or Rome first; he would be crowned emperor at Bologna. The spectacular ceremony took place on 24 February, his thirtieth birthday. Two days before, he was crowned king of Italy with the iron crown of Lombardy by a Flemish cardinal, Guillaume Enckevoirt. This was an ancient imperial title and ceremony, not an assertion of hegemony. The elaborate rites of the imperial coronation were conducted according to the rituals that would have been used in Rome. Only one German prince, Duke Philip of Bavaria, was present, which left room for Italian princes to play a conspicuous part in the ceremonies. The marquis of Monferrato carried the imperial sceptre, the Duke of Urbino the imperial sword; the Duke of Savoy the crown itself.

The ceremony has been much discussed and studied. Did Charles V see himself either as the successor to the medieval emperors, as the papal, ecclesiastical rituals suggested, or as the successor to the emperors of ancient Rome, as the classical iconography of many of the decorations in the streets of Bologna implied? There is no direct record of what the emperor himself thought of the significance of the ceremonies and their settings. No indication has survived that he felt the coronation enhanced his power, or conferred a new role on him. There is evidence of one practical consideration behind his wish to be crowned by the pope: that once he was crowned, he could arrange for his brother to be elected King of the Romans. If this was not done soon, he feared their opponents in Germany might elect someone else.[9] In fact, he had his brother elected in 1531.

The Duke of Ferrara had not been present at the coronation, for he was still unreconciled to the pope. After Charles obtained a safe conduct for him from Clement, he came to Bologna in early March. The most Charles could achieve was to get both parties to accept his arbitration.[10] On 22 March, the day after this was agreed, Charles left for Mantua, where he stayed for a month, enjoying a chance to relax after the formalities and hard bargaining in Bologna. While he was being entertained there he elevated his host, Federico Gonzaga – who had not attended the cor-onation because he did not want to cede precedence to the marquis of Monferrato – to the status of duke. He also agreed that Alfonso d'Este could retain Carpi, for a payment of 100,000 ducats. Once Charles left Mantua, he travelled without further delay over the Alps to confront the daunting problems in Germany.

The siege of Florence, 1529–30

The major piece of unfinished business he left behind was the matter of Florence, which had been under siege by the Prince of Orange since October 1529. Preferring to see the siege ended by a settlement with the payment of a heavy indemnity rather than the destruction of a great city, Charles was still concerned the pope should be satisfied that he had kept his promise to support him. Clement was ambivalent about the efforts of Orange and his army. Determined as he was that the Medici should dominate Florence once more, the longer the army was encamped outside Florence, the higher the cost to Clement, for he was responsible for paying 60,000 ducats a month to them. Yet he did not want the city sacked and ruined, or bled dry for the benefit of the imperial army.

Nor was the Prince of Orange able to press a vigorous siege. In the early stages, he had around 10,500 infantry, 500 light horse and 300 men-at-arms.[11] Many more would be needed to besiege the city completely, he stressed to Charles: if he did not have more men, it would take ten years to conquer it. And he would need more artillery, for most of the pieces he had broke after firing a few shots.[12] Lack of money to pay the men he did have meant that he could make little use of them; nothing like the sums due from the pope was being sent. With the end of the war in Lombardy, reinforcements gradually arrived at the camp. By early February, Orange was reported to have 14,000 Italian, 6,000 Spanish and 8,000 German infantry, 800 men-at-arms and 2,000 light horse.[13] Naturally, this did not make it any easier to find the money to pay them all.

Although some Florentine citizens and many Florentine subjects were not averse to the return of the Medici, and supported the Imperial army by giving them intelligence or supplies, or even fighting on their side, the regime in Florence was dominated by men hostile to the Medici. The broadly based, popular government aroused great loyalty, fanned by religious fervour in the Savonarolan tradition. Known or suspected supporters of the Medici were persecuted. It was more acceptable to favour a settlement with the emperor than coming to terms with Clement.

A citizen militia was raised from the beginning of the siege. From 4,000, its numbers grew to around 10,000.[14] They showed themselves willing and able to confront the enemy outside the walls, as well as to man the defences. Most of the fighting, however, was done by mercenaries, nearly all Italians, many with some sense that they were fighting 'for the liberty of Italy', according to the committee that supervised them.[15] Several of the commanders came from the Papal States, including Stefano Colonna, Mario Orsini and Malatesta Baglioni, who was appointed captain-general in January 1530. Numbers fluctuated around 10,000 in the first months of the siege, falling to around 6,000 by the end.[16]

Orange established his camp to the south of the city in mid-October 1529. To the north-west, a force of landsknechts were positioned on the routes leading to Prato and Pistoia, and Spanish troops on the main route north to Bologna. The Florentines sacrificed all the buildings for a mile or so around the city, to deprive the attackers of cover. There was some artillery bombardment of the city, which could be intensified when fresh, more reliable guns were sent to the camp at the turn of the year, but no great damage was done. Much work had been done on the defences on the south side of the city, under the direction of Michelangelo, acting as a military engineer. The bombardment, and the Florentine defiance of it, became more of a symbolic exchange, albeit one in which men died (including Mario Orsini, killed while inspecting fortifications). There were some assaults on the city, but only one, on 11 November, a large-scale one and that, intended to be a surprise attack, was driven back by artillery fire. Sallies from the city against the enemy camp were infrequent, but effective enough to force the besiegers to take precautions.

Most of the fighting took place not around the city itself but in the territory – a battle for control of supplies and of the routes along which they came. The most important route ran along the Arno valley through Empoli to Pisa. By the beginning of 1530, only Pisa, Livorno, Empoli and Volterra, of the major subject towns, were under Florentine control. From his base at Empoli, the commissioner Francesco Ferrucci had been leading effective raids against Imperial forces in the area. After Volterra surrendered to Alessandro Vitelli in late February, Ferrucci was sent to retake it and relieve the garrison that was holding out in the fortress there, but only at the end of April when Empoli was thought to be secure from attack. Ferrucci reached Volterra in a day with a force of around 2,000 infantry and 200 horse,[17] was admitted into the fortress and from there took the town. On 29 May Empoli fell to del Vasto, who then went in mid-June to invest Volterra, joining the Neapolitan captain Fabrizio Maramaldo whose company of infantry had already been attacking the town. Valiant defence of Volterra by the Florentine forces caused the siege to be lifted. Humiliated, del Vasto left Tuscany.

In Florence supplies of food were running low and ever harder to replenish. The Imperial army was also weakened by shortages and disease. One vigorous sally, and the Florentines could annihilate this skeleton of an army, Orange warned the emperor in early April.[18] Orange was having to give leave to companies of his unpaid men to leave the camp, which by the end of April was reduced to 4,000–5,000 men.[19] Not that this helped the Florentines much, for it only increased the numbers of troops ravaging the territory. Ferrucci was ordered to gather what men could be spared from defending Volterra and Pisa and, with Gianpaolo da Ceri who was based at Pisa, to try either to capture Prato or Pistoia as a base for operations north of the Arno, or to attempt to break through to Florence. Orange learned of this plan, ordered Maramaldo to intercept Ferrucci's forces or, if he could not, to join up with Alessandro Vitelli and with some Spanish infantry who were in the area, and himself led from the camp 2,000 infantry and what light horse remained. Marching east from Pisa with about 3,000 infantry and 300 light horse, Ferrucci had reached the vicinity of Pistoia on 3 August when the Imperial forces, around 8,000 infantry and 1,500 horse in total,[20] converged on them near the walled village of Gavinana. After a hard-fought battle in and around the village, the Florentine forces were overwhelmed. Ferrucci and Gianpaolo da Ceri were among the last to surrender. Already gravely wounded, Ferrucci was killed by Maramaldo. His exploits made him a hero to Italian patriots for centuries to come. For the Imperial army, the victory was marred by the death of the prince of Orange, killed by arquebus shots while leading his light horse in a charge.

Baglioni was now set on salvaging his own interests in Perugia, and saving the city of Florence by arranging a negotiated surrender. After the news of Gavinana reached Florence, he and Colonna sent envoys to Ferrante Gonzaga, who had taken command after Orange's death. Gonzaga stipulated that the Medici must be restored, but also suggested that the emperor should arbitrate. The government rejected this, and ordered an assault on the camp, which Baglioni and Colonna refused to mount. As Baglioni prepared his men to surrender the city, much of the militia sided with them, and the remainder stood down after a few hours. It was evident that many Florentines did not share the fanaticism of the diehards who would rather see Florence destroyed than the Medici return. Supporters of the Medici were coming out into the open. Negotiations were opened with Gonzaga, and by 12 August the terms of capitulation had been agreed, terms vague and provisional enough to leave some hopes alive for the proponents of a moderate republican government. Charles V was to decide within four months what regime Florence should have; the liberties of the city would be secured; the Florentines swore obedience to the emperor. There was no clause explicitly allowing the Medici to return: that was taken as read.[21]

Neither Clement nor Charles were wholly content with these terms. Charles had wanted more money from Florence, at least 200,000 ducats; Clement would rather that Florence had surrendered to him, not the emperor. The pope was worried that Florence might still be sacked, for it took a month to raise enough money to induce the soldiers in the Imperial camp to move on. Baglioni's reward for his part in the city's surrender was permission from Clement to return to Perugia. A force of about 600 Italians under Alessandro Vitelli provided enough security for the new regime.

A week after the capitulation, the oligarchs and the Mediceans had taken control of the government of Florence. The interim regime lasted several months, for Charles's arbitration was not published until the beginning of July 1531, when Alessandro de' Medici came from the Imperial court. His decree was that the regime should be as it was before 1527, with Alessandro and his heirs at its head in perpetuity. It was stressed that this decision was founded on the emperor's authority over Florence; if the Florentines flouted it, they would be treated as rebels, and Florence would devolve to the Empire.[22] What form the new government should take was not specified. The constitution settled in April 1532 was a compromise between the aristocrats' wish for an oligarchic regime, and Alessandro's desire to be a prince. He was to be 'duke of the republic of Florence', like the doge of Venice, the statute said.[23] He soon showed he wanted to rule as a duke, not just hold the title. To strengthen his position, he increased the garrison under Vitelli's command, and built an imposing fortress on the northern edge of the city. Construction of the fortress began in July 1534, just before the death of Clement, and continued rapidly, so that the guard could move there in December 1535.

The siege of Florence and the presence of the Imperial army in Tuscany for a year had repercussions for the other Tuscan republics. On leaving Florence, the army went to Siena. During the siege, the Sienese had been called on to provide much of the supplies for the Imperial camp. Willingly or not, they had done all they could, but not enough to satisfy the Imperial agents. Exiles from Siena had appealed to Charles to arrange for their return, and he had ordered Orange to see that they did. Imperial agents recommended that Charles should reform the government of Siena, perhaps appointing a governor, while maintaining the republic, but he did not want force used to bring about change. It was not on his orders that the army had gone to Sienese territory. Gonzaga did not know where else he could take it for the winter, and consequently had no wish for a speedy resolution to the question of the exiles. Both Gonzaga and Lope de Soria, the Imperial envoy in Siena, thought it would be essential when the army moved on for a garrison of Spanish troops, paid by the Sienese, to remain behind to secure the reform of the government and ensure that the returning exiles felt safe enough to stay. Agreement was reached in late November that the exiles could return, and that there would be a garrison under the control of Soria as the representative of the emperor, at Sienese expense, for as long as the Sienese or Charles thought necessary.

An outbreak of faction-fighting in January 1531 produced fresh exiles, however, and Soria left for the Imperial camp. Although Charles reiterated his order forbidding the use of force,[24] Sienese envoys who came to the camp were arrested, and Gonzaga proposed to introduce over 1,000 more troops into the city by night, and to disarm the Sienese. Charles did not approve. His advisers at court told him Siena could be a bulwark for the kingdom of Naples, and an observation post for affairs throughout Italy, but they also told him he could become 'absolute lord' of Siena by keeping the devotion of the Sienese, rather than by force.[25] Both Soria and Gonzaga were to be replaced; del Vasto was to come from Naples to assume command of the army, and take it to Lombardy once Siena was settled.

A new agreement was made in April 1531. The exiles were to return, none of the political factions were to be excluded from the government, and a garrison of 350 Spanish troops was to guarantee the security of all. Del Vasto's brother-in-law, Alfonso Piccolomini, duca d'Amalfi (from a branch of that Sienese family that held estates in Naples) was to be captain-general of the republic and effectively the emperor's representative in Siena. The presence of Spanish troops in Siena would do little to curb the turbulent animosities dividing the citizens, but reinforced the belief of Imperial agents that they had a duty to watch over the government there and, if possible, bring the city under the control of the emperor.

Some thought of Lucca in the same way. During the siege of Florence, a Spanish official, Juan Abril de Marzilla, had been sent there to see to the provision of supplies for the Imperial army. After the siege ended, he stayed on with no defined role, but he tried to exploit political troubles in Lucca in 1531–2 to assume the powers of an Imperial representative, if not a quasi-governor. The Lucchese government denied he had any authority from Charles to issue orders to them.[26] Marzilla backed down and left Lucca. In early 1533, when Charles was again in Italy, Marzilla signalled his intention to return to stay in Lucca. The Lucchese made it clear he would not be welcome, and said they had no need for any representative of Charles in their city.[27] Marzilla did not come, nor did Charles send anyone else.

The second Congress of Bologna, 1532–3

Charles had arrived in Italy in late 1532, travelling through on his return to Spain from Germany, and asked Clement to meet him again. Knowing that the principal business Charles wanted to discuss was the need for a general council of the Church, the pope reluctantly agreed to a second meeting in Bologna. After waiting a month at Mantua for Clement to arrive in Bologna, Charles joined him there on 13 December.

To the emperor's mind, the congress, which lasted until the end of February 1533, was not a success. Not only did Clement refuse to summon a council soon, his attitude to the king of France also troubled Charles. In June 1531 Clement had agreed to a marriage between Caterina, the daughter of Lorenzo de' Medici, and Francis's second son, Henry, duc d'Orléans. This followed Clement's disappointment at the decision by Charles to award Modena and Reggio to Alfonso d'Este. While Clement and Charles were in Bologna, Francis sent to have confirmation of the marriage and to ask the pope to meet him at Nice or Marseilles, and Clement agreed.

High on the emperor's agenda at Bologna was a general league with the pope and other Italian states. Supposedly, it would be to maintain the peace of Italy; in fact, to constrain Francis, when he saw Italy united with the emperor, to observe the terms of the treaties of Madrid and Cambrai and to swear not to involve himself in the affairs of Italy. It also revived the attempt to get Italian states to make regular contributions for the upkeep of the Imperial army in Italy, under the guise of paying for an army of the League. Milan, Mantua, Ferrara, Genoa, Siena and Lucca were to be brought into alliance with Charles and Clement (and, through Clement, Florence) to oppose anyone who disturbed the peace of Italy. The pope gave his unwilling assent, and his representatives took part in drawing up the terms of the League, but other Italian states were not consulted, just told what contributions were expected from them.

None of them acquiesced in what was demanded. The Duke of Ferrara refused to be included at all. To please Charles, the Sienese would accept their inclusion and pay a lump sum, but nothing more. The Lucchese refused to be nominated as principals in the League; Charles included them as his 'adherents', but they would still not commit themselves to regular payments. The Genoese were also included as 'adherents', and Charles promised on their behalf that they would fulfil their obligations under the treaty. They objected strongly. It had already been suggested to them that Charles could protect Genoa more effectively from French claims if they accepted their republic was subject to the Empire, but they were adamant they would not compromise their independence in this way. In order to get them to ratify the League, Charles had to concede substantial changes in their obligations. When he was in Genoa in early April, about to leave Italy, he issued letters patent confirming their liberties and privileges as inviolable. Only then did the Genoese formally ratify the treaty.[28]

This Italian League existed only on paper, although Charles and his officials would invoke it when it suited their purposes. The failure of this attempt to dragoon Italian states into supporting and subsidizing the emperor's interests and army is an instructive illustration of the limits of his power in Italy.[29] It did have one significant outcome – Antonio de Leyva was left in command of a body of troops, nominally of the League, stationed in Lombardy.

On leaving Bologna, Charles spent a few days in Milan, at the invitation of Francesco Sforza. A marriage between the duke and one of Charles's nieces, a daughter of the king of Denmark, was agreed. The duke had managed to raise enough money to redeem Como and the Castello of Milan in March 1531. Now a compromise was reached over the money for the investiture still outstanding, after he showed Imperial officials details of the poor state of the Milanese finances. No one expected the ailing duke to live long or father an heir; there was a sense that the future of the duchy was still uncertain.

Francis I's designs on Italy

Far from renouncing his interests in Italy, as Charles wished him to do, Francis was determined to recover at least some of the ground he had lost. He still had many partisans in Italy, and other potential supporters in opponents of the emperor. His abandonment of his allies at Cambrai, reinforcing the reputation of the French for disregarding their promises, made some wary of becoming involved in his schemes. The French are not reliable friends, the doge of Venice, Andrea Gritti, was reported to have said: they care only for themselves.[30] Nevertheless, the Venetians came to be regarded as natural allies of the French; they were not invited to join the League in February 1533. A longstanding ally of the French, the Duke of Ferrara, had also been aggrieved by the neglect of his interests at Cambrai. In any case, he had to cultivate good relations with Charles for support against the pope's pretensions to his lands.

The king still firmly believed that Genoa, Milan and Asti were all rightfully his. Paradoxically, he supported the idea of Genoa becoming subject to the emperor, apparently so that Charles could turn Genoa over to him when, as he hoped, the emperor would give him Milan. Recovering Milan was the king's primary goal in Italy. He had no serious plans for another campaign to recover it, but spoke often and forcefully of how the duchy was his rightful inheritance, and should be held by one of his sons, if not by him. Asti had been granted by Charles to his sister-in-law, Beatrice, duchess of Savoy, in 1531. This grant was one of the grounds for the king to quarrel with his uncle, the duke. Francis also laid claim to half of the lands of Savoy as heir of his mother, Louise, who had died in 1531, and he claimed Nice and Villefranche as heir to the Angevin counts of Provence, and Vercelli as rightful Duke of Milan. There was no true legal substance to these claims. He was not the first king of France to covet Savoy, or to feel it would be useful to control the territory through which French armies had to pass on their way to Milan or Genoa.

The same consideration underlay his interest in the marquisate of Saluzzo. On the death of Marquis Michele Antonio in Naples in 1528, the succession to the marquisate was disputed between his brothers Gian Ludovico and Francesco. Gian Lodovico went to France to plead his case before Francis – who considered Saluzzo a dependency of the Dauphiné – only to be arrested. In January 1531 the king declared Saluzzo had devolved to the French crown, but then changed his mind after Francesco was recognized as marquis in Saluzzo, and invested him with the marquisate.[31] He also backed his claims to Monferrato, when the Paleologo dynasty ended with the death of Marquis Giangiorgio in late April 1533. Francesco occupied most of Monferrato, only to be ordered to withdraw by the emperor, who sent de Leyva with troops to take control there. Monferrato was an Imperial fief and Charles asserted the right to decide what should happen to it.[32]

As a consequence of the marriage of his son Henry to Caterina de' Medici, Francis also began to put forward claims on behalf of Henry to Urbino and Florence. This marriage took place at Marseilles at the end of October 1533, when the pope and the king met there from mid-October to mid-November. Caterina was only 12, her groom but three years older, yet the pope wished to see the marriage completed. The match was a misalliance for a son of the king of France, and the pope possibly feared Caterina would later be repudiated. The king's hopes for an alliance with the pope for the conquest of Milan were not realized, but it was reported that Clement approved Henry's claim to the duchy of Urbino.[33]

The pope and king discussed a council of the Church, agreeing it was not desirable to summon one. Francis was intriguing with German princes and cities, Protestant as well as Catholic, against the Habsburgs. For some years, the king had been in contact with the Ottoman sultan Suleiman the Magnificent and the Muslim corsairs on the north coast of Africa, seeking to stimulate attacks on Ferdinand in Hungary and Austria and on Charles's Mediterranean lands, including Naples and Sicily. This was no secret. Francis even made a virtue of not attempting to thwart or exploit the expedition Charles led against the corsairs in the summer of 1535. Much to his chagrin, the capture of Tunis in July, after a hard-fought siege, was one of the high points of Charles's reign.

The devolution of Milan

Francesco Sforza died during the night of 1–2 November 1535. He had no heirs: his brother Massimiliano had died in 1530. So bad had his health been that his death came as no surprise. The emperor's representatives took charge of the duchy. There were no protests, or uprisings among the population of the duchy, nor were there any objections from the other Italian powers. Not even Venice was prepared to start another war to try to keep Milan an independent state under an Italian prince.

De Leyva urged Charles to keep the duchy for himself, but this opinion was not shared by all Charles's advisers. Some argued that it was in his own best interests, and in the interests of peace, for him to give the duchy to a new duke, and that if he kept it under his direct rule, this would be bound to cause another war.[34] Charles could see the force of both options. Milan was an important link between his other dominions, facilitating communications between Spain and the Empire. But keeping it for himself in the long term was likely to cause jealousy and discontent among the other powers, and it might, therefore, be preferable to grant it to another. Characteristically, Charles's initial decision, taken at the end of December 1535, was to keep possession of Milan for the time being, and wait to see what the Italian powers and Francis would do.

The French invasion of Savoy and Piedmont, 1536

About that time, Francis told his council that he had allowed Charles to become too powerful in Italy.[35] The takeover of Milan by the emperor's men intensified the king's desire to recover the duchy, and the lands of the Duke of Savoy were a bridgehead to it. Francis was primed to exploit a war that Duke Charles had launched against Geneva. The king sent an envoy to the Bernese, who had intervened on behalf of Geneva, warning them he planned to conquer Savoy for himself, and another envoy to the duke to demand he should surrender all the territories the king claimed. In mid-February 1536, two legions[36] of French infantry under Saint-Pol were sent into Bresse, the area of the duke's lands to the north-east and east of

Lyon. By the end of the month, they had occupied it all, and moved on to Savoy.

Francis sent to demand that Nice, Vercelli and Turin be surrendered to him, warning that if they were not, he would take them because he needed them.[37] In late March, the main French army under Philippe de Chabot, seigneur de Brion, advanced into Piedmont and entered Turin in early April. According to French official sources, this army numbered around 24,000 foot and 3,000 horse,[38] but these figures may be exaggerated, for the king had difficulty assembling all the troops he boasted he would raise. Nevertheless, there was not a great deal that the duke or his subjects could do.

Asti was also taken from the duke, occupied not in the name of the king, the French claimed, but by forces loyal to Francis. Openly to take it for Francis could be seen as a direct challenge to Charles. The French expected opposition from the emperor, but he had insufficient troops in the region to confront an army of that size. He ordered de Leyva to send 1,000 infantry, a force that could do little and withdrew to near Vercelli, where the Duke of Savoy had fled. Vercelli was on the border of Lombardy, and Chabot was under orders not to cross that border. He was ordered by the king to lead his army back to France, leaving garrisons in Turin, Pinerolo, Fossano and Cuneo. Marquis Francesco of Saluzzo was appointed lieutenant-general in Piedmont. The king said that his plan was to fortify a few places in Piedmont, but also to leave 25,000 troops there and wait to see what would happen. Piedmont was his, he argued, and he had taken Savoy to get from the duke what was his by right; nothing belonging to Charles had been attacked.[39] Yet he was conscious that Charles was making his way north through Italy, and the presence of the emperor was bound to raise the stakes.

Charles V's journey through Italy, 1535–6

The victory at Tunis had enhanced the emperor's reputation, and convinced him more than ever of the justice of his cause. From Tunis, he sailed to Sicily, where he landed on 22 August 1535. He was fêted by the Sicilians, after his triumph over the corsairs who were a very real threat to the island. In Naples, too, which he reached in late November, the people were glad to see their king, still feeling the relegation of their kingdom to a viceroyalty. Charles spent four months in Naples. Without touring the kingdom, he conducted careful enquiries into its government and administration, which had been taken into the firm hand of Pedro de Toledo, viceroy since 1532. While in Naples, Charles heard of the death of Francesco Sforza, and of the French occupation of Savoy; he gave orders for the recruitment of Spanish, German and Italian troops. Having left Naples on 22 March 1536, on his way to Rome he then heard of Chabot's invasion of Piedmont.

The new pope, Paul III, wanted the spectacle of Charles's entry into Rome, which took place on 5 April, to be worthy of a pope welcoming an emperor to the city. A carefully planned route took Charles past the major surviving monuments of ancient Rome, but as well as classical allusions, the iconography of the decorations in the streets gave prominence to Christian Rome. The pope's own family, the Farnese, were minor Roman barons. He had fathered several children, of whom a son and a daughter survived. His family's interests were never forgotten, but he took a more statesmanlike approach to international relations than Clement had done, and was resolute that his duty as pope was to remain neutral and promote peace.

From the early days of Paul's pontificate, Charles and his envoys had urged him to join the 'Italian League'. Knowing Francis would regard that as a hostile gesture, Paul refused. For his part, Francis wanted an explicit declaration of the pope's support for him against Charles, alleging that the emperor aimed to become lord of all Italy. Charles, of course, consistently denied he had any such desire. At the end of his stay in Rome, on 17 April, the emperor invited many people, including the French and Venetian ambassadors, to attend a meeting with the pope and cardinals in the Vatican. The normally taciturn emperor spoke for an hour, mainly of his relations with the king of France. Francis was never satisfied, Charles said. Now he had attacked the Duke of Savoy, without cause, and his pretensions to the duchy of Milan risked causing another major war. If the pope judged Charles to be in the wrong, let him back Francis; otherwise, he appealed to the pope against the king. Paul replied that if either sovereign refused a reasonable peace, he would side against him.[40] After Charles had left Rome, Paul formally declared he would remain neutral.[41]

Responding to the emperor's denunciation, in a letter to the pope Francis justified his occupation of Savoy and asserted that Charles had agreed to cede Milan to his son Henry, that he would not insist on holding the duchy himself, and that Milan need not be an obstacle to peace.[42] But he did not respond to the emperor within the time set by Charles – who therefore considered himself free to make war on the king.[43]

Charles V and Francis I again at war in Italy, 1536–7

Even before that time had expired, de Leyva led his army from the camp at Vercelli, heading for Turin. He now had a substantial force – 15,000 Germans, 2,000 Spanish, some Swiss volunteers and what Charles described as a 'good band' of horse, Italian and others, and more troops were being raised.[44] The French had retreated from all places in Piedmont except Turin, Fossano and Cuneo, and Cuneo was lost to them when Saluzzo surrendered it on 17 May. Saluzzo changed sides, hoping that Monferrato would be his reward from the emperor.[45] Charles himself arrived at Asti in late May, already intent on invading Provence. He would have liked the French to have been expelled from Piedmont before he took his army into France. Fossano surrendered on 24 June, but Turin held out, and a detachment had to be left behind to continue the siege of Turin when the invasion of Provence began.

On 25 July the Imperial army crossed into Provence, taking the coast road through Nice; an invasion of Picardy under Henry, count of Nassau was launched at the same time. Naturally, Francis concentrated his attention on the south, although his council dissuaded him from joining Montmorency at the head of his army. Adopting a scorched-earth strategy, Montmorency devastated Provence to deprive the Imperial army of supplies. Aix fell to Charles on 13 August, and then he made camp there with his army, the French blocking all the routes along which he could advance to Marseilles, which was his goal. Thousands of men died in the camp from disease, among them de Leyva. On 11 September, Charles began to withdraw from Provence, unaware that Nassau was also on the retreat from Picardy.

During this fruitless expedition to Provence, ground had been lost in Piedmont. Reinforcements for the French there had arrived in a force of 10,000 Italian infantry and a few hundred horse.[46] This had been raised by Guido Rangone and other members of the military nobility of southern Lombardy, including Galeotto Pico della Mirandola. Galeotto had gained control of Mirandola by killing his uncle Gianfrancesco in 1533, and his little state would become an important haven for French partisans and allies in Italy, and a gathering-place for troops in the service of France. Cesare Campofregoso was also with this band, and its first target was Genoa. They approached Genoa at the end of August, but the garrison had been reinforced and there was no uprising of Fregoso partisans among the people. Moving on to Piedmont, they had more success. They took

Carignano and with the munitions found there restocked Turin, and also occupied other places between Turin and Saluzzo, including Pinerolo, Chieri and Carmagnola.

As he returned to Italy, Charles detached part of his army under del Vasto to go to Piedmont and join the Imperial forces remaining there and fresh landsknechts recently sent from Germany. With these men del Vasto set about recovering territory in Piedmont. Charles himself went to Genoa, where he stayed from mid-October to mid-November before sailing for Barcelona. While in Genoa, he announced his decision concerning Monferrato, in favour of the Duke of Mantua, who claimed it in the right of his wife, Margherita Paleologo. French troops moved quickly to occupy Casale, the main town in the marquisate, but del Vasto's forces intervened and took Casale, enabling Federico Gonzaga to gain possession of his new state.

Francis was looking to open up other areas of conflict with Charles in Italy, making use of exiles and of the Turks. As soon as he heard of the assassination of Alessandro de' Medici on 6 January 1537 by his distant cousin, Lorenzino de' Medici, Francis decided to support the Florentine republican exiles in order to prevent Charles taking over Florence for himself.[47] Lorenzino had killed Alessandro because of his misrule, not to take his place, and had left Florence immediately. A group of Florentine aristocrats procured the election by the main council, the Forty-Eight, of Cosimo, the 17-year-old son of Giovanni de' Medici, as head of the government – not as duke. Envoys were despatched to Spain to seek the emperor's approval. Alessandro's ties to Charles had been strengthened by marriage in 1536 to his daughter Margaret, and the envoys were also to ask for her now to marry Cosimo.

Charles would not agree to his daughter marrying Cosimo, and he was uncertain whether to endorse what had been decided in Florence. Del Vasto sent 1,500 infantry, and Pirro Colonna to take command if any military operations were needed, and in Rome the Imperial ambassador the conde de Cifuentes busied himself seeking to obstruct the plans of the exiles. Alessandro Vitelli, the captain of the guard in Florence, took over the fortress there and declared he held it for Charles and for Cosimo. Securing this fortress and those of Pisa and Livorno, which Alessandro had promised would be put at the disposal of the emperor in the event of his death, was one of Charles's priorities. But he wished to avoid provoking Cosimo and his backers into turning to France for support, and hoped to settle the problem of the exiles by negotiating their return.[48] Cifuentes went to Florence with detailed instructions from Charles and confirmed that Cosimo could exercise the powers granted to Alessandro but without the title of duke. He had Vitelli swear to hold the fortress in Florence for the emperor, and got possession of the one in Livorno, but the castellan of Pisa persisted in holding that fortress for Cosimo.

Negotiations with representatives of the exiles failed, however. They were planning a military expedition. By the end of July, 6,000 infantry and 300 horse were assembled at Mirandola.[49] The exiles hoped for a French contribution of money or men to their enterprise, which was supposed to be co-ordinated with a renewal of the campaign in Piedmont and an attack by a Turkish fleet and Neapolitan exiles on Naples. Cosimo sent troops to meet them as soon as news arrived that they were on the move, and before all their forces had barely entered Florentine territory the exiles had been decisively defeated at Montemurlo near Prato on 1 August. Several of their leaders were captured and executed. Already showing political sense and maturity beyond his years, Cosimo was able to consolidate his position. Two months after the battle, Charles granted him the title of duke.

While the attack on Naples was called off, the war in the north-west of Italy carried on with alternating fortunes, but no major engagements. It remained a war between the French and Imperial armies. The Duke of Savoy had little or no part in it. There was still much loyalty to him among the population and he kept up contacts with those in the areas controlled by the French from his refuge in the remnants of his duchy left to him, but there was small chance of success for an uprising in his favour and none was attempted. At the beginning of 1537, the French held towns and strongholds on the major routes from the Alps, such as Pinerolo, Turin and Moncalieri and the main crossing-points on the Po, and to the south occupied part of Saluzzo, but their hold on these places was not secure. Marquis Francesco held much of Saluzzo before he died in late March fighting the French outside Carmagnola, and the king invested his younger brother Gabriele with the marquisate in November.

In Piedmont there was discord between the French and Italian captains, and among the Italians. There were around 9,000 Italians and 4,000 French troops in the main garrisons,[50] but the countryside was controlled by the Imperial army, so there was a serious problem with supplies, and a shortage of money. As usual, the people paid the price in robberies and extortion by the troops, and there was concern they would rebel. In early March Jean de Humières was appointed lieutenant-general in Piedmont. When he arrived in late April, Guido Rangone, captain of the Italian troops, took offence at the authority Humières had been given over him and left.

Humières had brought only 2,000 men with him. Francis was ready to devote more resources to the campaign in Piedmont, but was fighting another Imperial army on the northern frontier and some troops destined for Italy were sent to Artois. Ten thousand landsknechts under the Duke of Wurtemberg were sent south, and with these reinforcements Humières took the offensive in early July. Anticipating Francis would concentrate his efforts on Piedmont, del Vasto and Doria urged an increase in the Imperial army there. Charles estimated that with the troops del Vasto already had with him, those who were at Florence and Nice and others who were on their way, an army of 30,000 could be mustered.[51] As usual, however, the soldiers' pay was in serious arrears, and it was recognized that they would not take the field if they went unpaid. Yet del Vasto was also expected to keep watch over Genoa, over the French machinations in Tuscany and on possible attempts to seize Parma and Piacenza for the French.[52]

As the French offensive began, del Vasto withdrew to Asti from his position near Turin. An attempt by Humières to take Asti failed, but he was able to take Alba in Monferrato and Cherasco and other places on the river Tanaro to the south, despite the disobedience of his troops. At the end of July the war on the northern border of France was ended by a truce, and Francis prepared to transfer forces from that frontier to Piedmont. Humières was ordered to hold out with his most reliable men in the strongest places to await relief, and to dismantle the walls of those places that could not be guarded. He had already concentrated 13,000 French and Italian troops at eight strongholds, and himself retired to Pinerolo.[53] Del Vasto began to recover control of the countryside and blockade the towns held for the French.

Only three towns – Turin, Pinerolo and Savigliano – were left in French hands when the relief army under Montmorency at last came to Piedmont in late October and broke the blockade on them. The king joined his army as they quickly took possession of the territory east of Turin to Monferrato and south to the Tanaro. Conscious that negotiations in Spain for a truce with Charles were nearing fruition, Francis wanted to be in possession of as much of Piedmont as possible before it came into effect.

Truce and peace

A three-month truce, covering Savoy, Piedmont, Lombardy, Genoa, Nice, the Dauphiné and Provence, signed at Monzón in Spain on 16 November 1537, was published in Piedmont on 27 November. The next day, del Vasto and Montmorency met at Carmagnola and agreed each side could garrison the places they held at that time and send superfluous troops away. Francis explained his acceptance of a truce rather than pressing home his advantage by the approach of winter, and the difficulty of sustaining such a large army and finding food for all the towns he held in Piedmont when so much of the crops had been ruined.[54] Charles was also ready for a truce in Italy: his more urgent concerns were the Turks and corsairs in the Mediterranean, religious and political troubles in Germany and a brewing rebellion in the Netherlands.

Peace talks covering all the issues between the emperor and the king were opened on the border between France and Spain, but Francis refused the proposals advanced by Charles. As usual, the crux of their differences was Milan. For the king, no peace was possible without immediate and preferably unconditional restitution of the duchy. Even if it were to come as the dowry of a Habsburg bride for his son, Francis wanted to rule Milan himself. For Charles and his advisers, even if cession of the duchy were offered, restrictions had to be in place to prevent it being united with the French crown. The death of the dauphin Francis in August 1536 had complicated this conundrum. Henry, the new dauphin, had come to regard Milan as rightfully his, but Charles would not cede it to the heir to the French throne, or admit Henry's claims through his wife to Florence and Urbino, or any French claims to Genoa.[55] Piedmont had joined the list of lands that Francis regarded as his inheritance, and he refused to agree that restitution of lands he had seized from the Duke of Savoy should be a condition of any cession of Milan, asserting that he held nothing that was not his. Neither Francis nor Charles was willing to compromise on these fundamental issues – which were not the only intractable problems dividing them – and there was no chance of a firm and lasting peace unless one of them backed down.

Both sides still wanted a truce, nonetheless, and it was renewed twice, up to 1 June 1538. Paul III was seeking to mediate between them, urging Charles and Francis to meet. Nice was suggested as a suitable venue where both could feel secure. Charles liked this idea more than Francis did, but the congress did finally take place. Charles arrived first at Villefranche on 9 May; the pope at Nice a week later; the king a fortnight after that at Villeneuve. While Charles and Francis each had separate meetings with the pope at Nice, they would not meet each other in his presence. Only their negotiating teams did, but their discussions were acrimonious and unfruitful, and commissions of cardinals the pope sent to either side made no progress either. The French position was that if Milan was ceded freely to the king immediately, he would undertake to support a general council of the Church, and make war on the Turks. The Imperial position was the emperor could only cede Milan after three years, during which Francis must demonstrate his goodwill by supporting the council and war against the Turks. To break the deadlock, Paul put forward four sets of proposals; Charles chose the one nearest to his own, that the duchy should be held by a third party for three years, but stipulated that should be his brother Ferdinand. Francis's reaction was that this was a joke.[56]

As a peace was obviously not attainable, discussion turned to a prolongation of the truce. Francis wanted one for twenty years or more, Charles for five at most; they compromised on ten. Each was to keep what he held in Italy at that moment. The Duke of Savoy could be included if he ratified the terms, and lands that were not considered important might then be returned to him. Genoa and Florence were expressly covered, as was Mirandola; exiles from Naples were excluded.[57]

The truce concluded, Paul left Nice on 20 June. Charles joined him in Genoa for further talks before sailing to meet Francis, an arrangement made during the congress at Nice. They met at Aigues Mortes on the coast of Provence for a few days in mid-July, with much outward show of goodwill and mutual trust. Discussions were confined to generalities, yet they agreed the ten-year truce was to be considered a peace. Any matters that could not be settled between their ministers would be left as they stood.[58]

According to Montmorency, Charles and Francis gave their word to each other not to go to war over Milan again as long as they lived.[59] They would not do so, but this did not mean that Milan was no longer a major cause of contention between them. For a while, Francis tried a new tactic, of conciliation. When the emperor travelled through France at the invitation of the king from November 1539 to January 1540, on his way to the Netherlands to deal with a serious revolt at Ghent, Francis hoped he might offer Milan to him as a gesture. For Charles, entrusting himself to the king's hospitality was gesture enough. There was further disappointment for Francis in March when Charles proposed the king's youngest son Charles should marry his daughter Mary with the Netherlands and Burgundy as her dowry, not Milan, and with the stipulation that Francis should give up his claims to Milan and the lands he had taken from the Duke of Savoy. Francis could not accept such terms.

In October 1540, Charles invested his own son, Philip, with Milan. This did not settle the issue: Philip was not to govern the duchy himself; Charles was still willing to discuss alternative arrangements; and Francis had not given up. He recommended trying to stir up opposition to the emperor in

Germany and negotiating a renewal of his alliance with Suleiman. He was already thinking of a future war with Charles, when he was given grounds to justify it by the seizure – it later turned out, the murder – of two French envoys by Imperial troops as they were passing through Lombardy in July 1541. One of them was Cesare Campofregoso, travelling to Venice, the other – the true target of the attack – was Antonio Rincon, a Spaniard in the service of France for many years, who was on a mission to Suleiman. Under the law of nations, the assassination of his envoys gave Francis grounds for protest, and he made the most of it. Del Vasto, then governor of Milan, denied it was on his orders, but it plainly was.[60] Charles asserted that he had ordered no harm should come to the envoys, but that if Rincon had come into del Vasto's hands, he could be punished as a rebel.[61]

This affair was one of the subjects discussed by the emperor and the pope when they met at Lucca in September 1541, as Charles was passing through northern Italy from Germany to Genoa. Charles had suggested the meeting because he wanted to speak to Paul about the ecclesiastical council and about the Turks, and to urge him to join an Italian league against Francis.[62] Concerned about what Charles might say to the pope on French relations with the Turks, Francis sent an envoy to Lucca to ask Paul to adjudicate in the dispute over Rincon. After it was suggested Paul might arbitrate on all areas of dispute between Charles and Francis, the king changed his mind.[63]

The renewal of the war in Piedmont, 1542–4

Charles was on his way to lead a major expedition against Algiers, hoping to repeat his triumph at Tunis. This time it went badly, as a series of storms scattered and wrecked his fleet. By the end of November he was back in Spain. Encouraging the Turks to attack Sicily and Naples, Francis was also preparing for war. If his attempts to make alliances with Henry VIII and the German princes were unsuccessful, he did receive a promise of support from Suleiman. On 12 July 1542, he declared war on the emperor. The main theatre would not be in Italy. Francis concentrated his attacks on Perpignan to the south of France and Luxembourg to the north. The military commander in Piedmont, d'Annebault, was ordered to take the bulk of his men to Perpignan.

This left 14,000 infantry, about half of them Swiss, 500 French and Italian men-at-arms and 700–800 light horse in Piedmont, who the king reckoned should equal del Vasto's forces in Milan.[64] Del Vasto still seized the opportunity of d'Annebault's absence to go onto the attack himself in Piedmont, aiming in particular for Turin, and to encourage Marquis Gian Lodovico to try to recover Saluzzo. Despite problems in raising enough money to keep the French soldiers in the field, the acting governor of Piedmont, Guillaume du Bellay, succeeded in containing the assault. Either more men would be needed to drive the Imperial troops out and then hold the countryside, du Bellay warned d'Annebault, or the king would have to be content with only holding the fortified towns.[65] Following the failure of the Perpignan campaign, d'Annebault returned. Probably on orders from the king to keep expenses down, he restricted his efforts to taking minor places around Turin. Rather than increasing the number of his troops, he was dismissing many. For several months there was no significant military action in Piedmont.

The weary del Vasto, in disfavour at court and short of resources, could not take advantage of the diminution of the enemy forces. He was so dispirited that he was ready to recommend the emperor should accept an offer on behalf of the pope to buy Milan for his grandson Ottavio Farnese. This offer was made to Charles in Genoa at the end of May 1543, when he was passing through northern Italy on his way from Spain to Germany. Paul was again attempting to mediate between him and Francis, as they were gearing up for another round of fighting in northern France and the Low Countries, and had invited them to meet him at Bologna. Saying he was too busy defending the frontiers of his kingdom to come to Italy, Francis refused.[66] As he would be in Italy anyway, Charles agreed to see the pope, and they met at Busseto, between Parma and Piacenza, in late June. He tried, again unsuccessfully, to persuade Paul to side with him against Francis. He had been tempted by the two million ducats Pier Luigi Farnese had offered in Genoa to purchase Milan for his son Ottavio, who was now the emperor's son-in-law, having married his daughter Margaret, Alessandro de' Medici's widow, in 1538. At Busseto the offer dropped to a less tempting one million ducats.

Charles had managed to raise some money to give to del Vasto, by agreeing to restore the fortresses of Florence and Livorno to Cosimo de' Medici in return for cash: 100,000 scudi were paid over in early July. Soon del Vasto was in action again, preparing to go to the relief of Nice. A French fleet commanded by François de Bourbon, comte d'Enghien had tried to take Nice from the Duke of Savoy in June, but had been driven off by Andrea Doria's galleys. In August, Nice was attacked again, by a combined French and Turkish fleet, and the town fell on 22 August, after a fortnight's siege. The fortress held out and the siege was lifted on 8 September as the relief forces of del Vasto and the Duke of Savoy were on their way. For Christians and Turks to be attacking a Christian town together was considered shocking, so Francis tried to play down the involvement of the

Turks, alleging that only French soldiers had been involved in the siege.[67] Yet he then did something even more scandalous, giving over the French port of Toulon to the commander of the Turkish fleet, Khair-ad-Din, known as Barbarossa, to overwinter his vessels and his men; most of the inhabitants of Toulon were told to leave to make room for them. Barbarossa stayed there until late May 1544, and then sailed to raid the coasts of Italy.

When del Vasto heard that the siege of Nice had been lifted, he diverted his troops to Piedmont, where the French under Guiffrey Guiges de Boutières and 7,000 Imperial infantry and 400–500 horse under Pirro Colonna had begun campaigning in earnest.[68] Del Vasto took Mondovi and ten days later Carignano, causing serious hindrance to communications between the French positions, and then ordered his men into winter quarters in Piedmont and Saluzzo. Displeased, Francis ordered reinforcements to be sent to Piedmont, saying he wanted 27,000 men to be there ready to campaign in the new year.[69] D'Enghien was sent to take command and recover Carignano. Deciding it was too strong to be forced, he set about blockading it. As del Vasto prepared to relieve it, d'Enghien sent to Francis for permission to give battle. Permission was granted, and many young courtiers hurried to Piedmont to join in the action.

The armies met near Ceresole on 14 April 1544. D'Enghien was looking for battle, del Vasto was aware the French were approaching, and both armies were in battle order. The terrain was open, with no hedges or ditches, so cavalry could be deployed and pike squares manoeuvre without hindrance from natural obstacles. Both sides had field artillery, but it did not play a significant role. Both sides were aware of the tactical use of handguns. Each army had three blocks of infantry alternating with three blocks of cavalry; the total numbers of troops may have been about equal, about 13,000–14,000 on each side.[70]

The opening exchanges of the battle, lasting some hours, were between forces of several hundred arquebusiers on each side, supported by their artillery, both trying to position themselves on the enemy's flank, 'as at Pavia'.[71] A group of Florentine horse under Ridolfo Baglioni (which had been sent by Cosimo de' Medici to support the Imperial troops) moved to attack the flank of the French infantry unit on the right wing, but was itself attacked by the French light horse who pushed them into the Italian infantry under Ferrante Sanseverino, principe di Salerno, on the Imperial left wing. In the confusion Termes, the commander of the French light horse, was captured. Salerno's infantry retreated, with the remains of Baglioni's company.

In the centre, the block of Imperial landsknechts divided into two 'battles', one against the French infantry and one against a body of Swiss infantry. The French and Germans put handgunners – arquebusiers and, among the Germans, pistoliers – in the second and third ranks of their pike squares, with the aim of killing the captains in the front rank of the enemy. This proved an effective tactic; casualties among the front ranks were high. Blaise de Monluc, who commanded the French arquebusiers, wrote that he instructed the French to hold their pikes well down the shaft, as the Swiss did, because they could not handle them holding them near the end, balancing them on their shoulders, as the Germans did. As the Germans advanced at a fast pace, some gaps appeared in their ranks. The French maintained a more compact formation; their pikes had shorter reach, but they would then gain greater impetus from the ranks behind pushing those in front. The Swiss waited until the Germans were closing on the French before charging their flank 'like wild boar'.[72] French men-at-arms who had been positioned by the Swiss also charged the landsknechts, creating breaches in their formation, and they were overcome.

On the left wing of the French the mounted archers from the units of men-at-arms charged the light horse on the Imperial right wing, most of whom turned tail without making any fight. The archers had been positioned by a unit of Grisons and Italian infantry, on the other side of which was d'Enghien with his men-at-arms, including the volunteers who had come from the court. These infantry wavered as the Grisons panicked when charged by the battalion of Imperial infantry on that wing, who were Spanish veterans and Germans who had been long in Spanish service. As the Grisons and Italians fled, d'Enghien led his company in two costly charges through the ranks of the Spanish and German veterans, who killed many of their horses. Separated by rising ground from the battle in the centre, d'Enghien could not see the defeat of the landsknechts, and thought the battle lost. But the news had reached the veterans, who had been grouping to attack what remained of d'Enghien's company, and they began to retreat. The victorious Swiss and French infantry from the centre joined d'Enghien's men in pursuit.

Throwing down their pikes in sign of surrender, many of the Spanish and German troops clustered round the French horsemen to be accounted their prisoners, seeking protection against the French infantry and especially against the Swiss, who were killing all they could find.[73] This ferocity was probably the main reason for the high casualty rate among the Imperial troops – according to du Bellay, all but 200 of the estimated 12,000–15,000 dead were from the Imperial army.[74] The actual total of dead may have been nearer half that figure.[75] The French also took more than 3,000 prisoners. Del Vasto was wounded, but what part he took in the fighting is not clear.

He later said that he had not believed that the impetus of French cavalry could not be contained and broken by the arquebusiers, nor that the shock of a battalion in close order could not overcome French infantry.[76]

A message was sent to Francis, telling him that if money and reinforcements were sent, the army could march on Milan. He considered this option, but Imperial troops were massing on the Rhine, and he ordered d'Enghien to continue the blockade of Carignano instead. D'Enghien sent his French infantry under Jean de Taix with 200 men-at-arms and some artillery to 'live off enemy territory'.[77] This force occupied much of Monferrato, except for Casale, Alba and Trino. Carignano was surrendered on terms to d'Enghien in late June.

Meanwhile, del Vasto was regrouping his forces and concentrating his attentions on the defence of the Milanese. Cosimo de' Medici helped by sending 2,000 infantry and funds to Baglioni to reconstitute his company of light horse.[78] Although the anticipated attack from Piedmont did not happen, Piero Strozzi, the most active of the Florentine exiles in the service of France, who had assembled several thousand infantry at Mirandola, advanced into the Milanese. When he realized that d'Enghien was not coming and that Imperial forces were preparing a trap, he led his men to the Apennines, intending to go to Piedmont, but his troops were defeated and dispersed at Serravalle on 4 June by Imperial troops under Salerno and Philippe de Lannoy, principe di Sulmona. Undaunted, Strozzi returned to Mirandola to assemble another force of 10,000 men, at his own expense.[79] Because del Vasto was on the alert to oppose their passing through Milanese territory, Strozzi took them via Parma, unobstructed by papal officials there who were under instructions to observe neutrality.

D'Enghien had no money and few men left, as the king, facing invasions by Imperial and English armies, had sent for 6,000 French and 6,000 Italian troops from Piedmont.[80] D'Enghien sent instructions to Strozzi to join him near Alba. With their combined forces, they laid siege to Alba, which surrendered to them. Del Vasto had been on his way to relieve the city, but arrived just too late, and turned back. Shortly after, he proposed a truce, which was agreed. It came into effect on 8 August, putting an end to this phase of the war in Piedmont.

The Peace of Crépy, 1544

Six weeks later, on 18 September 1544, peace terms between Charles and Francis were agreed at Crépy; Henry VIII, Charles's ally, was not a party to it, and would remain at war with France for another two years. All territories occupied by either side since the truce of Nice were to be restored; Francis renounced his claims to Naples, Flanders and Artois, and Charles his to Burgundy. The king was to help Charles against the Turks, and with the ecclesiastical council and the German Protestants. There was to be a marriage alliance between them – either the emperor's daughter would marry the king's son, Charles d'Orléans, with the Low Countries and Franche-Comté as her dowry (in which case the king would renounce his rights over Milan and Asti), or his niece, Ferdinand's daughter, would marry Orléans with Milan as her dowry. At the time that either of these arrangements came into effect, French troops were to evacuate Piedmont and Savoy, and the king's dispute with the Duke of Savoy would be submitted to arbitration.[81]

Neither side was pleased by these terms, but nor did they want to continue with the war. Charles had run out of money and wished to focus on Germany. Francis was preoccupied by the loss of Boulogne, which had fallen to the English on 13 September, and the effort to recover it was his military priority for the rest of his reign. The emperor did consider whether Milan or the Low Countries should be sacrificed for the marriage alliance and hope of an enduring peace, and asked his councillors in Spain for advice. Opinions were divided between those who saw Milan as a drain on resources, a cause of continual war, which should certainly be given up rather than lose the hereditary Habsburg lands in the Low Countries, and those who argued that Milan was an essential corridor of communications to Germany, vital to the defence of Naples and Sicily and of far more use to Spain than the Low Countries were.[82] Charles decided he would rather keep the Low Countries. His problem was solved by the death of Charles d'Orléans in September 1545; Francis's only remaining son was the Dauphin Henry. In July 1546 the emperor again invested his own son Philip with the duchy of Milan. This investiture, although definitive, was not made public for three years because of fears of the reaction not just of the French but also of the Italian states.

The promotion of Spanish interests in Italy

In the debate about whether Milan or the Low Countries should be given up, those who argued for keeping Milan were thinking of its role in maintaining Spanish, not Imperial, power in Italy. Charles's officials and commanders in Italy – nearly all by this time Spanish or Italian, not from his Burgundian dominions – might invoke his authority as the emperor, as they sought to extend his influence over Italy, yet they were doing so in the interests of Spain. They were mindful that, as King of the Romans, Ferdinand, not Philip, should succeed Charles as emperor.

Foremost among the champions of Spanish interests was an Italian, Ferrante Gonzaga. The son of Marquis Francesco Gonzaga, he had been sent at the age of 16 to live at Charles's court in Spain. There he found a kindred spirit in the reserved and grave young emperor, and became thoroughly acclimatized to the ethos and the values of his court. He made his career in the service of Charles, as a soldier, a commander of light horse, then a general, from 1535 to 1546 viceroy of Sicily and from April 1546 governor of Milan. The emperor had great faith in his loyalty, energy and abilities, explaining that he had appointed him governor of Milan because he could rely on him to do whatever was necessary.[83] As well as securing Genoa, he proposed that Charles should swap the Low Countries for Savoy and Piedmont, take over Siena, Lucca and Piombino, and recover territories that had been part of the duchy of Milan from the Swiss cantons, from Venice and the pope.[84]

The emperor's approach was more cautious. He did not want to go to war with the Swiss or Venice to recover former Milanese territory. His vision of security in northern Italy was based on the possession of Milan with Parma and Piacenza, and the fidelity of the Duke of Florence.[85] Aware of the limitations of his resources and the many other calls on them, he would rather rely on persuasion and the cultivation of goodwill than the use of force. Yet he would certainly consider using force, or subterfuge, to achieve security. His agents in Italy tended to be quicker to advocate turning to violent means to achieve the goals they proposed. Often inclined to strike a high-handed attitude as representatives of the emperor, they regarded dissension or refusal of their diktats by the lesser Italian powers as disobedience to be repressed, if need be.

Siena was still a prime target for being brought under the direct control of Charles and his agents in Italy. The republic had been on the agenda Granvelle had been left to deal with while Charles was engaged in his expedition against Algiers in 1541. Under his direction, the government of Siena had been reformed yet again, with provisions for Imperial officials to nominate to several important posts. The recommendation of Juan de Luna, appointed the Imperial representative in Siena in 1543, that Charles should take over the fortresses on the Sienese coast was rejected by the emperor as inexpedient.[86] De Luna considered the emperor to be too careful in his handling of the Sienese,[87] yet his own handling of them resulted in an uprising in 1546, and he and the Spanish garrison withdrew from the city. His replacement, Francesco Grasso, told the emperor that reform in Siena had to be backed by troops, and that fewer troops would be needed if a fortress were to be built there.[88] Ordered by Charles to intervene, Ferrante Gonzaga demanded the Sienese should accept several hundred Spanish troops, but only in late September 1547 did they finally admit 400, after warnings from several quarters that if they did not agree, force would be used against them. Diego de Mendoza, the Imperial ambassador in Rome, was given the task of representing the emperor in Siena as well. Soon, he was applying pressure on the Sienese to build a fortress, to be paid for by them but held for the emperor.

The same proposition was put to the Genoese. Charles liked the idea of securing a hold over Genoa, but did not want to upset Andrea Doria. The question came to the fore after the failure in early January 1547 of a conspiracy against Doria led by Gianluigi Fieschi, who aimed to recover the predominant position in the republic of Genoa his family had enjoyed for generations. The conspiracy was encouraged by Francis and by the pope. Fieschi drowned as he seized Doria's galleys in the harbour, and Doria's nephew Giannettino was killed but, crucially, Doria himself escaped. The surviving Fieschi brothers joined the host of Italian exiles in France. In the aftermath, Doria and the Genoese government stressed that once the Fieschi had been uprooted from Liguria, there was no threat to the regime. On the other hand, Charles's ambassador in Genoa, Gómez Suárez de Figueroa, and Ferrante Gonzaga argued the need for heightened security, for a garrison, a governor and a fortress. Charles ordered a careful sounding of opinion there, following which Figueroa became more cautious, recognizing the strength of attachment among the Genoese to their independence. Gonzaga, however, favoured pressing ahead and proposed infiltrating troops into Genoa. Charles was ready to settle for a more oligarchic government and the establishment of a garrison, and then work towards a fortress. No garrison came, and no fortress would be built. Doria pushed through a modest reform of the government and was adamant that was enough.

The spur to fulfilling the promise of reform in Genoa had been Ferrante Gonzaga taking over Piacenza in September 1547. Piacenza was taken not from the pope, but from his son, Pierluigi Farnese, who had been granted Parma and Piacenza by his father in fief, as two separate duchies, in August 1545. To overcome opposition among the cardinals to this grant, Paul had to agree to his family giving up Camerino, which had been granted to his grandson Ottavio in 1540. Charles never recognized Pierluigi's title to Parma and Piacenza. To him, these cities were part of the duchy of Milan. Gonzaga urged their strategic importance and the contribution they could make to the duchy's resources, and fostered Charles's concern that Pierluigi was inclining to France. He suggested using Piacentine nobles sympathetic to Charles and hostile to Pierluigi's efforts to impose his authority on the nobility, to encourage them to conspire against him and then to call on Gonzaga to occupy the city for the emperor. Stipulating that Pierluigi should not be harmed, if possible, Charles gave his approval to these plans.

He was not concerned about offending the pope, for his relations with him were already bad. Paul had been angered by Charles's alliance with the heretic Henry VIII (worse, the pope said, than the alliance of Francis with the Turks[89]), and by the concessions he had been prepared to make to the German Protestants over the nature and location of the ecclesiastical council that had finally opened at Trent in 1545. The pope had been discussing a league with France and with the Venetians (who did not wish to be drawn into it). Knowing of this proposed league, Charles was also angry with the pope for withdrawing troops he had sent to help in the war against the Protestants in Germany in February 1547.

On 10 September Pierluigi was assassinated by the conspirators in the citadel of Piacenza, and the next day Gonzaga came to take possession of the city, with only a few troops. The intention was to make it appear that he was responding to an appeal, but it was widely suspected that he was behind the assassination, and that Charles too was implicated. Implementation of the plot had been delayed until Ottavio Farnese, the emperor's son-in-law, had left Piacenza. On hearing of the assassination of his father, Ottavio went to Parma, where he was accepted by the population as their lord. Gonzaga occupied much of the territory of Parma, but would not risk starting a war with the pope by attacking the city itself. His failure to take Parma would make holding on to Piacenza more difficult, and costly.

Gonzaga's engineering of the coup at Piacenza, and Mendoza's arrogant assumption of authority over Siena, would both backfire. Rather than consolidating Spanish power in Italy, they made other Italian powers more wary of Charles's intentions, and they would create opportunities for French intervention there at a time when Charles would be hard-pressed elsewhere in Europe, and the last thing he wanted was a renewal of the Italian Wars.

Notes

1 De Leva, II, 560.

2 *Ibid.*, 352: Charles to his ambassadors in France, 28 Oct. 1529.

3 Lanz, I, 367–8: Charles to Ferdinand, 11 Jan. 1530.

4 D'Amico, 68–76; *CSPSpan*, IV, i, 234–5.

5 *CSPSpan*, IV, i, 374–5.

6 Lanz, I, 367–8.

7 Sanuto, LII, 383–6.

8 Lanz, I, 360–73: Charles to Ferdinand, 11 Jan. 1530; a not entirely accurate English summary and translation of this important letter is in *CSSpan*, IV, i, 396–409.

9 Lanz, I, 364–5.

10 Molini, II, 295–6.

11 Roth, 194.

12 Bardi, 68, 73: Orange to Charles, 25 Oct., 8 Nov. 1529.

13 Roth, 254.

14 *Ibid.*, 194–5.

15 *Ibid.*, 194.

16 *Ibid.*, 193.

17 Monti, 101.

18 *Ibid.*, 97.

19 *Ibid.*

20 Roth, 313.

21 Sanuto, LIII, 501–3.

22 Rubinstein, 167–8.

23 *Ibid.*, 172–3.

24 AGS, Estado 1457, 103–4.

25 *Ibid.*

26 ASLucca, Anziani, Reg. 618, ff. 127–8.

27 *Ibid.*, ff. 385–7.

28 Pacini, 301–4.

29 Shaw, 'The other Congress of Bologna'.

30 De Leva, III, 95.

31 Mola, 13–16.

32 Lanz, II, 59, 64–5, 68–9.

33 De Leva, III, 110–1; Knecht, 230.

34 Chabod, 51–5.

35 Lestocquoy, *Correspondance … 1535–1540*, 106.

36 An ordinance of 1534 created seven legions of retained infantry in frontier and coastal provinces of France, each of 6,000 men (Potter, 112–13).

37 Lestocquoy, *Correspondance … 1535–1540*, 148.

38 Potter, 66.

39 Lestocquoy, *Correspondance … 1535–1540*, 164.

40 Brandi, 377–8.

41 *CSPSpan*, V, ii, 102–3.

42 *Ibid.*, V, ii, 116–7.

43 *Ibid.*, 400.

44 Jover, 398–9.

45 Lanz, II, 239.

46 Pacini, 311; de Leva, III, 172.

47 Lestocquoy, *Correspondance … 1535–1540*, 231.

48 *CSPSpan*, V, ii, 328–33.

49 Spini, 116.

50 Bourrilly, 241.

51 *CSPSpan*, V, ii, 356–7.

52 *Ibid.*, 366–8.

53 Bourrilly, 252–3.

54 De Leva, III, 235.

55 *CSPSpan*, V, ii, 393–415.

56 Turba, I, 111, 124–7, 130–1.

57   *Ibid.*, I, 152–3; Jover, 375.

58   Lanz, II, 284–9; de Leva, III, 246; *CSPSpan*, V, ii, 561–6.

59   Lestocquoy, *Correspondance … 1535–1540*, 387.

60   *CSPSpan*, VI, i, 335–8, 340.

61   Lanz, II, 316–17.

62   *CSPSpan*, VI, i, 267.

63   Lestocquoy, *Correspondance … 1541–1546*, 91.

64   *CSPSpan*,VI, ii, 56.

65   Bourrilly, 358.

66   *CSPSpan*, VI, ii, 265.

67   Lestocquoy, *Correspondance … 1541–1546*, 251–2.

68   Courteault, 137.

69   Lestocquoy, *Correspondance … 1541–1546*, 293, 297.

70   Hall, 186. According to du Bellay (Bourrilly and Vindry, IV, 217–8), the Imperial army was far larger, around 25,000 infantry and 2,500 horse.

71   Bourrilly and Vindry, IV, 219.

72   Monluc, I, 267.

73   Bourrilly and Vindry, IV, 214–29; Monluc, I, 256–77; Roy,104–17; Giovio, ff. 375–8 (the main account from the Imperial perspective); Courteault, 152–71; Rabà, 'Ceresole'.

74   Bourrilly and Vindry, IV, 228.

75   Lot, 85.

76   Giovio, f. 378r.

77   Bourrilly and Vindry, IV, 230.

78   De Leva, III, 506.

79   *Ibid.*

80   Bourrilly and Vindry, IV, 236.

81   Dumont, IV, 2, 279–87.

82   Chabod, 97–113; *CSPSpan*,VII, i, 478–93.

83   Turba, I, 486.

84   Chabod, 123–30.

85   *Ibid.*, 30, note 1.

86   AGS, Estado, leg. 1461, 154, 166: Juan de Luna to Charles V, 2 Nov., 29 Oct. 1545, Siena; 192: Charles V to Juan de Luna, 2 Dec. 1544, Brussels.

87   AGS, Estado, leg. 1464, 31: instructions Juan de Luna to Antonio Gilberte, 15 Feb. 1546, Siena; Juan de Luna to Philip, 28 Feb. 1546, Siena.

88   AGS, Estado, leg. 1464, 89–91: Francesco Grasso to Charles V, 27 Aug. 1546, Siena; 76: Franceso Grasso to Granvelle, 11 Oct. 1546, Siena.

89   De Leva, III, 522.

Bibliography

Bardi, Alessandro, 'Carlo V e l'assedio di Firenze', *Archivio storico italiano*, Ser. 5, 11 (1893), 1–85.

Bourrilly, V.-L., *Guillaume du Bellay, Seigneur de Langey, 1491–1543* (Paris: Société nouvelle de librairie et d'édition, 1905).

Bourrilly, V.-L. and F. Vindry (eds), *Mémoires de Martin et Guillaume du Bellay*, 4 vols (Paris: Renouard, 1908–19).

Brandi, Karl, *The Emperor Charles V. The Growth and Destiny of a Man and of a World-Empire*, trans. C.V. Wedgwood (London: Jonathan Cape, 1939).

Calendar of State Papers, Spanish (HMSO, 1862–1964) [*CSPSpan*].

Capasso, C., *Paolo III* (Messina: G. Principato,1924).

Chabod, Federico, *Storia di Milano nell'epoca di Carlo V* (Turin: Giulio Einaudi, 1971).

Courteault, Paul, *Blaise de Monluc historien: Étude critique sur la texte et la valeur historique des Commentaires* (Paris: Alphonse Picard, 1908).

D'Amico, Juan Carlos, *Charles Quint maître du monde entre mythe et réalité* (Caen: Presses Universitaires de Caen, 2004).

de Leva, G., *Storia documentata di Carlo V in relazione all'Italia*, 5 vols (Venice: Naratovich, 1863-Bologna: Zanichelli, 1894).

Dumont, Jean, *Corps universel diplomatique du droit des gens*, 8 vols (Amsterdam, 1726–31).

Giovio, Paolo, *Delle istorie del suo tempo* (*Historiae sui temporis*, trans. Lodovico Domenichi), 2 vols (Venice,1581).

Hale, J.R., 'The end of Florentine liberty: the Fortezza di Basso', in J.R. Hale, *Renaissance War Studies* (Hambledon Press, 1983), 31–62.

Hall, Bert S., *Weapons and Warfare in Renaissance Europe* (Baltimore: Johns Hopkins University Press, 1997).

Jover, José Maria, *Carlos V y los Españoles* (Madrid: Ediciones Rialp, 1963).

Knecht, R.J., *Francis I* (Cambridge: Cambridge University Press, 1982).

Lanz, K., *Correspondenz des Kaisers Karl V*, 3 vols (Leipzig: Brockhaus, 1846).

Lestocquoy, J. (ed.), *Correspondance des Nonces en France Carpi et Ferrerio, 1535–1540* (Rome: Università Gregoriana, 1961).

Lestocquoy, J. (ed.), *Correspondance des Nonces en France Capodiferro, Dandino et Guidiccione, 1541–1546* (Rome: Università Gregoriana, 1963).

Lot, Ferdinand, *Recherches sur les effectifs des armées françaises des Guerres d'Italie aux Guerres de Religion 1494–1562* (Paris: SEVPEN, 1962).

Mola, Aldo Alessandro, *Fastigi e declino d'uno Stato di confine. Il marchesato di Saluzzo dalla fine degli equilibri d'Italia al dominio francese* (Milan: Marzorati,1986).

Molini, G., *Documenti di storia italiana*, 2 vols (Florence: Dante,1836–7).

Monluc, Blaise de, *Commentaires*, ed. Paul Courteault, 3 vols (Paris: Alphonse Picard, 1911–25).

Monti, Alessandro, *La Guerra dei Medici. Firenze e il suo dominio nei giorni dell'assedio (1529–1530). Uomini, fatti, battaglie* (Florence: Nuova Toscana Editrice, 2007).

Pacini, Arturo, *La Genova di Andrea Doria nell'Impero di Carlo V* (Florence: Leo S. Olschki, 1999).

Podestà, Gian Luca, *Dal delitto politico alla politica del delitto. Finanza pubblica e congiure contro i Farnese nel Ducato di Parma e Piacenza dal 1545 al 1622* (Milan: EGEA,1995).

Potter, David, *Renaissance France at War. Armies, Culture and Society, c. 1480–1560* (Woodbridge: Boydell Press, 2008).

Rabà, Michele Maria, 'Ceresole (14 aprile 1544): una grande, inutile vittoria. Conflitto tra potenze e guerra di logoramento nella prima Età moderna', in Alessandro Buono and Gianclaudio Civale,

Battaglie. L'evento, l'individuo, la memoria (Palermo: eBook Mediterranea, 2014), 101–40.

Rabà, Michele, 'La nuova "porta d'Italia". Il Piemonte di Carlo II tra Francia e Impero: un'analisi geopolitica', in Marco Bellabarba and Andrea Merlotti (eds), *Stato sabaudo e Sacro Romano Impero* (Bologna: Società editrice il Mulino, 2014), 213–32.

Raba, Michele M., *Potere e poteri. 'Stati', 'privati' e comunità nel conflitto per l'egemonia in Italia settentrionale (1536–1558)* (Milan: FrancoAngeli, 2016).

Raviola, Blythe Alice, *Il Monferrato Gonzaghesco. Istituzioni ed élites di un micro-stato (1536–1708)* (Florence: Leo S. Olschki, 2003).

Roth, Cecil, *The Last Florentine Republic* (Methuen, 1925).

Roy, Ian (ed.), *Blaise de Monluc. The Habsburg-Valois Wars and the French Wars of Religion* (London: Longman, 1971).

Rubinstein, Nicolai, 'Dalla repubblica al principato', in *Firenze e la Toscana dei Medici nell'Europa del '500*, 3 vols (Florence: Leo S. Olschki, 1983), I, 159–76.

Sanuto, Marino Sanuto, *I Diarii*, ed. R. Fulin et al., 58 vols (Venice: Reale Deputazione veneta di storia patria, 1879–1903).

Shaw, Christine, 'The other Congress of Bologna', in Machtelt Israëls and Louis A. Waldman (eds), *Renaissance Studies in Honor of Joseph Connors*, 2 vols (Florence: Villa I Tatti, 2013), II, 114–9.

Shaw, Christine, 'The return of the Sienese exiles, 1530–1531', in *Paroles d'exil. Culture d'opposition et théorie politique au XVIe siècle (Laboratoire italien*, 14 (2014)), 13–30.

Simoncelli, Paolo, *Fuoriuscitismo repubblicano fiorentino 1530–54 (Volume primo -1530–37)* (Milan: FrancoAngeli, 2006).

Spini, Giorgio, *Cosimo I de' Medici e la indipendenza del Principato Mediceo* (Florence: Vallecchi, 1945).

Storia di Milano, VIII, *Tra Francia e la Spagna 1500–1535* (Milan: Fondazione Treccani, 1957).

Turba, Gustav (ed.), *Venetianische Depeschen vom Kaiserhofe (Dispacci di Germania)*, 3 vols (Vienna: F. Tempsky, 1889).

von Albertini, Rudolf, *Firenze dalla repubblica al principato: Storia e coscienza politica* (Turin: Einaudi, 1970).

CHAPTER 7

The French challenge, 1547–59

During the last decade of the Italian Wars, Imperial and Spanish hegemony in Italy was under challenge from the French, whose forces had the upper hand in Piedmont, extended their base in central Italy from Mirandola to Parma, became entrenched in Sienese territory, and attacked the kingdom of Naples. Charles V lacked the energy to respond adequately to these threats, and gradually handed over the government of his Italian lands and oversight of Italian affairs in general to his son Philip. But Charles found it hard to let go, and Philip had to struggle for the control and direction of the resources needed to combat the French in Italy. In the event, it was the outcome of the war on the northern frontier of France that put an end to the French challenge in Italy, and to the Italian Wars.

From April 1547 there was a new king of France, Henry II. Henry spoke Italian fluently; his court, like that of his father, was full of Italians, many of them exiles. His Italian wife, Caterina de' Medici, had close ties to Florentine exiles, especially her cousins, Piero Strozzi and his brothers. Henry was not as interested as his father had been in planning campaigns to recover Milan and Naples, but he was determined to hold on to Savoy, Piedmont and Saluzzo, lands he regarded as a defensive bulwark for his kingdom against attacks from Italy. The recovery of Boulogne and then Calais from the English was the king's military priority, and he also became involved in Scotland, fending off English attempts to establish dominance over their northern neighbours and protecting the young Mary, Queen of Scots who was betrothed to the dauphin. Henry did not have to deal with his English namesake, for Henry VIII had died in January 1547, but with the government of the young king Edward VI, and then from July 1553 Queen Mary. From 1554, when Mary married Philip, to her death in November 1558, Henry had to reckon with a Habsburg king of England; fortunately for him, Philip never got full control of English policy and resources. Nevertheless, in these circumstances it is understandable why Henry's attention was directed to the north of his kingdom, not the south.

The French challenge in Italy during his reign was in large part the outcome of the interests and initiatives of his agents and representatives in Italy, of the Italian exiles in his service, of his wife and his favourites, the brothers François and Cardinal Charles de Guise. The brothers had been loyal companions to him during the years when he was kept on the side-lines at his father's court, and were allies of the king's influential mistress Diane de Poitiers. François de Guise married Anna d'Este, daughter of the Duke of Ferrara, a match Henry helped to arrange. The duke's brother, Cardinal Ippolito d'Este, had been a favourite of Francis, and he kept Henry's favour, becoming an influential representative of French interests in Italy. Counterbalancing the Guises and their allies was another favourite of the king, the Constable Montmorency, who opposed their adventurism. Henry had great respect for his experience and judgement, and Montmorency assumed the role of chief minister and tried to control foreign policy.

Affairs in Germany were still the emperor's major preoccupation, together with the connected question of the affairs of his own family. He wanted to break the longstanding family compact, and to have his son Philip rather than his brother Ferdinand succeed him as emperor. There was also ill-feeling among the Habsburgs over the question of who should inherit which parts of the family lands, especially the Netherlands, which Charles detached from the Empire, enlarged by incorporating recently conquered territory, and set up as an independent state in 1548. In March 1551 the brothers reached a secret accord that Ferdinand would succeed Charles as emperor and then seek to have Philip elected as King of the Romans; Philip as emperor would then procure the election of Ferdinand's son Maximilian. But Ferdinand would not agree to Charles's wishes about the division of the family lands, relations between the brothers remained tense, and Charles could not rely on his co-operation in the German wars.

Like his father, Henry was ready and willing to form alliances with Charles's opponents in the Empire. He hated Charles, because he and his brother had been badly treated when, as boys, they were hostages for their father in Spain. He was also ready to maintain his father's understanding with Suleiman, and to co-ordinate his campaigns on land and sea with the

Turks. But it was in Italy that the war between Henry and Charles would begin, at Parma and in Piedmont.

The War of Parma and Mirandola, 1551–2

The matter of Parma and Piacenza had become very complicated. After the assassination of his son Pierluigi and the seizure of Piacenza by Ferrante Gonzaga in September 1547, the pope made no attempt to recover the city by force. He urged Charles to restore it, as belonging to the papacy, but the emperor refused, denying that the pope had any legal title to it. As Charles knew, Paul was negotiating an alliance with Henry. Although the king would not commit himself to sending troops to take Piacenza back, he was ready to commit to the defence of Parma, provided it was given to Orazio Farnese, Ottavio's younger brother, who was betrothed in June 1547 to Henry's natural daughter Diane. Paul said he could not invest Orazio with Parma until the French army was in the field, because the investiture would be bound to cause a war.[1] Negotiations continued, on and off, for the rest of the pontificate.

As Charles was not only keeping Piacenza but claiming Parma too, Paul at last decided to resolve the problem by revoking the grant of both cities to his own family, arguing that Charles then had no grounds for refusing to restore Piacenza to the Church.[2] Ottavio was to have Camerino, Orazio the family lands which had been elevated into the duchy of Castro. Opposed to this solution, Ottavio left Rome for Parma clandestinely in October 1549. On hearing of this, Paul ordered Camillo Orsini, the commander of the papal troops stationed there, to hold the city for the papacy. Having been refused admission to the fortress, Ottavio left Parma. He contacted Ferrante Gonzaga to ask for support, and wrote to the pope saying he could not in honour consent to renounce it. His letter infuriated Paul, who fell ill, and died a few days later. As the pope lay on his deathbed, Cardinal Alessandro Farnese induced him to sign an order to Camillo Orsini to give Parma to Ottavio.[3]

Paul's last order was reiterated in late February 1550 by his successor, Giovanni Maria del Monte, Julius III, soon after his election. Changeable, given to outbursts of temper, the new pope preferred a life of leisure to grappling with affairs of state. He was not especially ambitious for his own family, or hostile to the Farnese, provided they would show him respect. Yet Ottavio did not feel secure. Imperial troops held some of the territory of Parma, as well as Piacenza, and the emperor still wanted both cities for himself. Julius would not accept that Charles should have Parma. While

Piacenza could be said to form part of a chain of defences for Milan, linking the Ligurian Apennines to the river Po and Cremona, the pope argued, Parma constituted a forward defence for Bologna and the Papal States.[4] The Farnese were in a dilemma. Ottavio and Cardinal Alessandro did not want to lose the lands and benefices they held in Charles's territories, or to surrender Parma to him. At length they agreed to Orazio's proposal that they should turn to Henry. The king was happy to take the Farnese into his protection, with the prospect of being able to use Parma as another base for operations in Italy. He would have preferred it should be held by Orazio, but was content to make an agreement with Ottavio instead. Julius argued that to approve Henry's protection of Ottavio would endanger the Papal States, which was surrounded by the emperor's lands. Ottavio had been offered Camerino in exchange for Parma, so Henry had no pretext for intervention if Parma were to return to the Church. In the circumstances, Julius said, he had to ask Charles for help.[5] Charles was ready to agree: if the Farnese refused to leave Parma, they should be forced out, he said.[6]

The pope was not keen on the prospect of a war, warning Charles from the first that he had no money to pay for it. Charles himself was less keen than Ferrante Gonzaga was, but nevertheless advised that the crops around Parma should be destroyed. The major impetus towards war was coming from Henry. He sent Piero Strozzi in early May 1551 to put the defences of Mirandola in order, and also sent Orazio Farnese to Italy, giving him the command of 1,000 light horse. Before Orazio left, he married Henry's daughter Diane. In late May, Henry concluded a treaty with Ottavio, declaring himself the protector of the Farnese family, and undertaking to provide 2,000 infantry and 200 light horse to defend Parma, and an annual subsidy of 12,000 écus.[7]

Ferrante Gonzaga had anticipated events by seizing Brescello, a possession of Cardinal d'Este, on 1 May on the grounds that it would have been used to defend Parma. He was eager to press on with spoiling the crops there, but Julius thought this would only serve to make Ottavio more reliant on the French, and help them to link Parma with Mirandola as a base for French forces in Italy.[8] What tipped Julius into a more committed prosecution of the war in mid-June, was a raid on Bolognese territory by the forces of the Italian exiles fighting for the French, among them the Bolognese exile, Cornelio Bentivoglio; Orazio Farnese also took part. Papal troops under Gianbattista del Monte, the pope's nephew, who had just joined up with Ferrante Gonzaga, were ordered to go to defend Bologna, and the armies separated again on 26 June. Gonzaga decided to leave the papal troops to confront the forces based at Mirandola, to deepen the hostility between the pope and king.[9] As matters stood, Henry and Julius were not at war – Henry was only supporting Ottavio Farnese. Nor were Henry and Charles at war – Charles was only supporting the pope.

The siege of Mirandola by the papal army under the command of Camillo Orsini (Gianbattista del Monte had fallen ill) began in early July; the defenders were commanded by the veteran French soldier Termes. Around Parma, Gonzaga took the stronghold of Colorno on 3 July. Piero Strozzi and Cornelio Bentivoglio had left Mirandola before the arrival of the papal troops there, to go to relieve Colorno, and managed to enter Parma with 300 horse and around 1,500 infantry.[10] The papal forces were insufficient to besiege Mirandola effectively from their encampments, which had been constructed too far from the walls, even before Ferrante Gonzaga had to ask for the return of the cavalry he had lent del Monte, and Julius had ordered they be reduced to 4,000 infantry. Reinforcements of 4,000 German infantry arrived in mid-August for Gonzaga, and after dismissing many Italian infantry, Gonzaga was left with 8,000 foot and 1,000 horse[11] to continue the systematic devastation of the territory of Parma, despite objections from Julius, who did not want Parma ruined. Gonzaga dismissed the objections, arguing that this was a justifiable way to wage war.[12] Once he had prevented the sowing of crops for the next season, he proposed to settle his men into winter quarters.

His plans had to change in early September and he had to hurry to Piedmont, where the French had launched an attack. The marchese di Marignano was left to continue the campaign against Parma with 6,000 foot, including 1,000 papal infantry, and 300 horse.[13] The number of troops available was further reduced when Charles ordered a cut in expenses in late October, which did not help in accomplishing another order from the emperor, to finish off the campaign against Parma and Mirandola by the spring. Not enough men were left to prevent supplies reaching Parma, where Termes had taken over the command, or to block sorties from the city, and the Imperial troops were restive for lack of pay. In Mirandola, the defenders stood firm, making successful sallies against the papal encampments. The expense of the war made Julius uneasy. He suggested to Charles in late December that Gonzaga should take over the siege of Mirandola, offering to contribute 2,000 infantry and 200 horse.[14] Gonzaga did not leave Piedmont, and before a solution could found, the pope came to terms with Henry.

Julius announced the agreement on 15 April 1552 (his nephew Gianbattista was killed in a skirmish the same day). During the fortnight before it came into effect, Gonzaga ordered attempts be made to occupy the positions that were about to be vacated by the papal troops before the French did, but these attempts failed. When Charles consulted Gonzaga about whether he should accede to the truce, Gonzaga reluctantly advised that he had to, and Charles duly ratified it on 10 May. There was to be a truce for two years, at the end of which Ottavio would be at liberty to come to terms with the pope; Castro, which had been occupied by papal troops, was to be restored to the Farnese. These terms signified a clear victory for the French. Ottavio Farnese was to stay in Parma, and there was no stipulation that the French forces had to leave there or Mirandola.

The war in north-west Italy, 1551–2

The truce did not cover Piedmont, Monferrato and Saluzzo. Like the earlier wars in this region, the war there was mainly one of short campaigns, whose aim was to take towns and fortresses which were often won in a few days, but could be rapidly lost again. Neither side had enough men to garrison and hold on to all their gains. On the whole, the French had the advantage. Charles de Cossé, sieur de Brissac, Henry's lieutenant in Piedmont since July 1550, was a gifted military leader, always looking for opportunities, while Gonzaga was hindered by a chronic shortage of funds, which left him sometimes unsure of the temper and reliability of his men.

Henry had decided on a renewal of the war in Piedmont in late August 1551. Hostilities began before the formal declaration of war, on 2–3 September, with simultaneous attacks on three places, San Damiano, south-west of Asti, which was quickly taken; Chieri, south-east of Turin, which surrendered after a few days; and Cherasco further to the south, where the attack failed. Brissac's forces occupied several places in Monferrato, while his cavalry raided to the gates of Asti, where Gonzaga arrived with 2,000 German infantry and some cavalry from Parma to add to the forces already on the border. In October Gonzaga recovered some ground in Monferrato, but had no money to replace the troops he was losing to disease. Charles ordered him to put some Spanish and German troops in garrisons on the frontier, dismiss the Italian infantry and go to finish off the siege of Parma and Mirandola.[15] Gonzaga did not obey, responding that he needed Italian infantry to garrison outlying strongholds, and some men must be kept in the field. He had also heard that the French were sending reinforcements to Parma which would pass through the duchy of Milan, and so in early December he was encamped with 4,000 infantry between Vercelli and Casale to block them if they came.

Reinforcements for Brissac arrived from France, including many French noble volunteers, among them François de Guise, who came anticipating a battle.[16] As Gonzaga was in no position to give battle, Brissac was able to take the stronghold of Lanzo, to the north-west of Turin, at the end of November. The Imperial army fell back before his advance, leaving Volpiano as the only place in Piedmont held by Imperial troops on the left bank of the Po. But Brissac could not keep all he had won, because the king recalled the veteran French infantry companies, and dismissed 1,300 Italian troops. The noble adventurers returned to France, Guise carrying a protest from Brissac about the effects these economies would have.[17]

In the spring of 1552, Gonzaga decided he could go onto the offensive, and invade Saluzzo (held for Henry since 1548 when Marquis Gabriele had been arrested and deposed; he died in his French prison). At the beginning of May he marched on Brà, which Brissac had to evacuate, falling back on Carmagnola while the Imperial army took much of the marquisate. They then returned to Piedmont, and began to blockade Bene. So short of money were the Imperial soldiers that they were selling their arms and horses to buy food, and Gonzaga begged Charles to make better provision for the army. Having ratified the truce between Julius and Henry, the emperor ordered him to stay on the defensive, and to try for a truce in Piedmont. The French would not agree to one, and Gonzaga had to raise the siege of Bene on 15 July and retire to Asti.

Charles V at bay

The emperor ordered Gonzaga to hold back in Piedmont because his affairs generally were in crisis. Henry, in alliance with the German princes opposed to Charles, was pressing him hard. In late May 1552, Charles had to flee from Innsbruck to avoid being captured by his enemies. He did not feel he could safely take refuge in Italy, because his prestige there had suffered, the troops were restless, and he had no resources to bring with him to reinforce his authority. Recognizing the desperation of the people in Italy, that he had few friends there and many enemies, he believed he would be forced to retreat to Spain.[18] Two major causes underlay the discontent of the emperor's subjects and his lack of friends in Italy. One was the financial burdens imposed on his dominions to pay for his wars and to support the troops stationed there. The second major cause was the attitudes and policies of his lieutenants, viceroys and other officials, notably their tendency to subordinate local nobilities, accustomed to a large share in the governance of their states. Some individuals were able to make a career in the service of the emperor, or profit from the provision of goods and financial services to the administration, but many felt slighted and excluded.

Rivals and enemies of Ferrante Gonzaga, who was accused of financial malversation, portrayed the situation in Milan to Charles as being even worse than it was. In Naples, Pedro de Toledo's despotic ways provoked a revolt in the summer of 1547. The Neapolitans sent to Charles to tell him that their revolt was against Toledo, not him, but he listened to his viceroy, who kept his post. Diego de Mendoza, Charles's ambassador in Rome and representative at Siena, also held responsibility for Piombino, and saw himself as a quasi-viceroy. Such was his arrogance and discourtesy to the pope that Julius took to refusing to see him. In Piombino, which had been taken into Charles's hands on the grounds that the lord, Jacopo d'Appiano, could not defend it adequately against the fleets of the Turks and corsairs,[19] Mendoza failed to maintain, let alone improve, the fortifications. At Siena, his insistence on the construction of a fortress and his bullying of the citizens led to an uprising and the expulsion of the Spanish in July 1552.

All these problems, together with the setbacks for Charles at Parma and Mirandola, fired the ambitions of French agents in Italy and the Italian exiles in French service. Leading representatives of the king in Italy – Cardinals François de Tournon and Ippolito d'Este, Odet de Selve, his ambassador in Venice, and Paul de Termes – met with Ludovico Pico della Mirandola, Ferrante da Sanseverino, principe di Salerno, the most powerful noble in the kingdom of Naples, recently driven into exile by Toledo's hostility, and other exiles at Chioggia on the Venetian lagoon for four days in mid-July 1552. They discussed what use should be made of the forces freed up by the end of the war at Parma and Mirandola. Top of the list was the invasion of Naples, but it was decided this was not feasible. Henry had been attempting to form an alliance with the pope and Venice for an attack on Naples, but both had refused. It was agreed that Salerno should join the French fleet at Marseilles and sail to join the Turkish fleet that had been in the Tyrrhenian sea since June, to raid the Neapolitan coast. A bid for support by Sienese exiles was successful. This move into Tuscany would be a major enterprise. It is hard to imagine Charles giving his agents that degree of initiative, and it would have taken months of correspondence and deliberations before approval was given. Henry's agents were allowed – or took upon themselves – such freedom of action that they put the scheme into effect immediately.

The War of Siena, 1552–5

The French would claim the credit for the expulsion of the Spanish from Siena. Their support was timely, but discontent in Siena had reached the pitch where an uprising would probably have happened soon in any case. Mendoza had become fixated on the project of building a fortress there. He told Charles that it was the Sienese who were asking for a fortress, and the Sienese that it was Charles. The emperor agreed the plans Mendoza sent to him, and brushed aside the protests of the Sienese. Despite getting little money from Charles for the project, and very little money, materials or labour from the Sienese, Mendoza pressed on, paying for the work himself. He accomplished the apparently impossible feat of uniting Sienese of all factions and social classes behind one aim – but that aim was freeing themselves of Mendoza, the troops and the fortress. Given the attitude Charles was adopting, that meant throwing off their subordination to him, and that led to seeking the protection of the French.

Plans were laid for an uprising in Siena to coincide with incursions into Sienese territory by French troops from the neighbouring estates of barons sympathetic to the French, such as Nicola Orsini, conte di Pitigliano. False reports were deliberately circulated which deceived Mendoza into believing that it had been decided to attack Naples, so that he sent half the garrison to defend the Sienese ports.[20] One of the conspirators planning the uprising, Amerigo Amerighi, was a member of the main executive body in the Sienese government, the Balia, and he contrived to get orders from the Balia to raise the militia in the territory, supposedly to face the threat of the Turkish fleet. Even most of the captains had no notion of the real reason why the militia was being mustered, before they marched on Siena.

When the militia appeared beneath the walls on 27 July, the garrison (Mendoza was in Rome) were unsure what to do. One gate was taken by force, the others opened to the militia. On the following afternoon, French contingents began to arrive, as the Spanish troops, together with 400 Florentine militia who had been sent in their support, were concentrating within the curtain wall of the fortress, all that had been built. Cosimo prepared to send more troops but held them back on receiving a message from the French that to oppose the uprising would be to oppose them too.

Unwilling to enter into a war against the French, Cosimo began negotiating with the Sienese. Mendoza had to order his men to conform to whatever terms were agreed. These were concluded on 3 August. The troops were to leave the fortress; the Sienese could demolish it, and should send all other foreign troops away after the Spanish had cleared the state (in fact a Spanish garrison would stay in Orbetello). They were to remain loyal to the Empire – but the Sienese were careful not to pledge continued loyalty to Charles.[21] On 5 August, the troops left the fortress, and the Sienese began to tear it down with a will. Soon, the French were assuming greater powers over Siena than the Sienese wished them to have; Cardinal Ippolito d'Este, who came on 1 November as Henry's lieutenant-general there, was inclined to behave as though he were governor.

Absorbed in assembling a huge army for a campaign in Germany, the emperor had little attention to spare for Siena. Pedro de Toledo offered to mount an expedition to Tuscany from Naples. While not rejecting this offer, Charles refused to bear any of the costs. With difficulty, Toledo raised an army, scraping together what money he could. The men were still short of weapons, and Toledo had not found a competent commander for them when the emperor began to urge him to launch the campaign. The siege of Metz, where Charles had looked for glory, was going badly, and opening another front in Italy would, he hoped, distract the French.[22] Throughout January 1553, a total of 16,000–18,000 horse and foot made their way, some by sea, some overland, to Tuscany from Naples.[23]

Toledo was relying on Cosimo, his son-in-law, to provide substantial help for these troops, and Cosimo had little option but to support the campaign. When Toledo died in late February, Charles asked Cosimo to take command, but he refused. Pedro's son Garcia took charge, but lacked the personal qualities to impose his authority over his captains, and the campaign would be vitiated by a lack of drive. Most of February was taken up by the occupation of the Sienese part of the Val di Chiana, which was not defended by the Sienese. The army then began to besiege the fortified village of Monticchiello, suffering heavy losses before lack of food and ammunition caused its surrender after 20 days. Four thousand German troops from Lombardy sent in mid-March to the Maremma, where they were joined by 400 Spanish soldiers, were left to their own devices. After a group of 500 Germans escorting a supply train were killed or taken prisoner by troops from Grosseto, the others left to join the main body of the army at Montalcino. This small town to the south of Siena was at an important node of the road network with links to the coast and overlooked the main route to Rome. It was defended with spirit and ingenuity, although bombardment and sapping damaged the fortifications considerably. Toledo's soldiers lost interest, and began fraternizing with the defenders. On 15 June, the siege was lifted: Toledo had orders from Charles to take the army back to Naples to defend the kingdom against the French and Turkish fleets. The Sienese hailed the defence of Montalcino as a great victory.

Spanish troops remained in Orbetello; Cosimo felt he had been left in the lurch nonetheless. He quickly raised 2,000 infantry, sent to Germany to raise 5,000 more there and 500 men-at-arms,[24] appointed the marchese di Marignano his commander, and strengthened the defences on the Sienese frontier and the coasts. In fact, the French were not planning an imminent attack on him. The Franco-Turkish fleet came to Port'Ercole in August to take on board 4,000 infantry under Termes, to join an assault on the Genoese-held island of Corsica. This left them with only 700 men in the city of Siena and 2,800 in the territory.[25]

By the autumn, the duke was laying plans not just for the defence of his own dominions but for an attack on Siena, and asked Charles for his support. The emperor promised Cosimo a financial subsidy, 2,000 German troops from Lombardy and 2,000 Spanish infantry and 300 horse from Naples. In theory, Cosimo would be undertaking this campaign to serve Charles, not for his own benefit, and Charles agreed to repay the expenses he would incur. Until this repayment was made, or Charles granted him territory in lieu of the money, Cosimo would retain all the lands conquered.[26] This agreement was made in November, over a month before Piero Strozzi came to Siena in early January 1554 to take command as Henry's lieutenant-general in Tuscany. The arrival of the most dangerous Florentine exile gave Cosimo a spur and a pretext for the campaign.[27]

Strozzi had been appointed lieutenant-general of the king in Tuscany in October 1553, and Henry had ordered all the Italian exiles at his court to go there too. Nominally, Strozzi was to help relieve Cardinal d'Este of the burden of affairs, but he was really to replace him.[28] The cardinal knew it, and resented it. Throughout his time in Siena, he was opposed to attacking Cosimo, and he insisted reports that a campaign against Siena was being prepared in Florence were just rumours. Even when Marignano led his army across the border in late January 1554, he issued orders that the Sienese should not take up arms, which they ignored. His misguided over-confidence meant that a fort that the Sienese had expended much effort in building the year before outside one of the main city gates, the Porta Camollia, was inadequately guarded. It was taken by surprise by a squadron of Spanish horse as the army neared Siena on the night of 26–27 January; the Sienese would never succeed in recapturing it. Strozzi, who had been inspecting fortifications in the territory, hurried back to the city two days later.

Marignano had with him about 4,000 foot, Florentine militia and some mercenaries, 400 Spanish horse and pioneers; the troops promised by the emperor from Naples and Milan would not arrive until the spring.[29]

This was nowhere near enough men to surround a city the size of Siena. Situated on a Y-shaped ridge and surrounded by three miles of walls, the city was too strong to be taken by assault. Marignano made his camp to the north of the city, before the Porta Camollia. The French had recovered some of the ground lost outside the gate, and constructed earthworks to provide platforms for their artillery, most of which was newly founded in Siena. Although Siena was only a dozen miles from the Florentine frontier, Marignano's lines of communication were precarious, so in March after the arrival of 1,500 Spanish infantry he sent detachments to set about reducing the Sienese bases in towers and fortified villages that threatened his communications and supplies. His plan was to blockade Siena, when he had enough men. To do this he needed to bar the roads leading west to the Maremma and south to Montalcino by which the Sienese could receive supplies. By early April, his forces had control of the Maremma road, completing this by taking the stronghold of Monastero a few miles from Siena. This became the base for a second siege-camp; he still did not have enough men to bar the road south. His troops were constantly harassed by artillery and arquebus fire from Sienese outworks and sallies from the city.

Directing his efforts against Siena, Marignano did not attempt to conquer its territory. After a while, Cosimo became impatient with what he thought were the paltry gains Marignano could show for months of campaigning, but his general retorted that Cosimo's plans were those of an armchair strategist and would not work in practice.[30] An attempt by Ascanio della Corgna, the commander of some 3,500 Florentine troops in the Val di Chiana, to take Chiusi in late March, ended disastrously when Strozzi, informed of his plans, ordered an ambush to be set. Around 2,000 men fell prisoner, including della Corgna himself; Ridolfo Baglioni was among the dead. This victory was celebrated in Siena, but not followed up in time to prevent Cosimo sending fresh troops to the Val di Chiana. After the arrival of substantial reinforcements from Lombardy – 3,500 infantry and some cavalry[31] – in late May operations in the territory were stepped up. A succession of small places were taken, all the defenders, soldiers or civilians, killed or sent to the Florentine galleys. From the start, the war in the territory was conducted with vicious cruelty, on the direct orders of Cosimo. His ruthlessness (which only increased the determination of the people to resist) was fuelled by fear and hatred of the Florentine exiles who had so prominent a role in the defence of Siena. Piero Strozzi was not much liked by the Sienese, either. Aware that his priority was Florence, they could sense that their interests and welfare were being sacrificed to the exiles' vendetta against Cosimo, not to protect them or their liberty.

With great care and secrecy, Strozzi laid plans for a raid into Florentine territory, which was to be co-ordinated with the arrival by sea at Port'Ercole of German and Gascon troops from Piedmont and by land of troops from Mirandola. Meanwhile, Pietro's brother Leone and the Neapolitan exile, Gianbernardo da Sanseverino, duca di Somma were to take Orbetello and Piombino, gather large quantities of grain and revictual Siena.[32] On the night of 11 June, several thousand men, led by Strozzi himself, left Siena. They crossed into Florentine territory the next night and had reached the Arno before Cosimo had word they were in his territory. Strozzi ordered his men to pay their way and not to treat the Florentines as enemies, hoping to be welcomed as a liberator. Crossing the Arno, they were joined by the troops from Mirandola, and the combined army – now around 13,000 infantry and 1,000 horse[33] – made their way into the Val di Nievole on 17 June. Only then did Marignano manage to get a force of 7,000 men across the Arno, which was swollen by recent downpours. Strozzi failed to press his advantage by forcing Marignano to fight while he still had more men. Instead, he became discouraged by the late arrival of the French fleet with the reinforcements for him from Piedmont, while troops came from Lombardy and Corsica to support Cosimo. On 27 June he was back in Sienese territory, followed, but not pursued, by Marignano.

Arguably, the principal result of this expedition was that both sides had increased numbers of troops in Sienese territory. Strozzi sent the bulk of his army to the Maremma, where he joined them at the end of June after a fleeting visit to Siena. To his distress, his brother Leone had been killed during operations in the Maremma, although Somma had gone on to take Scarlino and Suvereto. Leaving some troops in Port'Ercole, Strozzi moved the rest of his men to Montalcino; they were joined in mid-July by 4,000 Gascon and German troops disembarked from the Franco-Turkish fleet when it at last arrived. Cosimo insisted that Marignano must bring the enemy to battle. Strozzi was also looking for a battle. Judging that Marignano would have the advantage if this was fought outside Siena, he decided to draw him away from the city by another attack on Florentine territory.

On 17 July, he took his army, around 14,000 strong, towards the Florentine Val di Chiana, leaving behind in Siena only 1,200 infantry and 200 horse under the command of Blaise de Monluc.[34] After an unsuccessful attempt on Arezzo, the French took and sacked Marciano, and began to build a fort at the bridge over the Chiana. It was a week before Marignano, spurred on by Cosimo's protests, followed Strozzi. Joined by reinforcements from Naples, he had over 16,000 infantry, 1,000 light horse and 350 men-at-arms.[35] As the artillery was being prepared to recover Marciano, the French arrived.

In skirmishes over the next few days the French had the worst of it, and they were short of food and water. Strozzi decided to go Lucignano, where supplies intended for Siena had been collected. On 2 August he began to march his men along a line of hills, heading for Lucignano; Marignano's army followed along a parallel line of hills. A mile or so from Marciano, the hills converged, with only a little valley, cut through by a dry streambed, the Fosso di Scannagallo, between them. Both armies turned to face one another.

The battle began when the Imperial light horse, mostly mounted arquebusiers, on the left wing began to advance on the French light horse opposite them. At the sight of the Imperial men-at-arms preparing to join in the charge, the French light horse, who had no men-at-arms with them, turned and fled. The Imperial cavalry disappeared after the French horse. Marignano positioned his artillery on a height, and the guns were firing into the French infantry. Strozzi, having no artillery with which he could return fire, decided the best hope lay in trying to overcome the enemy infantry before the Imperial cavalry returned, and sent his men across the valley. They fought hard, but took heavy losses as they pushed across the obstacle of the stream bed. Once again justifying their reputation for being inferior troops to their Swiss neighbours, the corps of Grisons in the French army broke. The return of the Imperial cavalry completed the rout. Wounded, Strozzi had already had to leave the field. French losses overall were estimated at 4,000 dead, and as many wounded or taken prisoner, including many captains. Most of the prisoners were soon released and sent home, except for 400 German troops who were taken into the Imperial army. Imperial and Florentine losses were reckoned to be less than 200.[36]

Strozzi could not build up his army again, and was no longer able to take the offensive. Marignano brought his men back to Siena and tightened the siege; he could now construct and hold positions on the road south. Cosimo urged him to take Monteriggioni and Casole, near the Florentine border. Monteriggioni would have been very difficult to take by assault, but it was surrendered by its commander, a Florentine exile looking out for his own interests, on 29 August. Casole and other places between Siena and Piombino were taken during October. As 1,500 Spanish troops from Naples and 1,000 Florentine militia engaged in the conquest of the Maremma, Strozzi took his remaining cavalry there to direct the defence of Grosseto and Port'Ercole. Before the onset of winter hindered further expeditions, the fall of Crevole in mid-November removed the last French outpost between Siena and Montalcino.

Reports reached the Sienese that Strozzi was ready to abandon Siena and concentrate on holding Montalcino, Port'Ercole, Grosseto and Chiusi, and he said openly that if Siena surrendered or fell, he would retain Grosseto and Port'Ercole as conquered lands.[37] He based himself at Montalcino, not in Siena. It was becoming ever harder to bring supplies into the city; those caught trying to do so paid with their lives. Strozzi ordered the expulsion of 'useless mouths' – those too young or old or infirm to play any part in the defence of the city – and the citizens protested such measures should apply only to the poor and refugees, not to their own families. Those unfortunates who were expelled were not allowed through the siege lines. There were 30,000 troops encircling Siena, while the French had only 5,000 infantry and a few hundred horse.[38]

If many Sienese were ready to hold out, the resolve of the French was weakening. In Henry's mind, Piedmont took priority over Siena. In mid-January 1555, the French agents in Rome suggested the Sienese should send envoys to open talks with Charles's representatives there. Cosimo wrote assuring the Sienese he had no wish for their destruction,[39] and the Sienese government tentatively began negotiations with him, keeping them secret from the people. When it appeared that the famished and weary Sienese were about to yield in early April, Monluc organized an exodus of all the remaining exiles, with an escort of French troops.

On 17 April, Cosimo concluded terms with the Sienese envoys, declaring he had a mandate from Charles. The emperor was to accept the city and republic into his protection again, granting its liberty anew, and he could reform the government. There was to be a general pardon, excluding only rebels against the emperor, Philip or Cosimo. Siena was to accept as many troops of whatever nation Charles chose to send, but Charles would pay them. No fortress would be built without the consent of the citizens. The French were to leave no later than 22 April, and then Cosimo could introduce what troops he saw fit.[40]

On 21 April all the French in Siena left for Montalcino. Nearly 700 Sienese citizens and their families went with them. Some were so weak from the privations of the siege that they died on the road. The Sienese who had chosen to leave rather than face the return of the Spanish, set up a 'republic of Siena in Montalcino'. Theoretically, they would govern the parts of the territory still held by the French, but they were completely reliant on their French protectors. As soon as they had gone, Marignano entered the city with an escort of 300 horse, riding through deserted streets.

Before leaving for Florence, he installed a garrison of Spanish and German troops, under the command of Sforza Sforza di Santa Fiora, who was in the service of Cosimo.

The transfer of power in Italy from Charles to Philip

The Duke of Florence had hopes that his reward for all the money and effort he had expended in bringing the Sienese to submission would be Siena itself. Achieving that ambition would be complicated by the fact that Charles was engaged in a long drawn-out process of ceding his dominions in Italy and elsewhere to his son Philip, and Philip had ideas of his own about Italian affairs.

Philip's interest in Italy had been fostered by his investiture with the duchy of Milan, even though his father had not allowed him any part in its government. When Philip passed through the duchy on his way from Spain to the Imperial court in December 1548, Charles ordered he should not be acknowledged in Milan as duke. He did not go to Naples, where the people hoped he would come to remedy the injustices of Toledo's government. But he was already thinking of the extension of his dynasty's power in Italy, strongly backing the renewed pressure on the Genoese to build a fortress in their city. After he returned to Spain in 1551, the Imperial agents in Italy repeatedly asked him to intervene there, as they were being starved of resources by Charles. When the emperor's deteriorating physical health was compounded by incapacitating bouts of depression in 1553 and early 1554, so that he was unable to attend to business for months at a time, Philip did take the initiative in sending help from Spain to the Genoese in Corsica against the French invasion of the island.

On Philip's marriage to Mary Tudor on 25 July 1554, Charles transferred both Milan (ignoring his previous investitures of his son) and Naples to Philip. Philip celebrated only his investiture with Naples; he already considered Milan his own. Charles continued to make decisions about the affairs of these states for several months, without consulting him. Not until 1555 could Philip assume effective control. One of his first assertions of that control was his refusal to reappoint Ferrante Gonzaga governor of Milan, as Charles urged he should. Philip thought the situation in Italy so precarious that a strong man with authority over both Milan and Naples was needed, and he appointed a member of the powerful Toledo clan, Ferrando, duque de Alba.

It was Alba who was given the delicate task of finding a solution to the conflict between Philip, Charles and Cosimo over what should happen to Siena. Charles had granted Philip an imperial vicariate over Siena in May 1554, and Philip considered Siena his, but subsequently his father had favoured a return to the earlier position, with Siena as a republic under Imperial protection reinforced by a garrison. The emperor's councillors were opposed to his ratifying the terms Cosimo had negotiated, although in essence they were in accord with his views. Philip thought them unacceptable – he asked for investiture with Imperial powers over Siena. Eventually, Alba was given two letters, one ratifying, one rejecting the terms, and the power to decide which to use. After discussions with Cosimo, Alba ratified them in mid-July, but it was agreed that the Sienese should be induced to ask Charles to annul them, and that Charles would grant an Imperial vicariate over Siena to Philip, with powers to grant it in fief, which would keep Cosimo's hopes alive. Already Charles, against Philip's wishes, had appointed his ambassador in Florence, Francisco de Toledo, governor of Siena.

War from the sea

Henry II renewed his father's policy of alliance with the Ottoman sultan Suleiman to mount joint operations of the French, Turkish and corsair fleets in the western Mediterranean. For both sides, these naval campaigns had the same strategic aim, to weaken Imperial and Spanish power, but they had significantly different views on tactics. Destructive raids to garner booty and slaves were standard practice for the Turks and corsairs, but the French were often hoping to have the co-operation of local people. These differences meant that, even though the Imperial fleet – still under the command of Andrea Doria, now aged well over 80 – was outnumbered, their joint enterprises did not give the French and Turkish fleets lasting superiority in the seas off the coast of Italy. On the whole, collaboration with the Turks proved counterproductive for the French in Naples and in Tuscany, and not as helpful as the French hoped in the war in Corsica.

In 1552, after raids on the Neapolitan coasts, the Turkish fleet waited from mid-June to mid-July off Naples for the French to join them. Contrary winds foiled an attempt to sail to Piombino and Elba, but chance brought a notable victory on 8 August in a night attack on Doria's fleet, as he was transporting troops to Naples, unaware of the position of the Turks. Two days later, they left for the eastern Mediterranean, ten days before the arrival of the French fleet under Polin, baron de La Garde with Salerno on board. The French followed them, and overwintered with them in the east.

In early July 1553, the combined forces of 130 Turkish vessels under the corsair Dragut and 24 French galleys and three frigates returned to the coasts of Naples. Salerno insisted the people should not be harmed. In the end, he was able to have the population in areas where he had partisans spared, although other places were not so fortunate. In 1557, when an attack on Naples by land was being discussed, Salerno would tell Henry his Neapolitan friends had sent to warn they would not assist him if he came with a Turkish fleet, because of the harm that had been done in the past.[41]

La Garde persuaded Dragut to sail for Tuscany, where the fleet was welcomed at Port'Ercole on 9 August 1553. While the French prepared the force of 4,000 men Termes was to take from Siena to fight the Genoese in Corsica, Dragut pillaged Elba. The fleets transported the troops to Corsica, where the Turks blockaded the eastern coast of the island, while the French fleet attacked the west. When Bonifacio surrendered on 15 September, the Turks massacred the Genoese garrison and sacked the town. Frustrated because he could not enslave the inhabitants, Dragut exacted a ransom of 30,000 écus for them from the French, and then left. Disappointed by what he felt were meagre pickings from the expedition of 1553, Dragut brought his fleet into Italian waters only briefly in 1554, and refused to help the French in Corsica or in Tuscany. In 1555, an Ottoman fleet under a new commander, Piali Pasha, came to support the French besieging Calvi in Corsica, and disembarked 3,000 men for an unsuccessful assault on 10 August. A second unsuccessful assault, on Bastia, followed and then Piali received orders to leave. This was the last significant joint operation of the French and Turkish fleets. Another was planned in 1558, but Piali Pasha refused to attack any of the targets the French had in mind.

When unencumbered by their French allies, the Turks made the terrible raids for which they were so feared, ravaging, burning and enslaving. It was to deny them a potential base in Tuscany, as well as to deprive the French of their main supply route for the places they held on to in Sienese territory, that Marignano went to besiege Port'Ercole in late May 1555. His attacks were combined with Doria's fleet, which was patrolling off Tuscany, anticipating the arrival of the Turks. The French had surrounded Port'Ercole with several forts, and it took until 18 June to capture them all and secure the town. When the Turkish fleet arrived in Tuscan waters in mid-July, it was feared they might seize Piombino instead, but the raiding parties put ashore were driven off. Elba, however, suffered another attack before the fleet left for Corsica.

The defence of Elba (since 1548) and of Piombino (since 1552) was entrusted to Cosimo de' Medici, and he devoted much effort to building fortifications on Elba, constructing a stronghold at Porto Ferraio in which the people of the island could take refuge when the Turks or corsairs threatened. Cosimo hoped his possession would be permanent, but he would be disappointed. The activities of the Turkish fleet, and of the French in Tuscany, had given new strategic importance to Tuscan harbours. When Cosimo eventually succeeded in obtaining Siena from Philip in 1557, he had to give up Piombino and some ports on the Sienese coast.

Corsica

What made Corsica a target for the French was its potential as a naval base, impeding the sea routes between Spain and Italy, and providing safe harbours and ship's timber for galleys and supplies of food and fresh water for their crews. The island's maritime significance was still greater for the Genoese, who were determined to keep it. In itself, Corsica was poor, and it was in a state of semi-permanent rebellion against the Genoese, who governed it through their iconic financial institution, the Casa di San Giorgio. A leading rebel, Sampiero Corso, was with the French, and his contacts and supporters helped the Turkish and French fleets to conquer all the island except for the town of Calvi within a month of their arrival in mid-August 1553. La Garde wrote to the Genoese, blaming the Turks for the attack. The French would not occupy the island, he said, if the Genoese would undertake to be neutral between France and Spain.[42] Henry was annoyed that the Genoese refused to discuss neutrality, preferring to set about recovering the island by force.[43]

By the time the Genoese had gathered their forces and sent them to Corsica in November under the command of Andrea Doria, Dragut's fleet had left. Doria sent a squadron of galleys to relieve Calvi, disembarked the troops near San Fiorenzo and began to lay siege to it. Cosimo had sent around 2,500 troops and four galleys in support of the Genoese, and Imperial troops also came from Naples and Lombardy, while a French naval squadron bringing reinforcements from Marseilles was dispersed by a storm. Yet the Genoese did not find reconquering the island as easy as the French had found taking it to be. There were heavy losses, mostly from disease, in the siege camp at San Fiorenzo, before the fortress finally surrendered on 16 February 1554. Andrea Doria was resolute, but so physically infirm he could not leave his cabin on his galley.[44] He would have to return to Corsica repeatedly over the next few years; his failure to dislodge the French damaged his already diminished standing in Genoa still further. By late 1554, however, the Genoese had retaken most of the island. French hopes for help from Dragut were not realized, and their efforts were also hindered by mistrust of Sampiero Corso and by the inevitable complications attendant on reliance on a faction leader in an island so riven by factional disputes. On the other hand, they were aided by the abiding unpopularity of the Genoese with many Corsicans, a sentiment fostered by the reprisals against civilians by Imperial troops in response to the guerrilla tactics of the rebels.

By 1555, the Genoese held the eastern part of the island which had in the past generally been more under their control, and the French held the western side, where the powerful clans were dominant. The French offensive, aided by the Turkish fleet, in 1555, besieging Calvi and Bastia, did not break the stalemate. Henry ordered another push in early 1556, instructing his lieutenant in the island to seize as much territory as possible, before the general truce that Philip and Charles were seeking was concluded.[45] When this truce of Vaucelles came into effect in mid-February 1556, leaving each side in possession of the territories they held at that moment, a large part of Corsica was in French hands.

The war in north-west Italy, 1552–6

During the mid-1550s the French made considerable progress in the war in Piedmont, Saluzzo and Monferrato. The skilful Brissac remained in command of the French army there, which had better resources than the Imperial troops and better relations with the population. Piedmont was administered as though it was a province of the French crown, and Henry was determined to keep it. Spanish and German troops, on the other hand, mistreated the subjects of the Duke of Savoy in Piedmont and of the Duke of Mantua in Monferrato that they were supposed to be defending, and lived off them. The French could afford to keep smaller garrisons in the places they held when they wanted to put an army in the field because they could rely more on the goodwill of the people, who were not taxed too heavily, and their soldiers were paid with reasonable regularity. The perennial problems of paying the Habsburg troops continued, however, and after Ferrante Gonzaga was summoned to Brussels, the commanders who replaced him were no match for the astute Brissac.

Following Gonzaga's withdrawal from the siege of Bene in July 1552, Brissac soon went on the offensive, recovering in August the places in the marquisate of Saluzzo that had been taken by the Imperial troops, and then completing the conquest of the area to the north of Turin. Gonzaga countered, trying to open lines of communication to Volpiano, and recovering Ceva in the mountains towards Liguria, which the French had taken by surprise at the beginning of October. In mid-November the French took another significant stronghold, the town of Alba, by surprise; Gonzaga could neither recover Alba, nor take San Damiano, where he turned in January 1553.

For some months, Brissac was hampered by a shortage of men, as some companies returned to France and their replacements were slow to arrive. In June he advanced into the mountainous area of Le Langhe towards Liguria, taking several places, including Serravalle, with ease, before marching on Ceva, which surrendered on 24 June. A detachment was sent to besiege Cortemiglia, which fell on 8 July. These successes gave the French access to the Riviera. With no money to pay his troops, Gonzaga could do nothing to stop these operations. Having raised just enough cash in Genoa to keep his army in the field for a month, he made an unsuccessful attempt in late July to retake Cortemiglia, and then approached Brissac's army, which had withdrawn towards Turin. Neither side wanted a battle. Gonzaga had more troops, but could not be sure they would fight; Brissac had been ordered by Henry, who was faced by an invasion of northern France, to stay on the defensive and to send some of his experienced French infantry and a company of German troops back to France. On 3 August they agreed a truce, but it was not approved by Henry or by Charles, and it ended on 10 October. Soon after the expiration of the truce, Gonzaga scored a success in taking the stronghold of Valfenera to the west of Asti, but was outshone by the French, who made a daring raid on Vercelli, the administrative centre of the lands that remained to the Duke of Savoy. A few hundred French soldiers scaled the walls of the town on the night of 17–18 November, and ransacked what treasure Duke Charles, who had died in August, had left to his son Emanuele Filiberto. The garrison took refuge in the citadel, and Gonzaga sent a relief force. Brissac withdrew from Vercelli, taking with him the duke's lieutenant.

When Gonzaga was summoned to Brussels in February 1554, he was instructed to leave the Imperial ambassador in Genoa, Figueroa – an old man with little experience of military command – in charge of the troops. Brissac was not slow to take advantage. Committing 6,000 infantry and

500 horse to a siege of Valfenera, he sent other detachments on diversionary operations. By the end of August, Figueroa had managed to assemble 12,000 infantry, 400 men-at-arms and 600 light horse at Asti,[46] and could go to relieve Valfenera. Figueroa then returned to Asti and Brissac dispersed his men to garrisons. A few months later, having received reinforcements, Brissac began another offensive. Ivrea fell after a few hours of bombardment on 14 December 1554, and then Masino; Volpiano was blockaded. On 2 March 1555, the French entered Casale, where Figueroa was, by a trick. He risked capture, but managed to leave the fortress before it surrendered a fortnight later.

News of the fall of Casale brought the announcement of the immediate despatch from Philip's court in London of the duque de Alba to take up his duties as lieutenant-general in Italy[47], but Alba delayed, trying to ensure he would have adequate resources. His hopes were disappointed, and when he arrived in Milan in June 1555, he struggled to find the funds to mount a campaign, when the German troops, for example, were already owed ten, even twenty instalments of their pay.[48]

Leaving Milan in mid-July, Alba led the army along the Po, with the aim of relieving Volpiano. An attempt to take the stronghold of Santhià ended in failure. Brissac, suffering from fever and unable to leave Turin, sent his lieutenant, Claude, duc d'Aumale (another of the Guise brothers) to lay siege to Volpiano in early September. By the time Brissac had arrived there to accept its capitulation on 23 September, the garrison was reduced from several hundred to about fifty able-bodied men. Throughout the siege, Alba had stayed at Pontestura, but when d'Aumale was sent to attack him there, he retreated in disorder back to Lombardy. Troops he left to defend Pontestura repelled the French sent to reconnoitre the defences, but the Mantuan garrison of Moncalvo resisted d'Aumale for only a few days.

During the winter, the French busied themselves consolidating their positions near Casale and Vercelli, and increasing the pressure on Fossano and Cuneo, the most important of the few remaining places in Piedmont that still held out against them. Alba could do nothing with his troops, because he could not pay them. When he left for Naples in January 1556, he appointed the young marchese di Pescara, Francesco Ferdinando d'Avalos, to command the army in Lombardy. As the son of the marchese del Vasto, he was shown some loyalty by the Spanish troops, but not enough to pacify their clamour for pay, and a German regiment owed five months' arrears mutinied.[49] D'Avalos could not prevent Brissac taking Vignale in early February, and although he did manage to put an army in the field – some 9,000 infantry and 400 light horse – by mid-February,[50] he was afraid to risk battle with the French.

When the truce of Vaucelles was declared, the governor of Milan, Cardinal Madruzzo, feigned not to know about it. With the territories in which the Imperial troops had been accustomed to spend the winter now largely in French hands, and holders of Imperial fiefs no longer obliged to billet troops that were in the service of Philip, not the emperor, Madruzzo did not know how he could provide for the army in the duchy of Milan. Trying to keep his men busy in enemy territory, Pescara went to attack Brà, as Brissac protested about the failure to observe the truce. Eventually, on 7 March, a local truce was signed between Brissac and Pescara. The French were left masters of all Saluzzo, nearly all of Piedmont, and much of Monferrato.

The alliance between France and the papacy

The election to the papacy in May 1555 of the Neapolitan cardinal Gianpietro Caraffa brought to the papal throne an ascetic reformer, renowned for his militant defence of religious authority – and for his hatred of the Spanish government of Naples and of Charles V. Paul IV believed Italy would be better off if all foreign powers were expelled, but he thought the presence of the French a lesser evil than that of the Spanish. He would advocate that two French princes should be educated in Italy, one in Venice to become the Duke of Milan, the other in Rome to become the king of Naples. Unlike his predecessors, he made no effort to stay neutral between the powers, but was ready and willing to ally with the king of France against Charles and Philip. Apologists for Paul have laid the blame for his zeal for war on his nephew Carlo Caraffa, a soldier who he created cardinal a fortnight after becoming pope. Much of Carlo's military career had been in the service of Charles in northern Italy and Germany, but a quarrel with a Spanish soldier about a prisoner's ransom made him change allegiance, and he had served the French in the war of Siena. When he became in effect the chief minister of the pope, Florentine and Neapolitan exiles looked to him for support, adding to the anti-Spanish, anti-Imperial fervour at the papal court, although no one was more fervent than the pope himself.[51]

Henry was eager for an alliance with the pope. His campaign in the Netherlands in 1554 had not yielded notable gains, and he was facing financial difficulties which, if not as desperate as those of Charles and Philip, were nonetheless serious. He entered into negotiations with them in the summer of 1555, but these foundered on the usual rocks of disputes over rights to Milan, Piedmont and Savoy. Henry told his officials that he was determined to divert war from the frontiers of France to Italy;[52] he hoped that Venice, the Duke of Ferrara and other Italian princes would join him and the pope in an alliance against Charles and Philip.[53] His league with the pope was concluded in Rome on 14 October 1555. Many of the terms concerned how the kingdoms of Naples and Sicily would be divided up and governed – when they had been conquered. Paul would invest one of Henry's sons with these kingdoms, and another with the duchy of Milan. The king was to send to Italy 8,000 infantry, 500 lances and 1,200 light horse, and 350,000 écus. After some modifications, the League was signed in France on 15 December: the main changes were that a French prince was to command the forces of the League, and that should Siena be conquered, it would belong to the papacy and Paul could grant it to whom he chose. The pope was to provide 10,000 infantry, 1,000 horse and 150,000 écus.[54] A separate treaty with the Duke of Ferrara negotiated by Charles de Guise, Cardinal de Lorraine in mid-November 1555, was extraordinarily favourable to the duke. He was to receive an estate yielding 50,000 ducats a year in the duchy of Milan (Cremona, in the first instance), as well as estates in Naples and in Tuscany if they should be conquered. For the defence of the duchy of Ferrara, the king was to provide 100 lances, 200 light horse and 2,000 infantry, and as security for this provision, deposit with the duke the sum of 300,000 écus. Understandably, Henry did not like these terms, but nevertheless ratified them in January.[55]

Cardinal de Lorraine, his brother François, duc de Guise and the queen were all advocates for a league and an expedition to Italy to take advantage of the opportunity of having the pope as an ally; Montmorency was, as usual, an advocate of peace. Henry still listened to both sides. Soon after the conclusion of the alliances with the pope and Ercole d'Este, Montmorency persuaded Henry to accept the Truce of Vaucelles with Charles and Philip. Agreed for five years from 5 February 1556, it stipulated that each should retain what they held at that time, without undertaking any further fortifications; their adherents were included, and the pope was at liberty to join if he wished.[56] Paul could not formally denounce the truce, but his anger and disapproval were evident. He soon urged Henry to break it, and asked for French troops from Sienese territory to come to Rome. The French ambassador was instructed to urge the pope not to go to war, but Paul would not listen. When Paul provoked Alba into invading papal territory, Henry he had to support him.

Alba's invasion of the Papal States, 1556

Paul showed his hostility to Charles and Philip in deeds as well as words, imprisoning and persecuting their partisans, and even in July 1556 detaining an envoy they had sent to Rome and their postmaster who was based there, accused of inciting Alba to attack Rome. Sanctions against supporters of Charles and Philip began in August 1555, when Paul took umbrage at two galleys that brothers of Cardinal Ascanio Sforza di Santa Fiora had commanded in the service of France being taken from the papal port of Civitavecchia to Gaeta in the kingdom of Naples. The cardinal was imprisoned, and only released after the galleys were brought back to Civitavecchia in mid-September. Paul ordered several barons he regarded as suspect to dismantle their fortresses, or ordered their fortresses be confiscated.

His main target among the barons was the Colonna. They were no longer as influential as they had been in the 1520s, largely because of the erratic behaviour of the most powerful member of the clan, Ascanio. In 1553 Ascanio was imprisoned in Naples, accused of intriguing with the French, and his son Marcantonio took over his estates. His dispossession of his father was one of the accusations made against Marcantonio by the pope, but the principal offence of the Colonna was to be the leading pro-Imperial family of Rome. In April 1556, Paul declared the Colonna excommunicate, and all their estates and ecclesiastical benefices confiscate. A month later, he granted Marcantonio's lands to his own nephew, Giovanni Caraffa, creating him duca di Paliano, and to Giovanni's son Diomede, created marchese di Cave.

Immediately, the Caraffa set about strengthening the fortifications of these estates, particularly the principal stronghold, Paliano. Charles and Philip were seriously concerned by this. There were fears that Paliano would be used as a base for French troops who would become ensconced there, on the borders of the kingdom of Naples, as they had in Piedmont and Tuscany. Charles was readier for a war on the pope than was Philip, but some of Philip's advisers persuaded him that he had to help the Colonna if he wanted to establish a reputation as a king who supported his allies.[57] It was left to Alba to decide when to go to war. In late August 1556, he sent to Rome to tell the pope that unless Paul gave assurances that he had no intention of attacking the king's lands, he would take steps to defend the kingdom of Naples.[58] In early September he led an army from Naples into the Papal States.

The army consisted of 10,000 infantry (3,000 Spanish, the rest Neapolitan and Sicilian), and 4,500 horse (1,500 light horse, 500 men-at-arms, the rest Neapolitan barons and their men);[59] among the commanders was Marcantonio Colonna. It made easy progress, rapidly securing several key positions defending the frontier of the Papal States and the routes to Rome, including Frosinone and Anagni which were abandoned by their garrisons. Apart from Anagni, which was sacked, the places that were taken suffered little harm. Much of the area was part of the estates confiscated from the Colonna and the invaders were welcomed; it was papal troops the people attacked, crying 'Colonna'.[60] Paliano, under Giulio Orsini's command, and Velletri were well-provided with troops, but Alba left them alone, and they scarcely impeded the operations of his army.

Cardinal Caraffa took effective charge of the defence of Rome, as his brother Giovanni, who had been appointed commander of the papal troops, was bedridden with a quartan fever. Former soldier the cardinal might be, but he was not a skilled commander or organizer. At a muster held in Rome in early October around 7,000 infantry and 600 horse appeared,[61] but many of the men only turned out to collect their pay, and many had little experience of military action. Some Gascon infantry who had been brought to Rome were causing trouble by their disorderly behaviour. With such troops, it was difficult to organize a sortie, let alone confront Alba's army in the field.

While Marcantonio Colonna led his cavalry on raids up to Rome, Alba went to Tivoli, which was given up to him. Vicovaro was surrendered by the townspeople at the beginning of October, the Savelli stronghold of Palombara was taken and sacked after making a brief resistance, and all the Colonna places in the surrounding area submitted to Alba. Alba's plan was to take Ostia, blocking the supply route to Rome up the river and then to go to attack Civitavecchia.[62] Gallant defence by the garrison of the fortress of Ostia, who capitulated on the third assault on 17 November, gave time for Piero Strozzi to bring about 2,500 men to the northern bank of the secondary mouth of the Tiber, the Fiumicino. He was unable to prevent Alba's troops from taking the island between the Tiber and Fiumicino, but could prevent the army crossing the river.

Before Ostia fell, there had already been approaches from Rome to Alba, and on 18 November a ten-day truce was agreed. Cardinal Caraffa came to hold talks with him on the island in late November. The cardinal and his brothers had come to feel that their own interests would best be served by coming to some understanding with Philip, and Alba knew this; convincing the pope to make peace would be another matter. Although the truce was extended for forty days, it was evident that the question of Marcantonio Colonna's estates, and of Paliano in particular, would be hard to resolve. Cardinal Caraffa suggested that Paliano could be given up if his family were given Siena instead; such a suggestion had to be referred to Philip.[63] Having put in order a fort he had had constructed on the island, placed his Spanish infantry as garrisons in Ostia and the other major fortresses he had taken, and leaving part of the cavalry behind at Tivoli, Anagni and on the Colonna estates with the conte di Popoli in command, Alba dismissed the Italian infantry and the rest of the cavalry and returned to Naples.

The expedition of the duc de Guise, 1557

Whatever hopes there may have been that the truce would become a peace were nullified by the news of the imminent arrival in Italy of a French army led by François, duc de Guise, in support of the pope. Continuing his efforts to draw Venice into the war, Paul sent Cardinal Caraffa there in mid-December 1556. Despite offers of the cession of Ravenna and Cervia to the republic, the Venetians turned aside the request they should join the League, unmoved by Paul's argument that, as the two remaining truly independent Italian states, Venice and the papacy had a common interest in driving the 'barbarians' out of Italy. Understandably unmoved, for Paul had not only been urging on the French king to send a powerful army into Italy, but proclaiming he would call on the Turks to join in striking at the Spanish there.[64]

In sending an army under the duc de Guise, Henry was keeping his promise to support the pope, but Guise was not under orders to go immediately to Rome, and had some discretion in what he would do. Philip feared an attack on Milan, and troops were raised to strengthen the defences of the duchy. Guise, however, was thinking only of getting his army through before the Milanese forces might be strong enough to impede him.[65] Brissac was to create a diversion in Piedmont, after helping the expeditionary force open a route through the Po valley. On their way, the combined armies took Valenza, north of Alessandria, on 20 January 1557. After a few days there, Brissac and his army (said in France to be 4,000 Swiss, 4,000 French and 3,000 Italians) returned to Piedmont, while Guise and his army (said to be 6,000 Swiss, 6,000 French and 4,000 Italian infantry, with 600 men-at-arms and 800 light horse) continued along the Po valley.[66] By the end of January, they had reached the frontiers of the duchy of Piacenza.

Except for the fortress, Piacenza had been restored to Ottavio Farnese by Philip in September 1556, together with his estates in Naples and Milan.

Informing Henry of his rapprochement with Philip, Ottavio Farnese had told him that henceforth he would be neutral; Henry regarded this as rank ingratitude.[67] Guise had instructions to take Parma on his way south, but when he was in the area decided it could not be done. Although Ercole d'Este was urging Guise to attack Parma – hoping he could get it for himself – he had not prepared the artillery and munitions that he had been supposed to contribute.

Guise, d'Este and Cardinal Caraffa met at Reggio in mid-February to discuss what to do. D'Este's proposals for an attack on Cremona or Parma were rejected. Caraffa proposed an invasion of the kingdom of Naples; Guise argued it would be better to secure the army from attack from the rear by dealing with the Duke of Florence first. Anticipating such a threat, Duke Cosimo had been trying to avert it by diplomacy, proposing a marriage between his eldest son and a daughter of Henry. Believing Cosimo had been won over, Henry informed Guise of the negotiations.[68] Guise and Caraffa agreed that the army should proceed by short stages through the Romagna to the Abruzzi; if Cosimo was troublesome, a rapid diversion could be made against Florence.[69] But first, Guise wanted to be sure that the finance, troops and supplies the pope was supposed to provide for the campaign were ready, and so he travelled to Rome with Cardinal Caraffa, arriving at the beginning of March. He would be delayed there for several weeks.

In the Campagna, the war had recommenced in mid-January, when papal troops under Piero Strozzi captured the fortress of Ostia, which the Spanish had tried to destroy by mines. The Spanish withdrew to the earthwork fort they had built nearby, which was surrendered after a few days. Raids and skirmishes between papal and Spanish troops began; many places not defended by a Spanish garrison submitted to papal forces. Vicovaro was taken by assault on 14 February, and its garrison killed, and the conte di Popoli left Tivoli. He lacked the strength to counter-attack, but it was expected that he would be sent reinforcements from Naples, and the Spanish forces were not pushed out of papal territory.

When Guise came to Rome, still advocating a preliminary move against Cosimo, Paul insisted the French army should not be diverted from Naples. Guise did get agreement for some French and Italian troops to be sent from Rome to guard the Romagna and Marche.[70] He did not, however, get agreement to a longstanding request from Henry for the temporary cession of some places in the Papal States to be safe havens for the French army if need be; Guise asked for Ancona and Civitavecchia, the two main ports of the Papal States.

Rejoining his army in the Marche on 10 April, he now wanted to push on, to draw Alba into a battle that Guise was sure he could win before Alba received reinforcements that were on the way from Spain. His plan was then to head for the western provinces of Naples, where he expected support from the French and Turkish fleets and by troops sent from Rome.[71] He did not get past first base. His troops crossed the border but refused to advance far into the kingdom unless they received their pay. The army came to a halt beneath the hill-town of Civitella, where they arrived on 20 April. If vulnerable to bombardment from neighbouring hills, Civitella would be difficult to take by assault, and had been well-prepared during the winter for a possible siege; during the previous autumn papal troops under Antonio Caraffa, conte di Montebello, had tested the defences of that area. Montebello had joined Guise with some troops, but he soon left, having quarrelled with him.[72] The defenders of Civitella successfully beat off assaults – the simple expedient of throwing stones at the attackers proved very effective – and Guise raised the siege on 15 May, having heard that Alba had advanced along the Adriatic coast to Giulianova and was threatening to cut off the French supply routes. Reports reached him that Alba had 18,000 infantry to his 10,000 and 3,000 horse to his 1,800,[73] but he advanced to offer battle nonetheless; Alba did not oblige.

Then, in late May, a despondent Guise received orders from Henry to abandon the campaign in Naples, and, having ensured the security of the Papal States, to go to continue the war in Lombardy or Tuscany. The king thought the pope had not kept his promises, felt slighted by the refusal to hand over Ancona and Civitavecchia, and was annoyed that Montebello had left the camp. He wanted his army to be safely outside the kingdom of Naples, to use it for an offensive elsewhere in Italy.[74] Sending 2,000–3,000 infantry to Ferrara and lodging the rest in the Marche, Guise waited for further orders. Paul did not want him to leave – he was finally hearing the truth from Montebello about the improbability of a successful invasion of Naples, and was approaching the idea of coming to terms with Philip, but was concerned for the security of Rome in the meantime.

The war continued in the Campagna throughout the summer, where the young Marcantonio Colonna had been left in command after the conte di Popoli was recalled by Alba. Fired by his personal grievances, he was very active in raiding and taking what places he could, with forces reported in early July to consist of 2,500 Germans, 1,500 infantry from Calabria, 1,000 peasants (doubtless from the Colonna estates) and 500 horse.[75] This was enough to keep the scanty papal forces at bay, and Alba sent him Spanish and German reinforcements after the French had left the kingdom. In late July, 2,000–3,000 Swiss troops recently arrived in Rome, with other papal troops under the command of Montebello, were sent to relieve Paliano, only to be routed by Colonna, who came to find them in battle array. Arguing it was crucial that Paliano should be relieved, the Caraffa asked Guise to bring his army to Rome.[76] Guise was ill, so he sent the bulk of his men ahead to join up with the papal forces at Tivoli. On his own way south in late August, he received news of the catastrophic defeat of the French army on 10 August at Saint-Quentin in Picardy, with orders from the king to return to France. Urged not to leave the pope in danger, Guise would only agree to go to Rome for a few days, to give Paul time to make terms.

Having heard of the defeat of the papal troops, Alba decided to leave part of his army to watch the frontier and the French and take the rest to the Papal States.[77] In bringing his army to within striking distance of Rome, his purpose was to put pressure on the pope to make peace, rather than to seize territory. On 27 August, he brought his troops up to the walls of Rome, staying there for some hours. Piero Strozzi, one of the few with sufficient nerve to tell Paul unpalatable truths, warned him that the French army would have to leave, and spelt out to him the danger he would be in if he did not seek peace. If Paul showed he would be neutral and dismantle the fortifications on the Neapolitan border, Strozzi suggested, he could require obedience from Philip, and that he should not interfere with the pope's subjects.[78] For all his apparently dominant position, Alba was willing to make concessions to secure a peace, and by 9 September, terms along these lines had been agreed.

On Philip's behalf, Alba was to ask pardon of the pope, who would abandon his league with Henry and promise to stay neutral. All the places that had been taken in the Papal States would be restored to the pope, after their fortifications had been demolished. Everyone involved in the war was to be pardoned, except rebels against the pope; Paliano was to be placed in the custody of a man trusted by both sides. Paliano had been the main stumbling-block. Alba had argued it should be restored to Colonna, but when told the pope would never accept this, he sacrificed Colonna's interests. A secret additional agreement between Alba and Cardinal Caraffa, that Paul may not have known about, provided that Philip could opt for the fortifications of Paliano to be dismantled and Paliano to be handed over to whomever he chose, except an enemy or rebel of the pope.[79]

Alba agreed to the terms without consulting Philip; the king did not ratify the treaty until 28 February 1558, which suggests it was not entirely to his liking. Given Paul's intransigent nature and his firm sense of the dignities and duties of a pope, it is doubtful whether he would have agreed to any further major concessions. As it was, Alba went to Rome and satisfied Paul's sense of what was due to him as the vicar of Christ by a ceremonious apology, which was graciously received. Prisoners who were Philip's subjects, including the envoys, and some Roman barons were released as a favour to Alba.

Before Alba came, Guise had left Rome. French galleys had been sent to Civitavecchia to repatriate him and part of the army. Some of the captains and gentlemen embarked with him, and the companies of arquebusiers. Other infantry were sent to Montalcino and Ferrara, while the cavalry returned to France overland.

The final phase of the wars

Henry was disappointed with the fruits of his alliance with Paul, who henceforth was more inclined to favour Philip. He still had plenty of troops in Corsica, Piedmont, Ferrara and the territory of Siena. The critical conflict was taking place in northern France, however, and the king had little attention or resources to spare for Italy, even for Piedmont.

In Corsica, the French held on with the help of the Corsican rebels, but from the summer of 1558, after the threat of the Turkish fleet had passed, the Genoese went on to the offensive. In Piedmont, Brissac's last major offensive operation followed the passage of Guise's army south. In late April 1557, he took Valfenera and Cherasco, and then headed to Cuneo, the last city in southern Piedmont that was held for the Duke of Savoy, with 15,000 infantry, 1,500 horse and nineteen large cannon as well as other smaller artillery pieces.[80] After two months and several assaults, when news came that Pescara was drawing near, the siege was lifted on 27 June. Brissac lost 4,000 men before Cuneo, and was already finding it difficult to garrison all the places the French held. Henry continued to use Piedmont as a reserve of seasoned troops. After the defeat at Saint-Quentin, Henry summoned Termes from Piedmont, and ordered Brissac to retire into the fortresses, using his French troops for garrisons, and send his Swiss and Italians with 250 men-at-arms and 500 light horse to France; new Italian and Swiss troops were to be raised as replacements.[81] Brissac had to stay on the defensive, while the Spanish in Milan were able to recover some ground; in October 1558 Spanish troops under the duca di Somma, having taken and sacked Moncalvo in Monferrato, began to besiege Casale. The siege continued until the peace of Cateau-Cambrésis.

In Tuscany most of the Maremma, including the city of Grosseto and the port of Talamone, and most of the territory south of Montalcino was still held by the French and the nominal government of the 'Republic of Siena in Montalcino'. Much of the rest of Sienese territory was in the hands of Cosimo, with the Spanish based in the city of Siena having only a restricted area of devastated land under their control. In the autumn of 1556, Monluc came to take up the position of lieutenant in Tuscany, set about recruiting 2,000 infantry and 200 horse[82], and began a campaign of raids and ambushes on Spanish troops. During the summer of 1557, he used the 4,000 infantry and 300 horse at his disposal[83] to conduct another series of raids. He was outnumbered by the combined Spanish and Florentine forces under Alvaro di Sandro, and was forced to abandon some places, including the city of Pienza. His recapture of Pienza at the end of June was the last success of any note for the French in the Italian Wars.

In June 1557, Cosimo de' Medici finally got the prize for which he had worked for so long – the grant by Philip of the city and territory of Siena, in fief for himself and his heirs. Philip exacted a high price for this concession. Cosimo had to cancel the considerable debt he was owed by Charles and Philip, to give back Piombino and Elba to the Appiani, except for Porto Ferraio which he was to hold of them in fief. The king also took for himself the ports of Orbetello, Talamone, Port' Ercole and Porto Santo Stefano and Monte Argentario, which were to come under the jurisdiction of the viceroy of Naples. These would form the Presidi, an important staging-post on the sea routes between Spain and Naples. The French observed a truce with the new lord of Siena, but not with the coastal places held by the Spanish; an unsuccessful attempt on Orbetello was made in April 1558.

Cosimo persuaded Philip to send troops to take Talamone, the only harbour on the Tuscan coast remaining under French control. In early September 1,500 Spanish soldiers on their way from Naples to Lombardy were disembarked at Port' Ercole. With the support of the Spanish vessels, they easily took Talamone and Castiglione della Pescaia, each defended by about thirty men. Castiglione was handed over to Cosimo, who had bought it from its lord together with the Isola del Giglio off the promontory of Monte Argentario. The Spanish refused to attack Grosseto, and left. Cosimo was content to bide his time and maintain his truce with the French, who were ever more at odds with the Sienese exiles and the inhabitants of the places under their control. Francesco d'Este, who had replaced Monluc in March 1558, had come with secret instructions from the Guises to exchange the Sienese territories for Avignon with the Caraffa, or to sell them to Cosimo.[84] The troops went unpaid – by the beginning of

1559, they were owed nearly two years' pay – and consequently those who did not desert lived by extortion from the people.

For some time in 1556–7 yet another front seemed to be opening, in Emilia. As Alba prepared to invade the Papal States in 1556, a Spanish garrison was placed in the fortress of Correggio north-east of Reggio, with the putative consent of the lords, and in January 1557 the Spanish put troops in San Martino, which belonged to Sigismondo d'Este, from a cadet line of the Ferrarese dynasty, who was in the service of Philip. Ercole d'Este's brother Alfonso led 4,000 infantry and 300 horse to San Martino and, having permitted the garrison to leave, destroyed the fortifications.[85] He proceeded to Correggio, but the lords did not wait for a siege, preferring to come to terms. In April 1557, Ercole was again threatened by Spanish troops at Correggio, and he was also preoccupied by Guastalla, which belonged to Ferrante Gonzaga, especially when Pescara brought soldiers there and began to strengthen the fortifications. The Swiss troops Guise sent to him after the withdrawal from Naples were to help him attack Guastalla.[86] His attempt to take it failed, because he did not take enough men with him, placing too much reliance on contacts inside it.[87] When Guise's army was summoned back to France, Henry said Ercole could make use of some French and Swiss infantry and men-at-arms, but he would have to pay for them, although the king promised he would be repaid.

The Duke of Ferrara was not only threatened from Milan: Philip had been preparing an expedition against him, which he wanted Cosimo de' Medici and Alba to organize and the Duke of Urbino or the Duke of Parma to lead.[88] In the event, there was nothing more than a border war between Farnese, with the backing of a few Spanish troops, and Este, who had the use of some French troops, with the advantage going to Este. Neither the Duke of Parma nor the Duke of Ferrara was prepared to engage in a lengthy surrogate conflict, largely at their own expense, for the kings of Spain and France, and a truce was agreed on 29 March 1558.

Rather than join in the attacks on Ercole, Cosimo intervened for him with Philip, and in March 1558 negotiated terms between them. Ercole was to renounce his alliance with Henry, and the French troops still in Ferrara were to be allowed to pass unmolested through Milanese territory on their way home. All the French troops were recalled from Ferrara in May. A marriage had also been arranged between Ercole's son and heir Alfonso and Cosimo's daughter Lucrezia. Henry tried to prevent it, offering Alfonso his sister Marguerite, with a generous dowry including the Sienese territories in French hands. Although Alfonso married Lucrezia, he left almost immediately for the French court and remained in Henry's service – enabling him to press for repayment of the money owing to his father, which Ercole estimated to be 700,000 écus.[89]

Ercole warned Henry that his lack of attention to Italian affairs was causing him to lose his friends to Philip.[90] His warning was given just after his own agreement with Philip, and the acceptance of Philip's protection, and a *condotta* of 100 men-at-arms, 200 light horse and 200 infantry by Guidobaldo della Rovere, Duke of Urbino.[91] Della Rovere had declared the year before that, as he had no allies, he would willingly turn to Henry, but if the French king rejected him he would turn to anyone else who promised him assistance.[92] Cosimo had also had a hand in negotiating that agreement. If he was by no means submissive to Philip, who disliked him, Cosimo was still the strongest ally the Spanish king had in Italy. With the Farnese reconciled to him and the Gonzaga of Mantua counted as friends, Philip was now on good terms with all the major princes of Italy. The Pico della Mirandola, who remained loyal to the French king, were hardly a counterweight to this array.

The Peace of Cateau-Cambrésis

By the autumn of 1558 both Philip and Henry were ready for peace, for a comprehensive settlement of all their disputes. Since their defeat at Saint-Quentin the French had recovered sufficiently to take some initiatives, capturing Calais in January 1558 and penetrating into the Low Countries, but suffered another significant defeat, at Gravelines in July 1558. Both sides were exhausted.

The peace conference began in October at Cercamp in north-east France. There was much to resolve, but some issues that had formerly bedevilled relations between Habsburg and Valois could be set aside, for Charles V was not involved in the negotiations – he died in retirement in Spain in September 1558. Philip did not have to take account of the interests of the emperor or the Empire; Henry did not attempt to advance claims to Milan or Naples. Nevertheless, Italy was at the top of the agenda. Philip was determined that the king of France should not keep any territory there. For Henry and his advisers, who ignored the pleas of Corsican rebels and Sienese exiles, Corsica and the Sienese territories in French hands were at best bargaining-counters: they had no wish to keep them. Piedmont was a different matter. Henry thought of it as his. While he was ready to return Savoy to its duke, he hoped Emanuele Filiberto would accept some exchange for Piedmont, but the duke would not hear of renouncing his inheritance.

The talks all but broke down in November, because Philip insisted on Henry relinquishing all the lands he held in Italy, and Calais and the duchy of Luxembourg. Faced by the ultimatum, Henry declared firmly, dismissing the protests of his councillors, that he desired peace at almost any price, and would cede everything except Calais and some places in Piedmont.[93] All that remained to settle concerning Italy was which places in Piedmont the French would retain. Henry also insisted that Emanuele Filiberto should marry his sister Marguerite, who was in her mid-thirties and thought unlikely to bear children. Although the duke received this suggestion unenthusiastically, Marguerite became an effective advocate for him at the French court. At Philip's court, despite the services Emanuele Filiberto had rendered as a general – notably the victory at Saint-Quentin – he did not enjoy fervent support. If, with the security of the duchy of Milan in mind, Philip would not accept the French keeping Piedmont, he did not back Emanuele Filiberto's efforts to have his states given up to him in their entirety, and would insist on keeping some places himself to set against those to be held by the French.

The conference was suspended for two months at the end of November because of the death of Philip's wife Mary Tudor. Her death put a different complexion on the question of Calais, the main item of business when the talks resumed at Cateau-Cambrésis in February 1559, for Philip no longer had such a direct interest in England recovering it. The fate of the Sienese territories had become an issue again, however, as the Caraffa and the Duke of Ferrara had each renewed their efforts to persuade Henry to cede it to them. To the last, the Sienese exiles at Montalcino hoped they would be allowed to decide their own fate, and even hoped Siena itself would be a free republic again. Henry did at least get a written undertaking from Cosimo that the exiles would be pardoned and their property restored. This was more than the exiles of Naples and Milan got, for Philip insisted they should be excluded from the peace; there was no mention of the Florentine exiles.

The peace of Cateau-Cambrésis was officially declared on 3 April 1559. Henry kept Calais, and ceded Luxembourg. The French were to withdraw from the Duke of Savoy's lands on the French side of the Alps and from all they held in Italy except for the marquisate of Saluzzo and Turin, Pinerolo, Chieri, Chivasso and Villanova d'Asti in Piedmont; Spanish troops were to hold Asti and Vercelli. Emanuele Filiberto was to be neutral between the French and Spanish kings. Philip, however, made the duke agree to a secret accord with him: in return for Philip's consenting to hold only the two strongholds rather than five to match the concession to Henry, the duke was to undertake to be his permanent ally and to order the castellans of the fortresses in the ports of Villefranche and Nice to swear fidelity to Philip as well as to the duke.[94] The duke's marriage to Marguerite went ahead on 10 July in an almost private ceremony – held as Henry, mortally wounded in a tournament staged to celebrate their marriage, lay dying.

There was some resistance among the French troops in Italy to the orders to withdraw. In Piedmont, Brissac, furious and disappointed as having to surrender lands won and kept at such cost, left his soldiers unrestrained as they pillaged and maltreated the people. Systematically, he destroyed the fortifications he had built, careless if that meant whole towns were ruined by the mines used to bring them down, until Henry called a halt to this wholesale destruction. Emanuele Filiberto's territories were to be given up to him after his marriage, but on the news of the death of the king the French commanders in Savoy and Piedmont refused to leave before they received the orders of the new king, Francis II. He soon ordered the restitution to proceed, but it was August before the duke's officials took full possession. (Not until 1574 would the French give up the last places they held to Emanuele Filiberto.[95] This removed Philip's justification for keeping Santhià, which he agreed to hold instead of Vercelli, and Asti, and these places were relinquished to the duke in 1575.) Brissac had also destroyed fortifications in Monferrato until Henry ordered him to stop. The inhabitants of Monferrato were not happy at the prospect of being under the rule of the Gonzaga again; the people of Casale resisted receiving the Duke of Mantua's representatives for a week.

According to the peace terms, the French were allowed three months to evacuate the Sienese territories they held. The commander of the French troops there, Cornelio Bentivoglio, did retire from some places, including Montalcino and Chiusi, by the end of July, but then the soldiers in Grosseto and other places in the Maremma mutinied, refusing to leave the fortresses unless they were given the twenty-one months' back pay owing to them. Cosimo sent troops to support Bentivoglio's efforts to resolve the problem, and had to provide money and transport for the men's goods to facilitate their embarkation on the French galleys sent for them at the beginning of August. Once they were gone, Cosimo's representatives took possession of the lands they had held, and the Sienese in Montalcino resigned themselves to acceptance of the new regime.

The Italian states had not taken part in the official negotiations of the peace. Henry had abandoned his allies and those who had sought his protection. Fortunately for the Italians, Philip had not taken advantage of this to claim new lands for himself; had he done so, Henry might well have changed his mind, however strong his yearning for peace. In the end Philip's representatives had negotiated that Corsica be left to the Genoese (who still had the Corsican rebels to overcome), the Sienese lands to Cosimo, Piedmont (or most of it) to the Duke of Savoy, and Monferrato to the Duke of Mantua. All Philip had added to the lands acquired by his father in Italy were the Tuscan ports of the Presidi, and two towns in Piedmont that he would later return to the Duke of Savoy. Yet Philip's advisers were astonished and delighted by the terms that had been obtained. Men like Alba who still viewed Italy as a key indicator of the relative strength of the kings of France and Spain thought them too good to be true; they could not believe that Henry sincerely meant to renounce French interests in Italy so completely. Brissac was not alone among the French commanders and officials in being dismayed at the sacrifices Henry had made. There was widespread scepticism whether the peace would last.[96] France would soon be engulfed in civil war, and Philip would have enough to do to hold on to the states he had. For Italy, at least, with the Peace of Cateau-Cambrésis, the long years of the wars that had begun with the expedition of Charles VIII in 1494, were finally over.

Notes

1 Romier, I, 208.

2 *Nuntiaturberichte*, XI, 320–1.

3 *Ibid.*, 633.

4 De Leva, *Storia documentata*, V, 125.

5 Lestocquoy, *Correspondance des Nonces … 1546–1551*, 465–7.

6 *CSPSpan*, X, 274–6.

7 Romier, I, 242.

8 Lestocquoy, *Correspondance des Nonces … 1546–1551*, 492.

9 De Leva, *Storia documentata*, V, 208.

10 *Ibid.*, 210.

11 *Ibid.*, 217.

12 *Ibid.*, 216–18.

13 *Ibid.*, 224.

14 *Ibid.*, 303.

15 *Ibid.*, 244.

16 Courteault, 198–9.

17 *Ibid.*, 203.

18 Lanz, III, 159–61: Charles V to Ferdinand, 4 Apr. 1552.

19 Turba, II, 434.

20 Cantagalli, 18.

21 *Ibid.*, 32, 70.

22 *Ibid.*, 83–4, 111–13.

23 *Ibid.*, 90.

24 *Ibid.*, 138–41.

25 *Ibid.*, 150.

26 *Ibid.*, 151–2.

27 Spini, 136–7.

28 Romier, I, 393.

29 Cantagalli, 186, 202–3; Pepper and Adams, 118.

30 Pepper and Adams, 126.

31 Cantagalli, 222.

32 *Ibid.*, 242–3, 267.

33 *Ibid.*, 248.

34 *Ibid.*, 289–90.

35 *Ibid.*, 294, 315.

36 *Ibid.*, 297–307, 320–3; Roffia, 573–82.

37 Romier, I, 439, 442.

38 Cantagalli, 391–2.

39 Pecci, IV, 198–200.

40 Sozzini, *Diario*, Documenti, 467–71.

41 *CSP Ven*, VI, ii, 970.

42 Cantagalli, p. 169.

43 Lestocquoy, *Correspondance du nonce … 1552–1554*, 227–8, 238.

44 Cantagalli, 170.

45 Vergé-Franceschi and Graziani, *Sampiero Corso*, 315.

46 Segre, 'Il richiamo', 211–12.

47 *CSPVen*, VI, i, 26.

48 Alba, I, 235.

49 Segre, 'La questione sabauda', 393–4.

50 *Ibid.*, 397.

51 Numerous full summaries of these denunciations are in *CSPVen*, VI, i and VI, ii.

52 Romier, II, 21–2.

53 *Ibid.*, 29.

54 *Ibid.*, 30–1, 39–40; Rodríguez-Salgado, 148.

55 Romier, II, 35, 42, 56–7.

56 *CSPVen*, VI, i, 329–30, 334–7, 340–1.

57 *Ibid.*, 498; Rodríguez-Salgado, 152–3.

58 *CSPForeign, 1553–8*, 249–51.

59 'Summarii delle cose notabili', 355.

60 *Ibid.*, 357.

61 *CSPVen*, VI, i, 677.

62 *CSPVen*, VI, ii, 768.

63 *Ibid.*, 811–12, 815–17, 819–21, 823, 825–6, 828, 831–4.

64 See, for example, *CSPVen*, VI, ii, 851–6 for the arguments Paul advanced.

65 'Mémoires-journaux', 320.

66 *CSPVen*, VI, ii, 933.

67 Romier, II, 87–8.

68 *Ibid.*, II, 136–41.

69 François, 329.

70 Romier, II, 152.

71 *Ibid.*, 161, 163.

72 *CSPVen*, VI, ii, 1035–6.

73 'Mémoires-journaux', 340.

74 Romier, II, 166–78.

75 *CSPVen*, VI, ii, 1191.

76 Romier, II, p. 183.

77 Alba, I, 465.

78 *CSPVen*, VI, ii, 1268.

79 Nores, 215–7.

80 Ruggiero, 308.

81 *CSPVen*, VI, ii, 1251.

82 Cantagalli, 480.

83 *Ibid.*, 499.

84 *Ibid.*, 514.

85 Cittadella, 215.

86 'Mémoires-journaux', 363–5.

87 *CSPVen*, VI, ii, 1238.

88 Cantagalli, 551.

89 François, 349.

90 Romier, II, 212.

91 Dennistoun, III, 111.

92 François, 335–6.

93 Romier, II, 311–2.

94 Merlin, 76.

95 In 1562 they returned four of the five towns, holding on to Pinerolo and being given Savigliano and Perosa in exchange for the others.

96 Rodríguez-Salgado, 325–7.

Bibliography

Alba, Duque de (ed.), *Epistolario del III Duque de Alba Don Fernando Álvarez de Toledo*, 3 vols (Madrid, 1952).

Angiolini, Franco, 'Lo stato di Piombino, Cosimo I dei Medici, Carlo V ed il conflitto per il controllo del Tirreno', in Giuseppe Di Stefano, Elena Fasano Guarini and Alessandro Martinengo (eds), *Italia non spagnola e monarchia spagnola tra '500 e '600. Politica, cultura e letteratura* (Florence: Leo S. Olschki, 2009), 125–46.

Bitossi, Carlo, 'La Genova di Andrea Doria', in *Storia della società italiana*, X, *Il tramonto del Rinascimento* (Milan: Nicola Teti Editore, 1987), 169–212.

Calendar of State Papers, Foreign, 1553–8 (Longmans, 1861) [*CSPForeign*].

Calendar of State Papers, Spanish (HMSO, 1862–1964) [*CSPSpan*].

Calendar of State Papers, Venetian (Longmans, 1864–98) [*CSPVen*].

Cantagalli, Roberto, *La Guerra di Siena (1552–1559)* (Siena: Accademia Senese degli Intronati, 1962).

Ceccaldi, Marc Antonio, *Histoire de la Corse 1464–1560*, ed. and trans. Antoine-Marie Graziani (Ajaccio: A. Piazzola, 2006).

Cittadella, L.N., 'Ultimo decennio di Ercole II Duca IV, 1549–1559', *Archivio storico italiano*, Ser. 3, 25 (1877), 43–64, 208–27.

Courteault, Paul, *Blaise de Monluc historien: Étude critique sur la texte et la valeur historique des Commentaires* (Paris: Alphonse Picard, 1908).

de Leva, Giuseppe, 'La guerra di papa Giulio III contro Ottavio Farnese, sino al principio della negoziazioni di pace con la Francia', *Rivista storica italiana* 1 (1884), 632–80.

de Leva, G., *Storia documentata di Carlo V in relazione all'Italia*, 5 vols (Venice: Naratovich, 1863-Bologna: Zanichelli, 1894).

Dennistoun, James, *Memoirs of the Dukes of Urbino*, ed. Edward Hutton, 3 vols (John Lane, 1909).

Durot, Éric, *François de Lorraine, duc de Guise, entre Dieu et le Roi* (Paris: Classiques Garnier, 2012).

Duruy, George, *Le cardinal Carlo Carafa (1519–1561). Étude sur le pontificat de Paul IV* (Paris: Hachette,1882).

François, Michel (ed.), *Correspondance du Cardinal François de Tournon* (Paris: 1946).

Galasso, Giuseppe, *Il Regno di Napoli: Il Mezzogiorno spagnolo (1494–1622)* (*idem* (ed.), *Storia d'Italia*, XV, 2) (Turin: UTET, 2005).

González Palencia, Angel and Eugenio Mele, *Vida y obras de Don Diego Hurtado de Mendoza*, 3 vols (Madrid: E. Maestre, 1943).

Hernán, Enrique García and Davide Maffi (eds), *Guerra y Sociedad en La Monarquía Hispánica. Politica, estrategia y cultura en la Europa moderna (1500–1700)*, 2 vols (Madrid: Ediciones del Laberinto, 2006).

La fortuna di Cosimo I: La battaglia di Scannagallo (Arezzo: PAN, 1992).

Lanz, K., *Correspondenz des Kaisers Karl V*, 3 vols (Leipzig: Brockhaus, 1846).

Lestocquoy, J. (ed.), *Correspondance des Nonces en France Dandino, Della Torre et Trivultio, 1546–1551* (Rome: Università Gregoriana, 1966).

Lestocquoy, J. (ed.), *Correspondance du Nonce en France, Prospero Santa Croce (1552–1554)* (Rome: Università Gregoriana, 1972).

Losi, Simonetta, *Diego Hurtado de Mendoza, Ambasciatore di Spagna presso la Repubblica di Siena (1547–1552)* (Siena: Il Leccio, 1997).

Mallett, Michael and J.R. Hale, *The Military Organization of a Renaissance State: Venice c. 1400 to 1617* (Cambridge: Cambridge University Press, 1984).

'Mémoires-journaux de François de Lorraine, duc d'Aumale et de Guise, 1547 à 1563', in Joseph Michaud and Jean Joseph François Poujoulat (eds), *Nouvelle collection des mémoires pour servir à l'histoire de France*, Ser. 1, 12 vols (Paris: Guyot, 1850), VI, 1–539.

Merlin, Pierpaolo, *Emanuele Filiberto: Un principe tra il Piemonte e l'Europa* (Turin: Società Editrice Internazionale, 1995).

Nores, Pietro, 'Storia della guerra degli Spagnuoli contro Papa Paolo IV', *Archivio storico italiano*, 12 (1847), 1–512.

Nuntiaturberichte aus Deutschland 1533–1559, ed. W. Friedensburg et al., 19 vols (Gotha: Friedrich Andreas Perthes,1892; Tübingen: Max Niemeyer, 1970).

Pacini, Arturo, 'Tra terra e mare: la nascita dei Presidi di Toscana e il sistema imperiale spagnolo', in Elena Fasano Guarini and Paola Volpini (eds), *Frontiere di terra, frontiere di mare. La Toscana moderna nello spazio mediterraneo* (Milan: Franco Angeli, 2008), 199–243.

Pecci, Giovanni Antonio, *Memorie storico-critiche della Città di Siena*, 2 vols (reprint, Siena: Edizioni Cantagalli, 1997).

Pepper, Simon and Nicholas Adams, *Firearms and Fortifications. Military Architecture and Siege Warfare in Sixteenth-Century Siena* (Chicago: University of Chicago Press, 1986).

Rabà, Michele Maria, 'Gli italiani e la guerra di Parma (1551–1552): cooptazione di élite e "sottoproletariato militare a giornata" nella Lombardia di Carlo V', *Archivio storico lombardo*, 136 (2010), 25–48.

Rodríguez-Salgado, M.J., *The Changing Face of Empire. Charles V, Philip II and Habsburg Authority, 1551–1559* (Cambridge: Cambridge University Press, 1988).

Roffia, Girolamo, 'Racconti delle principali fazioni della Guerra di Siena', *Archivio storico italiano*, 2 (1842), 525–82.

Romier, Lucien, *Les origines politiques des Guerres de Religion*, 2 vols (Paris: Perrin, 1913–14).

Ruggiero, Michele, *Storia del Piemonte* (Turin: Piemonte in Bancarella, 1979).

Santarelli, Daniele, *Il papato di Paolo IV nella crisi politico-religiosa del Cinquecento. Le relazioni con la Repubblica di Venezia e l'atteggiamento nei confronti di Carlo V e Filippo II* (Rome: Aracne, 2008).

Segre, Arturo, 'La questione sabauda e gli avvenimenti politici e militari che preparano la tregua di Vaucelles', *Memorie della Reale Accademia delle Scienze*, Ser. 2, 55 (1905), *Scienze morali, storiche e filologiche*, 383–451.

Segre, Arturo, 'Il richiamo di D. Ferrante Gonzaga dal governo di Milano e sue conseguenze (1553–1555)', *Memorie della Reale Accademia delle Scienze*, Ser. 2, 54 (1904), *Scienze morali, storiche e filologiche*, 185–260.

Sozzini, Alessandro, 'Diario delle cose avvenute in Siena dal 20 luglio 1550 al 28 giugno 1555', *Archivio storico italiano* 2 (1842), 1–478.

Spini, Giorgio (ed.), *Lettere di Cosimo I de' Medici* (Florence: Vallecchi, 1940).

'Summarii della cose notabili successe dal principio d'aprile 1556, a tutto giugno 1557', in *Archivio storico italiano*, 12 (1847), 345–72.

Turba, Gustav (ed.), *Venetianische Depeschen vom Kasierhofe (Dispacci di Germania)*, 3 vols (Vienna: F. Tempsky, 1889).

Valente, Angela, 'I Farnese ed il possesso di Parma dalla morte di Pierluigi all'elezione di Papa Giulio III', *Archivio storico per le province napoletane*, 67 (1945), 157–75.

Verdiani-Bandi, Arnaldo, *I castelli della Val d'Orcia e la Repubblica di Siena* (2nd edition, Siena: Turbanti, 1926; reprint Siena: Edizioni Cantagalli, 1992).

Vergé-Franceschi, Michel and Antoine-Marie Graziani (eds), *La guerre de course en Méditerranée (1515–1830)* (Ajaccio: A. Piazzola, 2000).

Vergé-Franceschi, Michel and Antoine-Marie Graziani, *Sampiero Corso 1498–1567. Un mercenaire européen au XVIᵉ siècle* (Ajaccio: A. Piazzola, 2000).

CHAPTER 8

The transformation of war

The Italian Wars were fought for the conquest and retention of territory and economic resources, as well as for the prestige and dynastic concerns of rulers and the benefit of ruling elites. They involved the gathering of troops from all over Europe, from Scotland to the Balkans, the movement of armies across the Alps and across wide stretches of the Mediterranean, and the maintenance of those armies hundreds of miles from their normal billeting areas and supply chains. There was a transformation of war, partly a matter of the increased numbers involved, partly of a new emphasis on permanence and long service, and partly of the developing role of gunpowder weapons. Between the battles of Fornovo (1495) and Pavia (1525), the balance of numbers in the opposing armies shifted from an approximately equal division between cavalry and infantry, to an infantry predominance of 6:1. The overall increase in numbers was largely the result of a new perception of the value of infantry as battle troops, and not just as baggage train escorts and garrisons. It was the new effectiveness of the Swiss and German pike infantry, and of the massed Spanish arquebusiers, that encouraged the growth of infantry numbers and led to an extension to the infantry companies of the institutions of permanence and long service which had already been introduced into cavalry organization. The lower cost of equipping and training infantry was also obviously a factor in explaining the increasing numbers, as was the nature of the Italian Wars as wars of conquest, occupation and defence of conquests.

These factors all contributed to the sense of novelty and the willingness to experiment which characterized the warfare of the period. At the same time the scale and extent of the confrontation that developed between the major powers itself created a new atmosphere in which the main armies faced each other on neutral soil, far from their bases and supply points. This undoubtedly stimulated a willingness to seek battle solutions and a search for the decisive blow. It increased the problems caused by casualties and changed attitudes towards the treatment of prisoners. It imposed new pressures on the commanders and the captains, and hastened the professionalization of the military world.

Weapons and the balance of arms

The traditional weapons of most European infantry were the sword, the foot lance or spear, about nine feet long, and the crossbow, introduced extensively in the thirteenth century. During the fifteenth century the French had tended to focus on the crossbow while Spanish infantry had specialized in the use of short swords and round shields. The Swiss, meanwhile, had developed the use of the heavy sixteen-foot pike, supplementing it in their squares with a relatively small proportion of halberdiers, whose weapon was more suited to hand-to-hand fighting. The use of the pike spread rapidly through all armies, except the French, in the late fifteenth century, while the crossbow was gradually being replaced by hand firearms among Spanish and Italian troops.

Most accounts of the wars of this period focus on the pike as the predominant infantry weapon, and indeed Louis XI had begun to hire Swiss pikemen in the 1470s. He and his advisers were impressed by the successes of the Swiss in conflict with Charles the Bold, and at the same time dissatisfied with the fighting quality of the French free archers. Ferdinand of Aragon, on the other hand, had made little use of pike infantry in Granada, and it was only in Italy after 1495, that Gonzalo de Córdoba, the Spanish commander, began to train some of his infantry in the use of the heavy pike.[1]

Mass was the secret of the success of the pike; not just large numbers of pikemen but pikemen trained to march and fight in close order, to support each other, and to handle their heavy weapons for long periods. A well-organized pike square could quickly overwhelm other types of infantry which rarely had the same level of training and *esprit de corps*, and could also resist a cavalry charge and turn the tables on disorganized horsemen once their charge had failed. At the beginning of the wars the hiring of large numbers of Swiss pike infantry was seen as the best recipe for military success, although the cost was already changing the whole scale of military expenditure. In fact, however, the early years of the wars were marked more by attempts to catch up and imitate their tactics and to find other ways to combat them, than by further outstanding successes for their methods. Charles VIII's Swiss were little used in 1494–5, although they did win a significant encounter with the newly arrived Spanish infantry at the first battle of Seminara. The response of Gonzalo de Córdoba to this defeat was to arm and train a part of his own infantry with pikes, and to increase the numbers of arquebusiers. The landsknechts were also initially formed to respond to the Swiss infantry by imitating their formations and weapons, with the encouragement of Maximilian. They adapted more rapidly than the Swiss did to make greater use of handguns.

As with the pike infantry, the success of the arquebusiers, and later the musketeers, lay in their deployment in large numbers, and preferably with some protection in the form of a trench, or a wall or earth rampart. The early arquebus was far less accurate than the crossbow or longbow which it began to replace, but if used by large numbers firing regular and rapid volleys in several ranks taking it in turn to load and fire, it became a lethal weapon against both pike squares and charging cavalry. The battle of Cerignola in 1503 was the first example of the effective deployment of large numbers of arquebusiers,[2] and by 1522 at Bicocca the tactics and discipline required to make best use of the new weapons had been perfected. Shortly afterwards at Romagnano Sesia and at Pavia, the marchese di Pescara used arquebusiers as skirmishers, moving about the battlefield in loose order, taking advantage of natural cover, and harassing the flanks of the opposing forces. This was a decisive shift towards a more offensive role for shot infantry, but there was no way that firearms could replace pikes at this stage, even if, properly handled, they could halt and disperse a pike square. By the 1530s, as army commanders were further expanding their infantry contingents, the emphasis switched to finding ways of getting pike infantry and arquebusiers to fight in close co-operation. It was at this point that large mixed infantry units emerged with the French legions and the Spanish *tercios*.

In the early stages of the wars the French and the Swiss had shown little interest in the handguns and arquebuses. Early Spanish interest, already evident in the later stages of the War of Granada, was demonstrated by the infantry ordinance of Valladolid, issued by Ferdinand and Isabella in 1496, which called for infantry companies to be composed of one-third foot lances, one-third swordsmen and one-third shot infantry.[3] The infantry lances were quickly replaced by heavy pikes, while the shot element became predominantly arquebusiers by the time of Cerignola. The Black Bands of Guelders, one of the most prestigious landsknecht contingents, which fought for the French at Marignano in 1515, had 12,000 pikemen, 2,000 arquebusiers, 2,000 swordsmen and 1,000 halberdiers.[4] It was the co-ordination of pike and arquebus which ensured the dominance of infantry in European armies by the 1530s, and Spanish, German and Italian arquebusiers had a significant role in achieving victory in the battles of the 1520s in Italy.

This relatively sudden emergence of effective hand firearms in the early sixteenth century can be attributed to three factors. First, the development of the matchlock firing mechanism in the 1480s: this enabled the arquebusier to fire from the shoulder instead of one-handed from the hip, as had been the practice with the earlier handguns.[5] Second, improved and cheaper powder: the cost of gunpowder fell by 80 per cent in the fifteenth century, and improvements in quality gave greater range and velocity to the shot.[6] Third, the development of large-scale manufacture of firearms in south Germany and northern Italy linked up geographically with the emergence of the landsknecht companies as rivals to the Swiss.[7]

There is no doubt that the Spanish, and later the Spanish-Imperial armies, had an advantage over the French in terms of the quality and achievements of their infantry. It was often remarked that in most parts of France there was no tradition of infantry service and that the social gap between the landed nobility and the peasant classes inhibited the arming of a peasant infantry. Attempts were made during the wars to reorganize the French infantry into permanent regiments officered by nobles, and the legions of 1534 were the final stage of this.

The dramatic switch in balance of arms from cavalry to infantry was the result of a massive increase in the recruiting of infantry, not of any significant decrease in cavalry numbers. The numbers of men-at-arms available to the French crown changed little throughout the wars; the cavalry components of the great expeditions to Italy shrank only proportionately; the organization of the six-man lance remained unchanged until 1534.[8] In the lance unit which he led, the French man-at-arms had two mounted archers who would have normally dismounted to fight; the surviving musters reveal that this practice continued into the 1530s, although there is evidence that the archers of a cavalry company tended to be mustered as a single unit. These traditional practices were clearly something of an impediment to the emergence of separate infantry companies in the French army, and also to the acceptance of arquebuses instead of crossbows.

On the other hand the Spanish heavy cavalry was reorganized into companies of 100 men-at-arms under the direct control of the crown in 1493, which was the beginning of true permanence in the Spanish army.[9] The

Spanish lance consisted of two or three men – either a single man-at-arms with a squire (senzillo) or two men-at-arms with one squire (doblado). But the Spanish heavy cavalry never had the same reputation as the French, although their equipment was basically the same. They were rarely used as the spearhead of an attack in battle, but more commonly held in reserve to exploit a weakness in the enemy. In fact, this applied increasingly to the French as the wars progressed and tactics changed, but for the Spanish a reluctance to commit the heavy cavalry was there from the start.

One of the things that lay behind this difference was the fact that the Spanish made much more use of light cavalry. When Gonzalo de Córdoba was sent to Italy with the first Spanish expedition in 1495 he had no heavy cavalry with him, only 600 of the light horsemen known as genitors (jinetes).[10] The genitors were lightly armed with short lances, swords, and sometimes bows; their use by the Spanish kingdoms was the result of centuries of campaigning against the Moors, who relied entirely on light horsemen for their cavalry units. Five of the twenty-five cavalry companies formally established in 1493 were companies of genitors, and by the early sixteenth century there were twenty-six companies of genitors and only ten of men-at-arms. This rapid expansion of the Spanish light cavalry reflected the wide variety of tasks that were now entrusted to such troops. Apart from traditional roles like scouting and foraging, and harassing a retreating enemy, light cavalry were seen as much more suited to collaborating closely with infantry. Companies of mounted crossbowmen and mounted arquebusiers began to appear in Spanish service from early in the wars, and this was a development in which Italian influences on Spanish practice were particularly apparent.[11] The Venetians had led the way in the use of Balkan stradiots, equipped in a similar fashion to the Spanish genitors, and by the second decade of the sixteenth century genitors were being replaced by stradiots in Spanish service in Italy. The French also experimented with the use of stradiots but without great conviction; the traditions of the heavily armed lancer were too deeply embedded in French military culture to be eroded quickly. An erosion of that tradition was apparent by the middle of the sixteenth century, however, as the lancers began to be equipped with wheel-lock pistols in imitation of the German light cavalry Reiters and this led to a shift in cavalry tactics. The Reiters developed the tactic of the caracole, with successive ranks firing heavy pistols, whose shot could pierce armour, into infantry formations at short range, wheeling away after discharging their weapons to make way for the next rank.

While it is important to seek to identify the numbers engaged in the battles and to chart the increase in those numbers, what is more significant is the shift towards the role of mass in war and the implications that this had for the broader conduct of war. In this period the shift from armies which were predominantly composed of cavalry, and the back-up troops necessary for cavalry, to those made up largely of fighting infantry, took place. The ground was prepared for whatever expansion of quickly trained and cheaply equipped infantry the western European powers could afford.

The impact of gunpowder weapons

If the growing involvement of infantry and the consequent increased size of armies, contributed to a sense of novelty and dramatic change surrounding the Italian Wars, a more immediately striking factor in this assessment was the reactions of contemporaries to artillery. Guicciardini's insistence on the terrifying impact of the French guns – 'so violent was their battering that in a few hours they could accomplish what previously in Italy used to require many days'[12] – reflected a sense of astonished outrage, just as did the frequent cries of foul play that followed the death or wounding of a noble captain at the hands of a plebian arquebusier, although such utterances should not necessarily be taken at their face value as expressions of general opinions about guns.[13] How exceptional for its time was the French artillery? How great was its influence, or indeed that of any artillery, on the course of the wars? Was it that 'gunpowder revolutionised the conduct but not the outcome of wars'?[14]

Gunpowder weapons, having developed gradually in the fourteenth and early fifteenth centuries, improved dramatically in the middle years of the fifteenth century. The crux of this was improved and cheaper gunpowder, and the implications were most quickly apparent in the gun foundries and the artillery parks of the French crown. Stronger, lighter, more mobile guns, firing metal rather than stone shot with greater hitting power, were produced in France and Burgundy and quickly imitated elsewhere. Undoubtedly by 1494 Charles VIII had at his disposal the largest, best-equipped, and best-manned artillery train in Europe. But the inevitable reactions to these developments in terms both of the diffusion of the new technology and improved defence, had already started, and guns did not win the wars. For Guicciardini, the remorseless destruction of anachronistic defence works became the epitome of Italian weakness in the face of foreign invasion. Machiavelli accepted that the new guns reduced fortifications more quickly, but to him walls were always a poor protection to the faint-hearted, and he saw guns on the battlefield as little more than impediments.[15]

The experiences of the Italian Wars made both these positions questionable. The French artillery did not make a great contribution to Charles VIII's successful march through Italy in 1494–5. The main siege guns were being transported by sea at the time of the initial breakthrough in the Lunigiana, and their subsequent use in the occupation of Naples produced ambivalent results; small fortresses could be reduced quickly, but major defensive works in Naples itself resisted stubbornly.[16] Prolonged resistance, periodically of the Castello Sforzesco in Milan, of Pisa for fifteen years, of Barletta throughout the winter of 1502–3, of Padua in 1509, of Florence in 1529–30, and of Siena in 1555–6, has to be set against the moments of brutal force, the success of which often depended as much on morale and the overall strategic situation as on guns. But the evidence of the major battles suggests a growing role for the artillery, and particularly for the arquebusiers, which has to be contrasted with Machiavelli's rather negative opinion. Jacopo Guicciardini described the carnage caused by the artillery at the battle of Ravenna in 1512: 'It was a horrible and terrible thing to see how every shot of the artillery made a lane through those men-at-arms, and how helmets with the heads inside them, scattered limbs, halves of men, in vast quantity, were sent flying through the air.'[17] But these were Ferrarese guns as well as French, and all the evidence suggests that on the whole the French handled their firepower on the battlefield less effectively than the Spanish did.

The main improvements in the effectiveness of gunpowder weapons had already taken place by 1500, and that this was a period of diffusion of technology and techniques, rather than of further innovation. Equipment such as obsolete guns, bombards and stone-throwers represented an investment which could not be lightly set aside. Artillery trains were made up of a heterogeneous collection of old and new, which made it difficult to produce co-ordinated salvoes and accurate bombardment. The rate of fire of the larger guns remained very slow; nor is it true that the heaviest guns could move at the same pace as the army, although, of course, the speed of march of armies was itself being slowed by the growing proportion of infantry in their ranks. Guns on the battlefield remained extremely vulnerable to capture and counter-bombardment; their improved mobility gave opportunities to switch the focus of a bombardment, but at the same time put them out of action while they were being moved. Above all, cost was a key factor in replacement, modernization and expansion of artillery trains. Such trains, in fact, did not increase in size significantly in this period, and their operation did not greatly increase the number of trained men needed, although there was undoubtedly an increase in the number of pioneers required to dig emplacements and to service the guns. In the last resort, guns contributed more to a shift towards defence than to one towards blitzkrieg. The majority of the guns manufactured and employed by the European powers were sited in defensive works, on the walls of towns and castles, guarding routes, all encouraging the development of bastions and earthwork emplacements.

Fortifications and siegecraft

Concern about the impact of the new guns and the need for new fortification techniques were already clearly apparent in the second half of the fifteenth century. Initially the emphasis was on the scarping and thickening of defensive walls, and on the renovation and strengthening of individual fortresses. The northern parts of the Papal States, the whole of Tuscany and the city defences of Naples have been identified as the foci of active experimentation with strong, low, projecting bastions which could take the weight of heavy guns for counter-bombardment and provide extensive fields of fire. A whole generation of military architects, led by Francesco di Giorgio Martini and the Sangallo family, were at work in the two decades before 1494, stimulating an intellectual enthusiasm for the new ideas, and preparing the way for a new style of fortification, involving defence in depth through elaborate outlying earthworks. The new style became known as the trace italienne (the Italian plan), although the same ideas were evident, developed independently in fortifications built in Spain, France and elsewhere in Europe. During the wars attention switched from individual fortresses to rebuilding of city walls, including those of Padua, Treviso and Vicenza in the Veneto, Milan, Siena and Lucca. After 1530 it was the threat from the Turks which led to the building by the Spanish of a series of coastal fortresses in the new style in the kingdom of Naples and in Sicily.[18] The focus on Italy in this period of frantic refortification was not only an indication of where the main military pressure lay, but also provided a training ground for a new generation of military architects and engineers, many of whom began to work extensively outside Italy.

To some extent the gradual shift to a dominance of defence in the later stages of the Italian Wars was the result of the spread of the new fortifications which outpaced the rate of expansion of artillery trains and improvements in the effectiveness of guns. However, while besiegers relied on new mining techniques as well as guns to bring down the walls of fortresses and cities, effective defence depended as much on the skills of the garrison troops and on the determination of the entire population, as it did on defensive structures. Given the slow rate of fire of the siege guns it was possible for an active defence, with sufficient manpower, to convert breaches in the walls into potential death-traps for storming besiegers by using the rubble to create enfilade positions for arquebusiers behind the surviving walls. The fifteen-year resistance of Pisa to all the siege attempts of the Florentines, even aided in 1500 by a strong French army, and the nine-month resistance of Siena to the assaults of Imperial and Florentine troops in 1554–5, stand at either end of the wars as examples of what determined defence could achieve. Cities could be defended against the new artillery and 'fare come Pisa' became a byword for the new defensive possibilities.

Building new city walls and bastioned fortresses could take many years; often they would never be tested in war.[19] During the wars, the type of defence works that most frequently was tested in combat was earthworks. With the help of the local people, a city could be provided within a matter of days with defences of rammed earth strengthened by timber that could resist artillery fire effectively enough to keep besiegers at bay. On the battlefield, a trench or a rampart that might determine the outcome of a battle could be thrown up in a few hours. Unglamorous and impermanent as such constructions were, their significance in shaping the course of the wars should not be forgotten.

Permanence and professionalism

The first European standing armies since classical times had emerged in the fifteenth century. Medieval armies were mustered for particular campaigns, either on the basis of feudal obligation or as volunteers or mercenaries. Apart from small numbers of garrison troops and bodyguards, the first significant attempt to retain large numbers of men in permanent service was the reform of Charles V of France in the 1360s which set up permanent cavalry companies for service in the Hundred Years' War.[20] By the time that Charles VII recreated the *compagnies d'ordonnance* in 1445, some Italian states, notably Milan and Venice, were also maintaining significant bodies of troops in permanent service; that is, in peace as well as in war.[21] Such troops, in both Italian and French experience, were mostly heavy cavalry; there was not yet felt to be a need to maintain large numbers of trained infantry on a permanent basis, given the existence of militia traditions of part-time service and training, and the speed with which the infantry of the time could be recruited and trained.

It was only in the late fifteenth century that the superiority of the mercenary companies of Swiss pikemen, emerging from a local militia tradition, led to a recognition of a need for standing companies of trained infantry. Conscription was introduced in the Swiss cantons in the mid-fifteenth century and thereafter a proportion of recruits were expected to be ready for immediate service. It was, however, the continuity of the campaigns, the new demands of occupation of territory and constant threats of renewal of war, of the Italian Wars period, that really confirmed the need for substantial standing armies, with accompanying shifts towards professional military service. Spain had instituted permanent cavalry companies just before the outbreak of the wars, but the campaigns in Granada had already provided a framework of almost continuous service of infantry companies for a number of years. Indeed the conflict with the Moors did not end with their expulsion from Granada; further campaigns in North Africa were launched over the next twenty years by Ferdinand, and added to Spain's military commitments in Italy and on the Pyrenees frontier. For France, war on two or three fronts also became a characteristic of the period, although there was a considerable continuity about the captains and companies involved in the fighting and the garrison duties in Italy.

Military ordinances issued in both France and Spain could bind the troops to service during the king's pleasure. These were a novelty in Spain in 1493 but had been the framework for the maintenance of the heavy cavalry companies in France for more than fifty years. The promulgation of ordinances for the service of infantry was a product of the post-1494 period and completed the arrangements for comprehensive permanent service.[22] Standing forces were not restricted to the ruler's own subjects, however. They could include troops who were not directly recruited or paid by the state, but by their commanders, who held contracts or commissions to raise their own men. The extensive and continuous demand for the specialist Swiss and landsknecht pike infantry had the effect of creating some permanent companies of them, too, organized by entrepreneurial captains, not by their own state. War and the engagement of individuals in war was moving towards new levels of continuity and, necessarily, expertise.

The development of standing forces provided only the core of early modern armies. Numbers always had to be made up, new companies formed, often by issuing commissions to commanders who would recruit their troops themselves when war approached. Part-time militia service remained an integral feature of sixteenth-century military organization. Both French and Spanish armies also remained heavily dependent on 'adventurers', often young men from lesser noble families who usually served as heavily armed infantry or light cavalry for the duration of a campaign. Some 400 adventurers were present in the French army in the Agnadello campaign; the presence of the king and the possibility of catching his eye was thought to be a particular attraction for such service. In 1523 6,000 adventurers were said to be ready to join Francis I's expedition to Italy.[23] Swiss companies crossing the Alps to join the campaigns in Italy tended to gather new recruits on the way, and to arrive at the assembly point sometimes three times as large as when they left the cantons. This caused headaches for the paymasters, and inevitably tended to dilute the discipline and effectiveness of the companies.

Soldiering as a profession came of age during this period. The professional captain, the captain who owed his position more to his skills and experience than to birth or wealth, was already appearing by the beginning of the fifteenth century. The emergence of standing armies and permanent service tended to slow down this particular development as members of the aristocracy jostled for rank and reward in royal service. A survey of the French captains in Italy during the Italian Wars reveals very few who were not of noble birth; but at the same time it also reveals a continuity of service and experience which allows them to be classified as professionals. German commanders in the period of the Italian Wars were predominantly Imperial knights, owing allegiance only to the emperor, not to any other territorial prince or Imperial city, and claiming the freedom to raise troops and made contracts with any employer they chose. The commanders of contingents of Swiss troops, both those levied by the cantons and those raised by 'free' captains, were generally experienced men from certain noble families with a tradition of military leadership, for whom soldiering was a career.[24] For Italians from the military nobility, on the other hand, it was perhaps more difficult to make a career as a professional soldier than it had been in the fifteenth century, when the system of *condotte* had been fully developed. Some did establish themselves as valued and trusted captains, whose services would be sought after. But there were fewer opportunities to find long-term positions, fewer possibilities to move from one army to another without having to weather periods of unemployment, or come under suspicion of disloyalty.[25]

In the ranks, it is the artillerymen and handgunners who traditionally have been seen as the first true professionals in late medieval and early modern warfare, whose recondite skills seemed to set them apart from other soldiers. It was relatively easy to train a man to handle an arquebus. Militias could practise this, as they had been used to practising archery. Using an arquebus effectively in the field, in co-ordination with other units, would require more training and practice. Manipulating a pike, particularly in the crucial front ranks of a pike square, demanded a level of physical fitness and skill that implied a commitment to military service that made professionals of those who fulfilled this role. The armies of the Italian Wars were filled with men with new skills and long service, recognized by promotion through the ranks and by higher pay.

Training and skills

There has been a tendency in the writing of military historians about the early modern period to assume that serious and sustained training, and the refinement of skills, cannot be expected without organized training schools and printed manuals and drill books. The new printing industry did not produce the latter in significant quantities until the early sixteenth century, and the military academy was only a gleam in the eye until after 1600. Hence it has been common to belittle progress in the arts and skills of war in the absence of these supposedly essential guides and institutions. In fact, many classical military writings and manuals were available in manuscript in the Middle Ages, and these were to be found in the libraries of leading soldiers. At the same time the classical texts provided the models for the treatises of influential fifteenth-century military writers, like Jean de Beuil, Valturio and Cornazzano, and for much of the printed literature in this field in the first half of the sixteenth century.[26]

This apparent dominance of classical ideas and precedents in Renaissance military literature has contributed to another misconception – that the warfare of the Renaissance was shackled by the past, that military solutions only had validity if they conformed to classical precedent. But when Machiavelli, in his *Art of War* (1521) put into the mouth of Fabrizio Colonna the words 'I say again to you that the ancients did everything better and with greater prudence than we do, and if in other matters we make some mistakes, in matters of war we are always making them', he was putting an 'armchair' view which his distinguished mouthpiece would probably not have endorsed.[27] The learned soldier was indeed a Renaissance prototype, but the range of military literature which his learning was expected to embrace was rapidly spreading beyond the well-thumbed classical texts to interest in aspects of contemporary warfare, particularly artillery and fortifications.

The main purpose of the classical military literature was to create a belief in the efficacy of military and physical exercises as a means to instilling discipline, endurance and steadfastness in battle. It deeply permeated the educational programmes of the humanists, and hence the military interests of the nobility; it also had an impact on the rather more recent training requirements of mass infantry presided over by professional infantry constables, who were maintained in permanent service in order to train new recruits when needed. Drill, heavily influenced by classical example, took its place alongside archery contests and hand gun competitions in the training of infantry, and mock battles on foot became integral parts of many tournaments.

Nevertheless, the tournament was primarily the training-ground of the knights. Riding skills, horse management, and familiarity with basic hand-arms were expected of the nobility, but the use of the heavy lance, the main weapon of the cavalryman, was practised in informal lists in camps and castle grounds, and displayed publicly in tournaments. The military academies for the knightly class in the Middle Ages were the courts and noble households of medieval Europe where groups of young men congregated to receive their training in courtly pursuits, hunting and the skills of war. This remained the path to the military life for the 'officer class' in the sixteenth century. Meanwhile, the new arts of gunnery were being taught in informal gunnery schools set up in Venice and Milan as well as within the permanent artillery companies created in France.

A military literature with a strong emphasis on the need for skill and training, and suitable environments for the development of those tenets, were undoubtedly available in the fifteenth century. What changed was the nature and scale of the warfare, and above all its permanence. An emphasis on the acquisition of individual skills was subsumed into an expanding interest in the control, discipline and effectiveness of men assembled in companies, regiments and armies. Castle courtyards and lists were giving way to the parade ground where large units could be drilled, and the open country where large-scale military manoeuvres could be carried out. The tournament survived through this transition, as the public display of skills and training which initially provided opportunities for both the honing of individual expertise with arms, and for mock battles and sieges for restricted groups of soldiers; but by the early sixteenth century it did not give scope for the more extensive dimensions of training now required. By the late 1470s quarterly parades and training sessions for the standing units of whole provinces and regions were being held in France and in the Venetian and Milanese states. The tournament lost its military significance less quickly than is often supposed, and only gradually became little more than a vehicle for state and civic pageantry and propaganda. In the early years of the Italian Wars tournaments and serious jousting remained popular, particularly in Milan, where French and Italian military traditions came together.

The transition from an emphasis on acquired skill to one on imposed training was a part of the broader military transformation. Greater permanence of service, more stable companies, the growth in numbers under arms, the new emphasis on infantry, all contributed to the process, as did the higher levels of military alertness which characterized the years after 1494. While cavalry could not be drilled to the same extent as infantry, the need to control the lancers' charge so that maximum impact was achieved became a part of the training. This became even more important in the mid-sixteenth century when the pistol was introduced as a cavalry weapon, and the discharge of concerted pistol volleys at close range became for a time the main cavalry manoeuvre.

Tactics and strategy

While it would be wrong to belittle the role of planning and preparation in medieval warfare, it was on the whole true that battles were fought with reluctance, frequently almost by accident, or in desperation because they could not be avoided. Strategy tended to be dominated by the besieging, capture and sacking of small towns and castles, the wearing down of the enemy by attrition, the anticipation of the arrival of autumn and winter quarters with a minimum of loss. In the first thirty years of the Italian Wars, on the other hand, battle was sought and accepted with a greater sense of purpose and with the necessary preparation.

The objectives of the campaigns were to occupy territory, and to drive out or destroy the enemy; the warfare became more studied and more planned to achieve these objectives. Maps of the terrain and preparatory plans for battles became more common. Information had to be gathered on the state of mountain passes, on the viability of the roads for guns and carts, on the state of the rivers and the bridges over them. In an atmosphere of growing permanence of military organization commanders became more familiar with their subordinates, companies became more accustomed to marching and fighting side by side. The pace of war slowed somewhat as armies accommodated their advances and retreats to the increasingly dominant presence of foot soldiers and artillery trains. While it is true that small columns of cavalry could be accompanied by mounted crossbowmen and mounted arquebusiers, and hence still be used for surprise attacks and flanking movements, the main armies were inevitably tied down by baggage trains and marching infantry. This tended to add weight to the decision to risk battle; it reduced the uncertainties and gave time for careful preparation. Defensive positions could be prepared, and trenches dug to give shelter from artillery fire. The deployment of reserves and the provision of protection for them, became part of an increasingly complex series of strategic and tactical decisions.

Changes in battle tactics applied less to the cavalry than to the infantry, although the period certainly saw a changing role for heavy cavalry from being the main strike arm to taking up positions on the flanks or in reserve, ready to be used as occasion demanded. This fundamental development was apparent earlier in Spanish tactics than in those of the French. The ever-increasing numbers of light cavalry could act either as more mobile infantry or in harassing actions round the fringes of the battle. It was infantry tactics that developed most strikingly during the wars. From the moment at which the Spanish and Italian arquebusiers, protected by an earth rampart and ditch, cut down the Swiss mercenaries of the French at Cerignola in 1503, a solution to the problem of how to defeat the Swiss had been found. Once the gaps in the Swiss ranks had been created by the fire of the arquebusiers, then the cavalry could be used to exploit them. Collaboration became the key, collaboration between arms which traditionally had had little in common, either socially or in military practice. For many military experts massed pikemen remained the key arm, and the solution to the problem of their apparent vulnerability to heavy shot was to provide the pikes with powerful arquebus support. The evolution of the increasingly complex infantry tactics led to the emergence of a new military rank, that of sergeant-major, who had a particular role both in training the infantry, and in positioning them ready for battle. A hierarchy of command was emerging within the companies; a corporal for every ten men became the standard distribution of non-commissioned officers.

Leadership

The military commanders in Italy during the wars had a degree of independence of political control which was somewhat unusual. Ferdinand of Aragon and Charles V each visited Naples only once, as did Charles VIII; Louis XII never went to Naples, but was in Milan several times, and led the army at Agnadello; Francis I's visits to Italy were for military campaigns, one victorious at Marignano, one disastrous at Pavia, and a brief participation in the war in Piedmont; Henry II never went on a military expedition to Italy. The governors of Milan and the viceroys of Naples, appointed by these kings, were mostly soldiers and bore overall responsibility for the control and defence of the newly acquired territories, as well as for the campaigns launched to extend them.

In Milan Gian Giacomo Trivulzio was the first French governor in 1499, having led the army that had conquered it, but he was replaced after the unsuccessful Sforza counter-attack in 1500 by Louis's chief political adviser Cardinal d'Amboise. Soon the cardinal's nephew, Charles de Chaumont, an experienced soldier, was acting as lieutenant for the largely absentee governor. On Chaumont's death in 1511, Gaston de Foix was made governor and commander of the French forces in Italy. After the reoccupation of Milan by Francis I in 1515, first Bourbon and then Lautrec, both distinguished soldiers, were given overall authority. Spanish viceroys of Naples, at least up to 1530, were generally soldiers. Gonzalo de Córdoba, the Great Captain, was the first viceroy appointed by Ferdinand and Isabella. He was replaced by a political appointee, Juan de Aragon, a nephew of Ferdinand, but after 1509 a succession of soldiers – Ramon de Cardona, Charles de Lannoy, Ugo de Moncada and the Prince of Orange – followed each other as viceroy. Cardona and Lannoy were absent from Naples for long periods, commanding the Spanish and Imperial armies in northern Italy. The viceroy for two decades after 1532, Pedro de Toledo, did not have overall command of the Imperial forces in Italy. Once Milan came under the direct rule of Charles V in 1535, the military commander in the north of Italy usually held the office of governor of Milan as well. Antonio de Leyva, the marchese del Vasto and Ferrante Gonzaga were not subordinate to the viceroy. The duque de Alba was appointed both captain-general of Milan and viceroy of Naples in 1555.

The fact that soldiers were on the whole in charge in Italy is not surprising. Defence and the suppression of internal unrest were prime preoccupations. This did not indicate military occupation in the accepted sense of the word. The garrison forces of both areas were only partly made up of French and Spanish troops; the troops commanded by the foreign governors and viceroys were in part Italian, and the civil administrations remained significantly so. But as a result of the military leadership at the top, the armies garrisoning, defending and fighting for the occupied Italian lands were a good deal less subject to political supervision than had been normal in fifteenth-century Italian warfare.

One of the unresolved questions about the foreign armies in Italy is the extent to which the heavy cavalry companies on both sides were recruited by their captains from a territorial base back in France or Spain. Undoubtedly, loyalty to the captain would have been strengthened over years of permanent service, but such loyalty would have been increased by some sort of regional tie. In theory, the ordinance system was intended to place the standing companies of cavalry and infantry directly under royal control. Royal recruiting officers should have been responsible for finding recruits, and royal paymasters sought to pay men individually rather than giving lump sums to the captains. While the choice of captains in the French army theoretically lay with the Crown and royal officials, there was a strong tendency for there to be a natural succession in the leadership of the companies, and before 1494 each company had a regional base. The 1493 ordinance in Spain, and the establishment of the standing cavalry companies, must have led to the royal choice falling on those captains who had already served with their companies in Granada, and again the companies would have been originally recruited in specific areas.

Once again, however, it is clear that the real novelties of this period are to be found in the development of infantry forces. How did the leaders of the greatly expanded infantry companies emerge? In France the regional companies of the *francs archers* were commanded by nobles appointed by the crown, and the infantry regiments which were formed and trained for the 1509 campaign in Italy, and which fought at Agnadello, were led by cavalry captains seconded for that role. Francis I's legions instituted in 1534 were also largely officered by nobles. In Italy the rank of captain-general of the infantry had been created in the Venetian army in the first half of the fifteenth century, and by the time of the wars a number of noted infantry leaders had emerged. Again, they tended to come from noble backgrounds, but usually had made their careers in leading infantry, rather than being deputed to the role by higher authority. Giovan Battista Caracciolo, who commanded the Venetian infantry in the early years of the sixteenth century, came from a Neapolitan noble family, as did Ferrante d'Avalos, marchese di Pescara, who won a considerable reputation for his innovative tactics. Renzo da Ceri, from a Roman baronial family, the Anguillara, also commanded the Venetian infantry, and then became one of the most trusted Italian commanders in the service of France. The most distinguished militarily of all the infantry leaders in the wars, the Spaniard Pedro Navarro, was not a noble. His background was very obscure, and he was said to have been a sailor, indeed a pirate, in his youth.

Experienced and generally accepted leadership was an obvious result of a greater degree of permanence and continuity in military service. But at the same time the need for a commander to consult widely among his captains, particularly about plans and preparations for battle, gained added importance in the polyglot armies that characterized these wars. In landsknecht contingents widespread consultation was a feature of the democratic organization cherished by the Swiss and German companies. But all armies functioned with a council of contingent leaders and captains to advise on key decisions. When armies were composed of the forces of allied powers, the council could include generals and civilian commissioners in the service of several states.

The war at sea

The transformation of naval warfare was a much slower process than that of land warfare. The period of the Italian Wars cannot be described as formative in that process, although the role of the fleets during the wars was a good deal more important than is usually recognized. Transportation of troops, supplies and money was their main role, particularly for Spain. Charles V came to rely so heavily on the galleys of Andrea Doria that he held back from trying to bring Genoa under his rule, largely to avoid alienating Doria and losing his services. Galleys and river fleets continued to play a role in river and coastal warfare, as they had done in the fifteenth century, while the demand for small and medium-sized sailing ships to convey and supply troops, increased steadily. Early moves towards the building and deployment of very large carracks as gunships were abandoned because of the difficulties of collaboration between such ships and galleys, the traditional warships of the Mediterranean.

Naval blockade proved relatively ineffective and naval confrontations rare. The most important action involving a river fleet was the Venetian attack on the Ferrarese by a fleet making its way up the River Po in 1509, but it was defeated by artillery positioned on the bank of the river, not in action against other vessels. The one significant sea battle of the wars was the action at Capo d'Orso in the bay of Naples in 1528. From the 1530s, the war at sea became increasingly a matter of confrontation with the Ottomans, and with the Barbary corsairs. Their raids, sometimes conducted in collaboration with the French fleet, brought destruction and misery to many coastal settlements of the Italian peninsula and islands, and became a major concern, especially in the 1550s, to the Italian states.

The experience of war

How did changes in the nature and scale of warfare affect the ordinary soldier? In some respects, of course, there was little change. Fighting continued to occupy a relatively small amount of a soldier's time. Except for elite companies of bodyguards and castle garrisons, most troops spent their time in camps or billeted on civilian families. There was, as yet, little evidence of custom-built barracks. Boredom, hardship, occasional violence remained the soldier's lot.

What had changed was that institutions of permanent service were being introduced for some troops, and a greater continuity of service was becoming common. War was becoming a way of life and not just an occasional experience. At the same time the majority of those serving were now infantry rather than cavalry. The typical soldier was no longer the knight in his armour, attended by his squire and valet, and his two mounted archers, but the individual pikeman, bowman or arquebusier, dependent on his own resources and those limited communal services that his company could provide.

Longer periods of service tended to increase loyalty to leaders, if not necessarily patriotism and commitment to the employing state. Such service also created a greater sense of comradeship and interdependence among the soldiers, and it encouraged training and discipline. These are all issues which are difficult to define or to quantify. One implication of such service which can be defined more clearly, however, is the apparently changing attitudes towards winter campaigning. Traditionally, the campaigning season was quite short, from April to early October with, in Italy, a pause in mid-summer when fodder for the horses was in short supply. In October the troops were either paid off or sent into winter quarters on reduced pay. During the Italian Wars winter campaigning became much more common. Machiavelli deplored what he described as a modern practice, and his chief spokesman in the *Art of War*, Fabrizio Colonna, commented on the extent to which discipline declined in winter campaigns.[28] Winter campaigns had their particular hazards and discomfort which eroded the discipline even of professional troops.

Apart from exposure to winter weather or the heat of summer, overcrowded billets, poor hygiene, inadequate food supplies, lack of qualified medical attention and sustained siege campaigns all encouraged the spread of disease, and it was generally recognized that disease caused more casualties and deaths than fighting itself. Mortality rates also reflected the toll of camp brawls and bloody confrontations with outraged peasants and townsmen, as well as the victims of battle and disease.

What of the likelihood of death in battle? Much has been written about the restraints on killing in medieval warfare: ransom, brotherhood of arms, chivalry and plate armour, together with the relatively limited number of significant battles in the fourteenth and fifteenth centuries, all figure as factors in such discussions. It is widely accepted that the Italian Wars created some sort of watershed in battle mortality. One factor in this was the rapidly increasing number of infantry involved in battles, and infantry were always regarded as more vulnerable than cavalry because they wore little armour and were relatively immobile. But the infantry of the Italian Wars were often a good deal more professional and better equipped than their predecessors. The pike square and field fortifications gave protection to the infantry companies, while the cavalry – who could not crouch down to avoid incoming fire as the infantry sometimes could – presented better targets to artillery fire and arquebusiers.

Cannon, properly handled, could cause severe casualties if directed at massed troops, cavalry or infantry. The growing number of captains and commanders killed and wounded by arquebus fire by the 1520s is also very striking. Certainly the wounds caused by gunpowder weapons could be difficult to treat, crushing bones and tending to create infections. Indiscriminate maiming and killing of captured gunners in the early stages of the wars reflected the hostility and fear their weapons caused. The killing of prisoners in general became more common, especially by German and Swiss mercenaries who had neither the inclination nor the resources to deal with them. The storming of cities, once guns had opened up breaches in their walls, led to particularly bloody encounters.

Another situation which posed special dangers was the moment of defeat and possible rout in a battle. Although it was always dangerous to turn one's back on the enemy, the evidence of the battles of the Italian Wars suggests that more slow-moving, but also more disciplined armies were less likely to turn and run, but rather to attempt a fighting, if often costly, retreat. The Spanish infantry at Ravenna extracted themselves with great bravery but heavy losses from that battle, as did the Swiss from the slaughter at Marignano in 1515. Troops fleeing in disorder were often hunted down by the victors. Those who were taken prisoner and then released after being stripped of their weapons, armour and horses, ran the very real risk of being killed by civilians. Nobles and captains of repute were kept for ransom or exchange, and had a better chance, if they survived the battle, of surviving their defeat.

It is probably true to say that army medical services improved signifi-cantly during the wars – there were plenty of opportunities for the small number of physicians and barber-surgeons attached to the armies to develop their skills. One of the best accounts of the Battle of Fornovo in 1495 was written by Alessandro Benedetti, chief medical officer with the army of the Holy League, who commented on the condition and treatment of the wounded.[29] His masterly surgery saved the life of Bernardino Fortebraccio, the Venetian second-in-command, who took an arquebus shot in the head. A substantial part of the military literature that appeared in the following years was devoted to the treatment of war wounds, but it would be idle to suppose that many of the rank and file wounded had much chance of receiving serious medical attention on the battlefield.

The experience of war was undoubtedly becoming more brutal for those who fought.

Note: This and the following chapter were substantially written by Michael Mallett. As he had only added footnotes to about two-thirds of his text of this chapter and none to his text of the next, I have tried to identify the sources of the quotations and statistics he cited, and compiled the bibliography from his notes. Additional references to recent works have been added, as well as to those used in the sections I have altered or added.

Notes

1 Pieri, 'Consalvo di Cordova'; Stewart.

2 Pieri, *Il Rinascimento*, 408–12.

3 Vallecillo, V, 281–94.

4 Knecht, 70.

5 Hall, 95–6, 129, 149; Tallett, 21–2.

6 Contamine, *War in the Middle Ages*, 196–8; Hall, 67–104.

7 Baumann, 3–48; Hale, *War and Society*, 219–24; Rossi.

8 Contamine, *Histoire militaire*, 248; Lot, 243.

9 De Pazzis Pi Corrales, 772.

10 García, 42–3; Quatrefages, *Los tercios*, 52–69.

11 Mallett, *Mercenaries*, 151–3, 158. Such companies, led by Italians, were also appearing in Spanish armies by 1504 (AGS, Contaduria mayor de Cuentas, la epoca, 177).

12 Guicciardini, Book I, Chap. 2.

13 Hale, 'Gunpowder and the Renaissance'.

14 *Ibid.*, 391.

15 Machiavelli, Books III, VII.

16 Pepper, 'Castles and cannon', 271–81.

17 Canestrini, 310: Jacopo Guicciardini, 23 Apr. 1512.

18 See pp. 378–80.

19 Parrott, 'The utility of fortifications'.

20 Contamine, *Guerre, état et société*, 3–131.

21 Mallett, *Mercenaries*; Mallett and Hale, 1–210; Covini.

22 Contamine, *War in the Middle Ages*, 165–72; Potter, *Renaissance France*, 95–123.

23 Contamine, *Histoire militaire*, 240. García, 41, suggests that the phenomenon of 'adventuring' was even more common in Spanish military experience.

24 Parrott, *The Business of War*, 49–54, 57.

25 Shaw, *Barons and Castellans*, 100–47.

26 Hale, 'Printing and military culture'; Eltis.

27 Machiavelli, Book VI, 491.

28 Machiavelli, Book VI, 491–3.

29 Benedetti, 106–9.

Bibliography

Baumann, Reinhard, *I lanzichenecchi. La loro storia e cultura dal tardo Medioevo alla guerra dei Trent' anni* (Turin: Giulio Einaudi, 1996).

Bazzocchi, Alessandro, 'Servizio militare e controllo del territorio. La milizia romagnola nell'età delle guerre d'Italia', in Dante Bolognesi (ed.), *1512. La battaglia di Ravenna, l'Italia, l'Europa* (Ravenna: Longo Editore, 2014), 85–99.

Benedetti, Alessandro, *Diaria de Bello Carolino (Diary of the Caroline War)*, ed. and trans. Dorothy M. Schullian (New York: Frederick Ungar, 1967).

Canestrini, Giuseppe, 'Documenti per servire all storia della milizia italiana', *Archivio storico italiano*, 15 (1851).

Contamine, Philippe, 'The growth of state control. Practices of war, 1300–1800: ransom and booty', in Contamine (ed.), *War and Competition*, 163–93.

Contamine, Philippe, *Guerre, état et société à la fin du Moyen Âge* (Paris: 1972).

Contamine, Philippe (ed.), *Histoire militaire de la France*, I (Paris: Presses Universitaires de France, 1992).

Contamine, Philippe (ed.), *War and Competition between States* (Oxford: Clarendon Press, 2000).

Contamine, Philippe, *War in the Middle Ages*, trans. Michael Jones (Oxford: Basil Blackwell, 1984).

Covini, Maria Nadia, *L'esercito del duca: Organizzazione militare e istituzioni al tempo degli Sforza (1450–1480)* (Rome: Istituto Storico Italiano per il Medio Evo, 1998).

Del Treppo, Mario (ed.), *Condottieri e uomini d'arme nell'Italia del Rinascimento* (Naples: Liguori, 2001).

de Pazzis Pi Coralles, Magdalena, 'Las Guardas de Castilla: algunos aspectos orgánicos', in Hernán and Maffi (ed.), *Guerra y Sociedad*, I, 767–785.

Eltis, David, *The Military Revolution in Sixteenth-Century Europe* (I. B. Tauris, 1998).

García, Luis Ribot, 'Types of armies: Early modern Spain', in Contamine (ed.), *War and Competition*, 37–68.

Glete, Jan, *Warfare at Sea, 1500–1650. Maritime Conflicts and the Transformation of Europe* (Routledge, 2000).

Guicciardini, Francesco, *Storia d'Italia* (various editions).

Guilmartin, J., *Gunpowder and Galleys: Changing Technology and Mediterranean Warfare at Sea in the Sixteenth Century* (Cambridge: Cambridge University Press, 1974).

Hale, J.R., 'Gunpowder and the Renaissance: an essay in the History of Ideas', in Hale, *Renaissance War Studies*, 389–420.

Hale, J.R., 'Printing and the military culture of Renaissance Venice', in Hale, *Renaissance War Studies,* 429–70.

Hale, J.R., *Renaissance War Studies* (London: Hambledon Press, 1983).

Hale, J.R., *War and Society in Renaissance Europe, 1450–1620* (London: Fontana, 1985).

Hall, Bert S., *Weapons and Warfare in Renaissance Europe* (Baltimore: Johns Hopkins University Press, 1997).

Hammer, Paul E.J. (ed.), *Warfare in Early Modern Europe, 1450–1660* (Aldershot: Ashgate, 2007).

Hernán, Enrique García and Davide Maffi (eds), *Guerra y Sociedad en La Monarquía Hispánica. Politica, estrategia y cultura en la Europa moderna (1500–1700)*, 2 vols (Madrid: Ediciones del Laberinto, 2006).

Knecht, R.J., *Renaissance Warrior and Patron: The Reign of Francis I* (Cambridge: Cambridge University Press, 1994).

Lot, Ferdinand, *Recherches sur les effectifs des armées françaises des Guerres d'Italie aux Guerres de Religion 1494–1562* (Paris: SEVPEN, 1962).

Machiavelli, Niccolò, *Dell'arte della guerra* in *Arte della guerra e scritti politici minori*, ed. Sergio Bertelli (Milan: Feltrinelli, 1961).

Mallett, Michael, 'Condottieri and captains in Renaissance Italy', in Trim (ed.), *The Chivalric Ethos*, 67–88.

Mallett, Michael, 'I condottieri nelle guerre d'Italia', in Del Treppo (ed.), *Condottieri e uomini d'arme*, 347–60.

Mallett, Michael, *Mercenaries and Their Masters: Warfare in Renaissance Italy* (London: Bodley Head, 1974; reprint Barnsley: Pen and Sword, 2009).

Mallett, Michael, 'The transformation of war, 1494–1530', in Shaw (ed.), *Italy and the European Powers*, 3–21.

Mallett, Michael and J.R. Hale, *The Military Organization of a Renaissance State: Venice c. 1400 to 1617* (Cambridge: Cambridge University Press, 1984).

Mollat du Jourdin, Michel, '"Être Roi sur la mer": naissance d'une ambition', in Contamine (ed.), *Histoire militaire*, 279–301.

Pardo Molero, Juan Francisco, 'La política militar de Carlos V', in Jean-Pierre Sánchez (ed.), *L'Empire de Charles Quint (1516–1556)* (Nantes: Editions du Temps, 2004), 167–91.

Parrott, David, *The Business of War. Military Enterprise and Military Revolution in Early Modern Europe* (Cambridge: Cambridge University Press, 2012).

Parrott, David, 'The utility of fortifications in early modern Europe: Italian princes and their citadels, 1540–1640', in Hammer (ed.), *Warfare in Early Modern Warfare*, 129–55.

Pepper, Simon, 'Castles and cannon in the Naples campaign of 1494–95', in David Abulafia (ed.), *The French Descent into Renaissance*

Italy 1494–5: Antecedents and Effects (Aldershot: Ashgate, 1995), 263–91.

Pepper, Simon, 'The face of the siege: fortification, tactics and strategy in the early Italian Wars', in Shaw (ed.), *Italy and the European Powers*, 33–6.

Pepper, Simon and Nicholas Adams, *Firearms and Fortifications. Military Architecture and Siege Warfare in Sixteenth-Century Siena* (University of Chicago Press, 1986).

Pieri, Piero, 'Consalvo di Cordova e le origini del moderno esercito spagnolo', in *Fernando el Católico e Italia* (V Congreso de Historia de la Corona de Aragon) (Zaragoza: Institución 'Fernando el Católico', 1954), 209–25.

Pieri, Piero, *Il Rinascimento e la crisi militare italiana* (Turin: Einaudi, 1952).

Potter, David, 'Chivalry and Professionalism in the French armies of the Renaissance', in Trim (ed.), *The Chivalric Ethos*, 149–82.

Potter, David, *Renaissance France at War. Armies, Culture and Society, c. 1480–1560* (Woodbridge: Boydell Press, 2008).

Quatrefages, René, 'La invención de la guerra moderna', in *Carlos V. Las armas y las letras* (Sociedad Estatal para la Conmemoración de los Centenarios de Felipe II y Carlos V, 2000), 73–84.

Quatrefages, René, *Los tercios españoles* (Madrid: Fundación Universitaria Española, 1979).

Quatrefages, René, 'Le système militaire des Hapsbourg', in C. Hermann (ed.), *Le premier âge de l'état en Espagne (1450–1700)* (Paris: Éditions du Centre national de la recherche scientifique, 1989), 341–50.

Rossi, F., *Armi e armaioli bresciani del '400* (Brescia, 1971).

Shaw, Christine, *Barons and Castellans. The Military Nobility of Renaissance Italy* (Leiden and Boston: Brill, 2015).

Shaw, Christine (ed.), *Italy and the European Powers: The Impact of War, 1500–1530* (Leiden: Brill, 2006).

Shaw, Christine, 'Popular resistance to military occupation during the Italian Wars', in Samuel Kline Cohn Jr and Fabrizio Ricciardelli (eds), *The Culture of Violence in Renaissance Italy* (Florence: Le Lettere, 2012), 257–71.

Stewart, P., 'The Santa Hermandad and the first Italian campaign of Gonzalo de Córdoba, 1495–8', *Renaissance Quarterly*, 28 (1975), 29–37.

Tallett, Frank, *War and Society in Early Modern Europe 1495–1715* (New York: Routledge, 1992).

Trim, D.J.B. (ed.), *The Chivalric Ethos and the Development of Military Professionalism* (Leiden: Brill, 2003).

Vallecillo, A., *Legislación militar de España antigua y moderna*, 13 vols (Madrid, 1853–9).

Viganò, Marino (ed.), *L'architettura militare nell'età di Leonardo. 'Guerre milanesi' e diffusione del bastione in Italia e in Europa* (Bellinzona: Edizioni Casagrande, 2008).

CHAPTER 9

The resources of war

A rmies changed greatly during the six decades of the Italian
Wars. The shift from an emphasis on largely aristocratic
heavy cavalry to a substantial numerical predominance of infantry had
immense implications in terms of cost and supply; the growing tendency
to draw recruits from many different regions and social and cultural
backgrounds also had widespread repercussions for the management
of the armies. Differing methods of recruitment produced soldiers with
differing incentives, preoccupations and obligations. In this chapter logis-
tics and resources are examined against the background of the development of early standing armies and widening participation in the military
life, with the principal focus on a comparison of the methods adopted by
France and Spain, the two main protagonists, for the creation, management and resourcing of their armies.[1]

An important factor in any comparison between these two states is
that they initially became involved in the wars with very different levels
of commitment and intensity. France was committed to massive invading
armies descending into Italy through the Alpine passes; Spain's initial
commitment was to very limited and carefully prepared expeditionary
forces dispatched by sea. The former approach produced problems of
inadequate administration of the armies and an undue dependence on
the existing military logistical structures in Lombardy, while the more
measured Spanish approach appeared to allow more careful preparation,
better record-keeping and less reliance on Italian, in this case Neapolitan,
logistical support. Responsibility for the administration of late medieval
armies tended to be divided between the army marshals and their staff who
presided over the musters and parades, and sought to maintain discipline
in the companies, and civilian officials, both royal and local, who managed
pay, supply and billeting. The tendency during the Italian Wars, for armies

operating for long periods beyond the frontiers of their employing states, was for many of these functions to be merged in the hands of professional commissaries and bureaucrats, often with military experience, who devoted themselves full-time to army administration. Paymasters, inspectors, commissaries of musters and lodgings, recruiting officers, camp masters, provisioners, increased in numbers and became an integral part of the military scene.

Recruitment and mobilization

The indications are that in the first half of the sixteenth century it was fairly easy to find recruits for the armies. Demographic growth was outstripping economic development in many areas of Europe, and the very fact of widespread warfare tended to cause temporary economic disruption, loss of work and social confusion, all of which aided military recruiting. Even though there were now substantial numbers of permanent troops, rapid mobilization for campaigns and equally prompt demobilization as soon as the pressures of war eased remained characteristics of the warfare. One inhibiting factor in the increased levels of recruitment was the growth of specialization in war and a growing pressure on recruiters to look for suitable and experienced men. While this contributed to refining the methods of recruiters, there is little evidence that it made their task significantly more difficult. The recruiting net widened substantially in this period. Both French and Spanish armies quickly included large numbers of Italians; the recruiting of Swiss and German infantry became essential; the development of the Habsburg axis meant that Netherlanders and Burgundians were also recruited into Spanish armies.

What particularly distinguished the early standing armies of the fifteenth and early sixteenth centuries was the use of royal warrants to guide recruitment. Captains chosen by the king held commissions to recruit companies of specific strength for service at the king's pleasure within a framework of ordinances and inspections enforced centrally. Common pay scales were established, at least in theory, for each category of soldier, and initially captains were responsible for recruiting from designated areas and in accordance with laid-down rules. It was soon apparent that the success of this system depended on service within the state under the eyes of royal and local officials. The Italian Wars inevitably stretched the tentacles of supervision and control and led initially to greater independence of the captains than had been originally intended, and eventually to the creation of bureaucratic posts and departments specifically responsible for various aspects of military administration, including recruiting.

Both the French and Spanish governments also had to employ the alternative voluntary recruiting method, contracting. The military contract or *condotta* had been widely used in Italy since the thirteenth century, and, as the *Bestallung*, in Germany for much of the fifteenth century. Contracts were drawn up between entrepreneurs and governments, initially for the raising of troops. The size of the company to be raised, the duration of the service, the levels of pay, and even who was to command the company formed part of the original negotiations, although governments increasingly insisted on rights of inspection and supervision. The prime function of such contracts was to raise troops quickly, indeed the contractors, particularly in the Italian contexts, often had a company already in being. Its effectiveness depended on the length of the contracts, and the increasing use of long-term contracts in Italy in the fifteenth century was an important feature of emerging standing armies. The system survived, not least because Italian states continued to use it to recruit their own forces, although both France and Spain preferred Italian *condottieri* to conform to the organization of their own standing forces and accept commissions which limited the size of their companies and the degree of their control over them. For much of the sixteenth and seventeenth centuries the recruiting of Swiss and German infantry continued to be carried out by contract.[2]

While the emphasis undoubtedly shifted to the recruitment of volunteers in the early permanent armies, previous methods based on obligation to king, local lord or city council continued to be exploited. The need for large numbers of relatively untrained infantry and pioneers led to a revival of militia obligations and indeed to the new development of select and partly trained militias, primarily for local defence. The right of the crown to call out large sections of the population for short-term military service was re-emphasized in the late fifteenth century with the Spanish ordinances in 1495 and 1496, and a resort to the traditional *arrière-ban* in France.[3] The mobilization of Swiss pikemen was, in fact, carried out by a combination of militia traditions and voluntary recruitment, and the Spanish infantry sent to Italy in the early expeditions of Gonzalo de Córdoba were mostly recruited as militia and subsequently transformed into permanent troops. The militia tradition survived particularly strongly in France for infantry recruiting, although ultimately the clear superiority of professional infantry, trained and skilled in the use of their weapons and subject to increasingly strict discipline, over the part-trained militias, became incontrovertible.

The move towards voluntarism in recruiting led initially to captains and contractors being expected to decide on the fitness of the recruits for their purposes, to be checked by government inspectors. Recruiting for militias, on the other hand, tended to remain the responsibility of municipal or government officials. But on the whole in this period the government recruiting officer became a shadowy figure, although it is hard to see how captains of the heavy cavalry companies, stationed in Italy, were able to retain control of recruiting for their companies, except by using local agents in their base areas.

Given the increasing internationalism of military recruiting it is not surprising that certain areas, traditionally noted for producing good soldiers, became widely exploited. The leading states made every effort to prevent their neighbours and rivals recruiting within their territories; but in frontier areas that was often difficult and the smaller states were learning that their manpower could be a profitable commodity. Switzerland was the classic example of both these situations, but Savoy, Navarre, Hungary and Scotland fulfilled the same criteria, as did the Romagna as part of the Papal States. In southern Germany, homeland of so many of the landsknechts, internal political divisions and the lack of central authority contributed to the emergence of the area as a major source of military recruits.

There has been a tendency to equate such areas with mountainous and upland economies where geographical and economic circumstances helped to produce hardy and available warriors. Pastoral economies have been associated with seasonal unemployment, hard living conditions and occupations like shepherding which could be left to women and children. This leads on to the idea that the bulk of infantry recruiting was conducted in the countryside, that soldiers of the sixteenth century were essentially countryfolk. Evidence from muster rolls and other lists of soldiers tends to challenge this assumption. Even in Switzerland the evidence is that the bulk of recruits came from the towns, and this certainly seems to be also true in south Germany. Artisans were particularly attractive targets for recruiters as every company needed its cobblers, tailors, carpenters and barbers. Crowded, and indeed by the middle of the sixteenth century overcrowded, towns were the natural ambience for recruiting drives. Towns were the natural focus for unemployed and underemployed countrymen, so those recruited there cannot necessarily be defined as townsmen. There was also a bureaucratic tendency to record the nearest sizeable town as the place of origin of a country dweller in official lists. The naming of a tiny hamlet or village as a birthplace meant little to the average official.

The question of motivation is mainly important for the infantry; the social composition and levels of recruitment of the cavalry changed very little in the first half of the sixteenth century. Despite a changing military role, cavalry companies remained elite units, members of which required special skills normally associated with gentry and noble families. For the infantry, no doubt, militia service was a natural preliminary to voluntary and professional service. This certainly seemed to happen in Switzerland; as the opportunities for regular military employment increased, cantonal militia service became a sort of apprenticeship for soldiering as a way of life.

For many, the initial signing-on fee was probably the greatest inducement; the promise of regular pay which accompanied it was rarely maintained in practice. The transition from booty and ransom as the main incentive for going to war, to pay and other regular handouts, was a slow one. Looting gradually became more circumscribed and frowned upon, and the possibilities of an ordinary infantryman winning a ransom declined as war became more lethal to officers and the practice of taking prisoners gained strength. But windfalls remained a distinct possibility, even if it was only stripping a few saleable items from a dead body. On the other hand pay, for the new recruit, was a diminishing incentive as the standard pay scales changed little in the first half of the sixteenth century, although the introduction of double pay for long-serving veterans must have done something to offset this.

Escape is often postulated as a factor in leading men to enlist; escape from debt and debt collectors, escape from the clutches of the law, escape from unsatisfactory family relationships. Patriotism certainly does not yet figure largely among these incentives, except perhaps in the surviving city-states, and neither do religious conviction and confrontation. Comradeship clearly counted in re-enlistments and long service. This was also a period in which greater literacy and greater awareness of a wider world were causing men to seek adventure and new experiences.

The ordinances: muster and control

The military ordinances in the statute books of France and Spain were primarily intended to establish firm royal control over the permanent elements of their armies. Large sections of them specifically applied to the ordinance companies of heavy cavalry, and the permanent infantry companies which were established a little later; but much of their content was also applied to the contract companies. One of the original purposes of Charles VII's ordinances was to prohibit the raising of troops by any subject without royal consent: and this remained an element of all subsequent ordinances. Following the French ordinances of 1439, 1445 and 1448,

Charles the Bold, Duke of Burgundy issued his first army ordinance in 1469, and Ferdinand and Isabella promulgated a series of ordinances in 1495, 1496 and 1503. Both Louis XII and Francis I marked the beginning of their reigns with updated ordinances in 1498 and 1515, and the French infantry legions were established by ordinance in 1534. Similar ordinances were issued by Milan and Venice in the fifteenth century.[4]

These ordinances laid down the terms of permanent military service. They defined the structure and size of the companies, the duties and responsibilities of the captains, levels of equipment and pay, arrangements for provisioning and billeting, disciplinary codes and specific punishments for infraction of those codes, and the obligations and rights of soldiers generally. The later ordinances make clear a shift from attaching treasurers and inspectors to each company to setting up groups of such officials for armies and large garrisons as a whole. Provost marshals and their retinues of mounted crossbowmen are given considerable attention.

Unfortunately, a good deal of the low-level administrative documentation generated by the ordinances, which would reveal how they were implemented, has not survived. Muster rolls, pay lists, safe conducts, cargo lists of transport ships, lists of prisoners, billeting lists, often created and used in the open air and in camps far from home territory, all form the sort of material which rarely gets conserved in the first place, and often gets discarded and destroyed in archives when its conservation was attempted. French military documentation has suffered particularly badly, Spanish and Swiss less so; nevertheless the task of creating a coherent picture of the efficiency of the administrative mechanisms of these early permanent armies is a daunting one.

At the heart of the attempts to organize and control these armies was the muster, the inspection parade when detailed lists of every man in a company, with his main weapon and his horse (if he had one) described, were drawn up and checked. Such inspections were scheduled every three months, or in the Spanish army after 1503 every two months. They were carried out in the early days in the presence of the army marshals, but later by professional muster commissaries. The intention was to ensure that the companies were up to strength, that the quality and fitness of the troops were being maintained and that they had the weapons that they were supposed to have. In theory, the muster was followed by a pay parade so that the presiding official could ensure that pay was being properly distributed. This was often a difficult link to maintain, particularly on campaign when troops were on the move and engaged in periodic fighting. In practice the first and last musters of the campaigning season were the important ones, and there is plenty of evidence of the formalities being carried out seriously with men and captains being fined, and even dismissed, for defects and incomplete numbers.

Billeting

In the absence of custom-built barracks in this period (itself an indication of the relative novelty of permanent military service), the provision of accommodation for soldiers was one of the key issues confronted by the ordinances. Protection of the civilian population from exploitation by the soldiery was a priority, and considerable care was taken in the ordinances to identify and seek to eliminate potential points of friction. This determination was particularly apparent in the decisions about whether to lodge troops in the towns and cities or in the countryside.

In France the cavalry ordinance companies had been billeted in towns from the beginning of their organization, and this intention was restated in the later ordinances. The justification was that it made it easier to muster and review the troops if they were concentrated in towns, and they could feed themselves more easily from the urban markets. This avoided the temptation for them to forage for their food supplies and alienate the local population. Italian practice was quite different and concentrated on billeting troops in the countryside. The custom of rural billeting seems to have been common to all the Italian states, where there was traditional widespread hostility towards soldiers, seen as the instruments of tyranny. Troops were spread round the villages of the countryside to avoid substantial concentrations, and to enable them to keep a low profile. This also made a good deal of sense for armies which were still largely made up of cavalry. Andrea Gritti, a prominent Venetian military commissary, commented in 1517 that the Venetian army should adopt urban billeting as its normal practice but he was a committed francophile and going very much against the normal Italian tradition.[5]

The use of civilian accommodation for soldiers applied particularly to winter quarters and to peacetime dispositions. On campaign, sleeping out in the open or in increasingly elaborate camps was the normal practice. On some of the long marches of the wars, however, it was not uncommon for the quartermasters and representatives of the individual companies to ride on ahead of the main columns, and identify temporary lodgings for the night. Inns and private houses were used for this short-term accommodation; for longer periods it was common to take over empty houses and fill them up with troops. The problem of billets for troops, in town and country, became a major source of friction during the wars. Regulations intended to discipline the behaviour of troops to the civilians they were lodged with in their own country in peacetime would be hard to enforce when they were in a different state on campaign, or even between campaigns.

Supply

The implications of more permanent warfare in the fifteenth century for logistical and administrative support for armies, had already been considered by Louis XI's government in France in the 1470s and 1480s. The solution worked out was designed for war within the frontiers; it involved compulsory contributions from communities all over the state being brought together by merchant provisioners under contract. The new arrangements had little relevance for the Italian campaigns when it was soon apparent that armies of 25,000–30,000 operating in hostile territory, presented quite different problems of provisioning and supply. The armies in Italy also attracted camp followers on an unprecedented scale; Lautrec's army besieging Naples in 1528 was said to number 80,000 although its fighting strength was under 25,000.[6] All these extra mouths had to be taken into account in the supply arrangements.

How, then, were these armies supplied and fed in Italy? The traditional answer had been that an army campaigning on foreign soil lived off the land; food was a form of booty to which the invaders were fully entitled. This might have been practicable and justifiable for the small scale and brief incursions of medieval warfare, but a scorched earth policy, that left the countryside bare and the barns empty, was an obvious response for the defenders and could quickly force an invading army to withdraw. Aggressive foraging was bound to arouse the local population and lead to violent clashes, and was particularly inappropriate if the intention of the invasion was long-term occupation of territory. It was widely recognized that wherever an army was deployed, it was a waste of time and a threat to its discipline to allow extensive foraging, but it remained the obvious resource for soldiers on campaign in hostile territory, or who had not been paid.

Local purchase – from urban markets and shops, from farmers and countryfolk, could be used by smaller garrisons established in Lombardy and Naples during the wars. But it was quite inadequate for large armies: for them, the initial solution was the use of wholesalers and merchant contractors to assemble supplies where needed and sell them to the troops. There was no shortage of such merchants in northern and central Italy where the provisioning of large and wealthy cities was a well-established part of the economic framework. What was different was the potential mobility of an army to which merchants had to become accustomed just as those who supplied a major court must have done. Italian armies and, by inference, Italian merchant provisioners, had relatively little experience of the particular problems of large-scale military provisioning.

The Italian Wars produced unprecedented mobility of large armies, but there were also long periods of inactivity and normality. The need for co-ordination of supply by experienced officials close to the military leaders, rather than reliance on entrepreneurs and the market, only gradually became apparent. Quartermasters and government provisioners inserted themselves between the merchants and the troops to prepare for moves of the army, to identify future needs and possibly commandeer essential supplies, to anticipate recruitment drives, and other changing aspects of strategy, and ultimately to set up deposits of supplies at appropriate places. This final stage of the development of supply systems was apparent by the 1550s; it reflects the extent to which the fighting had moved outside Italy to a wider European theatre, and it prepared the way for the organization of the stages on the Spanish Road to the Netherlands.

The last method of supplying armies used in this period was supply by sea. French armies in southern Italy occasionally received supplies by sea, but on the whole the use of the sea lanes for supplying and reinforcing armies was dominated by the Spanish, for whom it was essential. It is often not clear whether the supplies loaded in Spain were just for the troops on their voyage to Italy, or whether they were also supplies for the army already based there, but the range of commodities involved was considerable. By the late 1520s there was some concern about the security of this sea route across the western Mediterranean because of the growing activity of the Barbary corsairs. Spain always enjoyed the inestimable advantage of control of Sicily, with its supplies of grain, oil, wines, fish and fruit.

While centralized supply and distribution of victuals, including the baking of bread, clearly became an increasingly organized practice during the wars, the level to which distribution normally took place is more obscure. It is known that in some fifteenth-century *condottiere* companies the captain and his staff took responsibility for obtaining, preparing and distributing food to the company, and deducting sums from the pay of individual soldiers for this service. It must be assumed that practices of this nature prevailed in the armies of the Italian Wars period, alongside a move to increasingly centralized provisioning. It was standard practice in all armies of this period for soldiers to be responsible for paying for their food.

Together with the problem of providing food for the troops there was the problem of the provision of fodder for the horses, for draught animals as well as mounts. The use of horses for drawing guns and carts, as opposed to their use by the cavalry, was a new development for Italy. Traditionally oxen were used for this role, which meant slower movement but less voracious fodder demands. But the haulage needs of armies were rising steadily in this period, for the artillery and baggage trains. The decline in the role of heavy cavalry in the sixteenth century was balanced by the increased use of light cavalry and a growing tendency for infantry officers to have horses and small groups of mounted followers.

Fodder was provided free to the soldiers; in this respect armies did live off the land, either garnering what they needed as they passed by or commandeering it from local stocks. The main acquisition of horses took place at the start of a campaign or when the companies came out of winter quarters. The provision of horses and other draught animals became a task for the administrative officials in these large concentrations of troops in Italy. While there was considerable interest in breeding racehorses and war horses in Italy, there were few specialized suppliers of horses for ordinary military and agricultural use. Traditionally, horse merchants brought their stock over the Alps from northern Germany, Hungary and eastern Europe. The Spanish kingdoms also had difficulty finding horses for the army and this was one of the reasons why the Spanish heavy cavalry lacked the reputation and the prestige of the French. Traditional customs of the employing state being responsible for replacing horses killed in battle had gradually disappeared with the growth of permanence and it was now up to a captain to help his men maintain mounts of appropriate quality. The provision of draught animals for the artillery and the baggage trains was the concern of the central army administration.

Another issue of supply about which little is known is the provision of clothing and the emergence of uniforms. Obviously there was a link between increasing numbers of permanent troops owing direct allegiance to the crown, and the provision of some sort of uniform or device that emphasized that link. Royal guards were certainly distinguishable by uniform by the early sixteenth century, and at that time the newly formed Venetian and Florentine select militias were dressed in the colours of the republics. In France, the *francs archers* wore the liveries of their province or city, and the heavy cavalry of the ordinance companies, those of their captains. Some sort of clothing, and possibly a livery, often formed part of an enlistment package for new recruits, and in the fifteenth century Italian *condottiere* companies sometimes received a part of their pay in cloth. This provided the opportunity for a degree of uniformity in the appearance of the company. At the same time soldiers were encouraged to express their individuality and prowess by acquiring and displaying finery of all kinds; the landsknechts were particularly given to dressing flamboyantly.

The question of who owned the arms of the individual soldier cannot be answered neatly for this period. The ordinances laid down the equipment levels for the permanent troops, and governments were concerned to create stockpiles of arms both for the permanent companies and for large scale mobilization. Personally owned arms were widely distributed throughout the population and recruits often brought arms with them when they enlisted. The Spanish ordinance of 1495, reflecting a long tradition of military obligations imposed on the general population, not just the nobility, required all able-bodied men in the Spanish kingdoms to keep arms in their houses and be available for military service. Surviving muster rolls imply that, at least in the early phases of the wars, soldiers were responsible for their arms and could be fined for their loss. Captains also often assumed a personal responsibility for arming their companies.

While there was an undoubted expansion in this period of the arms industries and arms production at all levels, from daggers to cannon, the problem of supply was mitigated to some extent by the durability of much of the equipment. Even cannon balls and arquebus shot could sometimes be recovered. There was a tendency for troops to pawn their weapons, or sell them at the end of the campaigning seasons and this meant pressure for restocking and re-equipping in the spring. Much armour and weaponry also changed hands as a result of capture, and battlefields were regularly picked over by scavengers from the victorious army or by the local arms dealers.

Despite such recycling and re-use, the demand for weapons and military equipment escalated significantly in these years. Military equipment included not only weapons and armour, but also a range of tools for digging trenches, felling trees, and creating field fortifications. Governments became increasingly concerned to encourage production within their own territories, and to limit export through licencing systems. The tendency was for the number of major production centres to increase so that troops could be supplied quickly wherever their garrison or assembly points were. Thus the older centres of arms production, like Tours (the growth of which had been encouraged by Charles VII and Louis XI with special offers to Italian armourers to come and work there), Malines, Liège,

Malaga and Milan, were joined by a number of regional centres. The most spectacular growth was that of Brescia, supplied by the Val Trompia iron deposits and foundries; here, by the late 1530s the production of arquebuses and muskets had reached such a level that in 1542 Venetian government permission was given for the export of 7,800 guns after the needs of the republic had been fully satisfied.[7] By the 1550s fortunes were being made from arms production although many of the enterprises remained small scale. A major Spanish arms contract agreed in 1543 by the captain-general of artillery, Pedro de la Cueva, with an arms manufac-turer of Guipuzcoa in the Basque area was for 15,000 arquebuses, 15,000 helmets and 20,000 pikes.[8]

Pay

Paid service had been a common feature of most western European armies for over two centuries. The more novel aspect of fighting for money that distinguished this period was the extent to which large numbers of troops were paid not by their own central treasury but by that of another state. The vast majority of these mercenaries were infantry, professionals who derived their *esprit de corps* from living and fighting alongside fellow Swiss or Germans rather than from loyalty to their employing state. Companies of Spanish or French infantry who had been paid off in Italy could also look for employment in other armies operating there, such as those who served Francesco Maria della Rovere and Leo X in the campaign in the duchy of Urbino in 1517.[9]

It is apparent that while pay scales were remarkably similar across Europe in the first half of the sixteenth century, and rates of pay remark-ably static, certain bodies of troops got better treatment than others. While Swiss pikemen in French service received about three and a half ducats a month, and Germans about three, most other pike infantry were paid rather less than three ducats a month.[10] The real distinction lay in the number of 'pays' per year; the Swiss insisted on regular monthly payments whereas for other troops the gaps between pay parades could be subject to huge variations. French ordinance companies were paid only four times a year; eight pays a year was the normal regime in the Venetian army. In 1514 Spanish men-at-arms serving in Naples were paid 110 ducats a year, while Italians in the same army received 90 ducats, and French men-at-arms also received the equivalent of about 90 ducats a year.[11] Heavy cav-alrymen, however, bore the responsibility for paying at least two lightly armed followers out of their wages.

Common to all armies was a move towards greater variation of pay, particularly among the infantry. Long service and increasing numbers of non-commissioned officers meant that a proportion of the infantrymen began to receive double pay. In the French army in Piedmont in 1537 this proportion was about 10 per cent. Arquebusiers in the same army earned a third more than the ordinary pikemen, but by 1552 pikemen in Piedmont received six livres tournois a month, arquebusiers seven.[12] These disparities helped to cushion the effect of inflation for some soldiers, but by the 1530s the purchasing power of military pay was falling behind that of civilian artisan and manual occupations.

The distribution of pay was the most difficult problem facing an army administration. Even in time of peace when the permanent units were scattered in garrisons and billets across the state, it was not easy for the paymasters to extract funds from the local treasuries and to distribute them fairly among the troops. The ideal of the early ordinances was for paymasters to be attached to particular companies, so that they recognized the individual soldiers they were paying, and indeed to pay the wage directly to the soldiers. This system reduced the possibilities of frauds by the captains, but it opened the way to fraud by the paymasters and took up a large amount of their time. By 1494, a tendency towards greater centralization of military administration particularly in the Spanish army, and the increased prestige of the long-serving captains of the cavalry companies in France and in Italy, led to paymasters making more routine visits to companies to hand over the company's pay *en bloc* to the captain for him to distribute.

The long years of warfare after 1494 increased the pressure for this system. Pay parades became more irregular and dependent on the availability of funds, on the location of the company, and on the course of the campaigns. Pressure on supply of both food and equipment meant that the soldiers became increasingly dependent on their captains for advances and loans, and the long-awaited pay days became occasions when the bulk of the money available was retained by the captains as deductions from individual pay to settle the debts. These developments tended to increase the authority of the captains and put them in positions where they found themselves putting up their own funds to keep the companies in being. For these reasons governments seemed to accept the system despite the frauds that it engendered. Occasional voices were still raised for a return to state paymasters paying soldiers individually in order to control corrupt captains, but during the wars this was impracticable.

The other factor that gave added authority to the captains in this period was the institutionalization of the 'dead pay'. What had started as an early form of fraud, as captains delayed recruiting extra men to fill gaps in the ranks of their companies in order to make profit for themselves, became an accepted form of bonus, usually calculated as the equivalent of the pay of 10 per cent of the company strength. The captains were expected to meet the costs of the additional payments to non-commissioned officers and the specialist soldiers out of this bonus, but the arrangement left ample scope for captains to limit the number of promotions and the recruiting of specialists in order to line their own pockets.

The process of providing regular and adequate pay as a substitute for traditional rights of plunder and ransom was far from complete by the early sixteenth century. The ordinances did indeed seek to control and limit these rights, and place emphasis on organized sharing of booty and the rights of the employing state to take a major share. Exchange of prisoners became more common as they were increasingly regarded as having been captured by the army and its employer rather than by individual soldiers. The presence of provosts in companies meant a certain limitation on minor episodes of looting; but the possibility of major breakdowns of control often linked to failures of the pay and supply systems, remained very real. The army that sacked Rome in 1527 was owed 400,000 ducats in back pay; the sack of Milan by the imperialists in 1521, the decision of Lautrec to allow the Swiss to attack at Bicocca, and the acceptance by Pescara and Lannoy of the need to attack the French position at Pavia in 1525 were all influenced by threat of mutiny by unpaid troops.

Naval resources

After initial experiments with heavily gunned sailing ships, both France and Spain concentrated on the traditional Mediterranean galley as the most effective warship for the local conditions. These were accompanied by large numbers of small sailing ships for the transportation of troops, supplies and horses. Very few of the ships in the armadas were built or owned by the state governments; most were either hired or commandeered from merchants for particular expeditions, or hired on long-term contracts from naval entrepreneurs like Andrea Doria. The one state which maintained a significant fleet at public expense was Venice, but even in this case the bulk of its fleet, which numbered over 100 galleys in the early sixteenth century, was laid up in the Arsenal ready to be crewed and equipped in an emergency. A guard squadron of galleys based on Corfu, at the mouth of the Adriatic, was the only continuous naval commitment of the republic, and the same squadron had the task of protecting the Venetian bases in Apulia in the early years of the wars.

Arsenals, in the true sense of the word as state-controlled centres for the building and equipping of warships, with depots for naval equipment and arms, were relative novelties in this period, apart from those in Venice and, to a lesser extent, Genoa. The construction of ships, mostly by private initiative, was scattered round the coasts of the western Mediterranean and the Atlantic shores of Portugal, Spain and France in a myriad of small ports. Four separate 'admiralties' supervised French naval activities on behalf of the crown in the early sixteenth century, and similar divisions of responsibility applied in the Spanish kingdoms. Malaga, Marseilles, Toulon, Civitavecchia, Naples and Palermo were being partly converted into military arsenals in this period, but the commitment of governments to major naval expenditure was limited and spasmodic.

The key factor in terms of costs was the rapid expansion of galley fleets from the late 1520s, and the increasing use of galeasses packed with soldiers alongside the traditional war galleys. A war galley carried 150–180 oarsmen, together with a small number of seamen and as many soldiers as could be squeezed on board. This meant that a fleet of 70 galleys, such as those put together by Charles V for the Tunis and Algiers expeditions, required around 14,000 men. The raising of galley crews became a major problem for the maritime nations of the Mediterranean. The medieval custom was to employ volunteers as oarsmen, and this largely survived in the fifteenth century. Steady growth of Italian galley fleets as the Ottoman threat grew in the later years of the century, and the new requirements of France and Spain in the early sixteenth century, meant that conscription and other methods of enforcement were used to fill the benches on the galleys. Convicts began to be used in Neapolitan and Spanish galleys in the 1480s, and Ottoman and Barbary prisoners were being used as galley slaves by the 1520s. Venice drew heavily on its Balkan empire for galley crews, and also introduced the idea of a naval militia raised in the Terraferma.

The effect of these developments was undoubtedly to reduce the per capita costs; slaves and convicts were not paid, but still had to be fed. The bulk of galley oarsmen, and all the sailors, remained volunteers or conscripts, and the costs of naval enterprises inevitably accelerated with the growth of the fleets. It has been estimated that the Tunis expedition of 1535 cost Charles V over one million ducats of which almost half were naval expenses. A third of the 75 galleys involved are not included in this calculation because they were provided and paid for by allies, like Genoa,

Pope Paul III, the Knights of Malta and some of the Neapolitan barons. The cost of pay and victuals for the 26,000 soldiers involved in this expedition is almost excluded from this calculation of naval expenses, but also constituted the bulk of the larger half of the total expense.[13]

The costs of war

Who paid the costs of the wars? Did the financial burden of war fall significantly on the powers disputing control of Italy, or was it borne largely by Italy itself? Inevitably, the answers to these questions would depend on which period and stage of the wars is being considered.

All western European states in this period, with the possible exception of England, spent approximately half their normal peacetime revenue on defence and preparation for war. This expenditure covered the costs of permanent troops at peacetime rates of pay, of maintaining fortifications, of providing for part-time militia training, with tax exemptions for the infantrymen and wages for the instructors and constables, of maintaining the artillery, plus the cost of administration, inspections and so on. The additional costs of going to war were largely created by the need to recruit large numbers of new troops, mostly infantry on short-term contracts. In French treasury accounts the ordinary and the extraordinary accounts were kept quite separate and reflected the distinction between the costs of peace and war. Different groups of financial officials and inspectors presided over them. If the surviving records were more complete it would be possible to distinguish between long-term defence costs and the costs of actual war more effectively. As it is, it seems likely that when Chancellor Duprat told the Assembly of Normandy in 1517 that the campaign for the recovery of Milan, including the battle of Marignano, had cost 7,500,000 livres tournois (about 3,700,000 ducats), he was including the full cost of the permanent companies of the ordinance. Duprat's startling figure presents the costs of war in sharp perspective; it represented at least 75 per cent of the total French revenue for the two years; it also equalled 75 per cent of the total receipts of the Milanese exchequer during the period 1499–1521.[14]

It is said that when Gonzalo de Córdoba was asked by King Ferdinand to show him the military expenditure accounts for the Spanish occupation of Naples, Gonzalo supplied figures which highlighted payments to monks, nuns and spies for their undercover services, much to Ferdinand's indignation.[15] The accounts for the Spanish expeditions to Naples in 1495 and 1501–3 have largely survived, and give figures for 1495 of 200,000 ducats and 1501–3 of 1,000,000 ducats. It is worth noting that the latter figure represented four times the annual revenue of Naples at that time.[16] Charles V's campaigns in Italy in 1529–30, including the siege of Florence, cost between 1,250,000 and 1,350,000 ducats.[17] Extraordinary military expenses from the declaration of war in 1521 to the Battle of Pavia cost nearly 20 million livres tournois, and figures of this magnitude were recorded in the war years of the 1530s and 1540s.[18]

Fleeting as these glimpses of the cost of war are, they give some impression of the drain on national revenues. Some historians have suggested that France, in particular, was able to off-load the costs of the great expeditions to Italy onto the subjugated Italian states and Italian satellites like Florence, which were also forced to pay subsidies to the conquerors.[19] A combination of direct raids on the Italian treasuries, the payment of French garrisons from Italian funds, the allocation of confiscated lands to French captains in lieu of pay, when added to the subsidies, donatives and plunder which were extracted, make a strong case for wholesale exploitation. Successive French kings had promised that the initial costs of the invasions would be quickly recouped and individuals enriched by the Italian enterprises. Charles VIII had hoped to gain 1,500,000 ducats from the conquest of Naples, and Louis XII was counting on getting 300,000 ducats a month from the Venetian lands in 1509.[20] These were extravagant claims calculated to win the support of assemblies of taxpayers and military captains.

Ferdinand of Aragon, always a realist, referred in his will to Naples as 'a kingdom we recovered with such labours and hardship, and in whose acquisition and recovery we have put great sums of our own moneys which we had in our exchequer'.[21] Indeed, Ferdinand had no great hopes of quick profits from the occupation of Naples; he tried to reduce the Spanish occupying force as much as possible to save the kingdom's overstretched revenues. He limited his demands for special donatives to recoup some of the costs of expelling the French, and did his best to restrain potential French threats to try to retake the kingdom by agreeing an annual subsidy of 50,000 ducats to France in 1505.[22] Indeed these subsidies, and those subsequently promised by Charles after Ferdinand's death by the terms of the Treaty of Noyon, were clear gains for France from the whole adventure.[23]

Financial and military support to both contesting powers was given by other Italian states. The role of the Venetian army in supporting French expeditions in 1499, 1515 and 1526–7, and that of Spain in 1495–6, represented significant contributions to the campaigning, although whether they allowed the French and Spanish military authorities to make savings in their military expenditure is a moot question. The popes offered subsidies to both sides on different occasions but the promises were not always fulfilled. In 1527 Clement VII promised 400,000 ducats for the pay of the Imperial army, but only 150,000 was ever paid.[24] At the same time Florence totally failed to honour a promise to provide 300,000 ducats to the Imperial coffers, although in an earlier stage of the wars it had provided subsidies for the payment of French troops in Italy.[25] The pensions paid to King Federigo of Naples and Duke Massimiliano Sforza of Milan following their withdrawal to exile in France, and the 200,000 ducats promised by Louis XII to Maximilian for the investiture of Milan, also need to be accounted among French expenses in Italy.[26]

Chancellor Duprat in his address of 1517 spoke of 800,000 livres tournois (around 375,000 ducats) being taken from the Milanese exchequer since the reoccupation in 1515.[27] Once again this must have been music to the ears of his listeners. But what was being referred to here were the defence costs of Milan, with pay to both French and Italian troops, the costs of the administration of Milan, and some payments to the Swiss whose goodwill was crucial to its defence. The costs of French campaigns in the 1520s could not, in any way, have been met from Milanese revenues. Nor indeed could those of the Piedmont campaigns in the 1530s and 1540s when Milan remained firmly under Spanish control. In the 1550s over eight million livres tournois (over three million ducats) was sent to Italy by Albisse del Bene, the superintendent general of French financial affairs in Italy, to cover military expenses between 1551 and 1556.[28]

On the other hand, the contributions of the Neapolitan exchequer to Imperial wars after about 1532 began to pick up steadily as the kingdom became more settled under Spanish rule. The early years of Spanish occupation had been difficult financially because of long-term imbalances in the economy and the continuing hostility to Spanish rule of pro-French sections of the baronage. The turning point came in 1528 with the failure of Lautrec's expedition and the subsequent purges of the baronial opposition, and in 1532 substantial donatives to Charles V were agreed by the Parlamento.[29] The same period saw the final establishment of Habsburg control in Milan in 1535 and a gradual improvement of revenues there, although subsidizing the campaigns in Piedmont and against Parma placed a heavy burden on them.

There is no doubt that the successive invasions had to be financed largely from the invaders' homelands. The need in 1515 for Francis I to increase the *taille*, to sell demesne lands, and to raise extensive loans, was referred to in

Chancellor Duprat's speech. The contributions of the treasury in Castile to the imperial campaigns of the 1520s are also well documented. It has been calculated that 1,700,000 ducats were sent to Italy from Spain in the period 1522–8 to help pay the military costs, with a further 500,000–600,000 sent in 1529. The *cortes* in Castile was said to be infuriated by this constant flow of cash to the wars in Italy.[30] The 1520s were also the period when French military finances went into severe deficit, and tax rises and extensive loans had to be brought into play. In the last years of the Italian Wars, both sides were financially exhausted. Their realms were unable to sustain the levels of taxation imposed on them for decades, largely to pay for wars, and the monarchs' debts were increasing. By then both Henry II and Philip II were struggling to find credit; bankers and financiers had lost confidence that loans to their governments would be repaid.

This fragmentary evidence suggests that attempts to belittle the costs of the wars to the outside powers, and particularly to France, have been exaggerated and that, similarly, to emphasize the financial burden to Italy can be misleading. Money paid to soldiers from funds sent to Italy came into the local economy, particularly in situations of long-term garrisons and billeting. In this sense the flow of French and Spanish treasure into Italy was a reverse trend to that normally considered. Where the balance should be struck in deciding who ultimately paid more for the Italian Wars, the Italians or the taxpayers of France and Spain, is not easy to determine.

Notes

1 For changes in the military society of Italy during the wars, see pp. 375–8.

2 The continuing importance of military contractors and the companies they raised in early modern armies has been emphasized by David Parrott, *Business of War*; I have modified Michael Mallett's original argument in this section to reflect this important work, which appeared after his death.

3 Contamine, *War in the Middle* Ages, 169–72.

4 *Ibid.*; Potter; Quatrefages, 'La invención'; Covini, 355–91; Mallett and Hale, 101–52.

5 Hale, 'Terra Ferma fortifications', 171.

6 Arfaioli, 115.

7 Hale, *War and Society*, 220–4.

8 Quatrefages, 'Les industries'; 10; AGS, Estado 61, f. 1.

9 See p. 154.

10 Hamon, *L'argent du roi*, 26.

11 Mantelli, 420–1; Potter, 228.

12 Lot, 198, 202–9; Potter, 234.

13 Tracy, 154–5.

14 Hamon, 'L'Italie', 33

15 Giovio, 166; Ruiz-Domènec, 407–12.

16 Coniglio, 163.

17 Tracy, 128.

18 Hamon, *L'argent du roi*, 46–7.

19 *Ibid.*, 128–9.

20 Hamon, 'L'Italie', 26.

21 Galasso, 20.

22 Hamon, 'L'Italie', 27.

23 *Ibid.*, 27–8.

24 Tracy, 47.

25 *Ibid.*; Hamon, 'L'Italie', 29.

26 Hamon, 'L'Italie', 30.

27 *Ibid.*, 26.

28 Potter, 218–19.

29 Calabria, 225–34; Tracy, 79–80, 280–8.

30 Tracy, 128–9.

Bibliography

Arfaioli, Maurizio, *The Black Bands of Giovanni* (Pisa: Plus, 2005).

Bonney, Richard (ed.), *Economic Systems and State Finance* (Oxford: Clarendon Press, 1995).

Calabria, Antonio, 'Le finanze pubbliche a Napoli nel primo Cinquecento', in Aurelio Musi (ed.), *Nel sistema imperiale: l'Italia spagnola* (Naples: Edizioni scientifiche italiane, 1994), 225–234.

Coniglio, Giuseppe, *Consulte e bilanci del Viceregno di Napoli dal 1507 al 1533* (Rome: Istituto Storico Italiano per l'Età moderna e contemporanea,1983).

Contamine, Philippe, 'The growth of state control. Practices of war 1300–1800: ransom and booty', in Contamine, Philippe (ed.), *War and Competition between States* (Oxford: Clarendon Press, 2000), 163–93.

Contamine, Philippe (ed.), *Histoire militaire de la France,* I (Paris: Presses Universitaires de France, 1992).

Contamine, Philippe, *War in the Middle Ages* (Oxford: Blackwell, 1984)

Covini, Maria Nadia, *L'esercito del duca. Organizzazione militare e istituzioni al tempo degli Sforza (1450–1480)* (Rome: Istituto Storico Italiano per il Medio Evo, 1998).

Di Tullio, Matteo, *The Wealth of Communities. War, Resources and Cooperation in Renaissance Lombardy* (Farnham: Ashgate, 2014).

Esch, Arnold, *I mercenari svizzeri in Italia. L'esperienza delle guerre milanesi (1510–1515) tratta da fonti bernesi* (Verbania-Intra: Alberti Libraio, 1999) (original German version in *Quellen und Forschungen aus italienischen Archiven und Bibliotheken,* 70 (1990), 348–440).

Galasso, Giuseppe, 'Trends and problems in Neapolitan history in the age of Charles V', in Antonio Calabria and John Marino (eds), *Good Government in Spanish Naples* (New York: Peter Lang, 1990), 13–78.

Giovio, Paolo, *Le vite del Gran Capitano e del Marchese di Pescara*, trans. Ludovico Domenichi, ed. Costantino Panigada (Bari: Laterza, 1931).

Hale, J.R., 'Terra Ferma fortifications in the Cinquecento', in *Florence and Venice: Comparisons and Relations,* 2 vols (Florence: La Nuova Italia Editrice, 1979–80), II, 169–87.

Hale, J.R., *War and Society in Renaissance Europe, 1450–1620* (Aldershot: Ashgate, 2007).

Hamon, Philippe, *L'argent du roi. Les finances sous François Ier* (Paris: Comité pour l'histoire économique et financière de la France, 1994).

Hamon, Philippe, 'L'Italie finance-t-elle les guerres d'Italie?', in Jean Balsamo (ed.), *Passer les monts. Français en Italie – l'Italie en France (1494–1525)* (Paris: Honoré Champion, 1998), 25–37.

Kirk, Thomas Allison, *Genoa and the Sea: Policy and Power in an Early Modern Maritime Republic, 1559–1684* (Baltimore and London: The Johns Hopkins University Press, 2005).

Lot, Ferdinand, *Recherches sur les effectifs des armées françaises des Guerres d'Italie aux Guerres de Religion 1494–1562* (Paris: SEVPEN, 1962).

Mallett, Michael and J.R. Hale, *The Military Organization of a Renaissance State: Venice c. 1400 to 1617* (Cambridge: Cambridge University Press, 1984).

Mantelli, Roberto, *Il pubblico impiego nell'economia del Regno di Napoli: retribuzioni, reclutamento e ricambio sociale nell'epoca spagnuola (secc. XVI-XVII)* (Naples: Istituto Italiano per gli Studi Filosofici, 1986).

Parrott, David, *The Business of War. Military Enterprise and Military Revolution in Early Modern Europe* (Cambridge: Cambridge University Press, 2012).

Potter, David, *Renaissance France at War. Armies, Culture and Society, c. 1480–1560* (Woodbridge: Boydell Press, 2008).

Quatrefages, René, 'Les industries de la guerre en Espagne', paper to Sedicesima Settimana di studio, Istituto Internazionale di Storia Economica "Francesco Datini", 'Gli aspetti economici della guerra in Europa (sec. XIV-XVIII)', Prato, May 1984.

Quatrefages, René, 'La invención de la guerra moderna', in *Carlos V. Las armas y las letras* (Sociedad Estatal para la Conmemoración de los Centenarios de Felipe II y Carlos V, 2000), 73–84.

Quatrefages, René, 'Le systeme militaire des Hapsbourg', in C. Hermann (ed.), *Le premier âge de l'état en Espagne (1450–1700)* (Paris: Éditions du Centre national de la recherche scientifique, 1989), 341–50.

Rabà, Michele M., *Potere e poteri. 'Stati', 'privati' e comunità nel conflitto per l'egemonia in Italia settentrionale (1536–1558)* (Milan: FrancoAngeli, 2016).

Ruiz-Domènec, José Enrique, *El Gran Capitán. Retrato de una época* (Barcelona: Ediciones Península, 2002).

Shaw, Christine, 'Popular resistance to military occupation during the Italian Wars', in Samuel Kline Cohn Jr. and Fabrizio Ricciardelli (eds), *The Culture of Violence in Renaissance Italy* (Florence: Le Lettere, 2012), 257–71.

Tallett, Frank, *War and Society in Early Modern Europe 1495–1715* (Routledge, 1992).

Tracy, James D., *Emperor Charles V, Impresario of War. Campaign Strategy, International Finance and Domestic Politics* (Cambridge: Cambridge University Press, 2002).

CHAPTER 10

Propaganda and images of war

The Italian Wars were European wars, with Italy one of the chief arenas in which the rivalries and conflicts between the major European powers were fought out. Major campaigns and events, battles and sieges, were publicized not just throughout Italy but well beyond the bounds of the peninsula. In part, this was on the initiative of princes and their officials, endeavouring to raise support for the war effort among those who were called upon to bear the expense; in part, on the initiative of those hoping to attract favour or patronage by supporting the government's cause. Many of the publications dealing with aspects of the wars, however, were produced by printers and booksellers for commercial motives. Advances in printing technology, such as the use of moveable type, made it possible by the late fifteenth century to turn out, quickly and cheaply, hundreds of copies of leaflets and pamphlets, containing reproductions of official documents, letters giving news of the progress of campaigns, verses, songs or prophecies, often illustrated with woodcuts. Many of these publications, poorly printed on cheap paper, intended to satisfy an interest in the latest news, not to provide a permanent record, have been lost completely over the centuries since their appearance. Often only a handful of copies, even just a single copy, of a publication survives, or the text is known only because it was transcribed into a diary or a memorandum book. The wars were also publicized through more literary works, in Latin or a vernacular language, learned treatises or poems, sometimes running into hundreds, even thousands, of lines. Visual allegories and images of the wars could be commissioned by princes or their officials, or devised for celebrations of victories by municipal authorities, or to flatter princes making ceremonial entries into a city. Most images and texts produced and distributed outside Italy were patriotic in tone, celebrating the achievements of the armies of their prince, denigrating his enemies, if sometimes deploring the cruelties and sorrows of war. Patriotism in Italy could be expressed in similar ways, and the victories of foreign princes might be celebrated by Italians as well. But Italian texts and images referring to the wars often had a darker tone, lamenting the loss of life and the destruction brought by the wars, and the subjugation of Italians to foreign princes and foreign armies.

French Italy

When Charles VIII set out in 1494 on his expedition to conquer the kingdom of Naples which he claimed as his by right, he took with him André de La Vigne, Queen Anne's secretary, to chronicle the journey. Before their departure, La Vigne had already written a description of the delights of Naples, presented as a garden of unearthly beauty, in *La ressource de la Chrestienté*; the king was going there to right the wrongs of Christendom. But he also gave a voice to criticisms of the enterprise as unnecessary, an expensive adventure that was being urged on by nobles who thought of war as an opportunity of displaying their prowess, disregarding the cost, the danger and destruction it brought. If the Turks threatened Italy, let the pope defend it.[1] Such arguments did not prevail in La Vigne's work, but may help to explain the attention paid to publicizing the course of the campaign in France.

The circulation of news about the king's deeds and policies, in letters and copies of documents sent to royal officials, great nobles or municipal governments, was a long-established practice in France. Charles wrote directly to local authorities, to towns and Parlements, as well as to individuals. Queen Anne apparently ordered manuscript copies of some of the letters and reports from Italy that reached her to be circulated to her officials and others in her duchy of Brittany. Some of the material that was reproduced in printed bulletins may have originally been circulated in manuscript, and then printed on the initiative of the recipients. Several printed bulletins were made up largely of letters from the king to his brother-in-law, Pierre de Bourbon, and may have been printed on his orders; some bulletins were printed at Tours, a centre of royal government. Other printed bulletins were less official in nature, long letters from private individuals to family or friends; at least some of these may have been published as a commercial enterprise.

The course of the expedition provided little opportunity to portray the king as a warrior, leading his army into action. Most of what fighting there was as the army made its way south to Naples involved detachments of troops who were not with the king. This did not hinder compilers of the bulletins from laying stress on how he was pursuing his rightful cause in arms, or from exaggerating the strength of the opposition the French troops encountered. Accounts of the taking of strongholds emphasized the speed of the assault, inflating the numbers of the defenders killed, presenting these as gallant actions against redoubtable forces. No mention was made of the deliberate tactic of slaughtering civilians in order to discourage resistance. In one bulletin, a letter the king wrote to Pierre de Bourbon about the taking of Monte San Giovanni in the kingdom of Naples – the first time he saw action in the campaign himself – was altered to refer to the earlier assault on Montefortino in the Papal States, at which he was not present. The bulletin describing his first entry into the city of Naples was largely fiction. A letter from Charles to Pierre de Bourbon dated 22 February, saying that he had not wanted to make a formal entry, was followed by a lengthy description of the kind of triumphal entry that might mark a monarch's taking possession of the capital of a newly acquired kingdom, followed by the king's coronation by a cardinal legate, and a ceremonial pledge of homage and fealty from the Neapolitan barons, none of which happened. Three days of public rejoicing had been ordered by the Florentine government, it was said; greater celebrations should be held in France.[2]

No official bulletin of the king's return to France or the Battle of Fornovo survives. A letter dated 15 July from a French civilian, Gilbert Pointet, travelling with the baggage train, was printed, claiming that the French lost only fifty or sixty men, against 4,000 Italian dead, and that the French army had retired to lodge where they chose after the fighting, which would be taken as a token of victory, but it also described the anxious journey of the army to Asti, riding in battle order all the way. Charles himself, in letters to the authorities in Lyon, claimed the victory, but had to ask for a watch to be kept for any of the baggage that had been looted, including his personal jewels.[3] An engraving depicting the Battle of Fornovo was produced in France, perhaps in 1495, giving some impression of the confusion of battle while placing it in a stylized landscape, with the River Taro, which had so much influence on the course of the battle, reduced to a brook that soldiers were shown wading across in a couple of strides.[4]

Louis XII was much better suited than Charles to fill the role of a warrior king. He did lead his troops into battle. The major victories of his reign were in Italy; the Battle of Agnadello in particular confirmed his martial image. He had an official historiographer, Jean d'Auton, who followed the armies and chronicled the campaigns that secured the duchy of Milan for Louis, those that won and lost the kingdom of Naples for him, and Louis's own campaign to re-establish French dominion over Genoa in 1507. Queen Anne ordered the court poet Jean Marot to accompany the king to Italy and celebrate his victories over Genoa in 1507 and Venice in 1509. The result was 1,300 lines on the *Voyage de Gênes*, and around 4,000 lines on the *Voyage de Venise*. Although there was nothing that quite matched the systematic production of official bulletins in 1494–5 during these campaigns, many bulletins and leaflets were published on the orders of the authorities and as private commercial initiatives. Louis's reign was exceptional in the amount of literature, poems, histories, treatises and allegories informing the French public about Italy and what the French were doing there. Jean Lemaire de Belges, who moved from the court of Margaret of Austria to that of Louis, wrote of the need to address the people on the merits of the prince, to incline them to favour his just right, to aid him and pray for his victory, because to be at war unsettled them and gave rise to complaints.[5]

Louis's claim to Naples came with the French crown; his claim to the duchy of Milan, which concerned him more, was his personal inheritance. After the conquest of Milan, French authors wrote of the claims of Louis to dominate the whole of Italy, and continued to do so even after the French had been driven from Naples by the Spanish. The legitimacy of French claims over Italy were based on legends, such as the Trojan origins of the Franks (with the Trojans presented as the ancient rulers of Italy), and on history, including the conquests of Charlemagne, and more recent treaties and marriage alliances. It was argued that the Gauls were the true founders of the cities of Lombardy, 'Gallia Cisalpina', Cisalpine Gaul, cities that had been lost later to the Romans. During the war against Venice, Louis XII was said to be recovering from the Venetians cities that were legitimately French, as in Symphorien Champier's *Triumphe du tres chretien roy de France Loys XII*, which was published simultaneously in French, Italian and Latin. Italian humanists at Louis's court also referred to the original union of Gauls on either side of the Alps. The Milanese used the argument that Milan had been founded by the French, when trying to ingratiate themselves with Louis's minister, Georges d'Amboise, in 1500. According to a passionately pro-French writer from Asti (which had been held by Louis as duc d'Orléans), Giovan Giorgio Alione, there was no relationship between the Milanese and the French, however. The Milanese were merely descendants of the Lombards, who had driven the Gauls out and imposed their barbarous customs on a civilized land. Having conquered the barbarous Lombards, the French could now restore their civilization.[6]

The idea of the French bringing their culture to Italy, assimilating the Italians under French rule socially as well as politically, was promoted by writers in the service of Louis in particular. As under Charles VIII, it was asserted that it was God's will that the French should triumph in Italy, perhaps to promote a crusade, but also to rescue the benighted Italians from their tyrannous governments. In Naples, during Charles's reign, the tyrants were the Aragonese kings; under Louis XII, it was the Spanish nation, denounced as cruel and untrustworthy. Ludovico Sforza was a tyrant from an illegitimate dynasty, and guilty of poisoning his nephew, Duke Gian Galeazzo. The Venetians were tyrants because their republic, dominated by merchants, upset the social order and usurped princely rule. Genoa was the most anarchic city in an Italy riven by discord. Some authors imagined Italians pleading for the intervention of their legitimate prince. The French would protect the Italians from themselves, bringing proper social order, with the nobility supporting the monarchy, the only form of rule which could guarantee order. By adopting French social and political customs, they would gradually come to manifest French virtues and faith, and love of the king; learning French would be an important step. But the setbacks suffered by the French in Italy gave rise to some less roseate views of the relations between France and Italy, between French and Italians. Italy was viewed as quite distinct from France, as hostile and inhospitable. Italians were proud, avaricious, disloyal. Such opinions had been voiced as Charles's Neapolitan enterprise foundered, and they were expressed more frequently as Milan was lost to Louis. That Italy was the graveyard of the French became a stock phrase.[7]

The production of printed leaflets and pamphlets was most frequent during the campaigns led by the king in person against Genoa and Venice. There has not been any study of the bulletins that published letters from Italy to establish whether the texts were altered; the letters were often printed without explanation or elaboration. A printer in Lyon, Noël Abraham, was commissioned by the chancellor, Guy de Rochefort, to produce a number of pamphlets; his first commission was on the conquest of Genoa in 1507. Abraham published a variety of pamphlets in 1509, proudly emphasizing their official character. These included, before the campaign began, a translation of the papal bull against the Venetians, and a list of troops heading to Italy (a text also published in German, perhaps for the benefit of the Swiss and landsknechts with the army). Two reported the Battle of Agnadello, a brief one of letters sent from the French camp to the queen and the future king Francis, dated 14 May, and a more detailed, hastily put together account, with news of the taking of fortresses and cities from the Venetians, which was published in two editions, one with a note of news just received of the surrender of the fortress of Cremona. There were two editions of an account (the first to be published) of Louis's ceremonial entry into Milan after the battle. This was published in Paris as well, and in German translation. Abraham also published some of the literary works written about the campaign, including a collection of ballads by André de La Vigne concerning the alliance against Venice and the trepidation of the Venetians, letters and poems on the war by Jean d'Auton, and a poem by a Burgundian lawyer, Celse-Hugues Descousu, celebrating the high points of Louis's reign from his coronation and the conquests of Milan, Naples and Genoa, to the League of Cambrai and the attack on Venice. Three editions of a French translation of an Italian poem, possibly by a Milanese, Simone Litta, on the battle and the king's entry into Milan, were published within ten days.[8]

Abraham's output gives an idea of the range of material available to the French people during the period from 1509 to 1512 (there was not much good news concerning the French in Italy to be celebrated in the last years of Louis's reign). Other printers in Lyon, Paris, Rouen and elsewhere in the kingdom were active in diffusing information and commentary on the French in Italy, and the translation of some texts into German and Italian indicated that there was a market for their publications outside France as well. Anti-Venetian leaflets in Italian were printed at Lyon before Louis set out for Italy in 1509, for distribution in Lombardy as the army passed through.[9] There was much praise of the king, and support for his cause; defeat gave rise to lamentation, rather than criticism. His valour and the justice of his cause, approved by God, were not questioned. Louis was portrayed as an exemplar of chivalry, morally superior to his enemies.

The fact that many of the illustrations for the bulletins and pamphlets were stock scenes of knightly combat that could also be used to illustrate chivalric romances, would not have seemed inappropriate. More sophisticated illustrations than the clumsy woodcuts used for cheap leaflets, such as those in the manuscripts of Jean d'Auton's *Chroniques de Louis XII*, or his *Voyage de Gênes*, usually portray Louis and his nobles in fine armour, with plumed helmets, riding splendidly caparisoned horses.[10] A painting depicting the Battle of Agnadello by Jean Perréal, who was there, has been lost. Jean Lemaire, who saw it, described it as set in a precise and detailed background of castles, towns, rivers and mountains (which sounds more like an imaginary landscape than a faithful rendering of the battleground), and a realistic depiction of the fighting, of the wounded and those put to flight, as well as the victors.[11] The second edition of Claude de Seyssel's *La victoire du roy contre les Veniciens*, published in 1510, had a woodcut illustration of the presentation to the king of the captured Venetian commander, Bartolomeo d'Alviano, and the Venetian troops being driven from the field (the first edition, published in 1509, had a woodblock of a naval battle on the first page).[12] The only surviving illustration of the Battle of Ravenna produced in France is on a leaflet publishing a letter to the French governor of Genoa, but the woodcut depicts a generic scene of a king riding into combat, that had been used in the *Croniques de France* published in 1493.[13] Louis, of course, was not at Ravenna, and the battle was not celebrated in France. No letters were sent from the king to French cities announcing the victory, no Te Deum was sung in the cathedral of Notre-Dame in Paris.

Francis I's reign began with his spectacular victory at Marignano, fixing his image as a heroic warrior king. It was celebrated in France by an outpouring of poems and songs. One of these, the song *La Guerre*, later renamed *La Bataille de Marignan*, by the composer Clément Janequin, a vivid, graphic evocation of the different stages of the battle and the 'victory of the noble King Francis', became a model for other composers of 'battle pieces'. The victory was viewed as revenge on the Swiss who had expelled the French from Milan, and had been denounced as tyrannical peasants, incapable of fulfilling the role proper to a prince, and ungratefully fighting against the French after years of being in French pay.[14] Throughout his reign, Francis insisted on his right to the duchy of Milan, which was described as being an integral part of the lands of the crown, rather than the personal possession of the king (although in fact his claim rested on the inheritance of his wife, Claude, daughter of Louis XII). Even when the war in Milan was not going well for the French in the 1520s, some optimistic writers could still describe Francis as able to become the master of all Italy. In 1524 Guillaume La Maistre presented Francis as obliged to go to Italy, to respond to the appeals of the Italians, with 'Dame Italie' pleading to her lover Francis I to come to her.[15]

The French people in general, however, were by then less persuaded of Italy's desire to be French; Marignano did not change that. There were more references to animosity between the French and Italians, who would never be turned into 'good Frenchmen'. Claude de Seyssel (a cleric who was in the service of the crown for many years, and wrote a treatise for Francis, *La monarchie de France*, in 1515) had envisaged French influence extending from Italian lands throughout the Mediterranean in Louis's reign. But by 1516 he had changed his mind, arguing it would be impossible to establish a lasting French presence in Italy, particularly in Milan, because it would be seen as a threat to the balance of power in Europe.[16] Disenchantment with involvement in Italy naturally deepened after the Battle of Pavia and the capture of the king.

Propaganda on behalf of the king does not seem to have addressed this disenchantment directly, but might recognize that some reports on Italian affairs were not favourable. When Bonnivet's troops had been pushed out of nearly all the duchy of Milan in 1524, a letter was sent from the king to the principal cities of France on 8 May, denouncing those who 'altered the facts' by describing as a defeat what was an orderly withdrawal, sparing lives, in despite of the enemy. The letter was said to make known the 'real truth', correcting the accounts of those spreading reports at variance with how things actually happened.[17]

The conquest of the lands of the Duke of Savoy was justified on the grounds that the duke was the aggressor, having trespassed on the king's territory, threatening his subjects, so that Francis had had no choice but to respond in kind, and bring help to the Savoyards. Other arguments advanced were of the same nature that had been used to justify the conquest of Naples and of Milan. Some of the lands of the Duke of Savoy were said to belong to Francis through a right of succession of his mother, Louise of Savoy; Piedmont was part of Cisalpine Gaul. Guillaume du Bellay, who served as governor of Piedmont, claimed that Francis had rights to Piedmont and Nice through the Angevin inheritance, that the Dauphin had rights over Saluzzo, and that France had historic rights over Monferrato, Lombardy and Emilia.[18] Jean Thénaud, in his *Triumphe des Vertuz*, described French armies as composed of men coming from all the provinces of the kingdom, among which he counted Lombardy. Not just Milan but Piedmont and Savoy, the whole of Italy, were French lands.[19] But the conquest of Piedmont does not seem to have aroused much enthusiasm among the French, not least, perhaps, because the king did not take much part in the campaigns himself.

Imperial Italy

Although Maximilian was often held in low esteem by other princes, he devoted close attention to the presentation of his image as a wise and chivalrous ruler and military leader. His part, and that of his armies, in the Italian Wars, especially in campaigns against Venice, figured prominently in this self-promotion. He commissioned an illustrated romantic account of

his life, the *Weiss Kunig*, in which he appeared in the persona of the White
King, the king of France figured as the Blue King, and the doge of Venice as
the King of the Fish. Most of the illustrations of the wars in Italy were of
events in which he or his army had been directly involved, the exceptions
being depictions of the Battle of Agnadello and the Battle of Novara of
1513. The campaign of 1509 was also commemorated by scenes of the
sieges of Padua and Monselice, the attack on Cividale, and the occupation
of Venetian cities by Imperial troops.[20] He supervised the programme for a
series of miniatures of a procession of landsknechts bearing aloft banners
depicting battle scenes, the *Triumphzug*. These included a double spread
devoted to the 'Great Venetian War', showing the lion of St Mark being
driven into the sea by the Imperial forces, which have been described as
'the most purely propagandistic of the *Triumphzug* war scenes'.[21]

Maximilian was also concerned with more mundane propaganda,
aimed at a wide audience in Germany and Italy, being involved in writing,
editing, correcting and directing the distribution of bulletins. Leaflets were
distributed in the Veneto before and during the campaigns there. Some
were put in balloons to fly over the enemy lines; Imperial archers would
shoot to burst them, so that the leaflets fell among the enemy troops.[22]
A printed sheet, found in the streets of Udine in February 1508, declared
in Maximilian's name that he was coming to Italy to be crowned, to lib-
erate all Italy from tyrants, especially the Venetians, who had occupied
the lands of others, and to get rid of the taxes they had unjustly imposed,
leaving in place only true, Imperial taxes.[23] Pamphlets calling on the people
of the Veneto to rise against the Venetians were distributed; some calling
on the inhabitants of Venice to rebel found their way into the city on
several occasions, in 1509, 1510 and 1511.[24] Pamphlets intended for a
German audience were often aimed at arousing support for financial aid to
Maximilian from the Imperial Diet, but the members of the Diet were not
swayed. In the absence of Imperial victories in Italy, Maximilian edited war
bulletins describing victories in which landsknechts had a role, however
minor, such as the French occupation of Bologna in 1511.[25]

If Maximilian's war propaganda failed to convince the Diet to grant
him the money he wanted, it may have been more effective in influencing
the tone and approach of other publications in Germany concerning the
war in Italy, which supported his policy rather than that of the Diet. (How
the governments of the Imperial cities such as Nuremberg, Strasbourg and
Augsburg that were important centres of printing in Germany reacted to
this has not been studied.) The authors of these publications were also
influenced by the anti-Venetian arguments that were voiced in Italy; Italian

texts were translated and printed in Germany. Venice was criticized for taking lands that belonged to the pope or the emperor; Venetians had no legal right to hold territory in mainland Italy, and were consequently tyrants; they were proud and arrogant, corrupt and deceitful; they were in league with Turks.[26]

One German broadsheet included a woodcut representing Venice as a double-tailed mermaid, bearing a banner with the lion of St Mark, while Maximilian, the pope, Louis, and Ferdinand of Aragon stood on the shore on either side, grasping the banner and tearing it apart.[27] Other German illustrations of the war emphasized Maximilian's role. A German translation of Jean Lemaire's *Légende des venitiens*, despite the pro-French content of the work, had a woodcut on the title page in which Maximilian alone represented the League confronting the crestfallen doge and senators, while below Imperial troops advanced on fleeing Venetian soldiers.[28] In a volume of epigrams by the poet Ulrich von Hutten, published in 1519, his verses 'On the emperor and the Venetians' compare the Venetians with frogs being driven back into the water by Jupiter's eagle; the woodcut illustration shows a crowned eagle with a sceptre in its talons, hovering over the land, with an alarmed frog backing into the sea. Ten of the poems denounce the Venetians; two are directed against Bartolomeo d'Alviano; six celebrate the Battle of Agnadello, without any mention of its being a French victory, and with the Venetians again referred to as frogs, slain by an eagle. The illustration of the battle shows Venetian troops put to flight by landsknechts with the Imperial standard flying above them.[29]

Charles V was involved in the Italian Wars as the ruler of the Spanish kingdoms (and, consequently, of the kingdom of Naples) as well as emperor. He had more command of Spanish troops and Spanish resources to pursue his aims and policies in Italy than he did over those of the Empire. His officials and commanders in Italy, when they were not Italian, were usually Spanish, although they were often called 'agenti imperiali' by Italians. These Spanish Imperial agents were ready to employ arguments that Charles V was intervening in Italian affairs as emperor, and that he should be supported and obeyed by Italians in the regions of northern and central Italy which were considered to be part of the Empire, even if they were consciously working to establish Spanish dominance over Italy. They thought Philip, as future king of Spain, should have the duchy of Milan as well as the kingdom of Naples, and that Spain should be the hegemonic power in Italy.

In Spain, however, there was not a great deal of interest in Italian affairs. Other conflicts were more important to the people of the Spanish kingdoms. They were more concerned with the contest with the French on the frontier between France and Spain, than with the struggle for control of the duchy of Milan. They were particularly concerned about the Muslim powers and corsairs of the Barbary coast of North Africa. During Ferdinand's reign, news of the entry of the Spanish fleet into the port of Oran, three days after the Battle of Agnadello, and the capture of Bougie in 1510 and of Tripoli in 1511, would have been of much more consequence to them than the progress of the war in Lombardy and the Veneto. Nor did they identify with Charles's international interests as emperor: they wanted him to stay in Spain, make peace with other Christian powers and continue Ferdinand's fight against the North African corsairs. They were unwilling to grant him subsidies to fight the Turks, let alone for campaigns in Italy. Even the official royal chroniclers in Spain under Charles V did not write in his praise, and included criticisms of him in their work.[30]

Some effort was made to make persuade the Spanish to support his Italian policies. Cheap printed news leaflets had begun to appear in Spain in the late fifteenth century, and Charles used these *relaciones* to try to generate support for his aims. On the orders of the Imperial council, the chancellor Gattinara's secretary, Alfonso de Valdés, wrote a pamphlet, *Relación de las nuevas de Italia*, about the Battle of Pavia, which was presented as a victory for Castile. Published with a woodcut of Charles V's coat of arms, with the Imperial eagle and his personal emblem of the Pillars of Hercules, the bulletin was compiled from the letters sent by the Imperial commanders, and included five pages listing French casualties and prisoners, with the assertion that few Imperial troops had died. God had willed the victory, to put an end to war between Christians and permit Charles to go to fight the Turks and the Moors.[31] News of the Sack of Rome was not well received at the Imperial court, but efforts were made to present the shocking event to the people of Spain in a favourable light. In letters sent to municipal councils on 15 July 1527, the sack was blamed on the leaderless soldiers. Charles, an obedient son of the pope, was distressed by it, and wanted preachers to be instructed to explain this from the pulpits. For the more educated, Valdés wrote a 'Diálogo de las cosas acaescidas en Roma' ('Dialogue about what has happened in Rome'), placing the blame for the sack on the pope and justifying it as the only way to cleanse Rome, the 'Babylon of all the vices'; this circulated in manuscript. Much more widely distributed, were the verses *Triste estaba el Padre Santo* (*The Holy Father was sad*), which were also published with explanatory notes. Again, responsibility was laid on the pope, who had proved himself incapable of governing the Church. The sack was presented as being in the tradition of the glorious enterprises of the Castilians.[32] Naturally, no such hostile view of the pope was given in the several *relaciones* describing the Imperial coronation in 1530, and explaining its symbolism.

Charles also ordered the publication of justifications of his policies. In 1528, he ordered his secretary, Gonzalo Pérez, to publish a pamphlet concerning his exchange of insults with Francis I, emphasizing the emperor's magnanimity and good faith, and the baseness of the French king.[33] An 'address' by Charles to the Spanish and the Roman people, explaining the reasons for his journey to Italy in 1529, was published in Italian. Three reasons were given: the reform of the Church, the misery of Italy, and the crusade. Once peace had been established among Christian princes, Charles could command a crusade to reconquer Constantinople and drive the infidel from Jerusalem.[34] At least three *relaciones* concerning the emperor's speech denouncing Francis before the pope in Rome in April 1536 were published in Castilian. Two were in the form of anonymous letters recounting the event, one with the same woodcut of Charles's coat of arms used in earlier official *relaciones*, the other, published in Seville, with clumsier versions of the Imperial and papal arms (but the papal arms were those of Clement VII, rather than Paul III). After that, Italy was no longer a focus of Imperial propaganda in Spain.

No Spanish visual representation of the battles of the Italian Wars involving Spanish troops, even of the Battle of Pavia, are known. In Germany, a single woodcut of the Battle of Pavia, by Jörg Brau, was published in two versions, one with captions in German, and one with captions in Latin.[35] The major representation of the battle, presented to Charles by the marchese di Pescara, was a set of tapestries commissioned by Pescara in the Netherlands in 1531. The designer of the tapestries, Barnaert van Orley, was apparently given a detailed brief about the events of the battle from a Spanish perspective. Each of the tapestries shows the French army to disadvantage, including the attack on the French camp and, of course, the capture of Francis.[36] A painting of the battle, with labels in French identifying the different contingents and commanders was also possibly commissioned in the Netherlands by an Imperial partisan. Among the series of twelve fine engravings on the theme of *The Victories of Charles V*, perhaps commissioned by Granvelle, designed by Maarten van Heemskerck, and published in the Netherlands in 1556, was one of the capture of Francis at Pavia. Two of the series relate to the Sack of Rome, one depicting the death of Bourbon, shown falling from a scaling ladder, and one showing artillery levelled against the Castel Sant'Angelo, in which the pope had taken refuge. The Sack is alluded to indirectly in the first print of the series, in which Clement figures as one of the emperor's vanquished enemies, who stand encircled by a cord whose ends are held in the beak of an eagle at Charles's feet, as he sits enthroned above them.[37]

The papacy at war

The participation of the popes in the Italian Wars had a significant effect on how the popes and the papacy as an institution were perceived throughout Europe. That the popes should be actively engaged in making war against Christian powers in pursuit of secular ends, that sometimes they used the resources of the Church to fund military campaigns whose sole purpose was the elevation of their own family to the status of a princely dynasty, contributed to the disenchantment with the Church of Rome that fuelled the development of Protestantism. Even those who did not turn away from the Catholic Church might have to come to terms with the implications of the popes' involvement in the wars. Italians were accustomed to papal armies being deployed to further or protect the territorial or personal interests of the popes. The idea that this was a legitimate aspect of the role of the popes might have been easier for people elsewhere in Europe to accept if the pope was fighting on the same side as their own prince, but at some stage in the wars, French, German and Spanish publicists and writers might have faced the task of explaining why their prince, their soldiers, were at war with the Holy Father.

The martial image of the pope was most evident during the pontificate of Julius II. There was a positive aspect to this. Julius was hailed as the heir to the Caesars, as renewing the Christian Empire, in learned treatises, sermons, and in ballads and verses sung and sold in the streets. *Papa Iulio secondo che redriza tuto el mondo* (*Pope Julius II who puts the whole world to rights*) was the title of an anonymous ballad, published around the end of 1512 or the beginning of 1513, about the defeats inflicted on the French in Italy by the Holy League, and in France by the English. The woodcut illustration showed Julius, surrounded by the other members of the League, striking down the cock of France with his pastoral cross.[38]

On the other side of the coin, Julius could be presented as being more interested in war than in religion. His leading the papal troops to Perugia and Bologna in 1506, his presence at the camp besieging Mirandola in 1511, sharpened this image. In France, after Julius made peace with Venice and changed from being an ally to an enemy of Louis, the image of the warrior pope was contrasted with that of the Christian king defending the Church, and provided ammunition for those supporting the ecclesiastical council promoted by Louis to challenge Julius. French theologians concluded that the king had a right to defend himself militarily against a pope who was the promoter of an unjust war.[39] Writers associated with the French court portrayed the pope exchanging his vestments for armour, wielding a sword. 'What a fine sight to see an aged priest in arms ... besmirched with blood', urging on an attack, wrote Jean Lemaire in a treatise on church councils.[40] In Germany, Ulrich von Hutten directed even more of his epigrams, fourteen of them, against the pope than he did against the Venetians. Julius, 'murderer and spawn of hell', was accused of throwing the whole world into chaos, bearing sole responsibility for forcing peace-loving princes to take up arms. The accompanying illustration showed Julius wearing a full suit of armour with his papal cope and tiara.[41] Most famous of the denunciations of Julius was the *Julius exclusus*, published anonymously, but believed to be the work of Erasmus, in which the pope was described turning up at the gates of Heaven with the souls of those who had died fighting for him, demanding entrance of St Peter, boasting of his worldly power and of the wars he had stirred up. When St Peter refuses to open the gates of Heaven for him, Julius threatens to return in greater strength, confident that soon many thousands of men would die in battle and join with him to force their way in.[42]

So strong was the impact of the image of the warrior pope that it could also be applied to Leo X. A set of prints by Lucas Cranach, contrasting Christ and the Antichrist – in which the pope figures as the Antichrist – includes a pair in which Christ refusing an earthly crown is set against the power of the pope, in which a pope with the plump features and dumpy stature of Leo is surrounded by soldiers and artillery. The booklet, produced in 1521, was published in both German and Latin editions, and widely distributed. Luther considered it an excellent book for laymen.[43] But Leo was not regarded as a strong prince, as Julius had been. In a print which appeared in three versions in France and in Zurich, depicting a game of 'flux' (a card game along the lines of poker), in which the Swiss are presuming to take on the European powers, Leo is shown looking through a pair of eyeglasses, commenting that he cannot see how to get into the game.[44] Clement VII appeared even weaker. It was not only in Imperial propaganda that he was blamed for promoting the Sack of Rome by his impolitic, if not sinful, involvement in the wars, when the responsibility of his office was to promote peace among Christian powers. The idea of the pope as engaged in wars against Christian powers had become a familiar one, but no one could seriously consider him, or his successors who also were involved in the Italian Wars, as a warrior pope.

The woes of Italy

The Italian Wars prompted a myriad of publications in Italy itself, from popular songs to learned Latin treatises, conveying news and comment, prophecies and prognostications, satire and praise for rulers and commanders, celebrations of victories and lamentations for defeats, and for the suffering and destruction brought by the wars. Printers, booksellers, street pedlars evidently identified a market, an appetite, for information and comment not just on events and developments that directly affected their own state or region, but for what was happening elsewhere in Italy. The misfortunes of others could evoke some satisfaction, if the sufferer was a traditional rival or enemy, but more often commiseration, 'an anxious awareness of a common tragic Italian destiny reflected in the narratives of plundering and pillaging'.[45]

Italian governments did not promote the publication of the kind of official bulletins of news and propaganda that was organized by the ministers and officials of the kings of France or the emperors. On occasion, there were indications that some publication had been sponsored in some way by those in power. During the early years of the War of the League of Cambrai, for example, in Bologna leaflets reviling Cardinal Francesco Alidosi, the detested former legate who had fled the city as French forces approached in 1511, were distributed for free after his assassination. Poems in praise of Cardinal Federico da Sanseverino, one of those who had summoned the schismatic Council of Pisa, were thrown from windows into the crowds watching his entry into Bologna in March 1512. Leaflets mocking the pope and the Spanish (some in a mixture of Italian and Castilian) were launched from the city walls into the Spanish and papal troops besieging them.[46] Many of the flood of anti-Venetian publications produced in Ferrara in the early years of the war against Venice were printed with official approval from the ducal government, although it is not known if any were officially commissioned. They ranged from songs predicting the ruin of Venice, some in the form of mock laments by the Venetians, and celebrations of the Ferrarese victory at Polesella, to the text of a fictitious oration to Maximilian by a Venetian ambassador, informing him that his demands for the restitution of territories occupied by Venice and the republic's submission to Imperial authority were agreed. A large number of them were collected and annotated by a Ferrarese in Alfonso's service.[47] In Rome, papal officials, if not the pope, may have had a role in directing pro-papal publications. In 1509, a printed collection of pasquinades – the anonymous verses commenting (often satirically) on current affairs, which it had become customary to affix near a battered classical sculpture nicknamed Pasquino – contained many allusions to the League of Cambrai, with Julius hailed as its prime mover. The papal censor was apparently involved in choosing which verses should be included, and presumably in excluding criticisms of papal policy, which there may well have been among the pasquinades.[48]

Venice was a major centre of printing and publishing, and many publications concerning the Italian Wars were produced there. Yet even during the height of anti-Venetian propaganda, some of which found its way into the city of Venice, there was no sign of an official campaign to disseminate favourable works. When the government became aware of anti-Venetian publications, it banned their sale, but did not organize a printed response. Perhaps the Signoria and senators felt confident that they did not need to, that they could rely on Venetian writers and printers to produce the kind of response of which they would approve. Predictions of the demise of Venice were met by texts expressing confidence in Venetian strength and ultimate triumph. Open discussion of government policy in the streets and squares was not encouraged in Venice at any time, and there was some censorship. Incitements to war against Ferrara could meet with approval, but printed works critical of Maximilian, at a time when the Venetians were trying to negotiate terms with him, were censored by the Ten.[49]

Many of the works produced in Italy concerning the wars inevitably included comments, favourable or hostile, on the foreign powers involved. There were French and Imperial partisans, whose allegiance would persist through the changing fortunes of war. But most publications would reflect the shifts of sentiment that reflected the course of events; much depended on which side of the battle lines a writer and his prospective audience were at a given moment. Poets in Milan, Florence and Ferrara wrote favourably of Charles VIII and the French, at least in the early stages of the expedition in 1494, for example; those in Rome and Naples were hostile; those in Venice, neutral, at first, becoming more critical later. Stupefaction and apprehension at the size of the French army making its way to Naples, was turned to derision as poets celebrated an Italian victory at Fornovo.[50] All Italians could share in the horror at the Sack of Rome in 1527; and few seem to have believed that it had been perpetrated without the knowledge of the emperor; but how his presumed responsibility for it should be interpreted varied widely. Some held that he shared the guilt for the impiety and cruelty of his soldiers, that it showed him to be bent on the subjugation of Italy, that it showed he could not be the true emperor. But many people were ready to take a more favourable view of Charles, judging by

the wide circulation of prophetic literature, putting a pro-Imperial inter-
pretation on familiar prophecies of the Second Charlemagne, of a virtuous
prince who would come to cleanse and purify the Church and bring about
a golden age of peace and prosperity – the same prophecies that had been
used of Charles VIII when he came to Italy in 1494.[51]

Prophecies were an important element of the popular literature on the
wars. Complex prophecies with arcane symbolism which had been circu-
lating in Europe for a century and more, were re-worked and simplified
and applied to the events of the day, turned into verses that could be sung
and sold by street-singers. More educated people might read prophecies in
more sophisticated formats, but the basic ideas were the same. News of the
wars, of battles and sieges and sacks, of advances and retreats, of alliances
and treaties too, was the other staple of the popular literature. Even if it
was presented in the form of ballads, illustrated by generic woodcuts from
chivalric romances, the reports in the leaflets and broadsheets peddled in
the streets were often claimed to be reliable accounts of facts, not fanciful
tales of poets. Learned poets would sometimes accuse the street-singers of
retailing falsehoods, and assert in their poems that they were telling the
real truth, the exact truth. The emphasis in street literature was on the
bloodshed, the cruelty, the scourge of war, rather than heroic deeds. It was
difficult to accommodate the realities of contemporary warfare in more
literary works, whose authors looked to Latin poets, such as Virgil, and
chivalric epics for models. Ludovico Ariosto, in his long poem *Orlando
furioso*, for example, while ostensibly writing of the wars of Charlemagne,
between Christians and Saracens, introduced handguns and artillery into
the narrative. He made several direct references to contemporary events,
including a compliment to Alfonso d'Este on his tactics during the Battle
of Ravenna (he was in the service of the Este), and criticism of the French
for the sacks of Ravenna and Brescia. After he had retired from the service
of the Este, in revising his works he condemned the use of arquebuses as
unchivalric, destroying military glory.[52]

One of the main genres of Italian literature on the wars, at all levels of
sophistication and literary merit, was the *lamento*. Some *lamenti* were for
specific events, such as the fall of Naples in 1495, or the sack of Brescia
in 1512. Some were satirical, in which a defeated enemy was mocked by
being represented as bewailing their own misfortunes and humiliation.
Many were written as lamentations for, or by, Italy, personified in the
text and in the accompanying illustration as a woman, often as a young
woman, distraught, disconsolate, or a mother betrayed by her children, in
laments for the disunity of the Italians, the discords that divided them and

made them the prey of foreign princes and their rapacious, brutal armies. 'Italians, if you were united / nobody would engage in war with you / ... but if envy will reign / among you, be certain that / you will always be ruined by Infidels and Frenchmen', was the warning in a ballad, *Non dormite, o'taliani* (*Do not sleep, Italians*), published in Venice in 1510.[53] A collection of poems recounting the events of the wars from 1494, first published in 1522 as *Libro o vero cronica di tutte le guerre de Italia*, was re-edited and republished several times, acquiring the title *Guerre horrende de Italia*, the *Horrendous Wars of Italy*.

How patriotic Italians could move beyond lamentation, to find a way of coming to terms with the new political realities, was not a subject adapted to popular verses and songs. How difficult it could be was indicated by a dialogue written by the historian Paolo Giovio, who had been in Rome during the sack in the service of Clement VII, while being a supporter of the emperor. The dialogue reconstructs conversations he had after seeking refuge on the island of Ischia in the bay of Naples, with an Imperial commander, Alfonso d'Avalos, marchese del Vasto, whose family owned the castle of Ischia, and an official, a Neapolitan lawyer serving on the council of the viceroy, Giovanni Antonio Muscettola. Del Vasto had not been present at the assault on Rome, but had gone there soon afterwards to participate in negotiations with Clement. In the dialogue, he says that he served the emperor because he thought that victory for him would bring lasting peace to Italy, even if it meant renouncing dreams of the recovery of Italian liberty. He did think that Charles would restore the duchy of Milan to Francesco Sforza, although he conceded that the exactions of the Imperial soldiers were ruining Milan. Giovio vented his rage at the sack: Charles had reduced himself to the level of the Goths and the Vandals who had sacked Rome. He hoped against hope that Italians could recover their liberty, but everything depended on the moderation and justice of Charles. Muscettola took the line that the sack could have been a punishment sent by God. Italians should behave like discreet servants, with a cheerful demeanour, until the time came when they could be free again.[54]

Few visual representations of the wars were commissioned in Italy. Charles's daughter, Margaret of Austria, who was married to Ottavio Farnese, had a fresco of the Battle of Pavia in her palace in Rome.[55] She does not seem to have shared the scruples of the Cardinal-Bishop of Trent, who rejected the idea that he should decorate a room in his castle in Trent with scenes of the Battle of Pavia and the Sack of Rome: it would be awkward if the pictures should be seen by the pope or the French king, or their representatives, he said.[56] It had been suggested that the bodies of troops in the background to a portrait of Alfonso d'Este in armour by Battista Dossi represent a specific engagement of significance to him, the Battle of Ravenna, perhaps, or the Battle of Polesella, and that three panels of a fresco cycle of battle scenes commissioned by Enea Pio da Carpi for his castle of Spezzano in 1529 represent the Battle of Ravenna, but in both cases the scenes are too generic to be sure.[57] An engraving by an artist who signed himself NA DAT, produced in 1512, identified as being of 'la rota de Ravenna' (the defeat of Ravenna), is generally accepted as being by an unknown Italian artist; it shows the armies confronting each other before the battle. A 1518 copy of this print by Agostino Veneziano was later used as a model by Giorgio Vasari for his depiction of the battle in the Sala di Leone X in the Palazzo Vecchio in Florence.[58] The Battle of Marignano, which could be seen as a victory for Venice as well as for France, was celebrated by an eight-block coloured woodcut, printed in Venice by Zuan Andrea Vavasori. The blocks depicting the battle were added to blocks by a different artist, on a different scale, of the city of Milan; there are a few labels, and text in one corner lauding the victory of Francis and Venice. It was more akin to a news broadsheet than a work of art.[59]

Naive, slightly comic, as the drawing of the soldiers in this woodblock may be, it is in its way a more realistic depiction of contemporary war than works produced by more famous artists. Italian Renaissance artists were more inclined, if depicting soldiers, to dress them in classical, semi-classical, or fantasy armour, not versions of the clothing and armour of the soldiers of their own day, or to show them as svelte youths, gracefully decorating a scene. There was no equivalent in Italy of the German genre of prints, some of high artistic quality, of the life of soldiers, particularly landsknechts. When commissioned to produce representations of contemporary warfare, Italian artists could produce some beautiful, but iconographically curiously hybrid, mixtures of classical and contemporary arms. The panels for the tomb of Gaston de Foix by Agostino Busti, in the style of classical relief sculpture, show cavalrymen dressed in Roman armour, riding with no stirrups, carrying the weapons of Roman cavalry, alongside infantry dressed in semi-classical costume, with touches of the landsknecht or Swiss in their plumed headgear and slashed sleeves, bearing halberds, with modern artillery pieces.[60]

The triumphal entries organized for Louis XII by the authorities of Milan after his victories at Genoa in 1507 and at Agnadello in 1509 were also hybrids. As well as the usual apparatus of triumphal arches and allegorical figures, models representing captured towns and fortresses were borne in the procession, as scholars said would happen in a classical

Roman triumph, and the king was invited to mount what was described as a triumphal car. He refused to do this on both occasions, as possibly he was expected to do. The protocol for French royal entries was that the king should ride on horseback, under a canopy, and it was French protocol which prevailed in the order of the procession. In 1509, he also rejected a suggestion by the Milanese that Bartolomeo d'Alviano, as a captured commander, should figure in the procession as a prisoner, as the vanquished enemy of a Roman general would do. To Louis, such discourteous treatment of an honoured prisoner would be unchivalric.[61] Classical themes were considered even more appropriate for the formal entries of the emperor into Italian cities, and the imperial iconography devised by Italian artists for Charles V was adopted elsewhere in Europe. But the symbols, allegories and allusions could be obscure. Works of art produced for the Imperial court might have to be accompanied by a written explanation of their meaning for the emperor. Few spectators of the triumphal entries would have been able to decode the symbolism. Booklets were produced explaining the imagery of the entries of Charles V to Milan; without their guidance, spectators might well see no more than an arch with some figures on it, with little or no idea of what they were supposed to mean.[62]

After 1530, as with French and Imperial propaganda, many fewer news sheets, songs and poems about the wars were published in Italy. Prophecies suddenly ceased to circulate. The major issues – the fate of Milan and Naples – seemed to be settled, and Venice had withdrawn from active military involvement in the wars. The campaigns and sieges that there were, in Piedmont, Parma, Siena, Corsica, did not arouse the same level of interest in other regions of Italy as the campaigns in Lombardy had done, and the protests and exhortations and laments would be left to those who were directly affected by them.[63] There could still be a market for new editions of the *Guerre horrende de Italia*, and for images such as the broadsheet *Italia fui* (*I was Italy*), a woodcut produced in Venice, with a disconsolate woman personifying Italy threatened by foreign arms, with only Venice still free and able to defend her. But Italians in general had had more than enough of the wars, and, it would seem, had lost their appetite for hearing and reading about them.

Notes

1 Hochner, 'Visions of war', 240–1, 243–4.

2 Shaw, 'Wartime propaganda', 63–76; de La Pilorgerie.

3 Shaw, 'Wartime propaganda', 76–7.

4   Hale, 260.

5   Hochner, *Louis XII*, 71–2.

6   Dumont, 272–90.

7   *Ibid.*, 259–66, 291–302, 325–32, 360–98, 438–57.

8   Cooper, 'Noël Abraham'.

9   Rospocher, *Il papa guerriero*, 131.

10 Some of Jean Bourdichon's miniatures for the *Voyage de Gênes* are reproduced in colour in Taviani.

11 Hochner, 'Visions of war', 249–50.

12 Alazard, *La bataille oubliée*, 185, illustrations 21 and 18.

13 Vissière, 247–9, 251; Barreto, 171–2.

14 Dumont, 302–9.

15 *Ibid.*, 331–2, 345–6.

16 *Ibid.*, 344, 429–31, 449–57.

17 Le Gall, 34.

18 Cooper, *Litterae*, 5–6.

19 Dumont, 336, 346–7.

20 Mährle, 222–3.

21 Hale, 182–7; quotation, 184.

22 Rospocher, *Il papa guerriero*, 239.

23 Alazard, *La bataille oubliée*, 70.

24 Rospocher, *Il papa guerriero*, 239–42.

25 Scheller, 'Ung fil tres delicat', 25.

26 Mährle, 214–15.

27 Scheller, 'L'union des princes', 206.

28 *Ibid.*, 230.

29 *Ibid.*, 202, 219.

30 Redondo, 'La "prensa primitiva"'; Cárcel.

31 Redondo, 'La "prensa primitiva"', 252–4, 271; D'Amico, 'De Pavie à Bologne', 99–100.

32 Redondo, 'La "prensa primitiva"', 255–6.

33   *Ibid.*, 261–2.

34   D'Amico, 'De Pavie à Bologne', 105–6.

35   Hale, 190–1.

36   *Ibid.*, 250–1.

37   Rosier, 24–9.

38   Rospocher, *Il papa guerriero*, 158–63; Rospocher, 'Il papa in guerra', 146–9.

39   Rospocher, *Il papa guerriero*, 273–6.

40   Scheller, 'Ung fil tres delicat', 11.

41   *Ibid.*, 25–6.

42   Sowards.

43   Chastel, illustrations 31–2.

44   Rospocher, *Il papa guerriero*, 331–5.

45   Rospocher, 'Songs of war', 91.

46   Rospocher, *Il papa guerriero*, 196–7.

47   *Ibid.*, 205–13; Alazard, *La bataille oubliée*, 43, 114–15.

48   Scheller, 'L'union des princes', 207.

49   Alazard, *La bataille oubliée*, 116–17, 224.

50   Fiorato.

51   D'Amico, 'Charles Quint'; Niccoli, *Prophecy*.

52   Murrin, 79–92, 124–8.

53   Rospocher, 'Songs of war', quotation, 96.

54   Zimmermann, 88–95.

55   Bodart, 133.

56   *Ibid.*, 132–3.

57   Barreto, 190–3, 203–4.

58   Hale, 140–3.

59   Stermole, 116–22, illustrations 1–4.

60   Hale, 146; Barreto, 174–6, illustrations 4 and 5.

61   Scheller, 'Gallia cisalpina', 45–8; Scheller, 'L'union des princes', 237–9; Giordano.

62 Leydi, 227–54.

63 For Siena, see Glenisson-Delannée, 250–97.

Bibliography

Alazard, Florence, *La bataille oubliée. Agnadel, 1509: Louis XII contre les Vénitiens* (Rennes: Presses Universitaires de Rennes, 2017).

Alazard, Florence, *Le lamento dans l'Italie de la Renaissance. 'Pleure, belle Italie, jardin du monde'* (Rennes: Presses Universitaires de Rennes, 2010).

Balsamo, Jean (ed.), *Passer les monts. Français en Italie-l'Italie en France (1494–1525)* (Paris: Honoré Champion; Fiesole, Edizioni Cadmo, 1998).

Barreto, Joana, 'La battaglia di Ravenna nelle arti del Cinquecento. Modelli epici per la figurazione di una battaglia contemporanea', in Bolognesi (ed.), *1512*, 171–212.

Bodart, Diane H., 'L'immagine di Carlo V in Italia tra trionfi e conflitti', in Francesca Cantù and Maria Antonietta Visceglia (eds), *L'Italia di Carlo V. Guerra, religione e politica nel primo Cinquecento* (Rome: Viella, 2003), 115–38.

Bolognesi, Dante (ed.), *1512. La battaglia di Ravenna, l'Italia, l'Europa* (Ravenna: Longo Editore, 2014).

Bonali Fiquet, Françoise, 'La bataille d'Agnadel dans la poésie populaire italienne du début du XVIe siècle', in Balsamo (ed.), *Passer les monts*, 227–43.

Cárcel, Ricardo García, 'Los cronistas de Carlos V y la imagen del emperador', in Bruno Anatra and Francesco Manconi (eds), *Sardegna, Spagna e Stati italiani nell'età di Carlo V* (Rome: Carocci editore, 2001), 25–37.

Chastel, André, *The Sack of Rome, 1527* (Princeton: Princeton University Press, 1983).

Cooper, Richard, *Litterae in tempore belli. Études sur les relations littéraires italo-françaises pendant les guerres d'Italie* (Geneva: Librairie Droz, 1997).

Cooper, Richard, 'Noël Abraham publiciste de Louis XII, duc de Milan, premier imprimeur du roi?', in Balsamo (ed.), *Passer les monts*, 149–76.

D'Amico, Juan Carlos, 'Charles Quint et le sac de Rome: personnification d'un tyran impie ou Dernier Empereur?', in Redondo (ed.), *Les discours sur le Sac de Rome de 1527*, 37–47.

D'Amico, Juan Carlos, *Charles Quint maître du monde entre mythe et réalité* (Caen: Presses Universitaires de Caen, 2004).

D'Amico, Juan Carlos, 'De Pavie à Bologne (1525–1530): la prophétie comme arme de la politique impériale pendant les guerres d'Italie', in Augustin Redondo (ed.), *La prophétie comme arme de guerre des pouvoirs, XVe-XVIIe siècles* (Paris: Presses de la Sorbonne Nouvelle, 2000), 97–107.

Dumont, Jonathan, *Lilia florent. L'imaginaire politique et social à la cour de France durant les premières Guerres d'Italie (1494–1525)* (Paris: Honoré Champion Éditeur, 2013).

Fantoni, Marcello, 'Carlo V e l'immagine dell'imperator', in Marcello Fantoni (ed.), *Carlo V e l'Italia* (Rome: Bulzoni Editore, 2000), 101–18.

Fiorato, Adelin Charles, 'Complaintes, *cantari* et poésies satiriques inspirés par la campagne de 1494–1495', in Adelin Charles Fiorato (ed.), *Italie 1494* (Paris: Presses de la Sorbonne Nouvelle, 1994).

Fragonard, Marie-Madeleine, 'Le sac de Rome dans la poésie historique hispano-italienne: discours politiques et modalités littéraires', in Redondo (ed.), *Les discours sur le Sac de Rome de 1527*, 103–116.

Giordano, Luisa, 'Les entrées de Louis XII en Milanais', in Balsamo (ed.), *Passer les monts*, 139–48.

Glenisson-Delannée, Françoise, 'Esprit de faction, sensibilité municipale et aspirations régionales à Sienne entre 1525 et 1559', in Marina Marietti et al. (eds), *Quêtes d'une identité collective chez les italiens de la Renaissance* (Paris: Université de la Sorbonne Nouvelle, 1990), 175–308.

Gullino, Giuseppe (ed.), *L'Europa e la Serenissima. La svolta del 1509. Nel V centenario della battaglia di Agnadello* (Venice: Istituto veneto di scienze, lettere ed arti, 2011).

Hale, J.R., *Artists and Warfare in the Renaissance* (New Haven: Yale University Press, 1990).

Hochner, Nicole, *Louis XII. Les dérèglements de l'image royale (1498–1515)* (Seyssel: Champ Vallon, 2006).

Hochner, Nicole, 'Visions of war in the "terrestrial paradise". Images of Italy in early sixteenth-century French texts', in Christine Shaw (ed.), *Italy and the European Powers. The Impact of War, 1500–1530* (Leiden and Boston: Brill, 2006), 239–51.

Ilardi, Vincent, '"Italianità" among some Italian intellectuals in the early sixteenth century', *Traditio*, 12 (1956), 339–67.

de La Pilorgerie, J.L., *Campagne et Bulletins de la Grande Armée d'Italie commandée par Charles VIII 1494–1495* (Nantes: V. Forest and É. Grimaud, 1866).

Le Gall, Jean Marie, 'Ravenna: una disfatta senza vittoria. Riflessioni sull'esito delle battaglie durante le guerre d'Italia', in Bolognesi (ed.), *1512*, 25–49.

Leydi, Silvio, *Sub umbra imperialis aquilae. Immagini del potere e consenso politico nella Milano di Carlo V* (Florence: Leo S. Olschki Editore, 1999).

Mährle, Wolfgang, '"Deus iustus iudex". La battaglia di Agnadello e l'opinione pubblica nei paesi tedeschi', in Gullino (ed.), *L'Europa e la Serenissima*, 207–228.

Martines, Lauro, 'Literary crisis in the generation of 1494', in Stella Fletcher and Christine Shaw (eds), *The World of Savonarola: Italian Elites and Perceptions of Crisis* (Aldershot: Ashgate, 2000), 5–21.

Matarrese, Sabatina, 'Tra cantari e poema ariostesco: "la gran vittoria … / di ch'aver sempre lacrimose ciglia / Ravenna debbe"', in Bolognesi (ed.), *1512*, 159–70.

Mondini, Marco and Massimo Rospocher (eds), *Narrating War. Early Modern and Contemporary Perspectives* (Bologna: Società editrice il Mulino; Berlin: Duncker & Humblot, 2013).

Murrin, Michael, *History and Warfare in Renaissance Epic* (Chicago and London: University of Chicago Press, 1994).

Nardone, Jean-Luc, 'Le *Voyage de Gênes* de Jean Marot: définition du texte', in D. Boillet and M.F. Piejus, *Les Guerres d'Italie: Histoires, pratiques, représentations* (Paris: Université Paris III Sorbonne Nouvelle, 2002), 49–71.

Niccoli, Ottavia, 'Astrologi e profeti a Bologna per Carlo V', in Emilio Pasquini e Paolo Prodi (eds), *Bologna nell'età di Carlo V e Guicciardini* (Bologna: Società editrice il Mulino, 2002), 457–76.

Niccoli, Ottavia, *Prophecy and People in Renaissance Italy* (Princeton: Princeton University Press, 1990).

Piéjus, Marie-Françoise, 'Marignan, 1515: échos et résonances', in Balsamo (ed)., *Passer les monts*, 245–58.

Redondo, Augustin (ed.), *Les discours sur le Sac de Rome de 1527: pouvoir et littérature* (Paris: Presses de la Sorbonne Nouvelle, 1999).

Redondo, Augustin, 'La "prensa primitiva" ("relaciones de sucesos") al servicio de la política de Carlos V', in Christoph Strosetzki (ed.), *Aspectos históricos y culturales bajo Carlos V/Aspekte der Geschichte und Kultur unter Karl V.* (Frankfurt am Main: Vervuert; Madrid: Iberoamericana, 2000), 246–76.

Rosier, Bart, 'The victories of Charles V: a series of prints by Maarten van Heemskerck, 1555–56', *Simiolus: Netherlands Quarterly for the History of Art*, 20/1 (1990–1), 24–38.

Rospocher, Massimo, *Il papa guerriero. Giulio II nello spazio pubblico europeo* (Bologna: Società editrice il Mulino, 2015).

Rospocher, Massimo, 'Il papa in guerra: Giulio II nell'iconografia politica al tempo di Ravenna', in Bolognesi (ed.), *1512*, 139–55.

Rospocher, Massimo, 'Songs of war. Historical and literary narratives of the "Horrendous Italian Wars" (1494–1559)', in Mondini and Rospocher (eds), *Narrating War*, 79–97.

Scheller, Robert W., 'Gallia cisalpina: Louis XII and Italy 1499–1508', *Simiolus: Netherlands Quarterly for the History of Art*, 15/1 (1985), 5–60.

Scheller, Robert W., 'L'union des princes: Louis XII, his allies and the Venetian campaign 1509', *Simiolus: Netherlands Quarterly for the History of Art*, 27/4 (1999), 195–242.

Scheller, Robert W., 'Ung fil tres delicat: Louis XII and Italian affairs, 1510–11', *Simiolus: Netherlands Quarterly for the History of Art*, 31, 1/2 (2004–5), 4–45.

Shaw, Christine, 'Charles V and Italy', in C. Scott Dixon and Martina Fuchs (eds), *The Histories of Emperor Charles V: Nationale Perspektiven von Persönlichkeit und Herrschaft* (Münster: Aschendorff Verlag, 2005), 115–133.

Shaw, Christine, 'Wartime propaganda during Charles VIII's expedition to Italy, 1494/5', in Mondini and Rospocher (eds), *Narrating War*, 63–78.

Sherman, Michael A., 'Political propaganda and Renaissance culture: French reactions to the League of Cambrai, 1509–10', *The Sixteenth Century Journal*, 8/2 (1977), 97–128.

Sowards, J. Kelley (ed.), *The Julius Exclusus of Erasmus* (Bloomington and London: Indiana University Press, 1968).

Stermole, Krystina, 'Chivalric combat in a modern landscape. Depicting battle in Venetian prints during the War of the League of Cambrai (1509–1516)', in Mondini and Rospocher (eds), *Narrating War*, 113–30.

Taviani, Carlo, *Superba discordia. Guerra, rivolta e pacificazione nella Genova di primo Cinquecento* (Rome: Viella, 2008).

Vissière, Laurent, 'Lettere scritte, lettere stampate della campagna di Gaston de Foix (1511–1512)', in Bolognesi (ed.), *1512*, 237–52.

Zimmermann, T.C. Price, *Paolo Giovio: The Historian and the Crisis of Sixteenth-Century Italy* (Princeton: Princeton University Press, 1995).

CHAPTER 11

The legacies of the wars

As yet, there has been no focused historical debate about what the consequences of the Italian Wars may have been. Those who lived through them naturally lamented the destruction they brought, the ruined towns and devastated countryside that armies left in their wake, but economic historians have not made a concerted effort to assess what long-term damage or change may have been caused to the economy. It is significant that in discussions of long-term economic decline in the early modern era, the late sixteenth or early seventeenth century is generally identified as the period in which it became evident, not the period of the wars: this points to a swift recovery, when peace was established. Cultural historians have noted how the wars provoked a crisis of confidence among educated Italians, making them question whether the intellectual life as well as the political institutions and traditions of which they had been so proud might not have contributed to the disasters they suffered, might not have made Italians vulnerable to conquest by less sophisticated, more martial peoples from across the Alps. Yet Italian ideas and innovations in the arts, especially the visual arts, architecture and music, would be more influential in the rest of Europe in the century after the wars than before. The clearest long-term changes caused by the wars were political. Two of the major Italian states had become part of the dominions of the king of Spain, and the political role of the others had been fundamentally altered; the state system of Italy was very different after Cateau-Cambrésis from what it had been before Charles VIII's invasion of Naples in 1494.

Discrimination is needed between those changes in Italian society, politics, culture and the economy that can be attributed to the wars, and those that can be attributed to processes that would have happened irrespective of them. The Italian Wars lasted for more than sixty years – two to three generations – and it is inconceivable that such a dynamic society would have remained static for that length of time, even without their disruptive influence. Not every change that came about during the wars happened because of them.

Economic consequences

Perhaps the best known account of the effects of the wars is the report by two English ambassadors of their journey through Lombardy in December 1529. In the fifty miles between Vercelli and Pavia, they wrote, the best land for corn and vines that one could see, the country was so desolate that they saw no one working in the fields, and in large villages only five or six miserable people. The grapes were still on the untended vines, for there was no one to harvest them. Vigevano, formerly one of the 'goodly' towns of Italy was 'all destroyed and in a manner desolate', Pavia in the same pitiable condition. They were told that all the inhabitants of that region, and other regions of Italy, were 'dead and gone' due to war, famine and pestilence, so that, for want of people, there was no hope for many years that Italy should be restored.[1]

Such misery – the ruined farms, the fields gone to waste, the deserted villages, the towns burned and devastated by sack, the swathes of country stripped bare by foraging troops – was the most obvious economic consequence of the war. Less visible were the effects on trade of the disruption and insecurity, the loss of goods to looting – but also of the opportunities for some merchants to profit by supplying large numbers of men with food and drink, clothing and weapons. Not everything the armies consumed was stolen or forcibly requisitioned. Some merchants found their usual markets or sources of supply closed to them as routes were blocked, and frontiers closed or shifted, but new markets might also open up. Becoming involved in the financial transactions generated by the need to pay and supply the armies – taking on tax farms, making loans, cashing letters of credit – brought inevitable risks but also the chance of appreciable profits. It is impossible to make generalizations for all of Italy about the economic effects of the wars. Different regions, with diverse economies, suffered the impact of war at different times – and once peace returned, recovery from even the worst destruction could be surprisingly swift.

Of all the regions of Italy, Lombardy, as the main arena of conflict for the three decades of most intensive fighting, from 1499 to 1529, probably suffered the most. Some cities, such as Pavia, were sacked several times. In the intervals of peace or truce, the people of Lombardy had to support the French or the Swiss or the Imperial and Spanish troops. From the time that the French army first drive Ludovico Sforza out of Milan in 1499, the duchy was never free of foreign troops. Lombardy was one of the wealthiest and most fertile areas of Italy but, especially in the wake of the campaigns fought there, its people could not continuously support these armies. Even the commanders and officials of Charles V, who imposed the greatest burdens on the duchy of Milan, recognized that it was exhausted, and the burden placed on it intolerable.

After 1529, Lombardy was no longer a battleground, but for over twenty years the duchy of Milan was expected to provide for the troops engaged in the war in Piedmont. It was recognized that the duchy could not pay for the war without help. During the first three years of the war in Piedmont, from 1536 to 1538, over a million scudi were sent from Spain to pay for it, as against 616,000 scudi paid by the Milanese. Much less was sent in the 1540s: Charles wanted Naples and Sicily to supply what Milan could not. During 1550 to 1555, money had again to be sent from Spain to pay for this war, over two million scudi, about equal to the sum contributed by Milan.[2]

The war in Piedmont bore hardest on the west of the duchy of Milan, where the troops were concentrated. If the soldiers went unpaid, they could go on the rampage, as did the mutinous Spanish who in June and July 1537 occupied Valenza, assaulted Tortona and devastated the Alessandrino. In 1542, the governor, del Vasto, warned Charles that many peasants were abandoning their fields, which were lying untilled, and trade in Milan had in large part ceased. Two-thirds of the revenue squeezed from the duchy that year was spent on the army in Piedmont.[3] When Ferrante Gonzaga was governor, further costs were added, for the garrisons in Piacenza and the troops at Siena, and the war of Parma. After the French occupied Monferrato, the units that had been based there withdrew to the west of the duchy. The behaviour of the troops was insupportable enough when they were paid, an envoy from Milan was instructed to tell the emperor in August 1557; when they were not paid, as was usually the case, they truly could not be borne. The west of the duchy had been reduced to such a condition that a large part of the inhabitants, having lost their property, had left, and if some relief was not provided, the rest would be forced to follow.[4]

If for these areas of the duchy the war went on, the eastern regions, heavily taxed as they might be to support the military, had far fewer troops living among them, and enjoyed most of the benefits of peace. There, recovery could begin sooner, and the industrious people of Lombardy showed their resilience. Cremona, for example, in thirty years as well as changing hands several times between the Sforza dukes, the French, the Venetians and the Spanish, endured two major epidemics in 1511 and 1524, and a famine in 1518. Yet at the end of this 'infernal cycle',[5] enough people were left to revive the diminished manufacture of textiles, and there was enough capital to fund this, the production of soap, paper, silk and maiolica, and the nobility could afford to build themselves fine houses. By the 1540s, the population had already recovered to pre-war levels and by the 1550s Cremona could be described as flourishing, with a great number of merchants and an 'infinite number of artisans and workmen'.[6]

Even before Piedmont, Monferrato and Saluzzo became a theatre of war in 1536, they had seen a great deal of the armies that fought in Lombardy. French troops passed through them on their way from or to France, sometimes spending weeks in the region as they mustered there after crossing the Alps. Imperial troops were billeted there, mostly during the winter, for much of the 1520s. During the wars in this region, Monferrato saw less of the fighting than did Piedmont, but had to serve as the base for Imperial troops who treated the population they lived off much more harshly than the French treated the people of Piedmont and Saluzzo.

Nevertheless, by the end of the war, the lands of Piedmont were desolate, many places scarcely cultivated, the livestock driven off, the people dispersed. In several areas, canals and rivers had broken their banks for lack of maintenance.[7] In an edict of April 1561, Duke Emanuele Filiberto declared that the war 'had caused infinite damage to the people, the death of innumerable subjects and the flight of many inhabitants, artisans and agricultural workers', so that the land was left uncultivated, and 'our states without crafts and industry'.[8] Ten years later, he still attributed the difficulty he was experiencing in raising taxes to the poverty of men and lands.[9] But Piedmont was fertile, and the duke made efforts to attract immigrants to cultivate the land and ordered works on the waterways to improve drainage. His efforts to foster industry were less successful, and the controls and customs dues he imposed on trade made the Piedmontese look back nostalgically to the years of French occupation when they could sell their agricultural products much more freely.

Compared with their neighbours in Piedmont and Lombardy, the Genoese escaped lightly during the wars. The worst episode was the sack of 1522 by Imperial troops, and the greatest military effort they had to make was the war in Corsica in the 1550s. To the hard-pressed Milanese taxpayer, faced with paying off debts incurred by the Spanish administration in Milan to Genoese financiers, the Genoese appeared to have done well out of the war, enriching themselves by 'intolerable usury' to the great prejudice of the king and the ruin of his subjects.[10] Genoese financiers handled much of the money sent by Charles V to his armies in Italy, and the wars gave their bankers and merchants the opportunity to strengthen and develop the longstanding commercial bonds between Genoa and Castile. Their role in financing the Habsburgs was the foundation of Genoa's 'golden century'. For some years after 1528, the close connection with Charles V did bring economic problems to Genoa, as Francis I closed the French market to their merchants. This measure hit the silk industry hardest, for France was the major outlet for the luxury silk fabrics produced in Genoa. But the policy hurt Francis more than the Genoese, and in 1537, to obtain access to their credit to help pay for the war in Piedmont, he lifted the ban on the import of Genoese silks, and in 1541 reopened the French market to Genoa completely.

For Genoa's historic rival, Venice, the worst period of the wars was that during which Venice's Terraferma provinces were overrun for several years, from 1509 to 1516. Of all the republic's major subject cities on the mainland, only Treviso was not at some point lost to an enemy. The campaigns of the 1520s in which Venetian troops participated were largely fought outside Venetian territory, and after 1529 Venice avoided direct involvement in the Italian Wars, although the republic was involved in war against the Turks. The city of Venice itself was never besieged or attacked and for the citizens and nobles who did not serve with the armies on the Terraferma, the most direct effects of the war that they experienced – apart from the taxes levied to pay for it, and the sight of the refugees who came to Venice – was the disruption to trade.

When the French were at war with Venice during the War of the League of Cambrai, trade with areas under French control ceased. Trade with southern Germany was dependent on the grant of safe conducts by Maximilian, and even if he granted them, they would not necessarily be honoured; in 1513 he ordered the closure of all the passes over the mountains. Venice's role as a commercial hub between Europe and the Ottoman-controlled eastern Mediterranean was compromised by lack of goods to send east, and exclusion from traditional markets for the goods Venetian galleys brought back to Europe. The regular convoys that usually sailed east or west to Flanders and England were disrupted as galleys were used, sometimes damaged or lost, in naval operations. The patterns of trade of the Venetian subject cities that were occupied by French, Spanish or Imperial troops were also disrupted. During the French occupation of Brescia, for example, the Brescians hoped to send to Milan and other places in Lombardy goods that they had been accustomed to send to Venice, but the Milanese did not welcome competition from Brescian products, and saw Brescia as a market for their own goods. Brescian industry was suffering and trade contracting even before the city was devastated by the sack of 1512.

When the Venetians recovered their mainland territory, they had limited sympathy for their subjects' cries of poverty due to the losses and damage they had suffered during the war. The Venetians' priority was restoring the republic's own finances, and they expected their subjects to pay new and increased taxes, and both communities and individuals to make loans to the Venetian government. The commerce of the Terraferma was to be more than ever subject to that of Venice. Unlimited quantities of Venetian goods had to be accepted on local markets without tolls, while all local products were to be sent to Venice before they could be put on sale back home, their price increased by tolls and other levies. The Venetians could not make their city the focal point of all the trade of the Terraferma; their subjects were adept at finding ways round the restrictions, not least by smuggling. But such regulations and the increased taxes meant that the wars cast a long shadow over the economy of the Venetian Terraferma, long after the occupying armies had left.

Throughout the war, campaigns in Tuscany were in general of secondary importance to the major powers. That the Pisan War dragged on for nearly fifteen years from 1495 to 1509 was due to Florentine determination to recover the city, and the troops of other states – Milan, Venice, France and Spain – were involved only episodically. The Spanish troops who restored the Medici to Florence in 1512 sacked Prato, but left soon after; the Imperial army that restored them a second time, in 1530, was in Florentine territory rather longer, for about a year. The Pisans suffered most, the countryside around their city turned to waste year after year by Florentine troops.

From the Florentine perspective, the surrender of Pisa restored the economic status quo, with the Pisan economy treated as an adjunct to that of Florence. For the Florentines, the most obvious economic consequence of involvement in the wars and the alliances that shaped them – apart from the diversion of the citizens' wealth into paying taxes and forced loans – was probably the disruption to trade with France when they found themselves on the opposite side to the French king. It has been argued that, by weakening the economic resources of the political elite, the wars contributed to their political subjection to the Medici.[11] On the other hand, Richard Goldthwaite in his comprehensive study of the economy of Renaissance Florence concluded that episodes such as the siege of Florence 'rarely had more than a temporary impact on the economy', and that although war 'took its toll … usually these were only momentary disruptions, and however difficult, they rarely caused any structural damage to the economy'.[12]

The 'mala guerra' (bad war, dirty war) deliberately inflicted on the people of the territory of Siena in the campaigns of the mid-1550s has been held accountable for the depopulation of large tracts of land in later centuries.[13] For some villagers struggling to make a living from marginal lands, the devastation of their crops and homes and theft of livestock may have caused them to abandon their communities permanently. Yet an analysis of the population of Sienese territory in the fifteenth and sixteenth centuries found that it increased greatly overall during the sixteenth century, although in some areas such as the Maremma it grew markedly less than in others. The divergence of density of populations and the patterns of movement reflect those evident in the fifteenth century, and there was no marked effect from the troubles of the 1550s.[14] Nor did the loss of the harbours on the coast that were incorporated in the Presidi have any notable effect on the Sienese economy; they had not been of much economic significance to Siena.

For the kingdom of Naples, the first decade of the wars and the years of Lautrec's invasion and the siege of Naples in 1528 were the only periods in which campaigns were fought in the kingdom; Guise's incursion in 1557 barely qualified as a campaign. For invaders and defenders alike, control of one of the kingdom's major economic assets – the dues levied on the great transhumant flocks in the eastern provinces – was an important goal; the patterns of movement of the livestock may have been temporarily disrupted but there were no long-term effects. From the 1530s, coastal raids by Turks and corsairs were a greater concern for the government and people of the kingdom than any prospect of an invasion by the French. The need to build and man coastal defences against the Turks was used to justify a substantial increase in taxation. This was particularly marked in the 1550s, when several new taxes on foodstuffs, wine and other goods were imposed that became a permanent drag on economic activity. As well as being obliged to support the Spanish forces stationed in the kingdom, the people were also called upon to make grants, 'donativi', to Charles to pay for his wars elsewhere: 1.5 million ducats in 1536, 800,000 in 1541 and 1552, 600,000 in 1545 and 1549.[15] The costs of maintaining the garrisons in the Presidi in Tuscany were also charged to Naples.

In the late fifteenth century, Italy was probably the richest area of Europe. Initially, the French expected the costs of war could be recouped by subsidies and protection money paid by Italians, as well as ransoms and booty. Charles V's agents long hoped a system of regular contributions from Italian states could be set up to pay for the Imperial armies there. Sooner or later, the kings and their officials had to face the fact that, unless money was sent to Italy in very large amounts, their armies there would be dispersed or disintegrate. Most of the money raised in Italy, or sent to Italy to pay for the wars, was spent in Italy. Whether the influx of funds offset the damage and disruption caused by the wars is very doubtful. The wars were not an economic disaster for Italy – but it would be difficult to argue that any benefits were not heavily outweighed by the harm the wars caused.

A new state system

The political map of Italy in 1559 had changed considerably from that of 1494. Of the five major states whose alliances and conflicts had shaped the political system of the peninsula, Naples and Milan were no longer independent powers. Florence was no longer a republic, but was ruled by a duke who was the most powerful of the independent secular princes. Venice, formerly accused by rivals of aiming to dominate Italy, and always alert to opportunities to acquire more lands there, now kept a low profile in Italian affairs. No system of alliances bound the states together, either into a single Italian league or into two opposing blocks, as had so frequently been the case in the fifteenth century. Some of the smaller states had disappeared. The republic of Siena had become subject to the new Duke of Florence. The lordships in the Romagna, such as Faenza and Forlì, had been brought under the direct rule of the papacy.

But other minor powers had managed to survive. The city of Lucca was one, and it would preserve its republican government for centuries to come. Genoa, the third remaining republic, had emerged stronger and more stable from the wars, thanks to the constitutional reform of 1528 and the political acumen of Andrea Doria. The Dukes of Ferrara and Urbino and Mantua had also come through. Other lordships had appeared, notably the Farnese duchies of Parma and Piacenza. The lands of the Duke of Mantua were now girdled by a number of statelets belonging to cadet branches of the Gonzaga dynasty, including Guastalla and Sabbionetta. The Duke of Mantua was now also lord of Monferrato; attempts to exchange it for Cremona were unsuccessful. Monferrato was not only inconveniently detached from Mantua, but situated in what had become an area of strategic significance, and was expensive to guard. The Gonzaga had to allow passage through Monferrato to Spanish troops, receiving in turn help with the expense of fortifications. Largely as a result of the new strategic importance of north-west Italy – which had been on the periphery of the Italian state system of the fifteenth century – the Duke of Savoy had become one of the leading princes of Italy, one whose alliance was of consequence to the European powers.

The standing of the papacy among the European powers was also transformed by the Italian Wars. Popes had taken a major role in the political and military affairs of Italy during the wars – one often driven by their family interests, rather than those of the papacy. This had changed the attitude of the ultramontane powers to the pope, whom they came increasingly to see as an Italian prince, as a potential ally or opponent. They expected the popes to join alliances and to wage wars, not just against Muslims or heretics, and were unwilling to accept that the pope should be neutral or an arbiter in conflicts between Christian states. As religious matters rose to the top of the international agenda, the papacy had a more prominent role in European diplomacy, but this did not make Rome the diplomatic centre of Europe, as it has often been described.[16] Popes and papal legates had no role in negotiating the most significant truces and treaties between the Habsburg and Valois monarchs during the wars.

Ultramontane powers began to try to affect the outcome of papal elections. Since the end of the conciliar crisis, no power outside Italy had shown any wish to do that before 1503, when French and Spanish factions confronted each other in the conclave as French and Spanish armies were confronting one another in the kingdom of Naples. The challenge of the Protestant Reformation only intensified the interest of the monarchs in trying to secure a pope they could work with. By intervening in elections, their concern was as much to exclude candidates thought to be undesirable – usually because of too close an association with an opposing power – as to place their own partisans on the papal throne. It became accepted in the later sixteenth century that the kings of France and Spain could exercise a veto on the election of individuals they did not wish to become pope.

Italy had become more closely bound into the state system of Europe, inescapably so, due to the bonds linking Naples and Milan to the Spanish monarchy, and the interest the kings of France and the emperor continued to take in Italian affairs. Northern Italy in particular would again become a theatre of war between the European powers, the possession of Lombardy a key strategic interest. The fate of Italian states would be decided by the diplomatic and dynastic arrangements of the kings of Spain and France and the emperors for centuries to come. The elaborate system of political patronage and allegiances, of 'protection' and 'adherence' that was so important an element in the fabric of relations among Italian states, large and small, was radically reconfigured. For Italian princes and nobles looking for pensions and honours, the king of Spain was the major patron and his approval could be crucial if any power sought to gain more territory. He could threaten to use force if he disapproved of an initiative – as when he made it clear to Cosimo I that he would not countenance his acceptance of offers by the Corsican rebels in 1564 and 1567 to make him king of Corsica.[17]

But Philip was not the sole patron available to Italian states. The revival of the significance of the emperor in Italian political life persisted after the king of Spain was no longer the emperor as well. If the emperor no longer directly held territory in Italy, his jurisdiction and authority could still be a valid defence and shield, especially for holders of Imperial fiefs; states could appeal to Imperial tribunals to settle their disputes. Philip did not succeed in getting the grant of the vicariate which would have enabled him to exercise the powers of the emperor in Italy. Theoretically, he respected Imperial prerogatives and jurisdiction there. In practice, he permitted the governors and Senate of Milan to claim jurisdiction over Imperial fiefs, only calling them to order when the emperor protested.[18] It was an option for Italian powers to find security under the dual protection of the king of Spain and the emperor, as Lucca did, without being called on to choose one or the other.[19]

For those looking for an alternative patron, the pope too could be a source of sought-after honours. It was Pope Pius V who granted Cosimo de' Medici the title of Grand Duke, which was later confirmed by the emperor, despite Philip's disapproval. Once the Wars of Religion in France were over, the king of France would become a powerful pole of attraction to Italian states again. Even before then, the maintenance of good relations with the French king was an option well worth considering for those who did not want to commit themselves to Spain. It would not bring down automatic retribution from Philip, or his forces based in Italy.

One notable element in the Italian state system, the influence of political exiles, was perhaps even more conspicuous during the Italian Wars than it had been in the fifteenth century. The upheavals and frequent changes of regime produced many exiles, and competing claims to states created opportunities for political exiles to get backing for their efforts to return. Exiles from the duchy of Milan and the kingdom of Naples, from Florence, the Venetian Terraferma, Siena and Genoa, from Bologna and Perugia, all, at some stage in the wars, played a significant role in fighting for control of their home state. Many of the Italian soldiers who served in the campaigns were exiles, including commanders such as Gian Giacomo Trivulzio and Piero Strozzi. While some patterns of political exile persisted – with Venice, Rome and the courts of Ferrara and Mantua continuing to be havens for exiles – the Italian Wars did cause some modifications. Exiles were much more likely to turn to the king of France or Spain or the emperor than they had been, and far more likely to receive a sympathetic hearing and active support.

The ultramontane monarchs and their representatives in Italy quickly appreciated the potential utility of the exiles, and they also acknowledged some obligation to aid those exiled because of support for their cause. Even the unreliable emperor-elect Maximilian helped Imperial partisans exiled from the Veneto during and after the War of the League of Cambrai, and Charles V continued this. The French kings were particularly welcoming. As they lost the contest for Naples and Milan and their hold over Genoa, they had a natural interest in fostering exiles from those states, and Florentine republican exiles benefited from the help of Caterina de' Medici, especially after she became queen in 1547. Venice also provided a valuable point of contact for Italian political exiles with representatives of the French king. Before the wars, Venice had been a prime refuge for exiles, and the Venetians had been generous in supporting and protecting them, holding them ready for use if the opportunity arose. During the wars, especially after 1530, political exiles in Venice were more likely to get a sympathetic hearing to their proposals from the French representatives than from the Venetian government.

The ranks of political exiles were primarily fed, as before the wars, by conflicts between political factions. Longstanding factional divisions that had their roots in purely local issues were given new scope for expression by the wars. Such existing divisions often influenced choices of allegiance in contested territories: if one faction was pro-French, their opponents could well be pro-Spanish or pro-Imperial. The infinite complexity of local politics in Italy, however, meant that the patterns of division and allegiance were frequently not so straightforward. Similarly, although Charles V's position as emperor gave renewed vitality to the association of Ghibellines with the Empire and Guelfs with the French, the play of local loyalties and rivalries complicated the alignment of the Guelf and Ghibelline factions that were still so conspicuous a feature of Italian political society. It was by no means certain that factions or individuals who, in their local context, would be firmly identified as Guelf would support the French or, if Ghibelline, the emperor or the Spanish. The play of faction at a local level influenced the course and the outcome of many campaigns and sieges of the wars in ways it has not been possible to describe in such a general survey of the wars as has been given in this book. After 1559 there was less scope for violent conflict between factions, but factional allegiances and divisions remained an integral part of Italian political life.

An oppressed nation?

To patriots in later centuries, the new political order established in Italy as a direct outcome of the wars was seen as a painful humiliation of Italy and the Italians, oppressed by foreign powers, with only Venice and the papacy retaining any true freedom of action. This is not necessarily how it appeared to Italians in the sixteenth century. To Venetian observers, for example, the picture was not of undisputed Spanish hegemony, but of the persistence, beneath the equilibrium guaranteed by the Spanish presence in Italy, of contrasting ambitions and interests that princes were ready to forward when they could.[20] If Italian states were constrained in their relations to others, in fulfilling their ambitions or acting aggressively towards their neighbours by considerations of how the king of Spain or France or the emperor would react, in the fifteenth century they had been constrained by considerations of how other Italian powers would react. And if many Italians considered it lamentable that Italians should be subject to 'barbari', there were many who considered subjection to a foreign power preferable to subjection to an historic Italian rival.

On occasion, there were attempts to use the sense that Italy should be for the Italians as a spur for practical action, a rallying-cry to bring Italian states together to drive foreign powers from Italian soil. This became a reality in negotiations for an 'Italian league' of Venice, the pope and the Duke of Milan in 1525–6. But these powers did not believe they could drive the Imperial forces out of Italy without the help of the king of France, and so the Italian league became the League of Cognac. Similarly, while Paul IV repeatedly called on the Venetians to join him in bringing peace to Italy by 'expelling these barbarians', gaining immortal glory as the liberators of Italy, he was also calling on the king of France to send an army to invade the kingdom of Naples – although he claimed he could stop them in Piedmont if the Venetians would rise to the challenge.[21]

Paul IV's invocations of Italian identity and appeals to Italian unity were grounded in his dislike of the Spanish regime in his native Naples – and most such appeals were probably grounded in other resentments and aspirations, in local interests. To the great majority of Italians, the politics that really mattered to them were local – local aims and local rivalries were what concerned them most. Even the 'regional' states such as Milan or Florence were comparatively recent formations, and many communities had not welcomed incorporation into them. Local elites in these states were accustomed to bargaining with the central authority – the Duke of Milan, the pope, the governments of Venice or Florence – in efforts to preserve as much autonomy as possible, and often had little sense of loyalty to it. During the wars, cities and barons who had resented attempts to subordinate them to a regional state had sometimes cherished the hope that a foreign prince would be content with recognition of his distant supremacy by a self-governing community, or by a noble ruling his own lands as a state in miniature. Usually, as in the Veneto in 1509, disillusion soon set in when they were faced by reality in the shape of occupying troops and incessant financial demands. But troops and tax demands could be equally unwelcome if they came from an Italian prince or republic.

If local elites and the population in general were treated with some respect, were not over-burdened and were left sufficient margin to manage their own affairs, as in Piedmont under French occupation, then sentiments of Italian identity would not override satisfaction with their personal situation. That decisions about high politics should be taken in Madrid rather than Milan had little interest for the civic elites of Lombardy; what mattered to them was what happened within the city walls and in the countryside around. Spanish dominion could be seen as 'a kind of protective umbrella' that allowed them to maintain the status quo.[22] It would be anachronistic to denounce them for lack of patriotism.

There were indications that the wars did provoke an enhanced sense of Italian identity in many people, not so much attachment to an abstract ideal of 'Italia' as a sense of themselves as being Italians, who were ethnically and culturally different from the French, Germans and Spanish. The distinction may be summed up by contrasting two comments, from the beginning and the end of the wars. 'You speak to me of Italy, but I have never looked it in the face', was Ludovico Sforza's response to the Florentine ambassador in March 1495.[23] 'I would like to see the French in France, the Spanish in Spain and the Italians in Italy', the Roman baron and soldier Camillo Orsini told the Venetian ambassador in October 1556.[24] What made the people more aware of their identity as Italians was not so much the experience of foreign rule, perhaps, as the presence of thousands upon thousands of foreign soldiers. They were accustomed to foreigners coming to Italy as traders, pilgrims or students, but these visitors would tend to travel certain routes and be concentrated in certain areas. But the soldiers penetrated to areas of Italy that normally would rarely see a foreigner of any description, and even if they were not on campaign, would usually not behave to the local population in a manner which would have made a favourable impression. Many Italians who met a Frenchman or a Spaniard, a German or a Swiss for the first time during the wars would probably not have seen the representatives of these nations at their best.

Stereotypes of other nations developed by Italians during the wars seem to have been based above all on their experience of contacts with soldiers. The common perception of the French as courageous, impetuous, but sometimes brutal, displaying the 'furia francese', also echoed comments of classical authors on the Gauls.[25] Avarice and pride were widely considered the distinguishing feature of the Spanish character. Acquaintance with the hidalgos, the impoverished petty nobles who filled the ranks of the Spanish infantry consolidated these opinions, especially after contact with the bisoños, the 'needy ones', the recruits who arrived from Spain with barely a shirt to their back, ready to take what they lacked from the Italians. In retrospect, to the people of Lombardy the French seemed to have been preferable. A Neapolitan proverb cited by Paul IV said that the Spanish were good fresh and the French good salted. The Spaniard, he explained, when he arrived entered doffing his hat, and honoured and caressed you, but once he had a firm footing, plucked you and skinned you. The Frenchman, on the other hand, at the beginning committed some outrages in his 'furia', but then quietened down and spent what he had with you as a good companion.[26] Some Italians, however, came to prefer the Spanish; after many years' experience, Camillo Orsini said, he had formed the opinion that the French were more insolent.[27] Among the nobility in particular, as it became evident that the Spanish were in Italy to stay, there was a readiness to look for affinities between Spanish and Italian values.[28] Whether Spanish nobles were ready to acknowledge such affinities is another question. Closer acquaintance during the wars seems to have confirmed some unflattering stereotypes of the Italians among other nations as crafty, perfidious, cruel, traitors and poisoners.[29] Above all they were viewed as traders, always looking for an opportunity to cheat or overcharge, and exploit the hapless soldier who needed to buy clothes or food or arms from them.[30]

For Italian civic elites, the contemptuous attitudes shown to them by French, Spanish and German nobles they encountered could be especially galling; it was more difficult for them to be accepted at their own estimation of their status than it was for the military nobility. A desire to establish a right to be held in higher regard may have accelerated the tendency, already apparent in the fifteenth century, among Italian urban political elites to become civic aristocracies, to claim noble status and in some cases to seek to exclude from their closed oligarchy those who lived by trade.

Comparisons with other states, France, Spain, Germany, Switzerland, became a frequent feature of discussions on the role and nature of nobility – such comparisons could no longer be a mere literary exercise, 'but became a theme of urgent and unavoidable political debate'.[31]

The calamities of the wars and the political failings of Italian governments that helped to bring them about provided ample material for satirists and versifiers throughout Italy. Uneasy reflections on the inability of politicians and diplomats to counter the military forces of the Spanish and French gave new life to the classic debate about the relative import- ance of arms and letters. In Francesco Guicciardini's *Storia d'Italia* the wars were the inspiration for perhaps the greatest work of history of the sixteenth century. They also provided the subject matter for countless chronicles and diaries produced by men of various social levels throughout Italy. Reflection on the wars and the changes they brought to Italy underlay the two works of Machiavelli – *Il principe* and *Dell'arte della guerra* – that made him famous throughout Europe.

Signs of disquiet and of uncertainty have been detected in the work of the generation of artists and writers born around the time the wars began, such as the painters Jacopo Pontormo and Francesco Parmigianino and the writer Pietro Aretino. 'The mood of this generation was characteristically an unstable, anxious one, veering between cynical acceptance and violent rejection of the world.'[32] Proponents of fixing an elevated form of Italian as a vehicle for literature, setting aside the rich variety of the many dialects of Italy, could be seen as aiming at 'winning in the mind … that superior state which could not be won in war and politics'.[33]

The wars did have a positive effect on Italian culture, nevertheless. Among the soldiers and officials who came to Italy were many educated men who were impressed and enchanted by the painting, sculpture and architecture that they saw. They bought and commissioned works from Italian artists. Leonardo da Vinci, dying in France in 1519, honoured by the king, and Titian, the portrait painter of choice for Charles V, are only the best known of the many instances of Italian artists serving for- eign patrons, who might well not have worked for them, had it not been for the wars. However uncertain the status of some Italian nobles in the eyes of other nations, Baldassare Castiglione's *Il Cortegiano*, translated into English, Spanish, French and Latin, became for centuries the classic guide on the culture and conduct of a gentleman. The Italian Wars did much to diffuse the culture of Renaissance Italy beyond the Alps. This was one field in which Italians could console themselves that they retained acknowledged supremacy.

The transformation of military society

The military society of Italy had been transformed by the wars. The careers open to those who made war their profession were greatly changed, and a much higher proportion of Italian men would be expected to spend some time undergoing formal military training in militia companies.

In the fifteenth century, Italian professional soldiers had predominantly been cavalrymen, although maintaining their companies was a problem for *condottieri* when they were between contracts. Infantry constables might be given retainers in peacetime by *condottieri* or by states, but only limited numbers of their men would be kept on. After the early years of the wars, the French and Spanish kings did not want to hire *condottieri* and their companies in the manner usual in Italy; if they were to hire Italian troops they preferred to have them fit into the existing structure of their own armies. Individuals given commands might be able to recruit at least some of their men themselves, or they might be given charge of an existing unit.

These changes applied to Italian *condottieri* princes as well as other captains. They might still be given military commands, but the system by which the maintenance of a military company was part of the patronage net-work binding subjects to their prince, and *condotte* were an integral element in the structure of relations between the Italian powers, weakened and lost much of its significance. Princes such as the Este of Ferrara or the Gonzaga of Mantua might be given commands or alliances in time of war, and might hope that these would become permanent, but they could also find them-selves expected to provide additional troops, artillery and munitions, food supplies and financial loans, as a gesture of loyalty to their patron or ally. Foreign monarchs were generally disappointed by the results of arrangements made with Italian princes. Often they did not get the commitment of the prince and the resources of his territory to the war that they expected. Italian princes, accustomed to regarding the primary purpose of troops paid for by *condotte* as the defence of their own states, could be reluctant to move far from home. In the later stages of the wars, Henry II, looking for friends and allies to help him keep a foothold in central Italy, placed great reliance on subsidies to Italian princes. The king could have all of Italy, if he would pay a million écus a year, his paymaster there, Dominique du Gabre, warned in 1556, but the trouble was that once such payments began they could not be stopped and seemed 'an hereditary contribution'.[34]

Italians looking for a military career would have found fewer oppor-tunities to serve in units of men-at-arms, as these were no longer the dominant element in armies. (At the beginning of the wars, the strength of armies tended to be defined in terms of the numbers of men-at-arms; by the end, principally in terms of the number of infantry.) Those who did become men-at-arms would find themselves last in line for pay, with their French and Spanish counterparts. The expectation was that men-at-arms would have means of their own, and could support themselves unsubsidized for long periods. Many nobles still preferred to serve as men-at-arms, because of the social prestige attached to it – serving as infantry commanders was one thing, serving as rank-and file infantrymen quite another – and their employment was to some degree a political as much as a military choice. By the mid-sixteenth century, the Venetians, for example, had 'accepted the fact that the retention of heavy cavalry was primarily an exercise in maintaining good relations with powerful Terraferma families and a diversion of their chivalrous pretensions into a form of public service'.[35] Italians did make a reputation for themselves during the war as light cavalrymen. But units of light horse tended to be hired or raised for specific campaigns, so many would be dismissed in peacetime. Mercenary infantry companies of the size and professionalism of the landsknechts and the Swiss pike companies did not develop in Italy. The arquebus rather than the pike became the weapon of Italian specialist infantry. Companies of Italian infantry could be raised for a campaign, but were generally less valued than other infantry units in field armies. Usually paid less, they were the first to be turned off when funds ran down. They were more valued as garrison troops, and it was acknowledged they could perform better under siege than the Swiss or Spanish.

As elsewhere in Europe, by the second half of the sixteenth century, some kind of military service in a militia was becoming a much more common experience for Italian men. It has been estimated that in the early seventeenth century one in fifteen Italian men was enrolled in a militia.[36] In Venice in the mid-sixteenth century, of the 200,000 men on the Terraferma believed to be fit for active service, one in seven was a militiaman.[37] Militias had fought in some of the campaigns of the Italian Wars – the Venetian militia in the War of the League of Cambrai, for example, and the Florentine during the last stages of the Pisan War, the siege of Florence and the War of Siena. Cosimo de' Medici was proud of his Florentine forces, 23,000 strong, 'a very fine band, all armed, some with corselets and pikes', he told the Venetian ambassador around 1560; another 7,000 were raised in his new Sienese lands: 'Sienese territory always produces good soldiers.'[38] For him, as for Emanuele Filiberto, whose military reforms in Savoy and Piedmont in the 1560s attracted the interest of other rulers, a strong militia, well-trained and well-armed, was an important element in the image of the strong and independent prince that they wished to project.

All the militias, theirs included, were intended to be primarily defence forces. For those in states with coastlines exposed to attacks from the Turks and Barbary corsairs, defence against raiders from the sea was their primary role. Venice had a separate galley militia, distinct from the forces in the Terraferma. The need to defend a long coastline was the primary reason for the formation of the militia in the kingdom of Naples in the 1560s; no permanent militia forces were raised in landlocked Lombardy until the seventeenth century. Service in the militia gave many civilians training in the use of military weapons, generally the arquebus and the pike. Permission to keep and carry arms was one of its main attractions. The cavalry unit formed in Naples in 1577 – initially 1,200, increased to 3,000 in 1520, alongside the 20,000–24,000 foot – seems to have been an exception to the general rule that militias tended to be infantry. Those selected for cavalry service were to serve at their own cost, and were to be expert horsemen already.[39] The many barons of the kingdom provided an ample pool from which they could be recruited. The cavalry units Emanuele Filiberto aimed to raise alongside his infantry militia were to be provided by fief-holders, in accordance with longstanding obligations of the landed nobility of Savoy and Piedmont.

Mastering the skills of horsemanship necessary to fight on horseback was becoming part of a fashionable education for members of the urban nobilities who had no intention of ever going to fight in a war. Learning the art of handling a sword and a rapier was also essential for those who affected a sense of personal honour to be defended and maintained by duel-ling, if need be, following a formal code of practice that developed among the military nobility and professional soldiers. Such social trends were evi-dent in other parts of Europe too, but the adoption by many members of the civic nobilities of Italy of the ethos of the military nobility was a notable development. Although the military nobility had often had close ties to towns and close association with members of civic elites, there had been acute awareness of a social and cultural distinction between them, on both sides, and sometimes a measure of mutual disdain. Contact with the nobles and soldiers of other nations during and after the wars spurred on members of the civic elites to assert their right not only to be considered as nobles, but as gentlemen with personal honour to be respected and defended. For a member of a civic nobility, becoming a professional sol-dier – serving in the cavalry or as an infantry commander – could be seen as conferring or confirming aristocratic status. The old landed nobility, on the other hand, became less military in character. Their ability to raise large numbers of fighting men among their tenants and partisans and their possession of fortresses, which had been the foundation of their political power before and during the wars, counted for much less in the new, more pacific political system.

After the wars ended, there was much less scope in Italy for those who wanted to have a military career, or to spend some time soldiering to enhance their credentials as a gentleman. There was ample scope for military service elsewhere in Europe, in the Netherlands, for example, or in campaigns against the Ottomans on land and sea, and many Italians went to serve abroad. Most spent some time in the service of Spain. For many Roman barons, serving the king of Spain or France was preferable to service in the papal army – just as serving the pope had often not been the first choice of earlier generations of the military nobility of the Papal States. Neapolitan and Lombard nobles who sought to win the favour of the king by military service had to leave Italy to do so, even though Naples and Lombardy had a significant military function within the Spanish empire as bases and training-grounds for troops. Three of the *tercios*, the permanent infantry corps who formed the backbone of the Spanish army were based in Italy, in Naples, Lombardy and Sicily. Charles V had ordered that each *tercio* should be formed of men from one nation only, to promote cohesion,[40] but they were recruited in Spain, not Italy. Neapolitans could serve only in the militia, or abroad. In Lombardy, Italians were not supposed to serve even as garrison troops; fortresses were supposed to be manned by Spanish soldiers. In practice, some Italians could be found among the garrisons, if they pretended to be Spanish.[41]

As the presence of foreign soldiers became a permanent fact of life for the people of Lombardy and Naples, and as a greater proportion of Italian men had undergone some form of military training as militiamen or as part of the education of gentlemen, so in many areas fortifications became a more dominant element of the landscapes and townscapes of Italy. Castles and fortified villages, walled towns and cities had been iconic elements of the medieval Italian landscapes portrayed in countless works of art, but the new principles of military engineering demanded radical changes to the appearance of the towns and cities provided with modern fortifications. These demanded broad swathes of cleared ground around fortifications and outside the lower, thicker city walls to provide clear sight and firing lines, and clear access to the walls inside the city, and the facility for defenders to move rapidly from one point to another. Older town walls were often integrated into the urban fabric, with buildings right up against them on the inside, and busy suburbs on the outside; often certain trades and industrial activities had become concentrated in the suburbs, where there was more space and less potential for annoying the neighbours. Building new fortifications could result in the levelling of many homes, business premises and religious buildings, and thriving communities would be swept away. It was easier for people to understand and tolerate such destruction in time of war; it was much more difficult to accept when there was no immediate threat.

Extensive programmes of fortifications, designed to be a coherent defensive system, were undertaken in several states. Some, like the fortresses and watchtowers built to defend the coasts of the kingdom of Naples, might well have been built even if the Italian Wars had never happened. But many were designed to strengthen defences whose weaknesses had been revealed during the course of the wars. In the duchy of Milan, the cities on the western frontier received particular attention, but other places such as Cremona and Milan itself, where Ferrante Gonzaga began the construction of new city walls when he was governor, were also given new defences. The Genoese initiated the building of a new circuit of walls and defences around their city after they came under threat from the French in 1536. In the city of Naples, the construction of a new fortress, Sant'Elmo, in the form of a six-pointed star, on the hill of San Martino was intended by the viceroy Pedro de Toledo to dominate the city as well as strengthen its defences (and an entire quarter of the city was given over to be lodgings for Spanish troops). A new fortress at L'Aquila was intended to assert control over an area of rooted Angevin sympathies.

The Venetians had begun modernizing their fortifications in the Terraferma in the late fifteenth century, but the programme was extended and accelerated after the shock of the defeat at Agnadello in 1509. Two of their commanders, Bartolomeo d'Alviano and Francesco Maria della Rovere, had great influence over the planning and design of these works. As well as providing protection for the population and Venetian armies, the fortifications were intended to discourage invasion. 'Fortifications and their garrisons provided the essential base from which to carry out Venice's on-the-whole successful policy of armed neutrality'[42] – the policy adopted by Venice from the 1530s. A programme of fortifications was an integral part of Cosimo de' Medici's presentation of his new duchy as a strong state. Apart from the fortress in Florence itself, his major works were the fortified naval base he created on the island of Elba at Portoferraio, which he named Cosmopolis, and fortresses constructed to control routes through the Sienese, as at Grosseto, and the city of Siena itself, where near the ruins of the fortress begun by the Spanish, a huge quadrilateral fortress, with great angle bastions at each corner, was begun in 1560.

The famous city walls and ramparts of Lucca, begun in the 1540s and finally completed a century later, still convey an idea of how impressive and striking the appearance of cities enclosed by the new style of fortifications could be. Even with the ramparts planted with trees, and turned into a park running the length of the walls, they still sharply divide the city from its environs, and magnificent as they are, can still give an impression of constraining the city, although Lucca has now expanded beyond the walls, albeit at a respectful distance from them. When the new fortifications first went up around the towns and cities of Italy during and after the wars, their impact on the lives of the population was considerable. Apart from the destruction they entailed, these projects typically took decades to complete, with hundreds, even thousands, of (often conscripted) labourers toiling away. Often there would be fewer gates through the new walls, familiar routes would be cut, the sense of difference between the world inside and outside the walls greater than before. Many of these elaborate fortifications were never tested in war, and people must often have become more aware of how they inhibited urban expansion, rather than of their defensive purpose. For many Italians, the new fortifications remained the most tangible legacy of the Italian Wars.

Italy in the Spanish empire

Of all the enduring consequences of the Italian Wars, it was, of course, the fact that large parts of the Italian peninsula were now subject to a foreign monarch – one who did not come to reside in Italy – that had the most far-reaching effects.

Historians have been analysing the role within the Spanish empire of the Italian states that came under the direct rule of the Spanish monarchy – Sicily and Sardinia as well as Milan and Naples – and how and to what extent Italians were integrated into the networks of officials and noble families that knit the disparate parts of the 'composite monarchy' together. There has been some work, too, on how those areas of Italy not under Spanish rule related to Spain. Genoa, and even Rome, have been seen as part of the Spanish empire, but this is to stretch the definition of empire further than is either justified or useful, and to oversimplify to the point of misrepresentation the complexities of the political and cultural integration of Italy into the new European state system. For many Italians, outside those regions where people had to come to terms with the permanent presence among them of Spanish troops and officials, the predominance of the king of Spain in Italy impinged little, if at all, on their lives.

In general, it was those levels of political society which formed the networks of dependence and patronage, rivalry and enmity, that linked and divided princes, members of the military nobility and civic elites throughout Italy that were most affected. This complex system of relationships had been thrown off balance by the entry into it of the most powerful monarchs in Europe, who were used to different rules. All parties had to adjust. Italians had to become canny in how they changed or balanced relations and alliances with states far more powerful than they, while preserving a substantial degree of independence and room to manoeuvre. The kings of Spain and France and the emperor had to learn there were limits to their capacity to control and direct Italian princes and political elites; they could not demand unquestioning loyalty and submission. Italian states and elites had been unable to set aside their differences and unite to exclude all foreign powers from the peninsula. They had been more inclined to treat the dynastic conflicts of the ultramontane powers as an opportunity, a vehicle for the pursuit of their own personal aims and disputes, and sometimes succeeded in making use of them, as much as they themselves were manipulated. Some Italians found it easy to adjust to the new dispensation after the wars, taking advantage of opportunities to make careers in a wider world, while others saw their horizons narrowing, and chafed at their loss of autonomy.

Any assessment of that new dispensation should take into account that it was not a foregone conclusion to the wars that the king of Spain would become the predominant power in Italy. The matter was certainly not settled by Charles V's visit to Italy in 1529–30 – before and after that, his armies were often on the defensive, his commanders struggling to hold on to positions with inadequate numbers of badly paid men, unable to take the field because they could not trust their soldiers to fight. The final outcome of the wars, and the settlement embodied in the Treaty of Cateau-Cambrésis, were not viewed by the Italians, the French or even the Spanish as the inevitable result of the inexorable victory of Spanish arms in Italy, but as something of a surprise. Italians need not have perceived the power of the Spanish empire as overwhelming and inescapable. The foundations of Spanish power in Italy would have looked considerably less substantial and secure, when viewed from the perspective of those who had lived through the Italian Wars.

Notes

1 *State Papers*, VII, 225–7.

2 Chabod, 128–32.

3 *Ibid.*, 112, 116.

4 Canosa, 29–32.

5 Vigo, 220.

6 Politi, 14.

7 Ruggiero, 316–18.

8 Merlin, 132–3.

9 *Ibid.*, 135.

10 Canosa, 38.

11 Von Albertini, 182–3.

12 Goldthwaite, 595–6.

13 Cantagalli, 227.

14 Ginatempo, 439–88.

15 Galasso, 77–84.

16 Shaw, 'The papal court'.

17 Spini, 195.

18 Cremonini.

19 Mazzei.

20 Fasano Guarini, 15.

21 *CSP Ven*, VI, ii, 851–5.

22 Politi, 452–3.

23 Segre, (1902), 260.

24 *CSP Ven*, VI, ii, 756.

25 Smith, 'Émulation guerrière', 166–9.

26 Romier, II, 85.

27 *CSP Ven*, VI, ii, 756.

28 Guidi, 150–2, 161.

29 Smith, 'Complots', 95–101.

30 Chabod, 217.

31 Donati, *L'idea*, 29.

32 Burke, *Culture*, 275.

33 Martines, 'Literary crisis',18.

34 Romier, II, 72.

35 Mallett and Hale, 369.

36 Rizzo, 'Istituzioni militari', 158.

37 Mallett and Hale, 355.

38 *La fortuna di Cosimo I*, 66–8.

39 Muto, 160.

40 Belloso Martín, 182.

41 Anselmi, 85–8.

42 Mallett and Hale, 409.

Bibliography

Alfani, Guido, *Calamities and the Economy in Renaissance Italy. The Grand Tour of the Horsemen of the Apocalypse* (Basingstoke: Palgrave Macmillan, 2013).

Angiolini, Franco, 'Diplomazia e politica dell'Italia non spagnola nell'età di Filippo II. Osservazioni preliminari', *Rivista storica italiana*, 92 (1980), 432–69.

Angiolini, Franco, 'Politica, società e organizzazione militare nel principato mediceo: a proposito di una "Memoria" di Cosimo I', *Società e storia*, 9 (1986), 1–51.

Anselmi, Paola, *'Conservare lo Stato'. Politica di difesa e pratica di governo nella Lombardia spagnola fra XVI e XVII secolo* (Milan: UNICOPLI, 2008).

Arcangeli, Letizia, 'Carriere militari dell'aristocrazia padana nelle Guerre d'Italia', in Letizia Arcangeli, *Gentiluomini di Lombardia: Ricerche sull'aristocrazia padana nel Rinascimento* (Milan: Edizioni Unicopli, 2003), 71–121.

Barbero, Alessandro, 'I soldati del principe. Guerra, Stato e società nel Piemonte sabaudo (1450–1580)', in Cristof Dipper and Mario Rosa (eds), *La società dei principi nell'Europa moderna (secoli XVI-XVII)* (Bologna: Il Mulino, 2005).

Belloso Martín, Carlos, 'El "barrio español" de Napoles en el siglo XVI (I Quartieri spagnoli)', in Enrique García Hernán and Davide Maffi (eds), *Guerra y sociedad en la Monarquía Hispánica*, II, 179–223.

Brunelli, Giampiero, 'Poteri e privilegi. L'istituzione degli ordinamenti delle milizie nello Stato pontificio tra Cinque e Seicento', *Cheiron* 23 (1995), 105–29.

Brunelli, Giampiero, *Soldati del Papa: Politica militare e nobiltà nello Stato della Chiesa (1560–1644)* (Rome: Carocci, 2003).

Brunetti, Oronzo, *A difesa dell'Impero. Pratica architettonica e dibattito tecnico nel Viceregno di Napoli nel Cinquecento* (Galatina: M. Congedo, 2006).

Burke, Peter, *Culture and Society in Renaissance Italy 1420–1540* (Batsford, 1972).

Calabria, Antonio, *The Cost of Empire. The Finances of the Kingdom of Naples in the Time of Spanish Rule* (Cambridge: Cambridge University Press, 1991).

Calendar of State Papers Venetian (Longmans, 1864–98) [*CSP Ven*].

Canosa, Romano, *Storia di Milano nell'Età di Filippo II* (Rome: Sapere 2000, 1996).

Cantagalli, Roberto, *La Guerra di Siena (1552–1559)* (Siena: Accademia Senese degli Intronati, 1962).

Cantù, Francesca and Maria Antonietta Visceglia (eds), *L'Italia di Carlo V. Guerra, religione e politica nel primo Cinquecento* (Rome: Viella, 2003).

Chabod, Federico, *Lo Stato e la vita religiosa a Milano nell'epoca di Carlo V* (Turin: Giulio Einaudi, 1971).

Cremonini, Cinzia, 'I feudi imperiali italiani tra Sacro Romano Impero e monarchia cattolica (seconda metà XVI – inizio XVII secolo)', in Schnettger and Verga (eds), *L'impero e l'Italia*, 41–65.

Cresti, Carlo, Amelio Fara and Daniela Lamberini (eds), *Architettura militare nell'Europa del XVI secolo* (Siena: Edizioni Periccioli, 1988).

Croatto, Giorgio (ed.), *Castelli in terra, in acqua e … in aria* (Pisa: Università di Pisa, 2002).

Dandelet, Thomas James, *Spanish Rome, 1500–1700* (New Haven: Yale University Press, 2001).

Dandelet, Thomas James and John A. Marino (eds), *Spain in Italy. Politics, Society and Religion 1500–1700* (Leiden: Brill, 2007).

Del Torre, Giuseppe, *Venezia e la Terraferma dopo la Guerra di Cambrai. Fiscalità e amministrazione (1515–1530)* (Milan: FrancoAngeli,1986).

Denis, Anne, '1513–1515: "la nazione svizzera" et les Italiens', *Revue suisse d'histoire*, 47 (1997), 111–28.

De Seta, Cesare and Jacques Le Goff (eds), *La città e le mura* (Rome: Laterza, 1989).

Di Stefano, Giuseppe, Elena Fasano Guarini and Alessandro Martinengo (eds), *Italia non spagnola e monarchia spagnola tra '500 e '600: Politica, cultura e letteratura* (Florence: Leo S. Olschki, 2009).

Donati, Claudio, *L'idea di nobiltà in Italia: secoli XIV–XVIII* (Rome: Laterza, 1995).

Donati, Claudio, 'The profession of arms and the nobility in Spanish Italy: some considerations', in Dandelet and Marino (eds), *Spain in Italy*, 299–324.

Fasano Guarini, Elena, 'Italia non spagnola e Spagna nel tempo di Filippo II', in L. Lotti and R. Villari, *Filippo II e il Mediterraneo* (Rome: Laterza, 2003), 5–23.

Firenze e la Toscana dei Medici nell'Europa del '500, 3 vols (Florence: Leo S. Olschki, 1988).

Galasso, Giuseppe, *Alla periferia dell'impero: Il Regno di Napoli nel periodo spagnolo (secoli XVI–XVII)* (Turin: Einaudi, 1994).

Ginatempo, Maria, *Crisi di un territorio. Il popolamento della Toscana senese alla fine del Medioevo* (Florence: Leo S. Olschki, 1988).

Goldthwaite, Richard A., *The Economy of Renaissance Florence* (Baltimore: Johns Hopkins University Press, 2009).

Guidi, José, 'L'Espagne dans la vie et dans l'oeuvre de B. Castiglione: de l'équilibre franco-hispanique au choix impérial', in Rochon, *Présence et influence de l'Espagne*, 113–202.

Hanlon, Gregory, *The Twilight of a Military Tradition: Italian Aristocrats and European Conflicts, 1560–1800* (UCL Press, 1998).

Hernán, Enrique García and Davide Maffi (eds), *Guerra y Sociedad en La Monarquía Hispánica. Politica, estrategia y cultura en la Europa moderna (1500–1700)*, 2 vols (Madrid: Ediciones del Laberinto, 2006).

Irace, Erminia, *La nobiltà bifronta. Identità e coscienza aristocratica a Perugia tra XVI e XVII secolo* (Milan: Edizioni Unicopli, 1995).

La fortuna di Cosimo I: La battaglia di Scannagallo (Arezzo: PAN, 1992).

Lamberini, Daniela, 'La politica del guasto. L'impatto del fronte bastionato sulle preesistenze urbane', in Cresti, Fara and Lamberini (eds), *Architettura militare*, 219–40.

Leydi, Silvio, *Le cavalcate dell'ingegnero. L'opera di Gianmaria Olgiati, ingegnere militare di Carlo V* (Modena: Panini, 1989).

Mallett, Michael and J.R. Hale, *The Military Organization of a Renaissance State: Venice c. 1400 to 1617* (Cambridge: Cambridge University Press, 1984).

Marino, Angela (ed.), *Fortezze d'Europa. Forme, professioni e mestieri dell' architettura difensiva in Europa e nel Mediterraneo spagnolo* (Rome: Gangemi, 2003).

Martines, Lauro, 'Literary crisis in the generation of 1494', in Stella Fletcher and Christine Shaw (eds), *The World of Savonarola: Italian Elites and Perceptions of Crisis* (Aldershot: Ashgate, 2000), 5–21.

Mazzei, Rita, 'La Repubblica di Lucca e l'Impero nella prima età moderna. Ragioni e limiti di una scelta', in Schnetter and Verga, *L'impero e l'Italia*, 299–321.

Merlin, Pierpaolo, *Emanuele Filiberto: Un principe tra il Piemonte e l'Europa* (Turin: Società Editrice Inernazionale, 1995).

Murrin, Michael, *History and Warfare in Renaissance Epic* (Chicago: University of Chicago Press, 1994).

Muto, Giovanni, 'Strategie e strutture del controllo militare del territorio del Regno di Napoli nel Cinquecento', in Hernán and Maffi, *Guerra y sociedad*, I, 153–70.

Najemy, John M., 'Arms and letters: the crisis of courtly culture in the wars of Italy', in Shaw (ed.), *Italy and the European Powers*, 207–38.

Pandolfi, Tullio, 'Giovan Matteo Giberti e l'ultima difesa della libertà d'Italia negli anni 1521–1525', in *Archivio della R. Società Romana di storia patria*, 34 (1911), 131–237.

Politi, Giorgio, *Aristocrazia e potere politico nella Cremona di Filippo II* (Milan: SugarCo Edizioni, 1976).

Rabà, Michele Maria, 'Gli italiani e la guerra di Parma (1551–1552): cooptazione di élite e "sottoproletariato militare a giornata" nella Lombardia di Carlo V', *Archivio storico lombardo*, 136 (2010), 25–48.

Rabà, Michele M., *Potere e poteri. 'Stati', 'privati' e comunità nel conflitto per l'egemonia in Italia settentrionale (1536–1558)* (Milan: FrancoAngeli, 2016).

Rizzo, Mario, 'Finanza pubblica, Impero e amministrazione nella Lombardia Spagnola: le "visitas generales"', in Paolo Pissavino and Gianvittorio Signorotto, *Lombardia Borromaica, Lombardia Spagnola 1554–1659*, 2 vols (Rome: Bulzoni, 1995), 303–61.

Rizzo, Mario, 'Istituzioni militari e strutture socio-economiche in una città di antico regime. La milizia urbana a Pavia nell'età spagnola', *Cheiron* 23 (1995), 157–85.

Rizzo, Mario, 'Non solo guerra. Risorse e organizzazione della strategia asburgica in Lombardia durante la seconda metà del Cinquecento', in Hernán and Maffi, *Guerra y sociedad*, I, 217–252.

Rochon, André (ed.), *Présence et influence de l'Espagne dans la culture italienne de la Renaissance* (Paris: Université de la Sorbonne Nouvelle, 1978).

Rodríguez-Salgado, M.J., 'Terracotta and iron: Mantuan politics (ca.1480–ca.1550)', in Cesare Mozzarelli, Robert Oresko and Leandro Ventura (eds), *The Court of the Gonzaga in the Age of Mantegna: 1450–1550* (Rome: Bulzoni, 1997), 15–59.

Romier, Lucien, *Les origines politiques des Guerres de Religion*, 2 vols (Paris: Perrin, 1913–14).

Ruggiero, Michele, *Storia del Piemonte* (Turin: Piemonte in Bancarella, 1979).

Schnettger, Matthias and Marcello Verga (eds), *L'impero e l'Italia nella prima età moderna* (Bologna: Il Mulino, 2006).

Segre, Arturo, 'Lodovico Sforza, detto il Moro, e la Repubblica di Venezia dall'autunno 1494 alla primavera 1495', *Archivio storico lombardo*, 3rd ser., 18 (1902), 249–317; 20 (1903), 33–109, 368–443.

Shaw, Christine, *Barons and Castellans. The Military Nobility of Renaissance Italy* (Leiden and Boston: Brill, 2015).

Shaw, Christine (ed.), *Italy and the European Powers: The Impact of War, 1500–1530* (Leiden and Boston: Brill, 2006).

Shaw, Christine, 'The papacy and the European powers', in Shaw (ed.), *Italy and the European Powers*, 107–26.

Shaw, Christine, 'The papal court as a centre of diplomacy from the Peace of Lodi to the Council of Trent', in Florence Alazard and Frank La Brasca (eds), *La papauté à la Renaissance* (Paris: Honoré Champion, 2007), 621–38.

Shaw, Christine, 'Political exile during the Italian Wars', in Fabio Di Giannatale (ed.), *Escludere per governare. L'esilio politico fra Medioevo e Risorgimento* (Florence: Le Monnier Università, 2011), 79–95.

Shaw, Christine, *Popular Government and Oligarchy in Renaissance Italy* (Leiden: Brill, 2006).

Shaw, Christine, 'The Roman barons and the security of the Papal States', in Mario Del Treppo (ed.), *Condottieri e uomini d'arme nell'Italia del Rinascimento* (Naples: Liguori, 2001), 311–25.

Smith, Marc H., 'Complots, révoltes et tempéraments nationaux: français et italiens au XVIᵉ siècle', in Yves-Marie Bercé and Elena Fasano Guarini (eds), *Complots et conjurations dans l'Europe moderne* (Rome: École française de Rome,1996), 93–115.

Smith, Marc H., 'Émulation guerrière et stéréotypes nationaux dans les Guerres d'Italie', in D. Boillet and M. F. Piejus (eds), *Les Guerres d'Italie: Histoires, pratiques, représentations* (Paris: Université Paris III Sorbonne Nouvelle, 2002), 155–76.

Spini, Giorgio, 'Il principato dei Medici e il sistema degli Stati europei del Cinquecento', in *Firenze e la Toscana*, 177–216.

State Papers during the Reign of Henry VIII, 11 vols (Record Commission, 1830–52).

Storia economica e sociale di Bergamo. Il tempo della Serenissima. Il lungo Cinquecento (Bergamo: Fondazione per la storia economica e sociale di Bergamo, 1998).

Valseriati, Enrico, *Tra Venezia e l'Impero: dissenso e conflitto politico a Brescia nell'età di Carlo V* (Milan: FrancoAngeli, 2016).

Viganò, Marino (ed.), *L'architettura militare nell'età di Leonardo: 'Guerre milanesi' e diffusione del bastione in Italia e in Europa* (Bellinzona: Edizioni Casagrande, 2008).

Vigo, Giovanni, 'Il volto economico della città', in Giorgio Politi (ed.), *Storia di Cremona: L'éta degli Asburgo di Spagna (1535–1707)*, (Cremona: Bolis, 2006), 220–61.

von Albertini, Rudolf, *Firenze dalla repubblica al principato: Storia e coscienza politica* (Turin: Einaudi, 1970).

Index

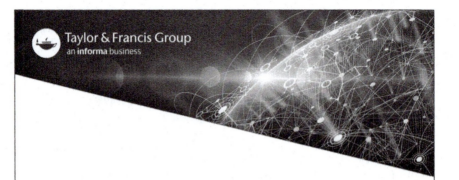